From Ally to Enemy

From Ally to Enemy
The Enigma of Fascist Italy
in French Diplomacy, 1920–1940

William I. Shorrock

The Kent State University Press
Kent, Ohio, and London, England

© 1988 by The Kent State University Press, Kent, Ohio 44242
All rights reserved
Library of Congress Catalog Card Number 87-22830
ISBN 0-87338-350-8
Manufactured in the United States of America

The paper in this book meets the guidelines for permanence and durability of the Committee on Production Guidelines for Book Longevity of the Council on Library Resources.

Library of Congress Cataloging-in-Publication Data
Shorrock, William I., 1941-
  From ally to enemy.
  Bibliography: p.
  Includes index.
  1. France—Foreign relations—Italy. 2. Italy—Foreign relations—France. 3. France—Foreign relations—1914-1940. 4. France—Politics and government—1918-1945. I. Title.
DC59.8.I8S48   1988   327.44   87-22830
ISBN 0-87338-350-8 (alk. paper)

British Library Cataloguing in Publication data are available.

For Marge

Contents

Preface ix

1	Introduction	1
2	France and the Emergence of the Fascist Era in Italy, 1920–23	17
3	Cooperation and Competition, 1923–32	31
4	Jouvenel Mission to Rome	59
5	From Jouvenel to Louis Barthou	79
6	The Laval-Mussolini Accords of January 1935	99
7	Military Preparations and the Stresa Front	117
8	Ethiopia and the Fall of Laval	141
9	Sanctions, the Rhineland Crisis, and the Inception of the Popular Front	170
10	From the Spanish Crisis to the *Anschluss*, October 1936–March 1938	196
11	France and the Anglo-Italian Easter Accord of 1938	220
12	From the Recognition of Empire to the Pact of Steel	237
13	To War	268
14	Conclusion	289
	Notes	297
	Bibliography	333
	Index	346

Maps

The Treaty of London in the Adriatic, 1915	8
Italian Claims and Acquisitions in Africa, 1919–20	13
The Hoare-Laval Plan, 1935	161

Preface

Although completely unanticipated, it is nevertheless appropriate that the final chapters of this book should have been written in Villefranche-sur-mer, a small community tucked into one of the loveliest bays along the French Riviera between Nice and Menton. This area circumscribes the chronological boundaries to the main body of the study. The story of modern Franco-Italian relations really begins with the French acquisition of Nice and Savoy in 1860 as the result of a bargain struck between Napoleon III and Count Camillo di Cavour—an important step in the building of a unified Italian nation. In many of the towns and villages along the Mediterranean coast and in the hills behind them are monuments commemorating the plebiscite of 1860 by which the inhabitants of these regions overwhelmingly endorsed their incorporation into France. Italian influence, however, is still pronounced, most notably in the spoken regional accent and the cuisine. The book concludes with the Franco-Italian armistice of 1940, whereby much of this same area fell into the fifty-kilometer demilitarized zone along the Italian frontier demanded by Mussolini.

The idea for this study began to germinate with summer research forays to France in 1973 and 1974, shortly after the French Ministry of Foreign Affairs Archives for the 1920s were opened. At that time my goals were decidedly less ambitious, for it seemed that a study of France's relations with Italy in the first post-World War I decade, although important, hardly warranted book-length treatment. But the subsequent declassification, in 1982, of the relevant archival materials for the 1930s made the larger work practicable and, in my judgment, essential. It also must be stressed that all of the projected volumes in the two series of *Documents diplomatiques français, 1932–1939* have now been published. This task has been accomplished by a team of French scholars and archivists under the general editorship of the *doyen* of French diplomatic historians, Jean-Baptiste Duroselle. Theirs is no mean achievement, since many important documents had been destroyed by the French in the courtyard of the Quai d'Orsay in June 1940 as the German armies advanced on Paris. The documentary record had to be painstakingly reconstructed, in many cases from copies of the originals retrieved from various French embassies and consulates around the world. The published volumes of documents also contain materials from the private papers of politicians, diplomats, military leaders, and so forth. It is relevant to point out that the work of reconstituting, reorganizing, and inventorying the archival record for the interwar years was an essential preliminary to making it available for general scholarly analysis. All of the people working on this period of contemporary history owe an enormous debt of gratitude for this effort.

It is well to mention at this point a fundamental problem confronting the researcher in modern French diplomatic archives. The paper trail to be found there is frequently less than satisfactory. There are a great many documents emanating from the various embassies and consulates abroad; less numerous but in adequate supply are Foreign Ministry instructions to embassy and consulate officials. What is missing is clear evidence of the policy-making process in Paris. The archives contain few internal Foreign Ministry memoranda that would help identify and trace the thinking of French policymakers. Furthermore, unlike the British, the French maintained no formal record of the proceedings of Cabinet meetings. The researcher, therefore, must draw inferences about the influence of recommendations sent to the Quai d'Orsay from diplomats in the field by comparing them with policy as it was ultimately applied. This problem is more acute for the 1920s than for the 1930s; for the latter decade a more abundant literature of memoirs and diaries, albeit frequently contradictory, is available to help fill the archival gaps.

As is to be expected, much of the best work published over the last

PREFACE

decade—dealing with French interwar diplomacy and employing the recently declassified archival materials—has focused chronologically on the early 1920s and geographically on France's relations with Germany and Great Britain. Little of a scholarly nature has so far appeared on France's relations with Germany's future Axis partner, Italy, except where the subject is treated in isolated chapters of more general studies, such as Duroselle's *La Décadence, 1932-1939*. The time for such a systematic examination has, therefore, arrived. I hope that this book will shed additonal light, not only on the origins of World War II, but also on the exigencies of the foreign-policymaking process in a democratic nation. It is appropriate to mention at this point, given my earlier caveat about less ambitious goals, that some of the subjects treated in this book have appeared in article form in the *Journal of Contemporary History, The Historian, Revue d'histoire diplomatique, International Journal of African Historical Studies* and *International History Review*. Most of these articles—all cited in the bibliography—deal with aspects of Franco-Italian relations in the 1920s, which explains why that important period has been condensed into two chapters in the present volume.

This book could not have been written without the cooperation and assistance of many different individuals and instititutions. In particular I would like to acknowledge the help received from the staffs and personnel of the Archives du Ministère des Affaires Étrangères, the Archives Historique de l'Armée de Terre (Château de Vincennes), and the Bibliothèque Nationale in Paris. Across the Channel, the British Library and the Institute for Historical Research in London provided much useful information. And, also, my gratitude is extended to the Public Record Office extension at Kew Gardens near London, not only for its treasure trove of meticulously maintained documentation, but also for the blissfully frigid quality of its air-conditioned environment on hot, humid August afternoons. The United States Library of Congress in Washington, D.C. was also helpful.

Finishing my research in timely fashion would have been impossible without the financial assistance afforded by the Commission for the International Exchange of Scholars in the form of a Fulbright-Hays Western European Research grant in 1983. The award permitted an uninterrupted three-month examination of archives in Paris and London. Closer to home, I would be remiss if I did not recognize the help afforded by the Freiburger Library of Case Western Reserve University in Cleveland for its excellent collection of contemporary works and memoir literature and for the congenial scholarly atmosphere in which much of the first-draft manuscript was written. Finally, my own institution, Cleveland State University, has been wonderfully supportive with grants of both money and time. Research awards in 1974, 1977, and 1985 made possible trips abroad to examine European archives. The University extended me a professional leave-of-absence for the academic year 1984-85 to complete the task of research and writing. My thanks also go to the Cleveland State Library staff for the timely acquisition of important secondary works and to the Interlibrary Loan Service for locating difficult-to-find published materials.

Much of the credit for the meticulous preparation of the manuscript belongs to LueVenia Richardson, the administrative secretary in the History Department at Cleveland State, who invested countless hours in front of her word processor. An acknowledgment of gratitude also goes to my colleagues in the Department of History for making it possible for their chairman to disappear for a year to pursue this project. And to John T. Hubbell, director of the Kent State University Press, and his editorial staff go my thanks for their many helpful suggestions in the final stages of composition.

To my wife, Marge, and children, David and Kim, who cheerfully acquiesced in their husband's and father's absence from home for several large chunks of time over the past decade, I give particular thanks. And last, but certainly not least, I would like to thank my colleague in European history at Ohio University, Professor James Chastain, for making available to me, during the final stages of manuscript composition, the inspiring tranquility of Villa les Lucioles, his charming eighteenth-century villa overlooking the harbor of Villefranche-sur-mer.

Cleveland, Ohio
December 1987

CHAPTER 1

Introduction

This book deals with France's reaction to what John C. Cairns has called "the enigma of Italy's position in Europe."[1] Materially the weakest of the European great powers from its consolidation as a national entity in the 1860s to the outbreak of World War II, Italy heavily depended on the maintenance of a balance of forces on the continent which would allow the country to maximize its influence by oscillating between various combinations of power. Geographically vulnerable, deficient in natural resources, and economically backward, especially in the southern half of the Peninsula, Italy proved an uncertain ally at best—yet with sufficient vigor, population, and strength to make it the object of a substantial diplomacy among the other European nations. Although this book focuses on the complex relationship between the Third French Republic and Fascist Italy between the two world wars, the diplomacy of that era can scarcely be understood independent from what happened before. Most of the problems that plagued Franco-Italian relations in the 1920s and 1930s originated in pre-1914 colonial rivalries and the bitternesses engendered by the wartime alliance and the "mutilated victory" recorded in the treaties of 1919 and 1920.

France played an important, albeit inconsistent, role in the drive for Italian unification in the nineteenth century. In 1849 the newly elected president of the Second Republic, Louis Napoleon Bonaparte, sent a French expeditionary force to Rome to restore Pope Pius IX to the throne of St. Peter. The Pope had fled in the wake of the revolutionary movement led by Giuseppe Mazzini and Giuseppe Garibaldi, which established the Roman Republic. Louis Napoleon's action represented a political gesture designed primarily to repay his clerical supporters in the December 1848 election, but French troops destroyed the Mazzinian revolution and remained in Rome as papal protectors—effectively delaying the incorporation of that city into a unified Italy until 1870. A decade later, in July 1858, Napoleon III met with Count Cavour, chief minister of Piedmont-Sardinia, at the conference of Plombières. There it was arranged that France would intervene militarily in behalf of Piedmont should the latter be attacked by the Austrian Empire. Cavour was planning the expulsion of Austria from the Italian Peninsula as a major step toward the unification of Italy under Piedmontese leadership. Should French intervention occur, Cavour promised at Plombières to cede the provinces of Nice and Savoy to France.

With the French alliance in his pocket, Cavour quickly found a pretext for war with Austria in 1859, and Napoleon III honored his commitment. French intervention proved decisive, but with the Habsburg army in full retreat, Napoleon III suddenly had second thoughts and arranged an armistice with the Austrians at Villafranca. The success of the war excited Italian nationalists elsewhere, and Italy seemed on the verge of unification. Napoleon III, at this point, had no desire to see a strongly unified nation on his Alpine frontier. Thus, by the Treaty of Villafranca, Austria gave the province of Lombardy to Napoleon III who then ceded it to Piedmont. Cavour achieved only half of what he had hoped to realize from the French alliance; the province of Venetia remained in Austria. Meanwhile, Napoleon III annexed Nice and Savoy to the Second Empire. Although Cavour failed to win his full objectives and died shortly thereafter, the events of 1858–1860 brought the Italian *Risorgimento* to fruition, and a unified Italian nation was born. Venetia was added in 1866 following Italy's intervention in the Austro-Prussian War, ironically via the mediation of Napoleon III. The Italians finally annexed Rome in 1870 when the French emperor found it necessary to withdraw his military contingent in order to buttress the French army in the Franco-Prussian War. Thus the final step in Italian unification coincided with the collapse of the Second French Empire at the hands of the Prussians. Both France and Italy were confronted thereafter with new political realities in the heartland of Europe represented by a

INTRODUCTION

consolidated, vigorous, and economically powerful German Empire. The German factor weighed heavily in future Franco-Italian relations.

Both France and Italy—the former a defeated power distracted by the domestic turmoil of the birth of the Third Republic, the latter a new and weak national entity—played effacing roles in international affairs throughout much of the 1870s. Their first major conflict of interest occurred in Tunisia, which was destined to play a long and important role in Franco-Italian relations between 1881 and 1940. Especially following the advent of the fascist era in Italy, Tunisia proved the single most intractable issue dividing the two Latin neighbors, and thus thwarting the desires of those in both countries who sought to establish a Franco-Italian common front against the mutually perceived German danger.

As late as the first week in March 1881, Premier Jules Ferry still had not been persuaded of the desirability of expanding the French Empire to Tunisia. Responding to such a suggestion by his foreign minister, Ferry said: "An affair in Tunisia in election year, my dear Saint-Hilaire, don't think of it." Yet, within three weeks he was preparing to send troops. A French expeditionary force from Algeria crossed the frontier on 24 April 1881, and the Treaty of Bardo, establishing the protectorate, was signed with the Bey of Tunis on 12 May. France's interest in Tunisia can be explained partially by its contiguity to Algeria, but in fact Ferry's motivation was essentially negative—to prevent the acquisition of Tunisia by another great power. French interests in the Mediterranean at this point coincided with those of England and Germany; at the Congress of Berlin in 1878, German Chancellor Otto von Bismarck actively had encouraged French action in Tunisia, both to distract her from the Vosges and to prevent the Italians from securing strategic control at the narrow midpoint straits of the Mediterranean.[2] Traditional balance of power considerations were, therefore, essential ingredients in thrusting France into the further partition of North Africa. It easily is understood why the French occupation of Tunis came as a rude shock to Italian leaders. Regarded by them as a logical first step in imperial expansion, acquisition of Tunisia would have afforded Italy strategic command of the central Mediterranean. Italians had established economic interests there, and Italian settlers constituted the largest European minority. At the time of French occupation in 1881, the Tunisian population approximated a million and a half. Of these, fewer than 20,000 were Europeans—708 French, 7,000 Maltese, and 11,000 Italians. The latter were to increase by 1935 to over 100,000, outnumbering the French by some 30,000 persons.[3] Caught inexplicably unaware by the French action, Italy refused to recognize the protectorate for fifteen years.

Italy's reaction took the form of *trasformismo,* that is, a shift from effacement to engagement in European affairs. The first step occurred in 1882 when Italy signed treaties with both Austria-Hungary and Germany. For Italy the main importance of the Triple Alliance was psychological; it constituted a sense of belonging to the European order and an end to isolation. The treaties guaranteed Italy against an attack by France in return for Italy's support for Austria-Hungary and Germany in the event they were attacked by Russia and France. The guarantee against France was useless, since the latter had no intention of attacking Italy and for much of the 1880s sought friendly relations. Only in the second treaty of the Triple Alliance, signed in February 1887, did Carlo di Robilant, regarded as one of Italy's most skillful foreign ministers, obtain from Bismarck the commitment the latter had resisted successfully in 1882—a guarantee that the *casus foederis* should apply against France in the event of war arising from an Italo-French quarrel in North Africa. This clearly reflected Italian concern over Tunisia and indicated that a second aspect of *trasformismo* was the demand for Italian security in the Mediterranean, a requirement drawing general support from both the right and left of the Italian political spectrum. Even those who opposed colonialism on ideological grounds were prepared to back armed overseas intervention if Italy's vital interests in the Mediterranean were felt to be at stake. If the French moved to occupy Morocco, then Italian leaders believed it essential to seize Tripolitania in order to maintain balance.[4]

These issues and others came to near crisis dimensions during Francesco Crispi's two terms as Italian premier and foreign minister from 1887 to 1891 and again from 1893 to 1896. Franco-Italian relations were extremely poor during this decade, degenerating at times to the verge of warfare. Crispi did not advocate war with France, but he was an ardent nationalist and colonialist whose leftist inclinations identified France with clericalism. Secure in the knowledge of German support and confident that Great Britain could be induced to follow suit, he saw no need to be deferential to the French. His first regime was dominated by an intense Italo-French tariff war that had severe repercussions on the economies of both countries. It was in this highly charged atmosphere of tension and recrimination that Paul Cambon, then serving as French ambassador in Madrid, wrote a remarkably prescient letter to his minister of foreign affairs. Dated 11 May 1889, the letter contains a number of themes that will be articulated in the following chapters and, therefore, deserves to be quoted at some length.

> I consider in effect [Cambon wrote] the reconciliation of France and Italy and later the entente of these two powers with England as the goal recommended for French policy. It is impossible for France to subsist with a double

INTRODUCTION

threat on the Vosges and in the Alps. . . . The estrangement with Italy puts a sword in our back on that day when the struggle with Germany arrives; it alienates us from England, who considers [Italy] our natural counterweight in the Mediterranean. Reconciliation with Italy means equality of forces with Germany and the acquisition of English goodwill. . . . Our policy with Russia is an empirical policy; that with England and Italy is the only rational and fruitful one. It would be a disastrous conjunction of circumstances and a fatal blindness not to seize by the hair the occasion presented by the Egyptian affair to reestablish straight away the entente of 1855 with England and make Italy a part of it.[5]

FRANCO-ITALIAN RAPPROCHEMENT

Crispi's demise, following the humiliating defeat of Italian armed forces by the Ethiopians at Adowa in 1896, paved the way for the Franco-Italian reconciliation sketched out by Paul Cambon seven years earlier. It must be emphasized that the new Italian leaders did not envision a change of camps at this time, that is, a substitution of an alliance with France and England for the Triplice. What foreign ministers such as Antonio di Rudinì and Emilio Visconti-Venosta wanted was greater flexibility. The French ambassador in Rome had no illusions on this score. He wrote to French Foreign Minister Gabriel Hanotauz in June 1897: "the ideal of M. di Rudinì and those who follow him is only to establish that Italian policy is not dependent on that of the German powers. . . . They want to add the benefits of a reconciliation with France to the advantage guaranteed by the Triple Alliance."[6] In short, improved relations with France would give Italy bargaining power with her German and Austro-Hungarian allies.

The altered atmosphere in Rome paralleled similar shifts in Paris. Although suffering from a static demographic situation and slow growth in industrial productivity compared with countries such as England and Germany—deficiencies in some important real measures of power—France nevertheless pursued an active and on the whole quite successful foreign policy after Bismarck's dismissal in 1890. France was aided by the skill of diplomats, such as Hanotaux and Théophile Delcassé at the Quai d'Orsay, Paul and Jules Cambon in London and Berlin respectively, and—most important for purposes of this work—Camille Barrére, who began a twenty-six-year career as France's ambassador to Rome in 1898. The work of these men was abetted by blundering German diplomacy, "which, more by awkwardness than by design, contrived to convey to others the impression of its aggressiveness and ultimately succeeded in creating the very danger that it professed to fear and was endeavoring to avoid, the much touted *Einkreisung."*[7] The Franco-Italian rapprochement, an acknowledged goal in both Paris and Rome following the fall of Crispi, took place in four stages over the course of the following six years.

The first matter to be resolved was the French protectorate in Tunisia. Official recognition was forthcoming in a series of conventions signed in 1896, in exchange for which the Italians acquired certain commercial advantages and nationality rights, among them the right to establish Italian schools and hospitals and to maintain Italian nationality. In short, the conventions of 1896 guaranteed Italians in Tunisia a completely autonomous national life within the context of the French protectorate.[8] It was an extraordinary situation, but one which marked the first step toward the resolution of Franco-Italian colonial differences prior to World War I. The 1896 conventions governed the two countries' relations in Tunisia until the Laval-Mussolini accords of 1935. France and Italy also settled their destructive tariff war in 1898 with an agreement assessing minimum tariffs on most goods exchanged between the two countries.

The most far-reaching agreements, however, were arranged secretly between 1900 and 1902. The first, negotiated by Visconti-Venosta and Delcassé, included a pledge that France had no intention of encroaching on Tripolitania or Cyrenaica and a corresponding Italian declaration of indifference in Morocco. By it, Visconti obtained French approval for an Italian move on Tripoli, conditional however on a prior French occupation of Morocco. Far more significant was the agreement negotiated by Barrère and Giulio Prinetti, actually signed on 30 June 1902 but dated 2 November to conceal its proximity to the renewal of the Triple Alliance, which occurred on 28 June. Prinetti obtained in this accord a French loan for Italy and a free hand in Tripoli, unconstrained by any prior French action in Morocco. The Italian foreign minister was anxious to move quickly in North Africa. In exchange Italy promised to remain neutral in the event of any attack on France or if France went to war as the result of direct provocation. It can be surmised that the latter clause, which was hardly consistent with Italy's commitment to the Triplice, would have raised eyebrows in Berlin and Vienna.[9] In fact, this agreement substantially weakened Italy's position in European affairs, and Prinetti's historical reputation is therefore not very high—particularly since his desire to move quickly on Tripoli was vetoed in Rome. On the other hand, the secret treaty of 1902 represented a diplomatic master stroke for Barrère. The sum total of these four arrangements weakened Italy's attachment to the Triple Alliance and provided essential preparation for the Anglo-Franco-Italian wartime alliance reached by the Treaty of London in 1915. This background weighed heavily in the minds of subsequent French statesmen who sought to repeat this

INTRODUCTION 7

pattern of colonial settlement in the wake of the revival of German aggressiveness in the 1930s.

The road to the Treaty of London, however, was far from direct. The Italians cashed in on their treaties with France by going to war with Turkey in 1911 in order to secure control of Tripolitania. The war lasted a year, and the Italians also occupied the Dodecanese Islands in the eastern Mediterranean. To men like Barrère and Paul Cambon, the prospect of Italy offering her German ally a naval base in the Dodecanese was too dangerous to ignore, and they advocated a more energetic effort to split Italy off from the Triplice. Their views, however, enjoyed no consensus at the Quai d'Orsay. The latter was strongly influenced at the time by young professional diplomats, called *bureaux,* who had been educated at the École Libre des Sciences Politiques for careers in the foreign service. Many had attended "Science Po" in the 1890s when the faculty there was highly nationalistic and anti-German. Hence these young *bureaux* frequently worked to thwart the efforts of old-line diplomats—Jules Cambon in Berlin or Barrère in Rome—to seek rapprochements with members of the Triplice. Hence, Barrère's pro-Italian policy was under constant attack from the *bureaux,* "who saw any flirtation with Triple Alliance members as an antipatriotic act."[10] Such ideological blindness to strategic reality was to reappear at the Quai d'Orsay in the mid-1930s, although with far more drastic consequences.

The outbreak of the First World War in 1914, accompanied by the original Italian stance of neutrality and the failure of early battles in the west to be decisive, made it apparent in both Paris and London that every effort must be made to bring Italy into the war on the side of the Entente Powers. The Central Powers recognized just as clearly the importance of keeping Italy neutral. But the latter's price for continued neutrality—the immediate transfer to Italy of the *Italia Irredenta* including Trentino, Alto Adige, Trieste, Gorizia, and much of the Dalmatian coast and its islands in the Adriatic—proved too exorbitant for Austria-Hungary to accept. At the same time the government of Prime Minister Antonio Salandra and Foreign Minister Sidney Sonnino was negotiating with the Russians, French, and English for the same objectives in exchange for Italy's active entry into the struggle against its Triple Alliance partners. Entente leaders had few scruples about offering Austrian territory in exchange for an Italian alliance. The Treaty of London, which brought Italy into the war, was signed on 26 April 1915 and provided for Italian acquisition of the following:

1. the Brenner frontier, including Trentino and the Alto Adige;
2. Gorizia, Trieste and Pola;
3. the eastern Istrian Peninsula up to, but not including, the city of Fiume

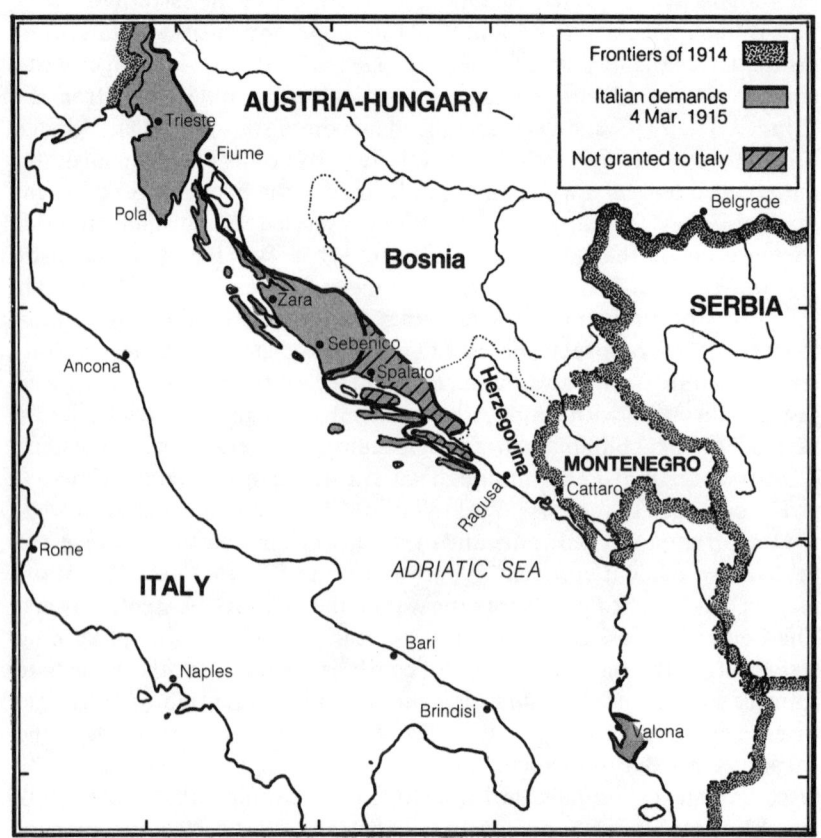

The Treaty of London in the Adriatic, 1915

(The latter was expected to become a port city for a self-governing Croatia or to be controlled by a weakened Habsburg Empire.);
4. northern Dalmatia, including the city of Zara;
5. control over central Albania and sovereignty over Valona;
6. the Dodecanese Islands, which Italy had been occupying since 1911, and "a just share" of territory adjacent to Adalia should the Ottoman Empire collapse.

In addition to these points, the London Treaty also included a vaguely worded Article 13, which subsequently gave rise to substantial Franco-Italian acrimony: "In the event of France and Great Britain increasing their colonial territories in Africa at the expense of Germany, those two Powers agree in principle that Italy may claim some equitable compensation, particularly as regards the settlement in her favour of the questions relative to the frontiers of the Italian colonies of Eritrea, Somaliland and Libya and the neighbouring colonies belonging to France and Great Britain."[11] It is relevant to note that implicit in Italian war aims was the assumption of the continued, albeit diminished, existence of the Habsburg Empire and the continued existence of the Russian Empire. The demise of both during the course of the war enormously complicated the task of Italian statesmen at the postwar peace conferences.

Although not included specifically in the Treaty of London, Italian war aims also included substantial French territorial concessions in Tunisia. Moreover, evidence suggests that some French ministers did not consider this too high a price to pay for an Italian alliance in 1915. "If I had listened to the Cabinet," Foreign Minister Delcassé later claimed, "I would have given half of Tunisia for Italian support." As usual, however, Delcassé did not listen to the cabinet, and the Italians settled for the vague colonial formulations of Article 13, which allowed the triumphant French foreign minister to crow, "I have brought in Italy without surrendering one iota of French territory."[12]

As it turned out, Italy intervened in the war at just the wrong moment. The Russian advance against Austria ground to a halt in the spring of 1915 and then reversed direction; the British suffered a serious setback with the failure of the Dardanelles campaign; and Serbia disappeared from the map. Italian leaders had planned for a timely intervention in order to capitalize on victory in a short war; they were not prepared for a long one. The Italian experience along the Isonzo front between 1915 and 1918 paralleled that of the French on the western front against Germany. The victories of 1918 went some way to ease the disastrous military defeat at Caporetto in the previous year, and Italians ended the war feeling that they had made a substantial contribution to the victory of the western powers. Their leaders approached the peace conference in Paris with every expectation that the Treaty of London would be fulfilled and the fruits of triumph awarded. They were to be bitterly disappointed, and much of their subsequent resentment focused on the French.

FRANCE AND ITALY AT THE PEACE CONFERENCE

As the peacemakers gathered in Paris in 1919, they faced a completely new set of political realities. The Habsburg, Hohenzollern, Romanov, and Osmanli dynasties had collapsed. In addition, the involvement of the United States—personified by President Woodrow Wilson—introduced a national self-determination ideology into the peacemaking process. The Wilsonian program, articulated in the famous Fourteen Points of January 1918, clashed at every juncture with the secret treaties arranged among the Entente powers and Italy before American entry into the struggle and with the exaggerated climate of expectations among the victor powers. So far as the Italians were concerned, one of the problems at Paris was that their claims against the then-defunct Austro-Hungarian Empire were set aside for several months while the negotiators worked on the German treaty. Moreover, Wilson was forced to compromise his principles so severely with regard to Germany—in the Rhineland, the Saar, and the matter of reparations in particular—that he was determined to hold fast to the Fourteen Points in the Adriatic. The Italian assumption of 1915 had been that Croatia and Slovenia would remain part of a reduced Habsburg Empire, which would retain Fiume as its outlet to the sea. But by 1918–19 there had emerged a vigorous, unitary, southern Slav state claiming not only Dalmatia, the Adriatic islands and Fiume, but also the Istrian Peninsula, Gorizia, and Trieste. Italian Premier Vittorio Orlando and his foreign minister, Sonnino, had to resist these claims. That, after all, was why Italy had fought the war.

The French and British remained consistent in their willingness to support Italy's Adriatic aspirations as articulated in the Treaty of London. But after forcing Wilson into so many compromises with regard to the German treaty, the French, in particular, were not anxious to antagonize the American president further by coercing additional concessions with regard to Italy. The promise, subsequently unfulfilled, of the Anglo-American guarantee of French security was too valuable to put at risk simply to satisfy Italian nationalist goals.[13] Georges Clemenceau and David Lloyd George contented themselves with tepid verbal support to Orlando for the Treaty of London program but essentially allowed Wilson a free hand to deal with Italian claims. Wilson refused to recognize the validity of the Treaty of London even though, by April 1919, Orlando was willing to make modest compromises.[14]

At first Orlando and Sonnino submitted a maximal program. Had they contented themselves from the outset with the Treaty of London, evidence suggests that they would have received more energetic support from their English and French allies. Wilson could have been worn down to an acceptable compromise, according to Italy far less than the Treaty of London provided but assuring her control of the Adriatic. However, the Italian leaders went to Paris with the port city of Fiume also on their agenda, claiming its acquisition on the perfectly respectable Wilsonian grounds of national self-determination; a clear majority of the city's population was Italian. Besides, its incorporation into Yugoslavia threatened to make the latter into a potent threat to Italian predominance in the Adriatic. But here Italian leaders found themselves in an impossible contradiction. It was clearly inconsistent to argue for Fiume on the grounds of nationality and at the same time demand the full London Treaty program in Dalmatia, where Italians numbered only some 19,000 in a population of over 630,000, on the grounds of strategic necessity and treaty rights. Orlando subsequently came to value Fiume more than the Dalmatian coast and indicated a willingness to sacrifice much of the latter. But Wilson would not be budged in his conviction that the economic viability of the new Yugoslav nation required its ready access to Adriatic port facilities. In fact, it proved impossible to arrange an acceptable compromise of the Fiume question at the peace conference itself. On 24 April 1919, Wilson so infuriated the Italian delegation by publishing his own compromise proposal in *Le Temps*—in effect going over Orlando's head to the Italian people—that the delegation left Paris and returned to Rome amid angry popular demonstrations against the "mutilated victory."[15] The question of Fiume remained a serious bone of contention between Rome and Belgrade until 1924. Its final resolution, largely in Italy's favor, involved substantial Franco-Italian diplomacy and is discussed in some detail in chapter three.

In the treaty of Saint-Germain (1919), signed with the truncated state of Austria, Italy received the coveted Brenner frontier, including Trentino, the Alto Adige, and southern Tyrol. In addition, Italy was allowed to absorb Gorizia and much of the Istrian Peninsula at the northern end of the Adriatic—but not Fiume. Given the situation in 1919 this probably represented as much as the Italians could have expected on the continent of Europe, and scant sympathy was felt elsewhere for the strident expressions of nationalist frustration emanating from Italy.

The angry cries of "mutilated victory" were far more justifiable with regard to the colonial settlement. The Treaty of London had promised Italy a "just share" of Turkey in the region adjacent to Adalia in Asia Minor. The St. Jean de Maurienne Agreement (August 1917) defined this as southern Turkey from Smyrna to Mersina, an area comparable in size to those former Ottoman territories turned over to Britain and France as League of Nations mandates. Paris and London, however, denounced the agreement in November 1918 on the dubious grounds that it had not been ratified by Russia. Article 13 of the London Treaty promised Italy "equitable compensation" if Britain and France absorbed any German colonies in Africa. However, these colonies were distributed during Italy's absence from the peace conference in the spring of 1919. As compensation Italy demanded French territorial concessions in Libya, Kassala, and Jibuti; British concessions in Somaliland and Jubaland; and recognition of Italy's sole influence in Ethiopia. What Italy received was paltry by comparison. France relinquished a small strip of territory along the Algerian border with Libya, which provided access to the two oases of Ghat and Ghadamès; the British eventually yielded Jubaland. But Paris absolutely refused to budge on Jibuti and Ethiopia, fearing potential Italian threats to French interests in French Somaliland and the Red Sea area.[16] This niggling response to Italian expansionist goals may be regarded as a blunder on the part of the western democracies, particularly France, who should not have been surprised to find Italy aggrieved in Africa and, therefore, among the "revisionist" powers in the interwar period. North and East African issues loomed extraordinarily large in the diplomacy of the two "Latin sisters" between the two world wars and are the subject of much analysis in forthcoming chapters.

THE POSTWAR ATMOSPHERE

Most discussions of French foreign policy in the early postwar era concentrate quite rightly on the "German problem" and the confrontation between England and France on how best to deal with it. Undoubtedly, *sécurité*— especially along the Rhine frontier—formed the most conspicuous leitmotif running throughout French diplomacy. France's political leaders, and not only those of the right-of-center Bloc national, were extremely reluctant to cooperate with British appeals to appease the Weimar Republic. This field has been well plowed,[17] but that of France's relations with Italy remains relatively virgin territory, which must be considered for the light it sheds on the main thrust of French policy in the 1920s and 1930s.

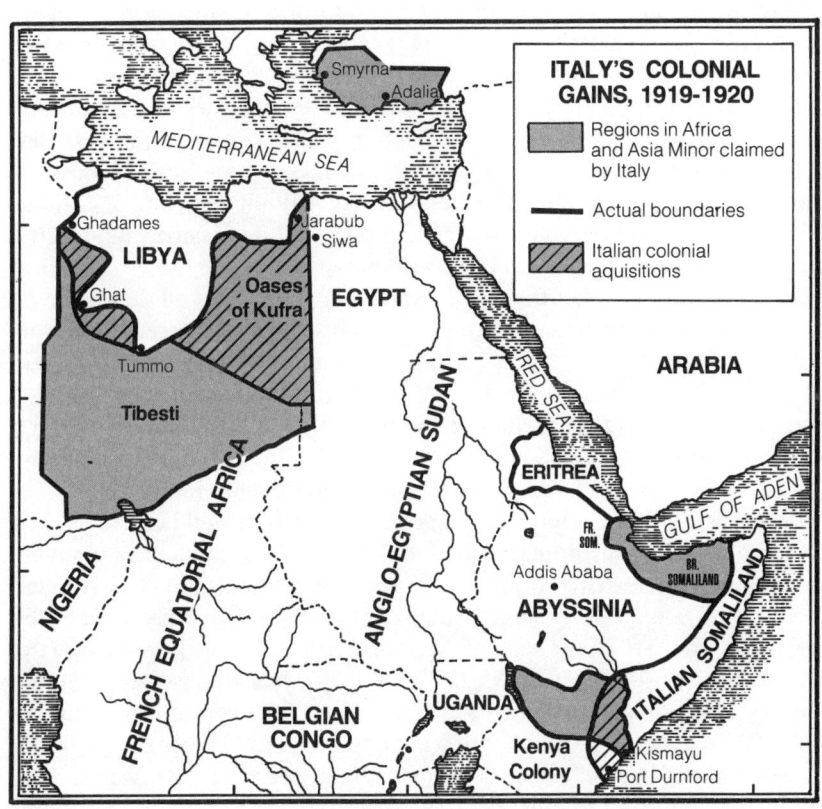

Italian Claims and Acquisitions in Africa, 1919–20

France's position in the Europe of 1919 was extraordinary. Since 1870, France had been in relative decline among the major powers of the world in terms of real measures of power—population increase, industrial growth, agricultural output, and so forth. The First World War exacerbated these trends incrementally. Thus, whereas *real* French power was severely impaired, the country's *apparent* strength as the major continental victor was enormously enhanced. The opposite condition prevailed for Germany whose absolute strength had declined because of defeat, but whose relative strength emerged more advantageous than before because of the demise of central and eastern European competitors. French leaders were painfully aware of Germany's vastly superior demographic and economic reserves. This potentially calamitous situation is one reason why France's postwar mood has often been interpreted as bellicose and uncompromising. Actually, archival materials that were assembled and declassified only in the 1970s show French policy to have been nervous and defensive—a natural reaction to the failure of the Anglo-American guarantee and the perceived inadequacies of the Versailles Treaty.[18] All of which reinforced the importance of France's relations with Italy, particularly her initial diplomatic reaction to the rise of Benito Mussolini's fascist movement.

Evidence presented in chapter two will suggest that whereas French leaders rejected the uncompensated appeasement of Weimar Germany, they proved anxious to take a tolerant and indulgent view of the Italian fascists. Should the latter come to power, they might well be enrolled in a common front against the Germans and thus act as a convenient counterweight to the British determination to appease. But it also must be stressed here that France's long-range strategy for dealing with Italy came to be predicated in part on the state of Anglo-French relations. In reviewing the brilliant twenty-six-year career of Camille Barrère, who retired from his ambassadorship in Rome in 1924, Albert Pingaud, a permanent official at the Quai d'Orsay, made the following observation: "He [Mussolini] had never exhibited more hostility to France than when the latter was at odds with Great Britain and more complaisance than when the entente between London and Paris seemed complete. In this sense, the state of Franco-Italian relations, according to M. Barrère, was and must remain conditioned by that of Franco-English relations."[19] These views came to prevail in the Ministry of Foreign Affairs only in the mid-1930s and help to explain the French thrust in those years to erect a common Anglo-Franco-Italian front against Nazi treaty violations. But the foundation for this strategy was laid in the immediate post-World War I era, when the Third Republic was forced to deal with the politically turbulent and treaty revisionist Italian nation.

Although France and Italy had fought side by side to defeat the Central Powers and shared a common interest in preserving the independence and integrity of Austria,[20] the preceding pages reveal a number of issues that hindered cordial relations between the two Mediterranean powers. Briefly, Italians were disgruntled at receiving no mandates over former German colonies in Africa and dissatisfied at the minor colonial compensations offered them by France in accordance with Article 13 of the Treaty of London. Many Italians also believed that their country was entitled to the Adriatic port city of Fiume and to further territorial gains along the Dalmatian coast. They held France largely responsible for their frustration, leading Frenchmen to fear that Italy would become a jealous rival of France in the Mediterranean, an adversary determined to stir up trouble among friends of France in south-central Europe, notably among the Yugoslavs. But, perhaps, the most serious issue dividing the two countries involved the rights of Italians in Tunisia. The French protectorate was a major area for Italian emigration, even more so after 1921 when the United States adopted stringent quotas on southern and eastern European immigrants. Italian nationality and special privileges had been protected in Tunisia since 1896 by the conventions that ironically marked the first step toward prewar Franco-Italian rapprochement. In 1918 France provisionally denounced the conventions of 1896 as an initial move toward the naturalization of all foreigners living in the Regency. Suffering from limited resources and a rapidly expanding population, Italians had long regarded their countrymen living in Tunisia as a major national resource. Their resentment of the French action was considerable.[21]

But in spite of these diplomatic tensions and the obvious anti-French bias of the postwar Italian government, Barrère succinctly underscored the importance of Italy to France in a long dispatch to Foreign Minister Alexandre Millerand on 3 May 1920. The ambassador pointed out how good relations with Italy had served France well in the period from 1902 to 1918. But since the armistice, French policy "has committed the greatest conceivable error—that of seeming to be more anti-Italian than it is in reality." Barrère observed that France's principal task for the foreseeable future would be to build and consolidate the new European order. Italy could perform useful services in this enterprise, but above all, she could hinder the French effort if she were to remain in opposition. "It is thus beyond doubt," he argued, "that our best interests lie in not alienating her, in not abandoning her to the maneuvers of our rivals, nor even sometimes to her own inclinations." Barrère concluded his dispatch by outlining a reasonable strategy for dealing with the Italians. Echoing Paul Cambon's recommendations of 1889, he advocated a close Anglo-French entente, to which

Italy could then be attached, as the best means of "disciplining Italy" and resolving the thorny problems surrounding Germany, the Adriatic, the Middle East, and North Africa. If such a policy were followed with regard to Italy, Barrère predicted that it would "ameliorate our present relations with this country and render it relatively amenable to our designs, during the period when the allies are unhappily becoming less united than one would like to admit."[22] Barrère's communication not only placed the problem of Franco-Italian relations in the context of European politics, it also demonstrated that some influential voices were anxious to bury the bitterness of the peace conferences and initiate a rapprochement. One of the most serious obstacles to such a development, however, was the virtually anarchical social and political climate in Italy during the immediate postwar period. It was an era in which the fear of growing leftist and Germanophile sentiment in Italy was a source of concern to French statesmen; the age was also marked by governmental instability that was severe even by French standards. These matters, and the French reaction to the rise of Mussolini and the Italian fascists are considered in the next chapter.

CHAPTER 2

France and the Emergence of the Fascist Era in Italy, 1920–23

B arrère viewed the postwar Italian government with serious misgivings. The wartime Orlando ministry gave way, in June 1919, to one headed by Francesco Nitti and Tommaso Tittoni, both of whom had been neutralist during the war and whose sympathies lay with Germany. Barrère notified the Quai d'Orsay on 23 June 1919 that the Nitti Cabinet symbolized the state of mind in Italy during recent months: "resentment against the Allies, explosion of Germanophile sentiments conceived by pique as well as by inclination, awakening all of the neutralist and anti-war elements whose tendencies are favorable to the Germans." The French ambassador blamed Nitti as well for prejudicing Italian newspaper opinion against France and for encouraging a bitter anti-French campaign. The French ambassador was particularly suspicious of the apparently close working relationship established between the Italian premier and Lloyd George, the British prime minister—a cordiality that Barrère feared would isolate France in the German question.[1]

The anti-French tone of the Italian press provided a constant source of annoyance to Barrère, who was inordinately sensitive to newspaper criticism. He and other French officials in Rome were also concerned about the efforts of German propaganda to capitalize on the tone of Italian newspapers in order to divide the wartime allies. Officials in the French Embassy, located in the historic Palazzo Farnese, noted on several occasions the irony of Germany's having so little money to pay reparations yet sufficient quantities to bankroll oppostion to France in Italy.[2] On 9 August 1921, François Charles-Roux, the French chargé d'affaires in Rome, wrote privately to Barrère, who was vacationing in Paris, that: "The Germans and Germanophiles are gaining here every day. Little by little, finance, industry, press, everything . . . is falling into their hands." He suggested that Barrère contact Philippe Berthelot, secretary general of the Quai d'Orsay, to urge that France counter the pro-German propaganda by subsidizing favorable commentary in the Italian press or by exercising some economic pressure on Italy. The Foreign Ministry rejected both suggestions. The extreme anti-French attitude abated somewhat with the fall of the Nitti government in June 1920. The new regime was headed by Giovanni Giolitti, the grand old man of Italian politics. France's concern about the return to power of this old pro-German and neutralist premier was modestly appeased by the appointment of Count Carlo Sforza to the Consulta. The latter's pro-French attitude was well known; he told the French chargé on 12 September 1920 that his sole "raison d'être in the [Giolitti] Cabinet is for having been an interventionist and for being a partisan of the alliance with France and England."[3]

This somewhat more favorable political climate, however, must be considered against the backdrop of an alarming expansion of social unrest throughout the Italian Peninsula in the years from 1918 to 1922. Strikes paralyzed the principal public services and severely affected industry and commerce as well. These activities were accompanied by the growth of the Italian socialist and communist parties. French officials watched these developments with considerable apprehension; they tended to place the blame for the social crisis on the activities of the maximalists and anarchists. The Italian Communist Party, founded in January 1921, was directly financed by Moscow, and French intelligence reports indicate that Russian money bankrolled strikes and disturbances in the large cities and industrial centers of Italy. The resurgence of socialist strength and activity dismayed Frenchmen working to ameliorate Franco-Italian relations. The socialists, the French chargé informed Foreign Minister Georges Leygues on 12 October 1920, had formally disavowed the Treaty of Versailles and identified Paris as the center of reaction par excellence. They are "the declared and implacable adversaries of French policy. . . . Their arrival in power, which they are working toward, is thus not desirable for us; and their influence on the present Government, which is looking at them more favorably . . . would not be favorable for us. . . ."[4]

The factor that compounded the socialist danger was the apparent inability of the Italian government to cope successfully with the social crisis. Barrère denounced the Nitti regime as weak and virtually helpless in combating the constant strikes. He refused to take a strong stand, as the press and the majority of the country demanded, and instead preferred to grant "concessions and accommodations while events demonstrate daily the uselessness of his efforts." By October 1920, the economic outlook had darkened considerably. Industry was paralyzed; agriculture was plagued by peasant land occupations; and exports had dropped. The Italian government, under both Nitti and Giolitti, argued that political and social discontent was the result of this prolonged economic crisis. The French, however, saw the cause and effect in reverse order. In a lengthy review of the Italian internal situation on 9 October 1920, the French chargé in Rome, Charles-Roux, informed Leygues that the agitation of socialists and anarchists rendered the development of normal economic life virtually impossible. Charles-Roux outlined the priorities very clearly: "Since it is socialist agitation, or rather revolutionary communist and anarchist agitation, which has caused the aggravation of the economic situation, this agitation must be attacked first."[5] But if the Italian government was either unwilling or unable to combat spreading leftist agitation, what alternatives remained? The evidence indicates that French diplomacy was likely to look with favor upon any force or movement capable of reestablishing order in Italy by challenging the left. French support would be enhanced if it was felt that such a force or movement could be expected to harbor a more optimistic view of France than that held by the Italian government in power.

The record demonstrates with striking clarity that French diplomats in Italy viewed the nascent fascist movement with almost unalloyed favor and enthusiasm. This attitude was especially marked among those, like Barrère and Charles-Roux, who were anxious to resurrect close ties between France and Italy. The tone was set in a dispatch from the French chargé in Rome to Leygues on 19 October 1920, which contained the first reference to the fascist phenomenon in the diplomatic correspondence. Charles-Roux first described the growing social agitation in the Peninsula, a condition bordering on anarchy. After ritually placing the finger of guilt on the combination of socialist extremism and governmental inaction, he noted that the socialists had begun to meet systematic opposition from a new political force: "These exploits are . . . the work of nationalist counter-demonstrators organized for this purpose into *'fasci di combattimento' (faisceau de combat)*. The peaceful population can look favorably upon them; but since they are peaceful, they don't participate. Because of this, it matters relatively little that the 'fascists,' on occasion, use truncheons, revolvers and hand grenades."[6]

Similarly sanguine analyses of the *squadristi* arrived in Rome from French consulates in various parts of Italy. But throughout the remainder of 1920 and on into 1921, the most uncritical appraisals of fascist activity arrived at the Quai d'Orsay from the pen of Camille Barrère. The prestigious French ambassador informed Leygues on 10 November 1920 that recent administrative elections had not resulted in the large gains anticipated by the socialists. This salutary result was due largely to the fascists, who have "drawn [the Italian voters] out of their torpor" as a result of their "protests by word and deed against the incessant provocations of the anarchists and bolsheviks." Thus, he concluded, although the fascists occasionally employed the same tactics as their adversaries, they nevertheless "have rendered the service of jolting those who intended to remain cautious out of their apathy." Referring again on 1 February 1921 to the fascist tactics of violent confrontation, Barrère advised the new foreign minister, Aristide Briand, that the vacillation of the Nitti and Giolitti regimes in the face of revolution from the left "fully justifies the energetic and resolute attitude of the fascists. . . ."[7]

Barrère's attitude revealed itself further in many other dispatches and telegrams to Briand. He referred to the fascists at one point as representing "the parties of order." Three weeks later he urged the foreign minister to plant a story in *Le Temps* lauding the "courageous struggle" of the fascists against the elements of disorder and dissolution and depicting them as "representing order, patriotism and security." Such a favorable analysis might have encouraged Francophile Italians to support fascist candidates at the next election. A few months later, in a long assessment of the socialist and fascist movements since the end of the war, Barrère argued that fascism had been caused by the excesses of the socialists and the deficiency of the Italian government. Since October 1920, when the fascists began openly to challenge the socialists, they became so effective that the latter requested state protection. But socialist appeals were in vain: "the fascists are continuing their work of purification and the Government is letting these improvised defenders of the public order act."[8]

It is clear, then, that the fascist movement's antisocialist activities undergirded Barrère's initial admiration; furthermore, it appeared to represent a force of order and stability, a situation regarded as prerequisite to establishing closer relations with Italy. In addition, fascist leadership seemed diplomatically acceptable to France. Mussolini was not an unknown quantity in the Palazzo Farnese. During World War I, he had been regarded as a force leading Italy away from her neutralist position and into direct alliance with France and England. Mussolini received financial support from the French Embassy during the interventionist campaign of 1914–15.[9] Barrère viewed the fascist leader as a force potentially favorable to French foreign policy goals in Germany, an attitude which emerged in his analysis of Mussolini's maiden speech to the Italian Chamber of Deputies. The fascist Duce became a deputy from Milan as a result of the election of 15 May 1921. His first speech energetically criticized the mild reaction of the Giolitti government to German propaganda activities in the Alto Adige and along the Brenner frontier. Barrère remarked on 22 June 1921 in a telegram to Briand that "the general anti-German tone of his speech . . . cannot be displeasing in France, any more than the fact that one cannot find here (this time at least) any word of criticism against our policy."[10]

The French Embassy's rather positive view of Mussolini as the skillful and controlled leader of a powerful but disorganized political force received reinforcement in later months. The disparate character of the early fascist movement occasionally led to outbreaks of violence, which even Barrère had to admit exceeded the limits of good sense. But Mussolini himself increasingly came to be depicted as the leader who might curb the violent elements within the movement and direct it into a creative political force. Barrère noted on 18 November 1921, in a dispatch to Briand, that the Duce's efforts to transform fascism into a unified political party demonstrated his concern about injecting serious political content into its program and eliminating the excessive and violent elements of disorder from the movement. Six months later Charles-Roux sent a telegram to Raymond Poincaré, Briand's successor as president of the Council of Ministers and minister of foreign affairs, which described in admiring terms Mussolini's skill at maneuvering within the Italian parliamentary structure.[11] These documents constitute early indicators of the future tendency of French foreign service personnel to view Mussolini as the most moderate man of his party, whose leadership was essential to discipline the movement and direct it into creative and peaceful channels.

The Italian political crisis deepened throughout the last half of 1921 and the first half of 1922. Electoral gains were registered by the socialists and the rural-based Catholic Popular Party, both of which were strongly antifascist and inclined toward a pro-German and anti-French stance in foreign policy. In July 1922, Giolitti declined an invitation to form another ministry on the grounds that the composition of the Assembly made any stable government impossible. His public letter to *Il Mondo* indicated that any government which continued to oppose the fascists would encourage civil war. Barrère repeated these views to Poincaré on 28 July 1922, and indicated that it was likely the fascists would have to be brought into the government. He expressed no alarm at this prospect. In fact, he suggested to Poincaré the following day that the French press be instructed to abstain from any critical analysis of the activity of the fascists during the Italian ministerial crisis. They, after all, were the ones blocking the anti-French Nitti from returning to power, and "we are going to have to adjust to them in the near future." Besides, Barrère added, fascist organs have abstained from attacking France for over three months and have supported French policy in Germany and at London. Barrère was by no means the only one to take such a salutary view of fascist foreign policy. The French consul general at Milan wrote on 12 September 1922 that, although the fascists were divided between nationalist extremists and "pure fascists" whose program was aimed at the reconstitution of national life in Italy, the latter were by no means unfavorable to France. This group, into which he placed Mussolini, might well be a useful element "toward consolidating good relations between the two countries."[12]

Barrère's favorable disposition toward the fascists continued right up to the eve of the "march on Rome," in spite of the increasingly belligerent domestic stance adopted by the movement. On 7 October 1922, he informed Poincaré about an article from *La Patria,* a fascist sheet strongly critical of German policy in Italy. It condemned Germany's support for *Il Paese,* a strongly pro-German, anti-French and antifascist newspaper. The latter's editorial policy was ill-advised, the fascist organ emphasized, because the fascists would shortly be in power. Without making any comment on the last observation, Barrère concluded simply: "We thus can only be pleased that a fascist organ is levelling such a frank attack on a newspaper like *Paese* and, behind it, those who are paying it with money from across the Rhine and who up to the present have not yet been unmasked." The French ambassador even deplored the appearance of an article critical of the fascists published in *Le Temps.* He maintained that the effect of such articles was unfortunate, since for several months "not only have we not had to complain about the fascists, but we have noticed that in matters of foreign policy they have declared themselves for us." Given the fact that the fascists were by that time one of the most important elements in Italian politics and were getting stronger every day, Barrère thought it was foolhardy to publish articles which could only prejudice Mussolini's party against France.[13]

Aside from *Le Temps* and the socialist press, however, the Italian fascist movement received reasonably favorable treatment from French newspapers on the eve of its takeover. Even *Le Temps* modified its views, admitting that if the fascists could form a coalition government with Giolitti, it could be a guarantee of social order and "its program will work quite naturally toward the rapprochement of our countries." *Le Petit Parisien,* politically moderate with the largest circulation in France, applauded the fact that Italy's next government was likely to be composed of those elements in the forefront of the fight against socialism. Predictably, the center-right and rightist press in France was more demonstrably enthusiastic about the possibility of a fascist government in Italy. *Le Matin* published a very favorable review of the movement, depicting it as "the new national forces thrown into the struggle against socialism and against the old political caste which abandoned the State to the mercy of socialism." *Le Gaulois* rhapsodized about the accomplishments of the *squadristi,* spurred on by the "magnificent inspiration" of warrior-poet Gabriele D'Annunzio and the "eloquent advocacy" of Mussolini; " . . . the cause they are defending is just and the spirit which it provokes is irresistible." Overall, substantial numbers of French newspapers sympathized with the fascist movement because it stood fast against bolshevism and because its foreign-policy stance appeared at least more pro-French than the government's. Some editorial reservations were expressed, however, about what impact Mussolini would have on Italy's treaty-revisionist ambitions.[14] Nevertheless, it should come as no surprise that neither the Quai d'Orsay nor many of the organs of French public opinion were greatly alarmed when, on 28 October 1922, the Italian king invited Mussolini to form a government. Rather, the contrary proved to be the case.

Mussolini's accession to power was not received at all poorly in France. It provided an occasion for the resurrection of old clichés about the two "Latin sisters," and there was a great deal of optimism about the Duce as a declared Francophile and reestablisher of order in the Peninsula. In addition, French officials at the Palazzo Farnese stressed in several telegrams to Poincaré the potential diplomatic benefits to France of the change in regime. Charles-Roux informed the president of the Council and foreign minister that the directors of the fascist party were favorable to France; the fascist press recently had supported France in Middle Eastern affairs and on the question of reparations and war debts. A functionary at the Italian Foreign Ministry told the French chargé that Mussolini was inclined to be moderate in his foreign policy initiatives, even in regard to Yugoslavia. The latter was a particularly sensitive point, since the Quai d'Orsay regarded the Kingdom of Serbs, Croats and Slovenes as a protégé, while substantial territorial disputes remained between the kingdom and Italy. Charles-Roux stressed the anti-German focus of the fascist mentality in his telegram to Paris, pointing out that the blackshirts had invaded the offices of several anti-French "Germanophile" and "Nittian" newspapers in Rome and burned recent issues.[15]

The main concern of French diplomats in Italy was how the French press would react to the commencement of the fascist regime in Italy. But just as in the United States,[16] the major mass circulation organs of the center and right in France either endorsed the new regime without qualification or took a reasonably favorable "wait and see" attitude.[17] Their editorials of the period from 29 October to 5 November uniformly emphasized the return of domestic tranquility, the marked decline of socialist activity, and the potentially favorable direction of fascist foreign policy. So far as France was concerned, the single most jarring event of the opening of the fascist era was the sudden resignation of Count Sforza as Italian ambassador to Paris on 31 October. Sforza resigned because he was bitterly opposed to what he presumed would be the major thrust of Mussolini's foreign policy; the Duce's maiden speech to the Chamber in June 1921 had been scathingly critical of Sforza's tenure as foreign minister, especially of his policy of reconciliation with Yugoslavia. Sforza had long been regarded as a strong partisan of the alliance with France, and his departure seemed to many to remove a moderating force in Italian policy. But evidence suggests that the ambassador's departure was not as serious as originally speculated. Charles-Roux noted that Mussolini was most worried that the hasty resignation would have a negative effect on French opinion of his government and that it might agitate Adriatic questions which he desired for the moment to keep tranquil. Mussolini attempted to keep Sforza at his post as a symbol of good Franco-Italian relations, but the latter rejected the Duce's overtures more, perhaps, because of personal antipathy than for any other reason. Besides, it was stressed that the unfortunate effects of Sforza's precipitate action would be muted in the long run by Mussolini's decision to retain Salvatore Contarini as secretary general of the Italian Foreign Ministry. Contarini's long experience and favorable disposition to France were well known at the Quai d'Orsay.[18]

The French diplomatic community, nevertheless, continued to harbor some apprehensions about the basic direction of the fascist regime. These concerns were momentarily exacerbated when the Duce presented his ministerial declaration to the Italian Chamber of Deputies on 17 November 1922. His speech had dictatorial overtones, and he defined the wartime entente as nothing more than a "diplomatic expression" and decried the "inferior way" that Italy had often been treated in the past. Mussolini enunciated his famous doctrine of "nothing for nothing" and indicated that unless the entente became "an egalitarian equilibrium of forces," Italy would seek her freedom of action. There are some indications that, if alarming, such bravado was not taken too seriously in high diplomatic councils. Mussolini's first meeting with western statesmen was scheduled for 20 November 1922 at the opening of the Lausanne Conference on the Near East. The Duce, however, took the initiative of inviting Poincaré and Lord Curzon, England's foreign minister, to meet privately with him in advance of the regular conference at the small Swiss city of Territet. He sought recognition and a statement of equality. Poincaré and Curzon, taken by surprise, agreed to go. The dinner conversation at Territet resulted in a rather innocuous communiqué alluding to the principle of equality among powers. Jules Laroche, a permanent official at the Quai d'Orsay, maintained that no one took Mussolini seriously at Territet or Lausanne. "Poincaré and Curzon scarcely hid their disdain. His success was considered ephemeral." But recent scholarship has arrived at a more realistic judgment. Alan Cassels concludes that Mussolini's accomplishments at Lausanne were considerable. He mitigated some of the suspicions in England and France about his belligerent speech of 17 November by showing his willingness to continue the entente in the eastern Mediterranean. Simultaneously, he compelled two of Europe's most influential statesmen to bow to his whim at Territet. "The deference shown to Mussolini by Curzon and Poincaré set the tone for the rest of the European diplomatic community."[19] Such a sweeping judgment may be somewhat exaggerated, but it cannot be denied that France became increasingly more deferential to the Italian leader as tensions with England mounted over the German question.

The prevailing tone of the dispatches from the French Embassy in Rome throughout November and December 1922 revealed increasing admiration for the completely altered social situation in Italy. Charles-Roux reminded Poincaré on several occasions that more Italians were rallying to Mussolini's support. To assess the significance of such a situation for France, he argued, one must compare the present calm and stability with the situation of the previous two years of governmental decrepitude, strikes, and socialist and communist defiance of law and order, when "the red flag floated from factory roofs, whose doors were defended by red guards. . . . " In contrast, Mussolini's movement is described as one of "audacity, will, decision, authority."[20] The extent of Mussolini's impact on socialist activity— which had so excited Barrère, Charles-Roux, and the Quai d'Orsay—can be gauged by reviewing the French document collection. The documents dealing with the Italian "Partis politiques, socialistes, action pacifiste et revolutionnaire" from June 1918 to 28 October 1922 are contained in four and two-thirds bound volumes. From the day of the fascist takeover, however, until the Law of Exception in November 1926 outlawed all other political parties, socialist and revolutionary activities formed the subject of only some seventy-two pages of documents.[21] Clearly, the fascists put an end to one of the most serious obstacles to Franco-Italian understanding, so far as the French were concerned.

Equally important to the French was the renewed possibility of integrating Italy into a common policy vis-à-vis Germany. Barrère worked diligently to foster a more conciliatory atmosphere between the two countries during the early days of fascist power. He arranged a special audience of the Duce with a group of exclusively French journalists in which Mussolini responded to all domestic and foreign policy questions "with simplicity and frankness." Since it was the Italian premier's usual practice to meet all foreign journalists together, Barrère described this gesture as "une gracieuseté spéciale pour la France." Events such as these led to favorable comments in the French press along with speculation that a new era in Franco-Italian relations was emerging. *Le Temps* remarked on several occasions about the common desire of both countries to cooperate in the Near East, concert their efforts in behalf of Austrian independence, and deal effectively with the German question. It appeared that relations could become even closer and more friendly.[22]

The diplomatic possibilities were stated even more explicitly when Charles-Roux responded on 18 December 1922 to Poincaré's request for detailed biographical information on Mussolini. The French chargé closed his dispatch with the observation that ever since the peace conference, fascist policy "has taken an anti-German attitude in the question of reparations and disarmament and of the execution of the Treaty of Versailles." Very thinly veiled was the suggestion that Italy's support might be valuable for France in the emerging showdown with England over the question of German reparations. The theme of a possible Franco-Italian entente reappeared in two important telegrams from Charles-Roux to Poincaré on 5 and 7 January 1923, on the eve of the Franco-Belgian occupation of the Ruhr. The first of these noted that virtually all the Roman and provincial newspapers had commented favorably and extensively on New Year's Day speeches by himself and the French ambassador to the Holy See. He interpreted this reaction as proof of the amelioration in Italian public opinion toward France, since some of the newspapers "have underlined particularly the necessity for a Franco-Italian entente." Two days later, the French chargé reported that Contarini advised him of his own personal interest in closer Franco-Italian relations and also commented that France has "everything to gain since the . . . disposition of fascism [is] currently favorable to the entente between the two countries."[23]

The documents cited above indicate that French officials in Rome were anxious to welcome the new fascist regime in exchange for Italian acquiescence in the French thesis on reparations. Their influence on the government became apparent when Poincaré presented his bill for the indulgent French attitude at the London Conference on reparations, which opened on 7 December 1922. Jacques Chastenet maintains that as late as the London Conference, Mussolini, a *"parvenu* whose shaved head and green-edged white spats bring smiles to the faces of the correct diplomats of the Foreign Office," was not yet taken seriously. Such assertions, however, are not consistent with those presented by the Comte de Saint-Aulaire, the French ambassador in London, who attended the conference on reparations. He maintained that Poincaré, as a lawyer, had no sympathy for Mussolini's tendency to hold himself above the law. But the systematic wooing of fascist Italy toward a common policy with France on the German question began at London. Poincaré neglected nothing to consolidate the cooperation with Mussolini already achieved the previous month at the Lausanne Conference. Saint-Aulaire maintained that the French foreign minister hoped, by building a Franco-Italian bloc, to goad the recalcitrant English into a common allied front on the German question—or at least to achieve a benevolent neutrality from England.[24]

The London Conference broke up in disarray. The French firmly maintained that Germany must pay reparations in full voluntarily or else be coerced to do so; the English, on the other hand, urged a moratorium. A further conference was scheduled for January 1923 in Paris. There was some concern at the Quai d'Orsay about the possible consequences of alienating England on the matter of reparations. Alexandre Millerand, president of the Republic, even suggested in two personal letters to Barrère that England might be brought around to the hard-line French position on reparations in exchange for a solution convenient to her in the Near East. A deal such as this never materialized, however, which only served to magnify the importance of the position that the Italians were likely to take on this matter. Since Belgium was allied to France, the Italian vote in the Reparations Commission would be decisive. There were those who feared that a direct clash between England and France would encourage Italians to adopt their historic diplomatic position of always maintaining close relations with England. In general, such fears were well grounded. But in this particular situation, the foundations for Franco-Italian cooperation had been well prepared. Mussolini was flattered by the enthusiastic reception his new regime had received in France. Poincaré succeeded in persuading his cabinet colleagues to approve economic concessions to Italy in Asia Minor in order to secure Italian cooperation in the Reparations Commission.[25]

In addition, several other solid Italian interests dictated her alignment with the French. Although, in the long run, fascist Italy was not averse to seeing Germany recover some of her strength in order to balance French hegemony on the continent, for the moment Italy recognized that France had power and the will to use it. If France should succeed in coercing Germany, Italian interests would be best served by supporting the French position. Hence, the decision was taken in Rome in December 1922 to support the Franco-Belgian occupation of the Ruhr as a means of forcing Germany to pay reparations. Italy would send no troops, but her presence was to be assured by sending several technicians and observers. This policy also found approval among northern Italian industrialists. These men, who had helped Mussolini to power, depended heavily upon continued coal deliveries from the Ruhr. They felt that if the French were alienated on the reparations question, the latter might use their exclusive position in the Ruhr to place pressure on Italy by hindering the flow of coal across the Alps.[26]

The Duce himself indicated the final Italian position on this matter in a conversation with Charles-Roux on 26 December 1922. Mussolini told the French chargé that, "'My position is that Germany must pay.'" He went on to denounce Germany enthusiastically and to label the current xenophobia of the Germans as "'bestial.'" Charles-Roux concluded: "I must say that during the seven years I have been here, I have never heard an Italian minister speak in such a tone about Germany." The chargé's chronology included the war years and must have been warmly received in Paris. On the same day, Louis Barthou, France's delegate to the Reparations Commission, put two motions to a vote before that body. The first simply noted that Germany had not entirely executed her responsibility for the delivery of timber to France in 1922; it was adopted unanimously as a simple statement of fact. Barthou's second motion, however, labeled Germany's nonexecution of her reparations responsibilities as a default according to Paragraph 17 of Annex II of the Treaty of Versailles. The British delegate strenuously opposed the motion, since its passage would empower the Commission to consider the use of coercive sanctions on Germany. The French, Belgian, and Italian delegates, however, supported the motion, and Germany was declared officially in default.[27] The Paris Conference on reparations met from 2 to 4 January 1923 and failed to resolve the Franco-British deadlock. When the Reparations Commission met again on 9 January, Italy once again voted with France and Belgium to authorize the latter's joint occupation of the Ruhr. Troops, along with several Italian technicians, entered on 11 January. France had secured Italian support against British opposition in the most serious crisis of the immediate postwar period.

It is quite true that Italian enthusiasm for the Ruhr occupation waned in the following months, as fascist leaders began to fear that a German financial collapse might prejudice reparations altogether. Mussolini even attempted briefly to mediate between Paris and Berlin. This maneuver irritated Poincaré but did no damage to his position with regard to England. Rome's support for the duration of the Ruhr crisis was assured by the regular delivery of Italy's share of German coal and by French support for Mussolini in the Adriatic. In addition, political figures of the stature of Henry de Jouvenel—who became ambassador to Rome in the 1930s—advocated a number of economic concessions to Italy in 1923 in order "to fortify . . . her economic resistance against Germany." Jouvenel proposed Italian participation in the coal and iron wealth of France; expansion of job openings for Italians in French colonies; the maintenance of Italian nationality rights in Tunisia; a Franco-Italian association to exploit oil resources in Turkey and southern Russia; and a customs agreement giving reciprocal trading advantages to France and Italy.[28] In short, Franco-Italian relations had rarely been as peaceful and courteous as they were during the opening months of the fascist regime. One French observer commented that "official Franco-Italian relations were ameliorated under the fascist regime and were no longer troubled by the very frequent coarse demonstrations which occurred before October 1922."[29]

French policy toward the Italian fascists in the period from 1920 to 1923 represented a first attempt to deal with the "Italian enigma" in the European foreign policy structure of the interwar period. The French documents illustrate quite clearly that the initial French admiration for the fascists derived from the antisocialist activities of the *fasci di combattimento* and the expectation that they would contribute to returning Italy to some semblance of order and stability, a necessary condition for the maintenance of a viable foreign policy. When it was perceived in Paris that fascist Italy could be enrolled in an anti-German combination with France on the reparations issue in opposition to England, relations between the two states became even more cordial. But the French attitude toward Mussolini's government, even among those who were most enthusiastic about a close Franco-Italian entente, was based upon more than optimistic expectations. The increasingly tepid Italian support for the Ruhr adventure implied a warning for France. In the long run the entire Ruhr episode, although technically a diplomatic victory for France, revealed the dangers of conducting French foreign policy in opposition to that of England. This realization, coupled with the historically close relationship between Italy and England, encouraged those who were most anxious to bring about a Franco-Italian entente to view it in terms of the state of relations between

France and England. Barrère, for example, advised Poincaré on 19 February 1924, fifteen months after Mussolini's advent to power, that so long as the fascist regime survived in Italy, "Franco-Italian relations will always be conditioned by the state of our relations with England. The effect of a Franco-British entente, if it is solid and based on the regulation of political interests, like the Entente Cordiale, will be to modify profoundly our relations with Italy and largely to diminish the importance of the differences which could arise in the Mediterranean as a result of the excessive pretensions of Italian policy."[30] Such thinking was to form the germ of the Locarno coalition in 1925, where England and Italy served as guarantors of the Rhine frontier. In this instance the Franco-Italo-British combination was designed to appease Germany. But Barrère's formula, after a hiatus of nearly a decade, reemerged in 1934 and 1935 when France attempted to erect a western coalition designed to contain Hitler's expansionism.

CHAPTER 3

Cooperation and Competition, 1923–32

The Ruhr episode was instructive in many important ways. Although technically a diplomatic victory for France, it has been interpreted by subsequent scholars as marking the apogee of French influence on the continent in the interwar years and demonstrating to Paris the dangers inherent in pursuing a single-handed policy independent of London.[1] Such views lead inexorably to Locarno and to the ever-increasing dependence of France on England, which was so characteristic of the years immediately prior to the outbreak of World War II. French archival evidence, however, belies such simple determinism and indicates quite strongly that policymakers at the Quai d'Orsay continued beyond 1923 to cultivate amicable relations with the new regime in Italy.

PROLONGING THE ERA OF GOOD WILL

An examination of French relations with Italy in the 1920s also brings into question conventional wisdom on the meaning and impact of France's system of alliances in eastern Europe. It is frequently maintained, for example, that given Clemenceau's failure at Versailles to separate the Rhineland into an independent buffer state between the historic Franco-German rivals and the subsequent failure of the joint Anglo-American treaty of guarantee, the French were forced to consider alternative methods of preserving the peace settlement. In order to bolster its military and diplomatic security, therefore, the Third Republic turned to the newly emerged succession states of eastern Europe. Under the guidance of Berthelot, France hammered out a series of defensive military alliances with Poland and the three members of the Little Entente between 1921 and 1927. The effect was presumably to buttress French security by encircling a potentially hostile Germany.

This familiar scenario, however, overlooks several factors. These east European states were small powers. Moreover, the raison d'être of the Little Entente was to ensure the preservation of the Treaties of St.-Germain and Trianon and to coordinate the efforts of Czechoslovakia, Romania, and Yugoslavia in order to prevent a Habsburg restoration. Their attention was riveted upon the Danubian rather than the German settlement. This explains why the treaties linking France with the Little Entente were concluded only between 1924 and 1927, that is, *after* the period of extremely tense Franco-German relations had run its course.[2] The requirements of French security clearly demanded the support of another major European power. Bolshevik Russia was out of the question. The Ruhr crisis demonstrated sharp Anglo-French divergence on precisely that issue most vital to France—the German question. These conditions encouraged leaders at the Quai d'Orsay to concentrate their attention on the remaining member of the allied wartime coalition, Italy, especially since the latter had so recently supported French policy vis-à-vis Germany.

The extremely cordial welcome accorded by the Ministry of Foreign Affairs and French diplomats in Rome to Mussolini and the Italian fascists when they arrived in power in October 1922 is analyzed in the previous chapter. It was felt, the new regime would provide stability and governmental continuity. But the extent of continued French efforts to appease the new Italian government, and thus align it with France in the diplomatic constellation of the 1920s, can best be measured by events in the Adriatic. The resolution of the thorny question of Fiume and the blatantly aggressive Italian occupation of Corfu were the first major initiatives in fascist foreign policy. The French reaction to them is both interesting and instructive, all the more so because both occured while French troops maintained their controversial punitive expedition in the Ruhr.

Fiume, Corfu and the Adriatic

As early as 14 February 1919 Barrère expressed the judgment that ". . . the Adriatic question remains the touchstone for relations between France and Italy." Barrère was most concerned at this point about the disposition of Fiume. The city, located on the gulf of Kvarner in the northern Adriatic, was decidedly Italian in nationality, but the suburbs and hinterland were overwhelmingly Slavic. The city's port facilities provided the only reliable trade and commercial outlet for the new state of Yugoslavia. Although Fiume had not formed part of those territories claimed by Italy in the Treaty of London of 1915, during the peace conferences, a spokesman for Italian Premier Orlando requested French support for the Italian acquisition of Fiume. Italy was willing to sacrifice most of the other Treaty of London stipulations for territorial gain in northern Dalmatia and to guarantee free port access to Yugoslavia.[3]

Although Barrère, who had initially received the Italian proposal, was inclined to consider it favorably in order to consolidate a Franco-Italian entente to balance the Anglo-Americans at the peace conference, the Quai d'Orsay took a different position on Fiume. A Foreign Ministry memorandum of 17 March 1919, while admitting France's interest in maintaining good relations with Italy, also underscored the importance of preserving equilibrium in the Mediterranean. This encouraged French diplomats to view Yugoslavia as a counterweight to Italian predominance in the Adriatic. An independent Fiume was considered indispensable for the economic and political development of Yugoslavia and also for Czechoslovakia and Hungary.[4] The Quai d'Orsay thus viewed the Fiume question as crucial, not only for Franco-Italian relations, but also for France's general influence in southeastern Europe. It avoided a strong stand on the issue and instead left the initiative at the peace conferences to the Americans. President Wilson refused to acquiesce in Fiume's incorporation into Italy; it became instead an autonomous free city.

Fiume rapidly became a cause célèbre among Italian nationalists who felt that Italy had been betrayed by her wartime allies. The French Embassy in Rome reported a dramatic upswing in anti-French feeling among all levels of Italian public opinion, which intensified even further following Gabriele D'Annunzio's seizure of Fiume in September 1919. Rumors circulated in the Italian capital that a military alliance between France and Yugoslavia designed to oust D'Annunzio was imminent. French policy in the Adriatic, however, was not nearly so assertive as that. The Quai d'Orsay, in fact, hoped that Italy and Yugoslavia would work out a compromise solution, which appeared quite possible when Giolitti appointed Sforza to the Consulta. Sforza, who later became ambassador to France, was highly regarded in Paris as a man of compromise and conciliation.[5]

Sforza's policies reached fruition in the Italo-Yugoslav Treaty of Rapallo on 12 November 1920. Rapallo laid aside many of the Italian territorial claims outlined in the Treaty of London. It accorded to Italy all of the Istrian Peninsula, the islands of Lussino and Cherso, and provided special privileges for Italians in the remainder of Dalmatia. But of greatest significance, Rapallo provided for Fiume's independence. The city was recognized to be of predominantly Italian character but it was to exist as an autonomous free city.[6] Rapallo did not resolve the Fiume question but it did provide the international settlement necessary for the ouster of D'Annunzio; Italian troops occupied the city on 18 January 1921. The removal of D'Annunzio's Legionnaires and the apparent willingness of Italy and Yugoslavia to work together seemed to have created a favorable environment for tackling other issues, such as outlining frontiers for the new free city, bringing its government into existence, and restoring its economic relations with the hinterland.

Problems such as these, however, guaranteed a short and chaotic life for the free city. From November 1920 until the fascist rise to power two years later, the domestic political scene witnessed repeated armed clashes between Fiumian Autonomists, who supported Rapallo, and the Nationalists, who wanted to annex Fiume to Italy. Domestic instability merged with a growing disparity between Italian and Yugoslav delegates to the Frontier Delimitation Commission. The Italians maintained that Port Baroš, a subsidiary port, and its delta, must be included in the new state of Fiume. The Yugoslavs disagreed, arguing that this was the only outlet to the sea through Yugoslav territory for the goods of Croatia and that, in any case, Sforza had agreed in a secret letter (12 November 1920) that Port Baroš and the delta should go to Yugoslavia. Failure to solve these problems led Italian troops to occupy Fiume on 17 March 1922. This development produced serious negotiations between Italy and Yugoslavia, resulting in the Santa Margherita Accords of 23 October 1922. The latter established a new machinery for implementing the Treaty of Rapallo; Italian troops would evacuate Port Baroš and an Italo-Yugoslav commission would meet to set frontiers between Fiume and Yugoslavia.[7] Three days later, on 26 October, the fascists staged their "march on Rome."

The official position of the French Foreign Ministry on the Fiume question, in the years before the rise of Mussolini, was essentially one of noninvolvement. Athough the Jurisconsulate of the Quai d'Orsay agreed that the

Italian plans for occupying Fiume in the spring of 1922 "appeared deprived of any legal basis" and thus had "no validity," Foreign Minister Raymond Poincaré refused to transmit this information to his consul in Fiume. The latter had been requested by the leader of the Autonomist faction to seek such information from Paris. Poincaré responded on 6 February 1922 that it would be "seriously prejudicial" to Franco-Italian relations for an official of the French government to furnish Autonomist leaders with arguments which could be used against the Italian government. He instructed the consul to say simply that France was not able to advise foreign governments on political matters. A long and technical legal analysis of the entire question was, however, forwarded to Barrère on the same day.[8]

Poincaré clarified his position on 1 April 1922, shortly after receiving a strongly worded telegram from the Fiumian government appealing for French support in the wake of Italian military occupation. The foreign minister notified his ambassadors in both Belgrade and Rome that he had no intention of acknowledging the telegram, since the government of the Republic "desires to abstain from any direct intervention in the question of Fiume." Barrère endorsed Poincaré's view, maintaining that French policy did not suffer by following a reserved policy in the question of Italo-Yugoslav relations. The thinking behind France's policy in the Fiume question emerges most succinctly in a dispatch to Poincaré from Charles-Roux, the French chargé d'affaires in Rome. He wrote on 29 August 1922 that although the Italians were obviously mishandling the situation, "the events which have taken place in this tiny Fiumian state have had such repercussions on the totality of Franco-Italian relations that it is certainly better for us to involve ourselves as little as possible in this question where our interests are not directly at issue; especially since every day witnesses the surfacing of delicate matters between France and Italy which are of vital concern to us."[9] Charles-Roux was alluding not only to issues of traditional Franco-Italian enmity such as Tunisia, but also to the intensification of the debate between England and France over German reparations. French diplomats saw little point in further alienating Italy over Adriatic issues when her support in the Reparations Commission would be vital.

The advent of the fascist era in October 1922 complicated the situation in the northern Adriatic. Before assuming power Mussolini and the fascists had stridently denounced the Rapallo formula. As a result, many feared that a fresh Italo-Yugoslav crisis was imminent. It seemed unlikely that Mussolini would ever submit the Santa Margherita Accords to the Italian Chamber for ratification. In fact Mussolini's initial gestures in foreign policy were far more conciliatory than had been generally anticipated.[10] But pessimistic expectations in the European chancelleries received reinforcement when Sforza, the symbol of Rapallo, abruptly resigned as Italian ambassador to France in protest against the ascendancy of Mussolini.

French sensitivity in this matter became evident when the Belgrade government, fearing fascist violence, officially requested France to assume the protection of Yugoslav citizens in Fiume. The request placed France in an awkward position. Both Mussolini and Contarini, then secretary general of the Italian foreign ministry, advised Charles-Roux that such an undertaking would be an affront to Italy since the latter fully intended to carry out all treaty obligations, including those outlined in the Treaty of Rapallo. Therefore, in spite of warnings from Belgrade that the Yugoslavs might be offended by a refusal of official French protection in Fiume, that was precisely the position adopted by Poincaré on 6 November 1922. He denied the Yugoslav request, promising instead to exert his influence on Belgrade's behalf in Rome, a decision with which both Mussolini and Contarini were reported to be "very satisfied."[11]

Satisfactory though the French attitude may have appeared in Rome, in Belgrade lingering suspicions persisted. Although the Fiume affair appeared to be moving toward a happy solution with the ratification of the Santa Margherita Accords by the Italian Chamber on 7 February 1923, the work of the Italo-Yugoslav frontier commission remained unresolved. At this point, with Italian support for the Ruhr operation secured, the Quai d'Orsay initiated a project to recoup French influence in Belgrade. It became known in April 1923 that France had approved a 300 million franc loan to Yugoslavia for the reorganization of the nation's army. In Italy the news aroused immediate distrust and touched off an anti-French press campaign, which expressed fears that the loan would be followed by the conclusion of a Franco-Yugoslav military convention directed against Italy.[12]

By July it was evident that Italian opinion had swung completely around against France in the Fiume matter. Contarini informed Charles-Roux that the loan was an embarrassment to the Italian government, which was trying to end the Italo-Yugoslav affair peacefully. It also threatened to weaken Mussolini's conciliatory attitude, as he was under considerable attack from his domestic opponents. Charles-Roux reported that the Peninsula was buzzing about the "threatening character of French policy toward Italy." The Fiumian impasse finally broke down in the summer of 1923 with the failure of the Italo-Yugoslav commission to implement the Rapallo Treaty. Mussolini, therefore, proposed an entirely new arrangement whereby Italy would annex Fiume; Port Baroš and the delta would go to Yugoslavia, which would be accorded special navigation and commercial advantages in the port. When Belgrade opposed the Duce's solution, the latter sought European support for it. In Paris, Romano Avezzana, the Italian ambassador, suggested to Poincaré that Franco-Italian relations could be ameliorated if France would champion the Italian formula at Belgrade.[13] Poincaré was in an awkward position. Mussolini's solution offered a quick way out of the impasse; yet to give wholehearted support to Italy might alienate Yugoslavian friendship. Such was the situation when the focus of Adriatic diplomacy shifted dramatically southward to the tiny island of Corfu.

The Corfu crisis, in September 1923, is frequently portrayed as the first blatantly aggressive example of fascist foreign policy, illustrating a disdain for both diplomatic convention and the League of Nations. The unpublished records suggest, however, that the French reaction to Mussolini's adventure was not only unusually mild, but that the Quai d'Orsay actually provided timely assistance to the Duce when his position in Corfu threatened to bring down the wrath of the League. France wanted to use the Corfu affair to rebuild relations with Italy, which had been prejudiced by the Fiume matter, and thus provide additional security for herself while the Ruhr occupation was in full swing. The background to the crisis is clear enough. The Conference of Ambassadors, composed of England, France, and Italy, had settled the fate of Albania by confirming the frontiers of 1913. But the task of delimiting those frontiers remained. On 27 August 1923 the Italian General Enrico Tellini and four companions, engaged in the task of delimiting the Graeco-Albanian frontier on behalf of the Conference of Ambassadors, were murdered on Greek soil near Janina. The Italian response was reminiscent of that of Austria-Hungary to the Sarajevo assassination, although far more prompt. Mussolini first requested that England and France, as joint members of the Conference of Ambassadors, join Italy in making remonstrances and demanding reparations from Greece. Although the British demurred, Poincaré supported the Italian point of view in an effort to avert a direct clash between Italy and Greece. Mussolini, however, acted unilaterally. On 29 August the Italian minister in Athens presented the Greek government with a set of demands calling for an apology, a funeral service for the victims, naval salutes for the Italian flag, a fifty million lire penalty, and a strict inquiry to be carried out quickly with the assistance of the Italian military attaché. Greece accepted all but the last two parts of the ultimatum, which appeared inconsistent with national sovereignty. The Italians replied by bombarding and occupying the Greek island of Corfu.[14]

French sources provide interesting insight into the contrast between French and British reactions to this incident. The British presented no demarche whatsoever in Athens following the Tellini murders. In contrast, although Poincaré felt that Mussolini's ultimatum was out of order, he did present a demarche in the name of the Conference of Ambassadors against the "odious and unprecedented attack" on the delimitation commission and articulated French support for sanctions and reparations to be paid to Italy.[15] In addition, the French press overwhelmingly denounced the Janina murders and announced its support for Italian demands. Even the fascist seizure of Corfu received mild treatment in the French press, which tended instead to flay the lack of outrage among British newspapers.[16] Charles-Roux reported from Rome on 30 August that Mussolini "has welcomed with great satisfaction" the indignant reaction of the French press, and he noted further that "the clearly friendly attitude of France has produced the most favorable impression here." In contrast, the British Foreign Office severely criticized the brutality of the Corfu occupation. The French ambassador in London reported on 1 September that all the major British newspapers, with the exception of the *Daily Mail,* condemned Italian policy.[17]

The British favored referring the entire Corfu matter to the League of Nations, where the Greek government had lodged an official protest. The Quai d'Orsay, on the other hand, opposed such a course of action for fear that it would provide a precedent for the League to engage itself in judging the French occupation of the Ruhr. France much preferred the adjudication of Corfu to rest with the Conference of Ambassadors where British opposition could be neutralized by the French and Italian delegates. Poincaré defined French policy in a telegram to the major embassies on 1 September 1923. He specifically rejected any comparison between Italy's action in Corfu and the Franco-Belgian occupation of the Ruhr. French troops were in the Ruhr, he maintained, to enforce a treaty of peace which Germany was obstructing, whereas Italy had responded to a particular incident where no direct responsibility of the Greek government had yet been demonstrated. He instructed his ambassadors to "maintain the greatest reserve on this matter and say nothing which could furnish Italy a pretext for discontent against us."[18] The stage was set for a confrontation between France and England over Corfu.

During the next few days, the issues were drawn sharply into focus. Although Cassels maintains that the Italians intended to occupy Corfu permanently, that was not the position that the Palazzo Chigi enunciated to the French. On 31 August Charles-Roux was informed that Italy had no intention of exercising a permanent occupation; its only purpose was to demonstrate her determination to obtain legitimate reparations. The French documents give no indication that the Quai d'Orsay believed that

Italian ambitions in Corfu were any greater than they were stated to be. But the real explanation for the mildness of the French reaction to Mussolini's behavior surfaced in a telegram from Poincaré to Hanotaux, then French ambassador to the League, on 3 September. The premier clearly underscored the connection between Corfu and the Ruhr. Poincaré's telegram reviewed the whole crisis, explained Mussolini's refusal to recognize the competence of the League, and reiterated the Duce's preference that adjudication be left to the Conference of Ambassadors. He concluded: "I add that, as President of the Reparations Commission, M. Barthou would see a very serious danger in a rupture between Italy and France on this question. He is convinced that [if a rupture should occur] the Italian delegate would receive . . . the order no longer to vote with us in the question of reparations." Charles-Roux buttressed these judgments the following day in reporting a conversation with Mussolini. The latter bluntly informed the French chargé that he intended to withdraw from the League should the Geneva institution intervene in the Corfu matter. He also indicated that continued Italian support for the French position on German reparations and the Ruhr occupation was contingent upon French aid in the Corfu affair.[19] The implications were obvious. Hanotaux must support the Italian position at Geneva in opposition to England in order to maintain Rome's endorsement of the Ruhr expedition.

Several other factors also contributed to Poincaré's thinking. The foreign minister was acutely aware of the fact that the British considered French action in the Ruhr illegal. It was likely, therefore, that if the Corfu affair were brought before the League, it would strengthen England's case for bringing the Ruhr question before that body. Poincaré understood that the European press regarded his Ruhr policy nearly as negatively as Mussolini's Corfu adventure. He wanted to avoid League censure at all costs. In addition, if France were to adopt an anti-Italian posture over Corfu, the Quai d'Orsay would be in no position to urge Italian moderation over the, as yet unsettled, Fiume question. On the other hand, Poincaré was anxious to preserve French credibility among the small powers of eastern Europe by safeguarding the rights and prestige of the League of Nations. All of these factors contributed to the policy adopted by the Quai d'Orsay and communicated to French diplomats in Geneva and Rome on 4 September. Poincaré's plan was carefully designed to prevent the question of League competency in Corfu from being raised in the Council. Instead, Hanotaux was instructed to urge the Council simply to take cognizance of all the facts of the case, including Italy's intention to evacuate Corfu once reparations had been made for the Tellini murders. The Council would not even raise the issue of competency but rather would recommend that the matter be resolved through direct Italo-Greek negotiations under the auspices of the Conference of Ambassadors. The League would be kept closely informed of all the negotiations. Hanotaux's papers show clearly that Poincaré's plan won enthusiastic support in Rome, and Salandra received instructions to work closely with Hanotaux in Geneva.[20]

Britain's Lord Robert Cecil mounted a campaign at Geneva to persuade the Council that the competency issue should be raised immediately before the entire Assembly, thus intensifying Italian bitterness toward England. Charles-Roux reported that the fascist press in Italy soundly denounced Britain's attitude and that the Italian government was becoming more reserved and distrustful of France's cross-channel neighbor—a development which might prove useful to France in the future.[21] Lord Robert's efforts were in vain, however, as Salandra and Hanotaux, with vigorous support from the Belgian delegate to the Council, managed to stifle the issue of League competency. Meanwhile, the Conference of Ambassadors in Athens, again under French leadership, began to move toward resolving the Corfu matter.

On 8 September the Conference presented its solution to the Athens government. The French delegate, Jules Cambon, acting on direct instructions from Poincaré, carefully shepherded the proposal through the Conference. It reflected the Italian point of view. The Conference ordered that funeral services and military honors be rendered in Athens to the dead Italians in the presence of the Greek government and the warships of Britain, France, and Italy. Furthermore, the latter three powers would comprise a commission of inquiry, under the presidency of a neutral Japanese, to work on Greek soil to investigate the Janina crime and to establish guilt and responsibility. Finally, the Permanent Court of International Justice at The Hague would determine appropriate reparations; in the meantime, Greece was to deposit fifty million lire in the Swiss National Bank. The Italians agreed that if Greece met all the stipulations, Italy would evacuate Corfu on 27 September.[22]

Although Cecil continued his efforts to bring the Corfu question before the Assembly of the League and even threatened to raise the issue of German reparations as a means of punishing France for the latter's support of Italy, the Corfu matter was, for all practical purposes, beyond League jurisdiction. The denouement may be rapidly summarized. As the 27 September date for the Corfu evacuation approached, it was clear that no progress was being made on the inquiry into responsibility for the Janina murders. Mussolini was reluctant to abandon the island on the basis of a simple pledge that the inquiry would persevere. In order to end the matter as rapidly as possible, therefore, the Conference of Ambassadors, on 26

September, took the position that Greece had failed to live up to its obligation to provide aid and support to the inquiry. Consequently, the Ambassadors ordered Greece to pay Italy the fifty million lire as reparations in order to clear the way for the timely evacuation of Corfu.[23] Since Athens had previously pledged to abide by the decisions of the Conference, the money was transferred immediately. Italian warships withdrew; the crisis ended.

Although minor and short-lived by comparison with the Franco-Belgian occupation of the Ruhr, the Corfu crisis nevertheless provoked some important consequences for European international relations in general and French diplomacy in particular. No doubt officials at both the Quai d'Orsay and Whitehall breathed heavy sighs of relief. Had the Italians remained on Corfu, it would have violated the principle of nationality and also upset the balance of power in the Mediterranean. But many felt the price paid in terms of League prestige far too high. In his generally pro-fascist book, Georges Christopolous pointed out that Mussolini's policies were widely saluted in Italy as an international success "which covered the nation with glory." French relations with England were strained still further as a result of its policies in the Corfu affair. On the other hand, Poincaré had won for France the gratitude of Mussolini's Italy, reiterated time and again throughout the crisis. The French foreign minister summarized the significance of these events and underscored his sympathy for the new Italian regime in a dispatch to Barrère in Rome on 20 October 1923, shortly after the Germans had capitulated in the Ruhr.

> I certainly appreciate . . . the satisfactory attitude observed on our behalf by Mussolini's Government since the beginning of the Ruhr affair. I think, as you do, that his Government has better intentions toward us . . . than those others which have held power in Italy since the war. But we must also not forget that we have been happy to lend it a helping hand in questions which interest it. I don't have to remind you that the attitude taken by the French Government in the Italo-Greek conflict has doubtless determined the favorable outcome for Italian prestige in this incident. . . . We are prepared to continue to give M. Mussolini similar proofs of our good will.[24]

But if Poincaré could congratulate himself on having preserved the good will of fascist Italy, he could only look with some concern at the rather more sombre appraisal of French policy emanating from the capitals of the small European nations—nations whom the Quai d'Orsay was anxious to cultivate as French protégés. Although the Greeks maintained that they regarded the outcome of the Corfu incident as a victory, this may be regarded as an attempt to put the best possible face on a difficult situation. As early as 5 September the Czechoslovak ambassador in Paris expressed to Laroche, at the Quai d'Orsay, his fears that the League of Nations might suffer irreparable damage if it chose to do nothing after a member nation had made an official appeal. He also feared that Mussolini might well be encouraged to undertake a coup de force in Fiume unless the League stopped him at Corfu. Hanotaux notified Poincaré the next day that Eduard Beneš, the Czech delegate to Geneva, was persuaded that if Mussolini escaped unpunished from the Corfu affair, he would likely unleash his expansionist program in Fiume and Dalmatia. Hanotaux's papers also contain several telegrams from French diplomats in Norway, Sweden, Yugoslavia, and Romania attesting to the horror of these nations at Mussolini's actions and their desire to see the League take strong action in condemning Italy. Hanotaux feared that French policy in this matter might drive all the small powers in the League to gravitate toward England. Cecil encouraged this trend at Geneva.[25]

The problem of France's relations with the small powers, particularly the Little Entente, emerged graphically in a dispatch from the French ambassador in Prague to Poincaré on 13 September 1923. The former reported the virtually unanimous denunciation of French policy in the Czech press. France, it maintained, had weakened the League by supporting Mussolini and had declared in effect that the League has no jurisdiction when the interests of the big powers are at stake. The dispatch concluded that ". . . we cannot deny that our attitude in this affair has provoked in Czechoslovakia and, I believe, among her Little Entente allies, a certain uneasiness which it would be useful for us to dissipate. . . ."[26] Such concerns reflected a fundamental dilemma in French policy vis-à-vis Italy—how to preserve the Italian connection without overturning the balance of power in the Mediterranean in Italy's favor and, at the same time, to nourish French influence among the small nations of eastern Europe. With these factors in mind, attention shifted back to the northern Adriatic and the still-unsolved problem of Fiume.

Shortly before Corfu came to dominate French and Italian attention, Mussolini had proposed scrapping the Rapallo Treaty formula for settling the Fiume question. Instead he suggested a new scheme which would incorporate Fiume into Italy while Port Baroš and its delta would go to Yugoslavia. Belgrade voiced initial reservations about the proposal, fearing prejudice to her commercial outlet on the Adriatic. Mussolini nevertheless demanded that the Italo-Yugoslav commission must arrive at a solution by 15 September. The day after the deadline passed, he appointed an Italian general as military governor of Fiume with instructions to maintain order in the city. Corresponding as they did with the Corfu crisis, these moves raised apprehensions in Europe that Italy was engaged in another coup de force in the northern Adriatic. The French reaction was clear and immediate. Poincaré informed Barrère on 18 September that France had no intention of intervening directly in the Italo-Yugoslav negotiations. Mussolini, however, should be aware that if he took an initiative analogous to the Corfu action, France ". . . could not support him as we did in the Italo-Greek affair, and it would be impossible for us to oppose an eventual intervention of the League of Nations."[27]

The possibility of League activity in Fiume was no more palatable to the Quai d'Orsay than in Corfu because it might well have created a similar precedent for League competence in the Ruhr affair. Consequently, the Quai d'Orsay worked energetically but discreetly to encourage both Rome and Belgrade to moderate their attitudes toward Fiume and to work toward a peaceful bilateral solution. French officials had the general impression that a direct accord between Yugoslavia and Italy would preserve the good relations of both with France, thus enhancing her prestige in the Adriatic region. Since the end of World War I, Italy had viewed Yugoslavia as France's pawn to be used against her in the Adriatic. But France's attitude in the Corfu matter had altered this perception.[28] Rome was anxious to take advantage of French goodwill to seek peacefully an advantageous solution to the Fiume affair. The matter was resolved with the Italo-Yugoslav Convention of 27 January 1924, an accord which incorporated most of Mussolini's program of the previous summer. Fiume went to Italy; Yugoslavia annexed Port Baroš, the delta, and the hamlets behind the city. Special provisions insured Yugoslav access to the port facilities of Fiume. A treaty of friendship between the two Adriatic neighbors supplemented the accord.

The Italo-Yugoslav Accord is generally portrayed as a striking diplomatic success for the fascist leader, achieved with moderation and thus effacing the fears engendered by the Corfu episode. It is also viewed as a precedent for the future expansion of Italian economic and political influence in Dalmatia. By allowing the port of Fiume to decline, Italy could foster the growth of Trieste as the single commercial outlet for a large hinterland. Barrère admitted that Mussolini had done well for his country by finally regulating a question that had seemed insoluble for so long. The Duce exploited this success to increase his personal popularity and that of his party. Barrère complained, however, that, following the accord, Mussolini ostentatiously conferred a title on D'Annunzio, attesting "that if Italy finally attained Fiume by pacific means in a well-regulated accord, this success was due, in large measure, to the adventure of the Poet-Condottiere who until very lately was considered an outlaw."²⁹ Which raises the question: what, in addition to the Ruhr affair, lay behind the French attitude in the matter of Fiume? Given the Quai d'Orsay's concern about French prestige among the small states of eastern Europe, why had the Italians been permitted a second major diplomatic triumph against a small power in less than three months? The answers to these questions involved a complex set of negotiations, progressing simultaneously with Italo-Yugoslav pourparlers, which hinted at the establishment of a triangular Franco-Italo-Yugoslav accord.

Accord à Trois

In October 1923 and twice again in December, Contarini queried Barrère about France's receptivity to the idea of a pact à trois among France, Italy, and Yugoslavia to stabilize the status quo in the Adriatic. These overtures were timely indeed, since they corresponded with growing French fears about Italian intentions for the Italo-Yugoslav accord. Since that instrument called for reciprocal compensation should one party acquire additional territory, Poincaré feared that Italy would encourage Yugoslavia to seek an outlet to the Aegean Sea at Salonika. This would allow Italy to claim compensation on the eastern shore of the Adriatic, perhaps in Albania. Such a scenario could well upset the entire structure of peace in the eastern Mediterranean. Barrère turned these fears into arguments supporting a favorable French response to Contarini's overtures. If indeed Rome and Belgrade were nurturing such expansionist notions, French participation in an accord à trois could act to thwart them. Above all, Barrère cautioned against moving toward the establishment of a Franco-Yugoslav agreement. Given Italy's fears of the previous summer with regard to the French loan to Yugoslavia, a direct Paris-Belgrade treaty would be viewed in Rome as a hostile act with the gravest consequences for Franco-Italian relations.³⁰

As it became clear, however, that the Italo-Yugoslav settlement of the Fiume question was near to signature, Italian enthusiasm for an accord à trois waned perceptibly. Contarini explained to Barrère on 13 January that such an accord was his idea alone and that Mussolini now considered it incompatible with relations between Rome and Belgrade. Italian reticence may have been attributable to the fact that France's security treaty with Czechoslovakia was also near completion (25 January 1924). But Poincaré nevertheless authorized a formal demarche in response to Contarini's earlier overtures on 21 January 1924. The document stipulated France's willingness to participate in an accord that would state the common will of the three nations to collaborate on the maintenance of peace and the execution of treaties. "The French Government therefore is ready to study, in concert with the Italian Government and the Yugoslav Government, the form to give to an accord à trois."[31]

France's eagerness to conclude such an understanding was clear. But French documents also indicate that the Palazzo Chigi had not formally raised the prospect of a pacte à trois in Belgrade, although the latter had been informed by the French minister. Italian bad faith in the matter was confirmed on 26 January 1924, the day before the signature of the Italo-Yugoslav Accord. Contarini told Barrère that Mussolini had definitely ruled out further consideration of a pacte à trois, since he believed that it would be poorly received by the Italian people, who would interpret it as a sign of French mediation in the Italo-Yugoslav accord.[32] The Duce wished to portray the settlement of Fiume as due entirely to his own efforts. He made a couple of attempts during the next two months to assuage French bitterness by proposing instead a vague accord à deux between Paris and Rome. The Quai d'Orsay responded favorably to these proposals, but Mussolini wanted a settlement of the question of Italian rights in Tunisia in exchange for his pledge of status quo in the Adriatic. The French took the position that the two matters were entirely separate and could be dealt with only in separate negotiations. By March 1924 all references to either a pact à trois or a pacte à deux had disappeared entirely.

The Italian ploy in this matter became painfully obvious even to admirers of the fascist regime. Barrère referred to the whole matter as a "comedy" and reported bitterly to Poincaré on 4 February 1924 that Italy had played fast and loose with French goodwill. The proposal for a tripartite accord had first been raised by Contarini in October 1923 and followed up on three or four subsequent occasions. It, Barrère now felt, had been made when Italy feared that France might impede the conclusion of the Italo-Yugoslav treaty. But once that instrument was assured, the Italians deemed French participation no longer necessary, and the proposal for an accord à trois was allowed to lapse—even though the Quai d'Orsay had welcomed it. Poincaré reflected his ambassador's bitterness in his instructions to French diplomats in eastern Europe. He underscored his suspicion that Italy's recent treaty with Yugoslavia was part of a larger drive to weaken French influence among the Little Entente nations and perhaps even to destroy that alliance. He ordered his representatives to keep him fully informed of Italian activities in their circumscriptions and admonished them about " . . . the interest we have in the maintenance of the Little Entente as an essential element in the conservation of the peace and the maintenance of the order established by the Treaties, which are as important to us as to our allies in central Europe."[33]

But if French suspicion of Italy had been intensified by the resolution of the Fiume matter, it was accompanied by a tinge of ambivalence—an unwillingness among some officials to abandon the Italian fascists as potential guarantors of French security. Barrère argued that the failure of the accord à trois should be followed quickly by a Franco-Yugoslav mutual security treaty in order to blunt Italian claims of reduced French influence in eastern Europe. At the same time he cautioned that great care should be exercised to make certain that such a treaty did not possess an anti-Italian character, which might stimulate an irreparable breach between the two Mediterranean neighbors. A carefully drafted Franco-Yugoslav treaty, on the other hand, might create the atmosphere for a general resolution of Franco-Italian problems. Charles-Roux sent Poincaré a long dispatch on 15 May 1924 which reflected a rather favorable interpretation of Italian foreign policy under Mussolini. He denounced as short-sighted those who debunked fascist Italy as anti-French. Charles-Roux emphasized that Mussolini's regime had been far less Germanophile than any of its predecessors since the war. He felt further that those who stressed Italy's irredentist ambitions toward Nice, Corsica, and Tunis had gravely overinflated the Duce's goals, which were not aimed so much at incorporation of these French territories into Italy as to guarantee the privileges of Italian nationals living there. Charles-Roux's report did not deny that Italy was engaged in preparing alliances in eastern Europe, but he did insist that it was not necessary to exaggerate the ambition of these projects or to view them as anti-French.[34]

EASTERN EUROPE

Despite some bitterness at the failure of the tripartite scheme, evidence indicates that the Quai d'Orsay viewed the Italo-Yugoslav accord of 27 January 1924 favorably in that it lessened tensions between Rome and Belgrade—a necessary precondition for security in the eastern Mediterranean.[35] Although Belgrade at this point harbored understandable reservations about moving toward an immediate Franco-Yugoslav treaty,[36] the French drafted the text for such an instrument during the summer of 1924. In form it was identical to the Franco-Czechoslovak pact, calling for treaty maintenance, common military action in the event either party were the victim of aggression, and arbitration by the Permanent Court of International Justice in all disputes between them. The Quai d'Orsay regarded such an accord as a logical complement to those with Poland and Czechoslovakia.[37]

Nevertheless, the European international atmosphere in the mid-1920s produced a degree of circumspection in Paris. The Locarno agreements of 1925 provided the guarantee of France's eastern frontier that had eluded Clemenceau in 1919-20. Italy's role, along with England, as a guarantor of those settlements was deemed an important aspect of French security on the Rhine. Conversely, however, eastern European leaders read Locarno's vague formulations regarding Germany's Polish and Czechoslovakian borders in much the same light as they regarded France's benevolent attitude toward Mussolini in the Adriatic. The two phenomena presaged a weakening of France's determination to preserve the territorial status quo in eastern Europe. Thus, in the wake of Locarno, an interesting reversal of priorities occurred. Belgrade, whose concern was to reactivate the French presence in the east, began to encourage an early signature of the proposed Franco-Yugoslav pact, while Paris became more prudent and cautious. Berthelot instructed the French minister in Belgrade on 7 December 1925 to delay signature of the pact, because "it would be imprudent to accumulate accords which, although complementary, could be interpreted differently, in Rome for example, where we must prepare the ground and act in a friendly manner, after the guarantee . . . that the Italian Government has given, along with England, to our frontier along the Rhine." In an effort to circumvent the impasse, Yugoslavian Foreign Minister Momchilo Ninchich resurrected the idea of a convention à trois between Belgrade, Rome, and Paris. Failing that, Yugoslavia also indicated a willingness to conclude separate identical arrangements with both Italy and France. The latter proposal aimed to undercut the only reason Mussolini could have for rejecting a tripartite pact, "which would be the desire to minimize French influence in central European affairs." Although the Yugoslavs had the clear impression on 21 January 1926 that the Italians accepted the principle of a tripartite accord, their efforts to include an article dealing with the maintenance of the political and territorial integrity of Albania could only serve to blunt Mussolini's enthusiasm. The Duce formally rejected the three-power accord on 26 February. René Besnard, Barrère's successor at the Palazzo Farnese, speculated that Mussolini believed the opportunity ripe to conclude a military pact directly with Yugoslavia. The latter would be an important step toward the Italian desire of "assuring herself a dominant influence among the Little Entente Powers and placing herself, with the support of England, at the head of Balkan politics."[38]

The thrust of events, however—particularly the intrusion of the Albanian question—belied these expectations. In 1925, Ahmed Bey Zogu led a successful revolution that resulted in his election as president of Albania. Although initially viewed as a development favorable to Yugoslavia, Zogu's elevation stimulated further Balkan intrigue. Once in power, he became a willing recipient of Italian financial assistance, thereby raising the spectre of this small Adriatic nation's acting as a Trojan Horse for the spread of Italian influence in the Balkans and eastern Mediterranean. For the previous two years the Quai d'Orsay had delayed the formal signature of a Franco-Yugoslav pact in the hope that the Albanian situation could be resolved amicably and result in a renewal of the Italo-Yugoslav accords of 1924.[39] But by November 1927, tensions between Rome and Belgrade had intensified to the extent that little was to be gained by further postponement. Given the earlier fears of abandonment among Little Entente leaders, France needed to demonstrate her commitment to the region. On 11 November, therefore, the Franco-Yugoslav treaty was finally signed. Predictably negative Italian reactions were not slow to materialize.

These were evident even before the formal signature of the pact. On 9 November the French ambassador in Rome had quoted at length articles from such leading government-controlled newspapers as *Corriere d'Italia, Tribuna,* and *Giornale d'Italia*—all were uniform in their condemnation of the announcement that France planned to sign in the near future a friendship and arbitration pact with Yugoslavia. According to the Italian press, this demonstrated France's hostility to Italy and unmasked its intention to make the South Slav state the vanguard of its policies in eastern Europe. A day later Ambassador Besnard, who had opposed signature of the Franco-Yugoslav treaty at this time, reported that his English colleague in Rome believed that Italian resentment would be prolonged and would have serious repercussions on relations between France and Italy. He added that he would not be surprised to see the Italians respond in some concrete fashion and noted that "germanophile elements are certainly not foreign to this Italian press campaign."[40]

Confirmation that Italy was inclined to play the German card in order to moderate suspected French initiatives in eastern Europe arrived from Berlin on 14 November. German Foreign Minister Gustav Stresemann told Pierre de Margerie that the Italian ambassador had been to see him to denounce France and to say that all of France's recent activity in eastern Europe had but one goal—to prevent any modification in the Treaty of Versailles, most particularly concerning the question of *Anschluss* with Austria. Although Paris repeatedly counselled Belgrade to refrain from responding in kind to Italian press diatribes, such advice met with modest success at best. Moreover, the French initiative aroused considerable alarm in London. Sir Austen Chamberlain openly expressed his dim view of a treaty he regarded as superfluous for France and which could only be viewed as an act of hostility by Italy. He feared that such actions might encourage Italy to leave the group of western powers she had willingly joined at Locarno and to orient herself instead toward a potential bloc of central European powers, namely Germany, Austria, and Hungary. The British foreign secretary admitted the difficulty of dealing with a man like Mussolini, but stressed that it was incumbent upon an established power like France to make "gestures of conciliation." Briand responded with a long communication detailing the whole evolution of the Franco-Yugoslav pact, and he concluded by assuring his British counterpart that France harbored no ill will toward Italy and hoped for an accord between the two countries, "thus guaranteeing one and all against all surprises."[41]

Despite such soothing words, however, Briand could not buffer himself against all disagreeable surprises. Within two weeks of the signature of the Franco-Yugoslav treaty, the Italians responded by signing a treaty of mutual assistance with Albania, a military pact completing the transformation of the small Balkan nation into a virtual Italian client state. From that point on, French efforts to smooth relations between Italy and Yugoslavia were rendered ever more difficult, a situation destined to complicate relations between Paris and Rome as well. The French ambassador in the Italian capital drew the inescapable conclusion from this series of events. He wrote ruefully to Briand in November 1927 that "we must not hide from the fact that the signature of the [Italo-Albanian] pact, intervening at a time of Italo-Yugoslav tension, will doubtless have serious repercussions over a long period of time on relations between France and Italy."[42]

The period from 1922 to 1925 had witnessed substantial measures of Franco-Italian cooperation in the Ruhr, at Locarno, and in the Adriatic region. This era of good will collapsed amid Balkan complications by the end of the decade. Besnard's prediction of stormy relations between the two powers held true for the immediate future. The breakdown of cooperation in eastern Europe also prejudiced efforts to resolve thorny colonial issues between the two Mediterranean powers.

TUNISIA

In many respects the question of Tunisia came to symbolize the colonial relationship between France and Italy, and it is regarded by some as the touchstone governing the entire relationship between the two Mediterranean neighbors. In November 1918, France announced its intention to denounce the Tunisian Conventions of 1896, which had guaranteed Italians living in the Regency a completely autonomous national life within the context of the French protectorate. Thereafter, they would no longer be extended year by year, as had been the case since 1905, but only every three months until a permanent arrangement limiting Italian nationality rights could be worked out. The official French position on this question was that such a denunciation had no political overtones; it was simply a matter of commercial and economic regularization. Until a new convention could be negotiated, the political rights of Italians in Tunisia would be maintained. It is clear, however, that this decision, coupled with French and British rejection of most of Italy's postwar colonial claims in Africa, was regarded as a political one in Rome. It exacerbated Franco-Italian relations at a time when some French diplomats, notably Camille Barrère, were encouraging Italy's firm association with the victory over Germany.[43]

Long a consistent advocate of close Franco-Italian relations, France's veteran ambassador in Rome advised against a denunciation of the accords protecting the rights of Italian nationals born in Tunisia, even though these provided for privileges more extensive than those accorded to French nationals. He advised that such an action would have serious repercussions and that "the present political circumstances require us to avoid discussions and polemics which would no doubt have an unfortunate backlash on our relations with Italy." His warnings acquired particular urgency when, on 8 November 1921, President Millerand and Premier Briand signed a decree abrogating previous conventions on nationality rights in Tunisia. Although the decree did not apply specifically to Italian nationals, its issuance was regarded as a precedent. It provided the occasion for a virulently anti-French press campaign in Italy and another opportunity for Barrère to advocate a policy of effacement on the volatile Tunisian question.[44]

Barrère's reservations were predicated upon a general concern among French diplomatic personnel in Rome that the alienation of Italy over the naturalization question might lead to "a junction of British and Italian action against our policy in Tunisia and against our administration of the protectorate." The Quai d'Orsay was anxious to avoid the internationalization of the matter, which might lead to a resolution unfavorable to France. Given the deteriorating domestic political situation in Italy in 1922, it was feared that the application of the naturalization decrees to Italians in Tunisia risked uniting *all* Italians against French policies in Europe at a time when "the centrist, rightist, conservative, nationalist, and Fascist parties are showing a marked disposition to seek a rapprochement with France. . . ."[45] Such a rapprochement became more desirable as a showdown with Germany and England over reparations became imminent.

The resultant cordial response accorded the advent of the fascist era in Italy by both the Quai d'Orsay and the French press has already been noted. Nevertheless, given the stridently nationalistic orientation of the new Italian government, Tunisia remained a convenient, logical focus and continued to be a bone of contention between Paris and Rome. Barrère, however, continued to caution prudence in dealing with the Tunisian question. His reasons, articulated in a telegram of 18 April 1923, are worth quoting at some length.

> The present Italian Government is more favorable to our interests than any in quite some time. . . . The attitude which it has taken toward our action in the Ruhr, while not satisfying us completely, is however more than another Italian government would probably have adopted. It is essential not to turn our backs at least not before the end of our difference with Germany, and not even after that; for if we alienate this Government, we shall have more difficulties with it than with any other.[46]

The ambassador's final words proved extraordinarily prophetic, and his references to Germany were telling. The Tunisian question blew hot and cold between Rome and Paris throughout the interwar years, but the intensity of the German question at any particular moment remained a fairly accurate barometer for measuring the two powers' willingness to be conciliatory on the issue.

On 25 May 1923, Millerand, Poincaré, Maurice Colrat, the Garde des Sceaux, and Minister of War André Maginot proposed a new naturalization law. It laid down a specific timetable for the naturalization of all foreign nationals in the Regency.[47] Although its stipulations again did not apply to Italians, the new proposal created a terrible impression in Italy and was profoundly disturbing to the Italian colony in Tunisia. Baron Avezzana formally protested to the Quai d'Orsay on 18 July 1923, indicating that Mussolini would press for a blanket renewal of the conventions of 1896. The Italian ambassador repeated his concern a month later to Charles-Roux, concluding with a thinly veiled threat that unless a satisfactory resolution of the Tunisian matter were forthcoming, he would urge the Duce "to do something . . . he did not say what" about the Ruhr situation. Barrère continued to urge caution, insisting that the timing for the new law on Tunisian nationality was unfortunate. It had been his intention to soft-pedal the Tunisian matter until the Ruhr occupation was settled. As it was, "the Italian press has declared a war against us, and the Quai d'Orsay must send M. Mussolini . . . more pleasant communications." The Tunisian law, he insisted, might imperil Franco-Italian cooperation in Lausanne and ". . . we must . . . act with prudence in order not to lose the benefits of the support of the Italian Government in the matter of reparations."[48]

Poincaré relented only slightly. He maintained, in the fall of 1923 as the Ruhr crisis headed toward a solution, that the general political situation made it desirable for the Italians to receive "all appeasements" relative to the Tunisian matter. He suggested that the accords of 1896 might remain in force for two more years, during which time negotiations for new conventions might take place. It was to be understood, however, that should this occur, it would be a final renewal; failure to achieve a new convention would mean that Italians in Tunisia would be subject to French law. There are some indications that the Duce was favorably inclined to such a two-year prorogation of the French denunciation of the 1896 accords. But when the proposed law on naturalization came into effect on 20 December 1923, following its final passage in the French Senate, it seemed to the Italians as though the French were bargaining in bad faith. The resultant buildup of anti-French feeling in the Italian communities of Tunisia prejudiced all the good relations established between Rome and Paris since October 1922. The documents for 1924 and 1925 record numerous examples of Italian nationalist activity and mutual recriminations between the French and Italian communities in Tunisia. Demonstrations and counterdemonstrations were weekly occurrences. The French government banned the wearing of black shirts in the Regency and suppressed several inflammatory Italian newspapers.[49] Until he fell from power in 1924 Poincaré was inclined to cut the knot and simply abrogate the 1896 conventions unilaterally. That such action was not taken, even after withdrawal of French troops from the Ruhr eased Franco-German tensions, is an indication that a long-term détente with Italy was still a desirable goal among key individuals at the French Foreign Ministry.

The years from 1924 to 1929 were difficult ones for Franco-Italian relations. In early 1923, conversations had been undertaken for an economic accord between the two countries. By 1925, French industry had established many new affiliates in Italy; fully one-third of all foreign companies located in the Peninsula were French. Yet, in spite of this, the grand project for an economic entente never saw the light of day. Mussolini's price for such an entente included unacceptable political guarantees—opening North Africa to Italian immigration, renewal of the 1896 conventions in Tunisia, participation in the administration of the Moroccan port of Tangiers. Aside from the latter, Poincaré regarded these demands as "proof of the megalomania" of Italian diplomacy, which was motivated by envy of

France's colonial empire. Concessions on these points would, he said, simply create "new pretexts for the colonial appetite which Italy manifests to our detriment." Other factors hindering the establishment of an economic entente included the disastrous collapse of the franc in the mid-1920s, Italian suspicion of the more cordial atmosphere between France and Germany following Locarno, and increasing American investment in the Italian economy.[50] This failure to reach an economic accord was characteristic of the tensions which plagued Franco-Italian relations in general in the late 1920s. The lack of mutual understanding on this issue presaged a similar failure on the crucial Tunisian matter, which developed with agonizing dilatoriness on both sides.

French efforts to deal with the large Italian population in Tunisia went in several directions, although each aimed subsequently at increasing the pace of naturalization. Lucien Saint, France's resident general in Tunis, submitted annual reports on the pace of naturalization. His figures show that between 1891 and 1923, there were a total of 4,128 naturalizations of foreigners in the Regency, of whom 2,632 were Italians. In 1923 he recorded 526 Italian naturalizations, a figure which increased to 1,025 in 1924. By the end of 1927, he noted that a yearly rhythm of 2,500 to 3,000 naturalizations had been established and was likely to continue. French schools in Tunisia acted as primary recruiting grounds. The resident general proposed a system of free tuition, books, and supplies as a means of attracting Italian students away from Italian schools, the number of which had been fixed by the 1896 conventions. Furthermore, he suggested that France might grant employment preference on Tunisian railroad projects to foreigners—especially Italians—who agreed to go through the naturalization process.[51]

These efforts proved marginally effective. They were heartily resented and energetically combatted by the fascist regime in Rome. For example, in 1923, when the resident general in Tunis reported 526 Italian naturalizations, immigration statistics revealed that over 2,000 new Italians had arrived in the Regency in the same year. Working from figures like these, Italian journalists argued that demographic realities clearly favored Italy. Sooner or later, speculated *Corriere d'Italia* in 1926, given France's failure to entice her own nationals to emigrate to Tunisia, Italians would be able to assimilate the French community. Under these conditions, the only way for France to continue to exercise political authority over Europeans in the protectorate would be to renew unconditionally the guarantees reserved to Italians by the conventions of 1896. Press polemics, albeit interesting, may occasionally be disregarded as for home consumption only. But the record also indicates that Fascist Party representatives were engaged actively in

Tunisia throughout the 1920s, campaigning among Italian communities against the French and threatening sanctions against those Italians who accepted naturalization.[52]

In mid-1925 the Quai d'Orsay initiated an effort to resolve the impasse. A lengthy Foreign Ministry note, dated 20 June, made a detailed and systematic review of the entire history of the Tunisian question. While recognizing the Italian desire for a blanket renewal of the accords of 1896, the author stressed that it was no longer possible to guarantee special privileges to Italians which, in effect, made them "a state within a state." A conciliatory policy toward the Italian government was still possible; indeed Besnard advocated such a course. He suggested that the full force of naturalization for Italians might be delayed for a generation or two; Italian schools might be progressively transferred to French authority rather than all at once; certain guarantees could be extended to Italian fishermen and those practicing the liberal professions. Nevertheless, the future of good Franco-Italian relations demanded a new Tunisian accord, one which would allow France "to collect the fruits of its labors over the past forty years."[53]

France's more conciliatory attitude appeared to be matched in Rome six months later. In an interview granted to the French newspaper *L'Avenir,* Mussolini said that all rumors about Italian ambitions in Nice, Savoy, and Corsica were without foundation and that the Tunisian controversy could be easily resolved if only France would consent to a renewal of the 1896 conventions on a year-by-year basis, or for a longer period of time, rather than at three-month intervals. The French ambassador commented that "it would be necessary to go back a long way to find such a clear expression of a desire for direct collaboration with our country in the mouth of a President of the Italian Council." In April 1926, Mussolini reiterated, in the wake of the signing of the Russo-German accord, his denial of any territorial claims on France and his desire to strengthen links between the two countries in the face of the German danger.[54]

The documents on file in the archives of the French Foreign Ministry contain no official response to these overtures by Mussolini, in spite of Besnard's repeated insistence that a favorable reply was in order. Nor, for that matter, were Italian initiatives repeated for several months, during which time Rome was preoccupied with negotiating an arbitration pact with Germany. Shortly after the signing of the pact, on 31 December 1926, the Duce repeated his desire for an entente with France. Besnard seized the opportunity to inform Briand that Italian policy currently was hesitating between two routes. One led to Berlin. However, following his recent conversation with Mussolini, Besnard was "more convinced than ever that some interesting perspectives remain open for our policy and that it is not too late to direct Italy on the path leading to France." Finally, on 12 January 1927, Besnard received instructions from Briand to welcome Mussolini's overtures of 31 December and to initiate conversations aimed at obtaining clarifications from the Duce on the form which such an entente might take. The foreign minister's cautious response was hedged still further. France, Briand wrote, was interested in a treaty of arbitration and conciliation on the Locarno model, stipulating a common desire to maintain the peace and existing treaties. The opportunity could also be used to regulate specific issues, such as Tunisia, between the two countries. But it was important, he stressed, to move neither too quickly nor too far; great care must be exercised to prevent any agreement with Italy from compromising French relations with "our most solid clientele" among the states of the Little Entente—particularly Yugoslavia.[55]

In this pronouncement, Briand identified the inextricable linkage between colonial issues and political problems on the European continent. The Franco-Yugoslav treaty and the Italo-Albanian accord of November 1927 could not be regarded other than with mutual suspicion in Rome and Paris. In addition, Italian officials became increasingly agitated at the failure of the French government to restrict the activities of antifascist émigrés in France.[56] This atmosphere of mutual distrust rendered any resolution of outstanding differences in Tunisia or elsewhere impossible.

The discord engendered by the Yugoslav and Albanian questions dissipated by the spring of 1928. Briand instructed his new ambassador, Maurice Beaumarchais, to begin a new round of negotiations with Mussolini. The foreign minister believed it was logical to work first toward regulation of specific differences between the two countries—Tangiers, Tunisia, Tripolitania—as a preparation for a more general treaty of friendship. But if the Duce insisted on reversing the order of priorities, Briand was disposed to defer to his judgment. Based on these instructions, formal negotiations between Beaumarchais and Italian officials began on 19 March 1928. Mussolini proposed that the two countries work toward an arrangement that would take the form of a general treaty of accord with three protocols annexed to it, dealing with Tunisia, rectification of the frontier between Tunisia and Tripolitania, and the acquisition of an Italian colonial mandate. Although resolutely hostile to any formula that would accord a colonial mandate to Italy, the French government, as a gesture of good will, prorogued for one year (instead of the usual three months) the denunciation of the 1896 conventions guaranteeing Italian rights in Tunisia. Mussolini noted in a speech to the Italian Senate that ". . . the state of Franco-

Italian relations has ameliorated considerably [in recent months] ... ," and the new French ambassador in Rome waxed enthusiastic about the possibility of a wide-ranging accord between the two countries.[57]

The state of apparent good will continued for the next six months. In August 1928, Beaumarchais verbally presented to Mussolini the first draft of a treaty of friendship and arbitration, which the Duce promised to study quickly. The two men discussed Tunisia and Libyan frontier rectifications. The French ambassador felt that Mussolini had made a favorable response to the French proposals; "he asked me to put them in writing as soon as possible and I have the impression that he is disposed ... to give conciliatory instructions to his services." It was clear from this conversation that Tunisia was the key to any all-embracing accord. With this as encouragement, a lengthy exchange of memoranda between Rome, Paris, and Tunis finally resulted in an elaborate document designed to replace the conventions of 1896. It provided the following:

1. most favored nation status for Italy in Tunisia and for Tunisia in Italy;
2. protection for Italians practicing the liberal professions in Tunisia;
3. progressive transformation of Italian schools to local administration over a period of ten years;
4. for five years, Italians accused at law could request a jury composed of at least fifty percent Italians;
5. fishing rights for Italians off the Tunisian coast and for Tunisians off the Libyan coast; and
6. two key articles on naturalization. These defined as a French citizen all individuals born on French territory from parents one of whom was born in French territory. But the proposed accord excepted from this rule all Italian children born in Tunisia within three years of the validation of the accord; these would conserve the right to repudiate French nationality.

This proposal, along with the text of a treaty of friendship and arbitration and a second convention granting territory to Italy in Tripolitania, was officially submitted to the Italian government on 21 December 1928. Beaumarchais, in a personal letter to Mussolini, expressed his hope that the documents would prove acceptable and would lead to the conclusion of a treaty.[58]

After all the hopeful preparations of the previous six months, Italy's totally negative reaction to the French proposals came as a shock. Raffaele Guariglia, director of political affairs at the Palazzo Chigi, expressed dissatisfaction by suggesting that the only solution for Tunisia was the continuation of the 1896 conventions. He told the French chargé d'affaires that the program was "disastrous." No official Italian response was forthcoming for over six months. The official explanation for the delay was that Mussolini, distracted by the spring elections and negotiations for the Lateran Accords with the Vatican, had not had time to study the French proposals. Beaumarchais felt that the delay was due to the Duce's embarrassment at the poor reception given the French proposals by his Foreign and Colonial Ministries, after he himself had been so encouraging in talks with the French ambassador. Nevertheless, the Duce's official response, contained in a personal letter to Beaumarchais, was delivered on 29 June 1929. It found neither of the proposed conventions acceptable. He contemptuously referred to the Libyan boundary rectification as a violation of the letter and spirit of the 1915 Treaty of London—"an absolutely worthless piece of sand." With regard to Tunisia, he refused to make a detailed examination of the French proposal because he disagreed with its basic principle. The Italian government's goal was "the amelioration or at least the maintenance of the situation of Italians in the Tunisian Protectorate." To that end, the Duce suggested in his letter, the best way to pave the way for a treaty of friendship would be for France to prorogue the renunciation of the 1896 conventions for a minimum of ten years. The totally negative Italian reaction brought a quick halt to all further official negotiations at this point.[59]

SUMMARY

The diplomacy concerning eastern Mediterranean and North African questions during the 1920s leads to a number of conclusions about the nature of French policy toward fascist Italy during its early years. The desire of the Quai d'Orsay, under Poincaré's stewardship, to cultivate Mussolini's good will was strikingly evident in both the Corfu and Fiume crises. In the former, France stood virtually alone in support of Italian action, and Mussolini's diplomatic triumph can be ascribed largely to French support against England at Geneva. The record shows clearly that Poincaré was willing to support Italy in exchange for continuing fascist endorsement of French policy in the Reparations Commission and in the Ruhr. France continued to take a favorable view of Italian policy after Corfu, and her counsels of moderation in Belgrade permitted Rome to engineer a satisfactory solution to the protracted Fiume crisis in 1924.

Poincaré's tenure at the Quai d'Orsay ended in June 1924. Direction of French foreign policy passed briefly to Edouard Herriot and subsequently to Aristide Briand, whose principal technique for guaranteeing French security lay in direct negotiation with Germany rather than in attempts to encircle her with hostile alliances. Only after the German problem appeared definitively settled by the Locarno Treaties of 1925—interestingly enough with fascist Italy as a guarantor of the settlement—did Briand move to buttress the French alliance system by attaching the Little Entente states of eastern Europe. But even then, sustained efforts were undertaken to avoid bruising Italian sensitivities. It becomes apparent, then, that the Franco-Czech, Franco-Romanian, and Franco-Yugoslav treaties were intended as much to refurbish French influence and prestige in the Mediterranean and Danubian areas (a prestige tainted, in the eyes of these small states, by France's endorsement of Italy's bullying of Greece and Yugoslavia) as they were to create an eastern bulwark against Germany.[60]

In any case, these eastern alliances, completed by November 1927, marked a temporary end to French attempts to enroll fascist Italy in an anti-German entente, even though influential voices continued to advocate such a policy.[61] Relations between Paris and Rome became progressively more strained over such intractable issues as Italian nationality rights in Tunisia and the stridently anti-fascist activities of Italian émigrés in France. Neither side proved willing to make substantial concessions to the other. Also, there was no real political pressure in the late 1920s to force the two nations to cut through the impasse. The German danger—calmed by the Dawes Plan, the Locarno Treaties, the Young Plan of 1929, and the early evacuation of French troops from the Rhineland in 1930—was momentarily quiescent. But active champions of a Franco-Italian entente emerged in positions of influence in France once again after 1932, when the German question heated up following the rise of Adolf Hitler. In the 1930s, men, such as Joseph Paul-Boncour, Henry de Jouvenel, Barthou, Laval, André François-Poncet, and Georges Bonnet, would attempt again to build the Franco-Italian entente that Poincaré, Barrère, Charles-Roux, and Besnard had pursued in the 1920s.

CHAPTER 4

Jouvenel Mission to Rome

Symbolic of deteriorating Franco-Italian diplomatic relations in the 1920s were the resignations, under pressure, of two men who had worked consistently to reconcile differences between their two countries—Contarini and Besnard. The former, veteran secretary general of the Palazzo Chigi, submitted his resignation in mid-March 1926; it was accepted immediately by Mussolini. The official explanation for Contarini's departure cited ill-health as the reason. The French ambassador, however, believed that the public announcement concealed deep-seated policy divisions between the Duce and the secretary general. Contarini had been wise, moderate, and devoted to good Franco-Italian relations. He had become impatient with Mussolini's tendency to conduct foreign policy by himself, without bothering to inform his chief Foreign Ministry official in advance of the content of his foreign-policy speeches to the Italian Chamber and Senate. Other analysts were even more alarmist. Charles-Roux, who recently had been named ambassador to the Holy See, warned Berthelot that the resignation constituted a signal that Mussolini might be contemplating violent action at an opportune moment in an effort to resolve Franco-Italian differences. A note prepared for the European section of the Quai d'Orsay pointed out that Contarini's replacement, Antonino Bordonaro, recently had held positions as embassy counsellor at Berlin and minister in Vienna. Although Bordonaro was not a noted Germanophile, his appointment might well be "an indication that the President of the Council intends to modify his policy."[1]

The Italians also were quick to find ulterior motives lurking behind a sudden personnel change. Besnard resigned from his position at the Palazzo Farnese in November 1927, shortly after the signing of the Franco-Yugoslav treaty, explaining that he wished to run for elective office in the next election. Given the French ambassador's reluctance to conclude that agreement, Italian editorial writers told their readers that the real reason for Besnard's departure was his frustration at being undercut by the Quai d'Orsay in his efforts to establish the groundwork for a genuine entente between Italy and France. Three leading Italian newspapers, *Tribuna*, *Giornale d'Italia*, and *Messagero*, regretted the failure of his mission.[2]

Personnel changes may or may not betoken alterations in policy. But it cannot be denied that the years from 1927 to 1932 were extraordinarily contentious ones for the two "Latin sisters." On the official diplomatic level, virtually every issue that offered the possibility of Franco-Italian competition was allowed to fester. The Adriatic and eastern Mediterranean questions, for example, became ever more exacerbated in the wake of the Franco-Yugoslav and Italo-Albanian accords of 1927. On 13 September 1928, the Deuxième Bureau of the French General Staff completed a lengthy, secret report analyzing Italian policy in Danubian Europe, the Balkans, and the Middle East, virtually every aspect of which constituted a direct challenge to Yugoslavian and French interests there. The main points of this study were as follows:

1. Italy's stranglehold over Albania guaranteed control of the Adriatic and a political, economic, and military base on Yugoslavia's southern frontier.
2. Italy's support for Hungary's revisionist ambitions was designed to solidify her influence on the northern border of Yugoslavia.
3. Rapprochement with Austria, in accord with Hungary, aimed to undercut the emergence of any Danubian economic confederation under the aegis of the Little Entente.
4. Italian activities in Prague and Bucharest sought to separate Czechoslovakia and Romania from Yugoslavia, thus disrupting the Little Entente.
5. Recent Italian activities in Bulgaria were designed to encourage the latter to pressure Belgrade on her southeastern border.

6. Conversations in Athens encouraged the Greeks to abandon any idea of according Yugoslavia transit privileges to the Mediterranean at Salonika.

Such an all-encompassing program was very likely beyond the capacity of Italy to carry forth consistently and systematically. Nevertheless, the perception that it represented Italian goals was regarded by the French General Staff as "a threat to peace in the Balkans and in Europe as a whole." A similar analysis of Italian foreign policy in that region was submitted to Briand a year later by the French representative at the Holy See, Charles-Roux, who was well-situated to hear all kinds of rumor and inside information concerning Italian foreign policy ambitions.[3]

Similarly, the Tunisian question remained apparently intractable. Fascist propaganda urging the Italian communities to preserve their "italianità" was on the increase. Italian adults were targets of stepped-up consular activities, lectures, newspaper articles, and so forth; young people were wooed through the Italian schools, sports, art and literary clubs, free vacation trips to the mother country, and free food for Italian school children. Each year a number of Italian officials arranged to vacation in Tunisia, after which they would be greeted effusively at the train station in Rome and occasionally even received by Mussolini himself. In 1932, the French chargé in Rome, Roger de Dampierre, assessed such activities: "These various demonstrations show that the Italian colony in Tunis is the object of special attention on the part of the Fascist government, whose excessive solicitude has created a delicate situation for Regency authorities. . . . In effect the Fascist government sees in these Italian communities not only a national element whose protection is regarded as a duty, but also a means of political influence which can be manipulated at the appropriate opportunity." Manipulation might also be applied to Mussolini's periodic preoccupation with the *fuorusciti*, Italian political exiles in France whose stridently antifascist activities the Duce blamed on a combination of French toleration and covert encouragement. All of these factors have led some observers, most notably Cassels, to conclude that Franco-Italian discord was "a basic assumption of Mussolini's diplomatic vision."[4] Such judgments are virtually irrefutable if one looks only at the surface rancor of mutually hostile press diatribes and official communiqués released by the French and Italian Embassies and Foreign Ministries between 1928 and 1932. But international relations are conducted privately as well as in the public arena. The record demonstrates clearly that informal, and occasionally covert, contacts between the French and Italians planted the seeds that eventually established the Laval-Mussolini accords of 1935 and the subsequent military collaboration between the two powers at precisely the same time that the public recriminatory atmosphere seemed least conducive to germination.

STRAWS IN THE WIND

Mussolini himself provided the context in which these informal contacts could be nurtured. On 15 December 1927, the text of an address by the Duce to the Italian Council of Ministers was leaked to the French embassy. In it he maintained that the Franco-Yugoslav treaty and the Italo-Albanian defensive military alliance only seemed contradictory to observers who were overly impressed by the fact that eleven days separated the signing of the two accords. "I believe," Mussolini told the government leaders,

> that it is possible, useful and I hasten to add, necessary [to achieve] a long, cordial, durable entente between France and Italy. But such an entente, to be solid, cannot be based on exclusively literary or purely sentimental formulas, but rather on the elimination of all concrete points of friction between the two countries. Normal diplomatic representatives will eventually confront these problems which are neither serious nor insoluable but only delicate. . . . When these diplomats will have accomplished their preliminary and necessary work, the next logical step will be a meeting between the responsible Ministers who, in a short conversation, can simply and solemnly consecrate an accord.[5]

Mussolini, not often credited with great foresight or political acumen, had accurately forecast the sequence of events that would bring a Franco-Italian accord to fruition seven years later.

General Pietro Badoglio proved to be a friendly source, who was monitored consistently by both the Quai d'Orsay and the French General Staff during the years of stormy public relations. As early as April 1925, Badoglio, then Italian military attaché in Rio de Janeiro, told the French chargé d'affaires that should he be recalled to Italy to take over a General Staff appointment, he would seek authorization to initiate conversations with the French General Staff aimed at concluding a military convention between the two countries. The Italian underscored his conviction that Germany, in association with Austria, was prepared for a war of revenge to be launched simultaneously on the Rhine and on the Italian Alpine frontier within ten years. For that reason, Badoglio believed that an alliance between France and Italy was indispensable. General Maurice Gamelin, Badoglio's French counterpart in Brazil, noted in his memoirs that he and the Italian frequently had discussed rapprochement involving a reciprocal recognition of interests in Africa. It is not surprising that the Italian military man's views on this subject took on considerably greater importance when he was named Chief of the Italian General Staff of the Army in May 1925.[6]

It seemed unlikely to French observers that Mussolini would have made the appointment had his own views been diametrically opposed to Badoglio's. The general never sought to conceal his Francophile inclinations. The new Italian Chief of Staff reiterated his views on the common German danger to French diplomats in Rome on several social occasions and in informal conversation with the French military attaché in 1925, even going so far as to invite the latter to contact him directly at any time, without going through the military liaison officer connected to Badoglio's office. Reports of all of these contacts were transferred immediately to General Ferdinand Foch, the French Chief of Staff and to the minister of war. The former, in a personal letter to Briand, advised that France ought to respond "without delay" to Badoglio's repeated overtures "for fear that these favorable dispositions toward us might become reoriented in another direction."[7]

General Badoglio repeated his views on at least eight different occasions between 1926 and 1930 to various French diplomatic and military officials in Rome. It is difficult to believe that so many overtures were not designed to elicit some sort of formal proposal from Paris. Why was none forthcoming? The answer can be deduced from the way in which the Quai d'Orsay reacted to Badoglio. Before his resignation, Besnard had observed that although he would welcome a military pact between France and Italy, it could only come about as the result of a political decision undertaken by the two governments, and neither Contarini nor Mussolini made any allusion to such a pact in their conversations with him. The ambassador argued that the perfect opportunity had arisen in the summer of 1925, during preparations for the Locarno Treaties, when he verbally told the Duce that France was prepared to investigate a pact with Italy which would mutually guarantee the Rhine and Brenner frontiers. The offer, however, elicited no formal response. Besnard concluded, therefore, that Badoglio's words did not seem capable of leading to practical conclusions "so long as M. Mussolini will not let us know whether he shares the ideas of his Chief of General Staff." Berthelot responded by recalling the same incident and instructing his ambassador to take no further initiative. "It is up to M. Mussolini," he wrote, "to reinitiate the conversation at the point where it has been suspended." Briand repeated these instructions a year later, adding that it would be advisable to await the reestablishment of normal Italo-Yugoslav relations before pursuing an accord with Italy.[8]

It seems reasonably clear that while both sides were interested in the military arrangements articulated by General Badoglio, neither was willing to make a formal written proposal to the other through normal diplomatic channels. To do so would have risked the embarrassment of rebuff and certainly would have alienated third parties, particularly Germany. In any case, such failures of communication and intellectual understanding would once again plague Franco-Italian relations in the late 1930s, when the diplomatic situation was decidedly more volatile.

Unpublished materials in the archives of the Quai d'Orsay also indicate that unofficial conversations on outstanding colonial differences between the two countries in North Africa ensued over a four-year period from 1928 to 1932.[9] The most important of these took place in Geneva between Robert de Caix, French delegate to the League of Nations' Mandate Commission, and his Italian counterpart and president of the Commission, the Marquis A. Theodoli. A number of suggestive bits of information can be gleaned from these documents. They contain, for example, the first substantial discussion of what the future might hold for Ethiopia. Theodoli did not disguise the fact that Italy coveted Ethiopia as the natural extension of her colonies in Eritrea and Italian Somaliland. He indicated to his French counterpart that "complete freedom of action" in Ethiopia would be acceptable as a basis upon which to liquidate all Franco-Italian colonial differences. De Caix pointed out that Ethiopia was a member of the League of Nations, but he suggested that France might not be totally hostile to Theodoli's Ethiopian ambitions if the Italians would, in turn, be willing to accept the naturalization of Italian immigrants in Tunisia and the withdrawal of special privileges for Italians in the Regency. Such, for France, would be "the condition *sine qua non* of an accord." This language subsequently was adopted by the Quai d'Orsay in official instructions to French diplomats in Rome after 1932. Both Theodoli and de Caix agreed that Libyan boundary rectification was a minor issue.

Ethiopia represented a sticky matter for the French from a number of perspectives. Paris had supported the African nation's entry into the League in 1923. Obviously, France could not openly sanction the demise of a fellow League member. Similarly, France had supported Haile Selassie as the best hope for a stable government in Ethiopia and essential for protecting French economic interests there. Unfortunately, however, Haile Selassie experienced some difficulty in controlling the "feudal anarchy" of his administration—thus encouraging the French to consider more seriously the prospect of making a deal with the Italians. The French, after all, had important economic interests in the Red Sea port of Jibuti and along the Jibuti–Addis Ababa Railway. The Theodoli-de Caix negotiations suggest, therefore, that any understanding with Italy, which was prejudicial to Ethiopian sovereignty, would have to be made secretly and would have to recognize French economic interests.

Taken together, the Badoglio hints about a Franco-Italian military arrangement and the Theodoli-de Caix pourparlers about a colonial trade-off in North Africa encapsulated nearly the entire package of accords, protocols, and General Staff agreements achieved by Laval and Mussolini between January and June 1935. These matters—far from being the sudden brainstorm of Laval who was anxious to demonstate his supposed profascist inclinations as some observers wrote at the time—had been under discussion unofficially at various levels in both France and Italy since 1925. All that was needed was a change in the European political climate sufficient to transform unofficial contacts between the two countries into official government determination to achieve an understanding.

TOWARD A MORE FAVORABLE CLIMATE OF OPINION

Under the direction of Briand, the Quai d'Orsay had become so enmeshed in collective security that it neglected some aspects of its own security system. Apart from the small eastern European states, France enjoyed the commitment of no other continental power. This situation, tolerable during the "era of illusions" of the late 1920s, became cause for alarm in light of European developments after 1930—the Austro-German customs union proposal, the spread of the Great Depression, and the waxing strength of Hitler and the National Socialists. Most particularly, growing popular support for radical nationalist elements in Germany encouraged French policymakers to alter their official attitude toward fascist Italy in order to forestall the possibility of an Italo-German fascist alliance. A similar concern about the German danger also became apparent in Rome. An indication that public opinion in both countries was being prepared for a policy change was evident in the popular press. Following the Lateran Accords of 1929, which regularized relations between the Papacy and the Italian state, the majority of Catholic newspapers in France abandoned their reservations about Mussolini's regime. In addition, a number of conservative and moderate newspapers, whose editorial policies frequently were inspired by the Quai d'Orsay on matters of foreign policy, seized upon the Lateran Accords to begin writing of a rapprochement between France and Italy. Similarly, the French Embassy in Rome alerted the Quai d'Orsay on a number of occasions in 1930 to a perceptible moderation in the tone of the Italian press, especially in the editorials of Virginio Gayda, editor of *Gior-*

nale d'Italia and well known as a foreign-policy mouthpiece of the Italian government. His pieces became "very moderate in tone," in striking contrast to the anti-French press diatribes of previous months.[10]

This changing atmosphere in public opinion also coincided with Laval's first ministry (27 January 1931–20 February 1932). Even though Briand and Berthelot remained in charge of foreign policy, the new French government seemed to encourage an improvement of relations. The English ambassador in Rome reported an almost imperceptible improvement in Mussolini's public stance toward France, and he suggested that the Duce was moving toward the view that Italy's best interests lay in collective security and better relations with France and England. A concrete indication of the altered atmosphere occurred in May 1931, when the Italian minister in Belgrade paid a spontaneous visit to his French counterpart. The former pointed out the common interest of both countries in opposing the idea of *Anschluss,* recently intensfied by the customs union proposal, and emphasized the joy with which the Italian government had greeted the Washington Naval Agreement. These factors, he hoped, would pave the way for a long future of friendship. Italy was approaching a crossroads and must look to the future. "Germany's power is increasing steadily; its influence is even on the rise in Yugoslavia. Let France not lose this occasion to get together with Italy, whose intentions have never been better."[11]

Shortly thereafter the Italians approached directly. On 14 July 1931, the Italian ambassador in Paris came to see Léon Noël, Laval's chief of staff, to present a *note verbale* from Mussolini. In it, the Duce affirmed his desire to seek an entente with France. He flattered the French premier, citing the common origins of them both and the parallelism of their political careers. In short, Mussolini implied, their personalities were such as to be able to deal with all the problems dividing Italy and Paris.[12] The Italian leader was not the only one to recognize that Laval differed substantially from Briand. Some Englishmen were concerned about the premier's evident lack of attachment to the British connection and his inclination to pursue European policies without consulting London. Poliakoff, pseudonym for the diplomatic correspondent of the *London Times,* wrote to Robert Vansittart, permanent undersecretary of state at the Foreign Office, on 4 August 1931:

> I have reached the conclusion that the French at present are on the verge of forming a foreign policy characterized by its independence from British influence. They are on the verge of deciding that the Entente with Great Britain is worthwhile preserving for decorative purposes, but that it is a thing of no great practical value. . . . As to Italy . . . I know that M. Laval wants peace with the Italians. Mussolini at heart has always been a francophile. If the two men can manage to get past their own officials, they will come to a full agreement quickly.

Poliakoff's observations were perspicacious enough, but Laval's tenure at the Matignon Palace did not last long enough to override lingering suspicions at the Quai d'Orsay. A novice in foreign affairs and reluctant to alienate the veteran diplomatic establishment in France, he allowed Mussolini's initiative to pass. According to Noël, Berthelot and other Italophobes at the Foreign Ministry worked hard to thwart this effort on the Duce's part to encourage a meeting between himself and Laval in 1931. They believed that too much tension still remained for such a summit gathering to be fruitful. The secretary general's attitude was symptomatic of the "systematic italophobia" which paralyzed many career diplomats at the French Ministry of Foreign Affairs.[13]

The year 1932 represented a turning point in French policy toward Italy, stimulated both by important changes in personnel and by the alarming electoral successes of Hitler's Nazis in Germany. On 27 March, André Tardieu, Laval's successor, spoke sympathetically about Italy in the French Senate. In November Henri Béranger chairman of the Chamber of Deputies' Foreign Affairs Committee, returned from a visit to Italy and called for a "total entente" as soon as possible. Shortly thereafter Premier Edouard Herriot, who also held the foreign affairs portfolio, at a Radical Socialist Party congress in Toulouse, advocated clearing up misunderstandings with Italy, "'with whom we perhaps have not been fair enough.'"[14] General Gamelin, chief of the French General Staff, recollected in his memoirs about this era: "I have always been a partisan of Franco-Italian collaboration. Italy is the European country nearest to us in general mores. . . . I have always thought that the logical complement to the French-British system was Italy."[15]

Other evidence also indicates that the Italians, concerned about the events in Germany in 1932, were willing to consider rapprochement with France. Mario Toscano, the noted Italian diplomatic historian, observed in his introduction to the diary of Baron Pompeo Aloisi that the latter's appointment as secretary general of the Italian Foreign Ministry on 20 July 1932 was meant as a signal that the Duce desired to ameliorate relations with France. Aloisi was married to a French woman and was widely recognized as an energetic Francophile. On 24 August 1932, the French chargé in Rome reported that the head of the European division of the Palazzo Chigi had bruited the possibility of a modification in Italy's fiercely anti-French public posture. If only Paris would take steps to control the anti-fascist activities of Italian emigrants in France, then "'I am persuaded that things would change and that you would see immediately a modification in our political attitude toward France.'"[16]

These impressions explain why Herriot's speech and Béranger's visit in

November met with generally favorable responses in the Italian Peninsula. Many there regarded these events as the first indications of a positive amelioration in the Franco-Italian atmosphere. According to Roger de Dampierre, Italian officials came away from their meeting with the French deputy no longer completely absorbed with the idea of clarifying specific points of detail on Tunisia, Libyan boundary rectification, and naval parity. These matters had fallen to second rank. "In the eyes of the fascist government, an accord between the two countries must be a general political accord, largely based and embracing the totality of European problems." The French Embassy advisor believed Italy to be at a crossroads of two paths—one leading to Paris and the other to Berlin. And although Italian officials still remained vague in responding to questions about what exactly Italy wanted in order to achieve an accord, Mussolini assured Béranger and others that any entente should be achieved within the cadre of the League of Nations and should aim toward establishing rapport among the four great European powers—Britain, France, Italy, and Germany. This entire analysis was heavily underlined and bracketed in blue pencil by officials at the Quai d'Orsay. Shortly thereafter Dampierre pointed out that Mussolini was viewed by the Frenchmen he met as the most moderate figure in the Italian government on questions concerning Franco-Italian relations. Therefore, he suggested that the time had come to follow up Herriot's and Béranger's words of good feeling toward Italy by some action. Silence would indicate to Rome an inability to translate words into deeds.[17]

THE JOUVENEL MISSION

Such was the situation when Joseph Paul-Boncour, who had recently resigned from the Socialist Party, was named premier and minister of foreign affairs on 18 December 1932. Although adamantly opposed to fascism in all its forms, Paul-Boncour nevertheless believed that any realistic analysis of the European situation demanded an amelioration of Franco-Italian relations. Such a development, he felt, would be a useful counterweight to both Germany and England. His first task, therefore, was to appoint people who could work enthusiastically for a rapprochement. Paul-Boncour made two quick appointments which showed clearly the direction of this policy. Since Beaumarchais's death, the ambassadorship in Rome had remained vacant. In his place, the new premier appointed his friend, Henry de Jouvenel, as a special ambassador to Mussolini. Jouvenel's appointment was for only six months—the maximum constitutionally allowable to a member of the French Senate. But Paul-Boncour was anxious to have an emissary in Rome who, "by his earlier functions, by his inclinations, by his winning personality, [could] put an end to the misunderstandings and the latent tension between us and our former ally of 1915, Italy."[18]

Bertrand Henry Léon Robert de Jouvenel des Ursins was descended from a line of Limousin barons who had come to prominence in France during the Hundred Years' War. A brilliant student, he had begun his political collaboration with Paul-Boncour in 1900. Politically Jouvenel was a man of the moderate left, although he avoided joining a political party. He had acquired a substantial reputation before the First World War as a writer, journalist, and editor of the influential Parisian daily newspaper *Le Matin*. Four years in the trenches magnified his determination to fight fiercely for peace once the war was over. In 1922 Poincaré had appointed Jouvenel a delegate to the League of Nations where he energetically supported his government's oppositon to sanctions against Italy in the Corfu crisis. His attitude at that time foreshadowed his activities as Paul-Boncour's special emissary to Rome in 1933: "Between the prestige of the League of Nations and the interests of peace [he had said], no hesitation is possible: peace first!" Jouvenel frequently spoke out in favor of Franco-Italian rapprochement thereafter and, beginning in 1930, used his new journal, *Revue des Vivants*, as a forum for urging better relations between the two countries.[19]

Jouvenel's appointment to Rome paralleled an equally important change in command at the Quai d'Orsay in Paris. Paul-Boncour persuaded the ailing Berthelot to resign, and appointed Alexis Saint-Léger Léger, the French poet. Whereas his predecessor had harbored a phobia against Italy, "Léger's mind, supple to excess, was quite incapable of any phobia whatever." By the end of 1932, therefore, a new team had seized control of French foreign policy—composed of Paul-Boncour, Jouvenel, and Léger—whose principal task was to seek "the basis of an entente [with Italy] which would not put in peril [France's] Mediterranean interests or other alliances."[20] Jouvenel's instructions reflected this goal. His major effort, to be carried out in direct negotiations with Mussolini, was to liquidate points of friction between the two countries in Africa and to harmonize their interests in Europe, especially in the Danubian region.[21]

Jouvenel arrived in Rome with great expectations on 22 January 1933. He was, if nothing else, well prepared to negotiate a general understanding with Italy. The Jouvenel papers, collected at the Ministry of Foreign Affairs Archives in Paris, contain detailed background reports on all the unresolved issues dividing the two countries—Libya, Italian nationality rights in Tunisia, Ethiopia, and especially the Danubian question.[22] Paul-

Boncour underscored his own high hopes for the mission to Rome in his official instructions to Jouvenel. "The important thing [Paul-Boncour emphasized] is not to ameliorate relations . . . for several months, but rather to use these months to define the principles of a durable entente which will associate the interests of the two countries over a long period of time." Accordingly, Paul-Boncour instructed Jouvenel to work toward an entente which would resolve the following problems: (1) Amelioration of public opinion in Italy in regard to France. Especially it was important that the Italian press tone down its demands for French territory (i.e., Corsica). (2) Resolution of the Italian demographic problem. Such a resolution must not rely on French territory (Tunisia), but Jouvenel should not reject out-of-hand any suggestions that Italy might make regarding Ethiopia. (3) A more active economic and financial collaboration. (4) Cooperation on European disarmament. (5) Amelioration of Italy's relations with France's Yugoslavian ally. This was a crucial question. France would not entertain any Italian claims to Yugoslav territory but would support Italian economic influence in Albania. Paul-Boncour concluded his dispatch by stressing the importance of preserving the sanctity of treaties, continued support for the League of Nations, collaboration with England, and the maintenance of France's links with Poland and the Little Entente.[23] He hoped that any future understanding with Italy would not violate any of these "permanent" aspects of French foreign policy.

Jouvenel had been handed an imposing assignment, difficult to achieve even in the best of situations. It was complicated by the fact that the Italians had some initial reservations about the Jouvenel mission. Mussolini was suspicious about the seriousness of a complicated mission that was forcibly limited to six months, and he felt that the Quai d'Orsay had probably sent a famous politician "to get him out of the way." Consequently, the initial conversations with Mussolini and his foreign minister, Fulvio Suvich, were not particularly fruitful. Jouvenel was frustrated at the Italians' insistence upon discussing small details of naval parity and relations with Yugoslavia. These matters would be easily resolved, he argued, if first the two parties could fall into accord on the general lines of a Franco-Italian entente. The whole negotiation appeared to have reached "a dead letter" following Hitler's rise to power in Germany. Jouvenel informed Paul-Boncour on 24 February 1933 that no breakthrough in Franco-Italian relations was likely until the German situation came into clearer focus. To force the pace of the negotiations might be viewed in Rome as a sign of French weakness and insecurity vis-à-vis the rise of the Nazis in Germany.[24]

On 3 March 1933 Jouvenel had a long and important conversation with

Mussolini, in which the Duce rejected the idea of any direct Franco-Italian alliance. Alliances, he said, divide Europe whereas the point is to seek a general "political entente" to deal with the large European issues. One can notice quite clearly the germ of what was shortly to become Mussolini's grandiose proposal for a Four-Power Pact among France, Italy, Britain, and Germany. First, however, it would be useful for France and Italy to bring together their points of view on the organization of Europe. For his part, Mussolini made the following proposals for the preservation of European peace: (1) Germany should be accorded a band of territory across the Polish corridor linking the Reich with East Prusssia; (2) the frontiers of Hungary should be revised; (3) Italian security in the Adriatic must be guaranteed by an Italian presence in Albania; and (4) the independence of Austria must be preserved. Once an agreement on these general matters was reached, the purely local issues directly affecting Franco-Italian relations could be resolved without difficulty. Mussolini's program was far more ambitious than anything the French had envisioned, and Jouvenel remarked in his summary of this conversation that "the time when Mussolini's ambition can be satisfied by a few palm trees in Libya has passed." But at least the issues had been clarified from the Italian point of view. "We have before us [Jouvenel concluded] the entire panorama of the negotiation and consequently the full extent of the difficulty." Aloisi underlined the difficulty when he noted in his diary that opposition to *Anschluss* was the only aspect of the Duce's program where French and Italian views coincided. Most of the other points involved treaty modification, to which France had been adamantly opposed since 1919. As he left the room after his conversation with Mussolini, Jouvenel seemed like "a man already resigned to the defeat of his mission."[25]

Esmonde M. Robertson, one of the few scholars to recognize method rather than simple opportunism in the evolution of Mussolini's foreign policy, sees this series of events as decisive. The list of priorities articulated above seemed to suggest that whatever ambitions Mussolini might have in North Africa, the *politica periferica,* were of secondary importance. Of first priority was some immediate dramatic success in Europe to drum up support within the Fascist Party. Although he was flattered by what he thought to be Hitler's imitation of fascism, the Duce recognized that a policy of fraternization with Germany would totally alienate the French. Conversely, he also dismissed, for the time being, the alternative of an agreement with France for fear that this would rule out all possibility of change in the territorial status quo for both Germany and Italy. He thus gave up—at least temporarily—his efforts to alter the territorial equilibrium by force in Italy's favor. Instead, he aimed to pursue a policy of "equidistance" with the other three main powers; his method proved to be the Four-Power Pact.[26]

Up to this point Jouvenel's mission appeared to be entirely frustrated. The talk with Mussolini uncovered little basis for a substantial Franco-Italian entente. Far from admitting defeat, however, Jouvenel proposed to Paul-Boncour that France try to turn Mussolini's grand scheme to her own advantage. He felt it would be dangerous to ignore the Duce's proposals or to delay a response, since any delay might encourage Italy to strengthen ties with Hitler's Germany. " 'To capitalize [on the situation],' " he said, " 'we need speed and optimism.' " Jouvenel saw Mussolini's sweeping program as an opportunity *first* to solve some of the specific Franco-Italian problems. In short, France's price for participating in Mussolini's general entente would be a settlement of the specific problems between the two countries. Paul-Boncour, although harboring severe reservations about a Polish counter-corridor and Hungarian frontier revision, concurred with his ambassador on 10 March and instructed him to pursue the matter further.[27] In the end, such a strategy proved extremely naive; Mussolini insisted on reversing the order of priorities—first the general entente and then the Franco-Italian settlement. But at least Jouvenel convinced the Duce of the connection between the two.

On 18 March 1933, Mussolini presented Jouvenel with the text of his Four-Power proposal. From the French point of view it was an extremely dangerous document. Although it paid lip service to the Kellogg-Briand Pact and the League of Nations, the Duce's draft called on the four powers to confirm the principle of treaty revision. In addition, it provided for equality of armament rights for Germany and implied the creation of a four-power (Anglo-Franco-Italo-German) directorate which could impose its will on other European states. The French were placed in rather an awkward situation by Mussolini's proposal, which had been presented simultaneously to the British and the Germans. To reject it outright risked assuming responsibility for the failure of a proposition aimed at consolidating the peace; furthermore, a French rejection might lead to an Italo-German agreement. It was, however, equally impossible to accept the proposal. To do so might harm the League, harness France to a policy of treaty revision, and prejudice France's relations with its eastern European allies. For the moment the Quai d'Orsay simply adopted the tactic of delay, hoping to gain time to modify the Italian proposal in conformity with French interests.[28]

Edouard Daladier, who had replaced Paul-Boncour at the Matignon Palace on 31 January 1933, and his foreign minister underscored their many objections to the Mussolini draft and prepared a counterproposal which eliminated treaty revision and restricted Four-Power collaboration to economic matters. Jouvenel, however, advised a much more hardheaded and practical response. Instead of delaying action, Jounvenel urged the Quai d'Orsay to make a quick and generally favorable gesture congratulating Mussolini on his initiative. It was more than likely that the British would propose concrete changes to the articles dealing with treaty revision and German armament. For Jouvenel it was essential to seize this moment to solidify a favorable Franco-Italian atmosphere. More fundamentally, the French ambassador saw the Four-Power proposal as "in reality . . . a pact for holding Germany in check."[29]

He developed this argument in a long and eloquent telegram to Paul-Boncour on 25 March. Registering impatience at the fact that the Quai d'Orsay had done nothing more than list its objections to the Duce's proposal, he urged the adoption of a more positive attitude. He pointed out that the League of Nations was becoming progressively weaker and that the stalemated disarmament talks were also in danger of collapse. If this were to occur, there would be nothing left to ensure peace unless some version of Mussolini's Four-Power Pact arrangement were adopted. Granted, France's small eastern allies would have reservations, but they must be made to recognize that their best guarantee of security lay in the creation of a forum in which the ambitions of Germany could be restrained. Jouvenel concluded his analysis with the following appeal:

> I fear that once again we are going to lose the opportunity for rapprochement with Italy. This had seemed to be one of the essential directives of your foreign policy, without which I would not be here. [The consequences of opposing the Four-Power Pact] would be to throw Italy into Germany's arms and to put distance between ourselves and England. It seems that we fear being isolated in the group of four whereas we shall always retain recourse to the Council and the Assembly of the League. How can one not see that we would be even more isolated if we remain outside of it?

No doubt Jouvenel was also motivated by indications from the Italians that progress on a Franco-Italian political accord would be considerably expedited once serious negotiations on Mussolini's Four-Power proposal were underway.[30]

The official French counterproposal to Mussolini's Four-Power Pact arrived in Rome on 11 April 1933. It contained a long preamble pledging allegiance to the principles of the League, Locarno, and the Kellogg-Briand Pact. Article II made no specific mention of treaty revision but referred instead to clause 19 (on revision of treaties) and clause 16 (on sanctions against aggressors) of the League of Nations Pact. The French draft insisted further that Four-Power decisions could not be foisted on outside parties without their consent; it also stressed the principle of disarmament as opposed to equality of rights in armament. Mussolini's initial reaction to the French draft was not unfavorable, and Jouvenel took the opportunity once again to stress France's interest in reaching a separate bilateral accord with Italy. A conversation ensued between the two men about several issues of concern to both countries. Jouvenel gathered the impression that "if the negotiation of the Four-Power Pact has the effect of appeasement that we have been looking for, we will be able to profit from the atmosphere it will create to push the negotiations à deux and finally liquidate our differences with Italy."[31] It is quite clear that the Four-Power Pact was valued by the French only insofar as it would act as a vehicle leading to a bilateral pact with Italy.

Numerous obstacles remained to be resolved. The Germans adamantly opposed the French version. The Quai d'Orsay was reluctant to move forward too quickly because of continued reservations among French allies in eastern Europe and because French public opinion at home was uneasy about the presence of Germany in negotiations whose purpose was rapprochement with Italy. Nevertheless, Jouvenel continued his efforts—with both Mussolini and the French Foreign Ministry. He continually emphasized, in his regular communications with Paris, how significant it was that Mussolini had abandoned his own draft in favor of the French version as the basis for discussions. Nevertheless, the Italians would propose changes and France must be responsive, since establishing a document acceptable to both France and Germany would be no easy task. Jouvenel argued, "more than France, it is Mussolini who is pressuring Germany, because of his desire to control German rearmament projects and submit them to the three western powers."[32]

For the next several weeks, negotiations for a Four-Power Pact continued in Rome. According to Jouvenel, who was anxious to speed France toward approval of the Pact in order to begin negotiations à deux before his six-month tenure expired, Mussolini was acting the role of mediator— meeting first with the German ambassador and then with the English and French ambassadors. Slowly the Germans were being brought around to a text acceptable to France. Given the anti-German state of French public opinion, Jouvenel was careful how he outlined the relationship between Germany and Italy. Mussolini regarded the Nazis as disciples but had only contempt for their anti-Jewish policies. He was, in addition, concerned about preserving Austrian independence as a buffer between the two fascist states. France also opposed *Anschluss,* but Mussolini viewed the Franco-Yugoslav alliance as hostile to Italy. The Duce's uncertainty about France, magnified by frequent outbursts of anti-Italian sentiment in the French press and by the fact that French political leaders rarely came to Rome for consultations, explained why he was anxious to construct a Four-Power forum in which he could maintain good relations with Germany but also have some input into decisions on armament and treaty revision.[33] These communications revealed Jouvenel's growing impatience with what he regarded as foot-dragging in Paris. His telegrams made constant reference to the fact that Mussolini was fully prepared to sign a bilateral accord with France within weeks of the conclusion of the Four-Power Pact. Paul-Boncour's responses stressed the fact that a Four-Power accord would be meaningless for France unless it led to a settlement of French differences with Italy. He continued to insist on the careful wording of Article II concerning treaty revision in order to reassure France's eastern allies. In addition, Paul Boncour argued, time was necessary to prepare French public opinion for entering a pact with Nazi Germany.[34]

On 30 May 1933 Jouvenel forwarded to Paris the final text of the Four-Power Pact, urging that he be instructed to initial it immediately. Article II expressed the French position; no specific reference to treaty revision was included—only a reference to clause 19 of the League of Nations Pact (on revision of treaties). Also included, however, were references to clause 16 (sanctions against aggressors) and to clause 10 (territorial integrity of the various states). Article II stipulated that the Four Powers would collaborate should it become necessary to bring these clauses into force. Whereas the French position was adopted on this matter, Article III partially incorporated the German thesis on rearmament. The first paragraph stressed continued efforts at disarmament, as the French had insisted. But a second paragraph recognized the principle of equality of rights for Germany and the other disarmed states, and further wording suggested that the Four Powers would collaborate to realize the principle of equality by stages if the Disarmament Conference should fail.[35]

On 3 June Jouvenel was shocked to find a telegram from Paul-Boncour in which the latter strongly objected to Article III. Since it mooted the eventual rearmament of Germany, he felt it would stand no chance of being accepted by either the French Parliament or public opinion. Paul-Boncour suggested that Jouvenel propose to drop this controversial article from the Pact. Seeing his entire mission imperiled, Jouvenel responded in an emotional and strongly worded telegram to the foreign minister. He argued that he had done everything humanly possible to direct every article of the proposed Pact in the direction of the French point of view. For two and one-half months he had, in line-by-line negotiations, cajoled Mussolini and the English ambassador in Rome to accept numerous French modifications of the Duce's original proposal. To argue now for withdrawal of Article III, or worse, to reject the entire Pact would make France look ridiculous and obstructive in world opinion. It would have disastrous consequences for the disarmament conference and would make impossible any future rapprochement with Italy. To underline his point of view, Jouvenel concluded his telegram by pointing out that it would be perfectly possible for the government "to disavow me and to replace me with another ambassador. . . ."[36]

Jouvenel's outburst produced the desired result. On that same day, Paul-Boncour authorized his ambassador to initial the Pact. But in so doing, the foreign minister reiterated his expectation that now direct conversations with Italy would be undertaken in earnest with an eye toward achieving an effective Franco-Italian entente. Paul-Boncour specifically mentioned the naval question as being in urgent need of regulation. He instructed Jouvenel to make it clear to Mussolini that the Four-Power Pact would stand no chance of parliamentary ratification in France unless "it could be legitimately considered as a certain step toward the rapprochement of the two countries." The Four-Power Pact was initialed in Rome on 7 June 1933, and in his speech to the Italian Senate honoring the occasion, Mussolini included several references to the contributions of the French government. It was clearly an effort to quiet any last-minute objections to the Pact. The evidence also suggests that the Duce's statements about moving forward on direct Franco-Italian questions were greeted with enthusiastic applause.[37]

Needless to say the Four-Power Pact was not uniformly welcomed in France. General Gamelin, the French Chief of Staff, supported the Pact and expressed admiration for Jouvenel and his achievement. He noted in his memoirs that the Four-Power Pact episode momentarily raised "a period of hope." Surprisingly, Paul-Boncour's policy also received support from the socialists. Socialist Party leader Léon Blum noted that although dictatorships were distasteful, one must deal with realities rather than cling to a futile moral resistance. It must be France's duty never to refuse a peaceful gesture even if it comes from dictators whose motives were suspect.[38] For the moment at least the Pact also had the indispensable support of Joseph Caillaux and Henri Béranger, chairmen of the foreign relations committees of the Chamber of Deputies and the Senate respectively. The Pact's most outspoken opponent was Paul Reynaud, future premier, who argued that it was a first step in the complete abandonment of the principle of the sanctity of treaties and thus represented a total contradiction of French foreign policy. Louis Barthou, who became foreign minister in 1934, also was in opposition, primarily because he felt the Pact represented an obstacle to the creation of an "eastern Locarno."[39] Despite this opposition, however, Paul-Boncour's policy prevailed, and France officially signed the Four-Power Pact on 15 July 1933.

The final version of the Four-Power Pact may be regarded as a victory for French diplomacy and a tribute to Jouvenel's tenacity. Mussolini's original proposal had been completely emasculated and the entire Four-Power "directorate" was harnessed to the League of Nations. In the end, the Pact, for all the emotion it generated and for all the optimistic hopes expressed in its behalf, came to nothing. It was never ratified by the French legislature. Some have suggested that the French failure to ratify reflected the growth of anti-Italian sentiment or that opposition from her eastern European allies encouraged policymakers to back away from the Four-Power commitment. Paul-Boncour argues quite plausibly, however, that the French Chamber failed to ratify the Pact solely because it became a dead letter after Hitler's withdrawal from the League of Nations in October 1933. From the French perspective, the Pact had been revised in such a way as to strengthen the League; it could not operate independent of Geneva.[40] Therefore the overt purpose of establishing a Four-Power collaboration had failed. This failure, however, was clear only after October 1933. Besides, the Four-Power Pact had never been the central issue for France, a fact made clear by all the correspondence between Jouvenel and the Quai d'Orsay. In the end the success or failure of the Jouvenel mission to Rome must be assessed on the covert purpose of France's support for the Pact— that is, how successful was it in stimulating direct negotiations between Paris and Rome with an eye toward reaching an entente?

Jouvenel's achievements in this regard may seem rather modest. He had achieved no concrete accord with Italy before his six-month ambassadorial mission came to an end in mid-July, but the process of negotiation was launched. Jouvenel began preliminary conversations with Mussolini on 13 June, a week after initialing the Four-Power Pact. The major priorities were a naval accord and a common Franco-Italian understanding on the reorganization of central Europe—a matter of increasing concern to both countries since the rise of Hitler in Germany. In central Europe, Jouvenel favored the formation of a large Danubian economic union that would unite Austria, Hungary, and the Little Entente. Granted, such a configuration would redound to the benefit of Italy and likely would cost France something in terms of a less favorable balance of trade with eastern Europe as a whole. But that was a price that France must be willing to pay to end chronic tensions between Italy and Yugoslavia and to strengthen eastern and southern Europe vis-à-vis Germany. "To undertake a Danubian negotiation repeating 'neither Italy nor Germany' is to return to checkmate. What must be said is 'either Italy or Germany.'"[41] Jouvenel's message was quite clear. In order to contain German influence, France must be willing to accept a Danubian situation favorable to Italy. He regarded this as less dangerous than the alternative.

On 12 July 1933 Jouvenel reported that he and Mussolini were fully in agreement on the general lines of a negotiation for a bilateral Franco-Italian pact: (1) opposition to *Anschluss;* (2) reorganization of central Europe; and (3) coordinated efforts to secure disarmament and a naval accord. He concluded that all obstacles had been cleared away and that, therefore, his job in Rome had been completed.[42] Jouvenel returned to Paris in mid-July.

How can one assess the political significance of the Jouvenel mission? From one point of view, the conclusion that its accomplishments were quite modest is inescapable. After all, the Four-Power Pact was never ratified; Jouvenel's grand scheme for the economic reorganization of central Europe never materialized; and no naval accord was reached—although lengthy negotiations continued on the latter two points for several months. But from another perspective, the potential payoff inherent in Jouvenel's mission is impressive. He had aimed to tie fascist Italy into the French security system to act as a further brake on Germany's potential ambitions. The fact that such an association failed in the long run does not belie the significance of the objective and cannot be blamed on Jouvenel.[43] What was important was the fact that the effort was made at all.

For the short run Jouvenel's mission was extremely important because it represented the continuation of a major tendency in French interwar policy. Just as Poincaré and Barrère had sought to tie Italy to France in the 1922-24 era, so Paul-Boncour and Jouvenel worked to recapture that policy in the period following Hitler's rise to power. Their efforts coincided with Italian desires as well. Aloisi remarked in his *Journal* on 17 July 1933 that Jouvenel's mission had "succeeded completely" and that the man himself had shown a courage and savoir-faire recognized by all Italians. Italian Foreign Minister Fulvio Suvich awarded him the grand cordon of Saints Maurice and Lazare shortly before his departure from Rome. Mussolini himself paid an indirect tribute to Jouvenel in a speech on 6 October 1934, shortly before the achievement of the famous Laval-Mussolini Agreements, which liquidated Franco-Italian colonial rivalries in North Africa and pledged each to continue to support the independence of Austria. The Duce said: "There is no doubt that for over a year our relations with France have been appreciably ameliorated." Mussolini recognized quite clearly, as did Jouvenel's successor as ambassador to Rome, Charles de Chambrun,[44] that the Laval-Mussolini accords of January 1935 followed logically from the Jouvenel mission of 1933.

CHAPTER 5

From Jouvenel to Louis Barthou

During the course of his mission to Rome, Jouvenel became a firm champion of the Four-Power Pact idea, feeling that France's security was better preserved in cooperation with the large powers than in continued alliance with the small powers of eastern Europe. Such an arrangement would work to keep German ambitions in check. He had at least this much in common with Pierre Laval. Paul-Boncour, however, a great friend of the Czech statesman Eduard Beneš, was more sensitive to the objections of the eastern states to a four-power directorate which excluded them. This helps to explain why the version of the Four-Power Pact signed on 15 July 1933 was completely anodyne, linking the entire project to the League of Nations and effacing all reference to the revision of treaties.

Nevertheless, Jouvenel's mission created the atmosphere wherein concrete steps could be taken toward a two-power Franco-Italian association. His successor, Count Charles Pineton de Chambrun, was named on 29 July 1933. A descendent of Lafayette, de Chambrun came from a family in which classical liberalism was a tradition, but his personality seemed entirely compatible with Mussolini's. He remained faithful, even after his recall from Rome during the Ethiopian crisis, to the idea that an arrangement with fascist Italy was possible. Jouvenel had indicated earlier that de Chambrun's appointment would be likely to please the Duce, and the new ambassador recorded his favorable impression of the fascist leader shortly after his arrival in Rome: "he has a positive spirit, clear expression and great seductive power, which he employs even in political conversations."[1]

DISARMAMENT, DANUBIA AND THE NAVAL QUESTION

The atmosphere was altered, but serious issues remained, among the most serious being disarmament and the future status of Danubia. The close relationship between France and Yugoslavia touched both of these matters. A year earlier, on 28 October 1932, Paris and Belgrade had renewed the treaty of 1927, thereby igniting violent anti-Yugoslav and anti-French press campaigns in Italy and rumors of an Italian troop buildup. By December 1932, Italians were concerned about indications that General Weygand, French commander-in-chief and confidant of Paul-Boncour, was contemplating a preventive war against Italy—to preempt the possibility of an Italian attack on Yugoslavia. The French were correspondingly fearful about alleged Italian activities. The Paul-Boncour papers for the period yield an intelligence report suggesting that Italy and Germany were secretly preparing "a vast cooperative effort" in central Europe which would encompass the following:

1. the dismemberment of Yugoslavia and the incorporation of parts of its territory into a Danubian confederation under the direction of Germany and Hungary;
2. formation of a customs union composed of this new Danubian confederation, Germany, Austria, and Italy, which Czechoslovakia would sooner or later have to join;
3. Romania, Serbia, Bulgaria, Albania, and Greece would form a Balkan federation under Italian influence.

The premier's informer said that the secret Italo-German agreement, then in negotiation, would call for the abandonment by Germany of the idea of political union with Austria and of expansion into the southern Tyrol. Germany " . . . would engage herself not to extend her economic penetration south of the Alps and east of the Carpathians. Furthermore, Germany would abstain from hindering Italian economic and political interests in the Mediterranean and the Adriatic."[2]

The complex question of disarmament was equally beset with mutual fears and suspicions. The close relationship between France and Yugoslavia, coupled with the suspicion that the two partners were heavily armed and in the process of coordinating their efforts against Italy, inevitably affected Rome's attitude toward disarmament. A speaker in the Italian Chamber of Deputies defined the Italian thesis on disarmament when he observed that since 1928, Mussolini explicitly had declared Italy's readiness to reduce her land armaments to any level whatever, "but not inferior to that of the most heavily armed continental power."[3] The French correspondingly were concerned about the potential impact of disarmament on their security. With the Maginot Line projected to stop at the Belgian border, the problem of securing the northeast frontier against Germany was important. Unless some universally acceptable disarmament formula were achieved, it was realized that France could maintain a military preponderance over Germany only if Italy could be either neutralized or converted to an ally.[4]

Disarmament negotiations, in fact, did not go any more smoothly after the signing of the Four-Power Pact. Italy enjoyed a strong position since her support was courted by both France and Germany. The French rejected an Italian proposal in September 1933 for a very restricted German rearmament that was to take place in stages. Paris was prepared to allow Germany some "sample" weapons but not aircraft in the early stages, as the Italian plan proposed. The Danubian problem, however, appeared substantially clarified in the wake of the Four-Power Pact. On 10 September 1933 France sent an aide-mémoire to the Italian government proposing a Danubian economic pact based upon an economic union between Austria, Hungary, Yugoslavia, Romania, and Czechoslovakia to be achieved by a series of bilateral accords calling for preferential tariffs and an amelioration of means of transport. The French proposal also called for coordinated measures in dealing with outside states. The Italian reaction, submitted in the form of a memorandum to the Economic Commission of the League of Nations Assembly, was decidedly favorable. Paul-Boncour pronounced the two powers entirely in agreement on general principles and that, therefore, the possibilities for an accord were enhanced. No such pact for Danubian confederation finally came to fruition. The various proposals foundered on opposition from members of the Little Entente and on the problem of the small nations' debts to France. The Quai d'Orsay, in the end, balked at the extent of the financial sacrifice that would have been necessary to redress the negative commercial balance between Italy and the small nations of the Danube region. Nevertheless, it was obvious that such an economic pact among Danubian states, achieved under joint Franco-

Italian tutelage, would have had as its main objective the limitation of German influence in the area. The new anti-German focus was underscored still further in an important conversation between de Chambrun and Mussolini on 11 October 1933. On that occasion, the Duce expressed his opinion that Hitler's regime was solidly entrenched and was likely to last a long time. He then expressed his loyalty to the Locarno Treaties and concluded: "Italy will remain faithful to her engagements for two reasons, because she intends to honor her signature and because she sees that it is in her interest to do so; German aggression on either Calais or the Brenner would pose an equal threat to her security. If you are attacked . . . we will be with you."[5]

Both the Danubian and disarmament issues acquired increased urgency when, on 14 October, Germany dramatically withdrew from the League of Nations and the disarmament conference. Hitler's action had two immediate repercussions. Ironically, Germany's withdrawal from the League tended to strengthen the latter's appeal among rightist elements in France; and, instead of a potential revisor of treaties, the Genevan institution could thereafter be viewed as an instrument for preserving the status quo.[6] But these events virtually destroyed the Four-Power Pact, which thereafter had little meaning, since clauses in the Pact had made it dependent upon the League of Nations. With Germany now out of that body, the raison d'être for the Four-Power Pact, insofar as the French were concerned, evaporated, and the political machinery aimed at parliamentary ratification of it ground to a halt. This series of events intensified French efforts to pursue a direct Franco-Italian accord.

The Hitlerian coup de théâtre in withdrawing from the League had a number of interesting repercussions. Mussolini continued for quite some time in his belief that Italy could act as a mediator between Germany and the western powers. As late as 4 January 1934, the Duce submitted an aide-mémoire to the Disarmament Committee proposing a meeting of the Four-Power foreign ministers in order to salvage some form of disarmament discussion. "The major practical question," he wrote, "is no longer to prevent the rearmament of Germany, but to avoid having it take place independent of all rules and all controls." It was sage advice, and Paul-Boncour was initially inclined to follow it up, but his tenure at the Quai d'Orsay came to an end on 30 January 1934. In fact, the future of Italian influence in Europe rested heavily on Mussolini's continued ability to limit Hitlerian ambitions. He had achieved relative success in restraining Hitler in Austria and had won the Führer's acquiescence for his earlier compromise stand on disarmament. Should Mussolini be able to maintain his tutor-student relationship, his prestige both at home and abroad would be considerably enhanced. If, however, Hitler moved toward a more independent position, an increasingly likely possibility, Italy's status as a power broker on the continent would be reduced to insignificance. In that case, the Duce would be forced to look elsewhere in his search for the greater glory of the fascist regime—most probably to North Africa.[7] It was apparent that any Italian expansion in North Africa would have to be achieved in confrontation or cooperation with France.

The realities of the situation in the fall of 1933 were also reflected in the French political milieux. In the Chamber of Deputies, Hitler's withdrawal from the League precipitated a strong reaction from the right. Georges Mandel, Colonel Jean Fabry, Henri Franklin-Bouillon, and Louis Marin all advocated a more aggressive strategy of maintaining the treaty structure based on alliances. Although some influential rightist newspapers, such as *Le Jour* and *Le Matin*, advocated rapprochement with Germany, most of the right wing press opposed such a strategy as tantamount to abandoning the principle of anti-revisionism. Opinion in these circles was that France must stand firm, even if it meant going against the Italians and the English. Others, however, viewed the increased fluidity of the European situation as an opportunity to move directly toward the resolution of those Franco-Italian differences that had divided the two nations since the end of World War I. De Chambrun, for example, urged that France not be put off by the critical tendencies of fascist political figures and the Italian press. On 17 October 1933, the French ambassador wrote that the leaders at the Quai d'Orsay "must not, in my opinion, do harm to a rapprochement which we are seeking with this country and which we have an interest in following through. In this respect it seems that we would be well advised to avoid demonstrating undue touchiness [for fear of prejudicing] the attempted efforts in Rome to reestablish a situation which Germany's gesture has seriously compromised."[8]

Paul-Boncour followed up two weeks later by instructing de Chambrun to begin negotiations with Italy for a bilateral naval pact. The foreign minister suggested that the two countries renounce the construction of naval programs already voted but as yet not laid down and agree further to limit their construction through 1936 on the following bases: (1) ships-of-the-line not to exceed 26,500 tons of displacement; (2) total tonnage of light ships not to exceed 30,000 tons, with new ships limited to a tonnage equivalent to overage ships; and (3) total tonnage for submarines not to exceed 8,000 tons. Buoyed by an apparently favorable Italian response, Paul-Boncour sought to move immediately beyond "a simple technical regulation" of naval armaments and toward widening the terrain by linking a naval accord to a larger Franco-Italian negotiation, which would involve the adoption of common positions on such important European considerations as arms limitation and German rearmament. Although de Chambrun believed the atmosphere to be ripe for engaging the Italians on these issues and on specific Franco-Italian colonial grievances in Tunisia and Libya, he repeatedly cautioned against linking complex and ill-defined objectives to a potential naval accord, the technical preparations for which were already well advanced. It was preferable, he argued, to use the latter as a stepping-stone to the former. Why? Because the Duce feared that a single all-encompassing accord with France would be viewed as anti-German, thus prejudicing his self-styled role as *arbiter mundi*. Negotiations on naval matters continued until February 1934, but the proposed agreement foundered on the parallel issues of parity and the precise wording of the preamble and a "safeguard clause" calling for renunciation or revision of the accord should nonsignatories of the Washington Naval Agreement increase the size of their fleets.[9]

LOUIS BARTHOU

Although differences of emphasis between Paris and Rome continued to be apparent—as the foregoing discussion of disarmament, Danubian, and naval questions demonstrates—nevertheless a common determination to negotiate à deux had come to the surface by the end of 1933. Such was the situation when Louis Barthou succeeded Paul-Boncour at the Quai d'Orsay on 9 February 1934. Frequently viewed as one of the few men of vision and creativity to occupy a position of diplomatic influence in France in the 1930s,[10] Barthou was determined to contain Germany by strengthening the French alliance system and by building a secure link to the USSR. Occasionally overlooked or undervalued were the new foreign minister's efforts to build a "Mediterranean Locarno" in cooperation with fascist Italy. The necessity for the latter became apparent to Barthou in the wake of the total collapse of European disarmament negotiations in April 1934. Barthou favored a mild response to Hitler's proposal to modify the disarmament clauses of the Versailles Treaty and even supported a plan submitted by André François-Poncet, France's ambassador in Berlin, calling for modest gains in German armament over a number of years. Neither man expected Hitler to live up to such an agreement, but both hoped that it might at least delay full-scale German rearmament. The proposal, however, won no support from Prime Minister Gaston Doumergue, whose insistence on entirely rejecting the German plan prevailed. The latter's government had come into power in the wake of the Stavisky scandal, and those who opposed such a blanket rejection went along with it anyway in the interests of preserving governmental stability.[11] The result was that France appeared unconciliatory and had to accept much of the blame for the total collapse of disarmament negotiations.

The latter magnified the importance of the Italian question. While France's desire for Franco-Italian negotiations had been apparent at least since the inception of the Jouvenel mission, the exact focus for such conversations was still a matter of debate within the government. Mussolini posed the issue with some clarity in a speech before the Italian Assembly on 17 March 1934. Relations with France, he said, had improved markedly over the past several months, "but truth obliges me to add that none of the large or small problems at issue over the last fifteen years has been resolved." Mussolini's speech was accompanied by a diplomatic initiative which served to focus the debate on strategy among French diplomats. Barthou himself responded to the Duce on 20 April, saying that there could be no discussion of specific Franco-Italian issues until a prior agreement had been reached on such fundamental European problems as armament, Austrian independence, and maintenance of political equilibrium in central and eastern Europe and of a durable economic order in those regions. Once these were resolved, Barthou was prepared to move immediately to the settlement of Tunisian and Libyan colonial questions and to the establishment of a treaty of friendship and arbitration.[12]

The French ambassador, however, argued strongly for the reversal of Barthou's priorities. Responding to the foreign minister's instructions on 29 April, de Chambrun proposed instead to revive the idea of a naval accord with Italy, which would mark an important step on the road toward entente. Furthermore, de Chambrun argued that the time was not yet ripe for a Franco-Italian accord on European disarmament and that it would be a mistake to subordinate all negotiations to such an understanding. He believed that Italy was prepared to talk about a pact of friendship with France, accompanied by protocols relating to Tunisia and Libya. De Chambrun also thought such an approach might bring ancillary dividends: "I am convinced that, in the present circumstances, a direct conversation is increasingly desirable and that it would contribute not only to dissipating the misunderstandings which still exist between our two countries, but also to boost along those tendencies which are beginning to become apparent in favor of a rapprochement between Italy and the Little Entente." At this point, preparations were well advanced for Hitler's first official visit to Italy in mid-June. It would have been quite awkward for the Italians to embark on full-scale negotiations with the French while at the same time entertaining the German Führer in Venice. Hence, Rome adopted a dilatory, but not unfriendly, posture vis-à-vis Paris that lasted until the Hitler visit was concluded. Italian undersecretary of state Fulvio Suvich, for example, told de Chambrun that a pact of friendship between Italy and France (with protocols on Tunisia and Libya) would have little value unless a prior accord could be reached on the question of disarmament. Mussolini repeated the same argument to Henri Béranger, chairman of the foreign relations committee of the French Senate. In the meantime, Barthou set about mollifying fears in Belgrade that a Franco-Italian rapprochement might be achieved at Yugoslav expense. On 15 May 1934, he instructed the French minister in Belgrade to inform the Yugoslav government that, although a rapprochement with Italy had become an important objective of French foreign policy, the Quai d'Orsay firmly believed a vital aspect of such an association was "necessarily a détente in Italo-Yugoslav relations going if possible toward a three-power enlargement of the accords linking France to Yugoslavia."[13]

As it turned out, the Mussolini-Hitler conversations in Venice in mid-May were far from satisfactory from the Italian perspective. The two dictators discussed many issues, but no concrete decisions were taken. De Chambrun seized this opportunity to declare the time ripe for a serious and aggressive French initiative. Hitler's alienation from Mussolini's insistent opposition to any form of *Anschluss* provided an excellent entrée for French proposals. In a strong telegram to Barthou on 14 June, de Chambrun urged the Quai d'Orsay to move directly toward the resolution of specific Franco-Italian problems; these must take precedence over more general European questions. Furthermore, the French ambassador energetically supported an idea originally put forward by Mussolini that matters might be resolved quickly by an official visit of the French foreign minister to Rome. In the present circumstances—the end of disarmament negotiations, the less-than-successful Hitler-Mussolini conversations in Venice, Franco-Soviet rapprochement—such a visit would be a useful sign to Italy that France had no intention of trying to isolate her. It would prove France's continuing desire for an entente. To delay, on the other hand, might force Italy to orient her European policies toward accommodation with Germany.[14]

Barthou indicated his readiness to go to Rome, but not until the ground had been well prepared in advance by substantive discussion of all major issues. Mussolini allowed in two subsequent conversations with de Chambrun that he would be delighted to welcome the French foreign minister in Rome during the month of October. In the meantime, he would work closely with the French ambassador to define the outlines of an agreement on specific Franco-Italian issues, such as Tunisia and Libya, and on matters of more general European concern, such as the future of Austria and

Danubia. Once such a framework of accord had been worked out (September was the target date), the Italian government would extend an official invitation to Barthou.[15]

By the summer of 1934, therefore, French leaders were fairly solidly behind the goal of seeking an understanding with Italy. Men as different as Tardieu and Herriot had expressed their desire for rapprochement, and their conviction that it could be achieved, as early as 1932. The British also offered their support. Barthou's major problem, however, was to square the need for a reconciliation with Italy with the latter's treaty revisionism aimed at Yugoslavia and on behalf of Hungary against the Little Entente. The Italians had substantial economic interests in the Danubian area which were likely to increase, and they had worked throughout the 1920s and early 1930s to expand that sphere of economic and political influence. France and the Little Entente had consistently opposed Italian efforts in this area. During the summer of 1934, therefore, Barthou visited eastern Europe in search of support for his program to strengthen French security by both an eastern and a Mediterranean Locarno. Failing to find support in Germany and Poland for an eastern Locarno, he focused his attention directly on the Mediterranean pact. In Bucharest and Belgrade the French foreign minister spoke out strongly for maintaining the status quo and denounced the principle of treaty revision. Although Yugoslav leaders were not entirely convinced that détente with Italy was a realistic possibility, Barthou was successful in persuading King Alexander to state his terms for acquiescing in a Franco-Italian accord. The Yugoslav monarch wanted a guarantee of Austrian and Albanian independence and an Italian pledge to respect his country's integrity. In exchange he would be willing to grant economic concessions to Italy.[16] A major stumbling block in the way of Franco-Italian rapprochement had been cleared away. At this point the shocking assassination of Austrian Chancellor Englebert Dollfuss and the decisive Italian reaction to it intervened to speed along the Mediterranean portion of Barthou's grand design.

THE AUSTRIAN QUESTION

Whereas Franco-Italian policies diverged on many questions, on that of the *Anschluss* the two powers' interests coincided almost exactly. Throughout the 1920s Italian leaders, while touting a revisionist point of view in other matters, had been categorical in their insistence upon the need to maintain an independent Austria. In 1922 the prefascist minister of war, Marcello Soleri, articulated his "firm desire" to enforce the Treaty of Trianon as it related to Austria and said that Italy would never permit its annexation to Germany or to any other power. Three years later, Mussolini flatly affirmed in a speech to the Italian Senate that any rumor of *Anschluss* was "inadmissable." Such a development would annihilate the Italian victory in World War I and, therefore, "Italy can never tolerate the annexation of Austria to Germany." For France, an independent Austria was a matter of principle insofar as it formed a part of the Versailles system, and in 1925 Briand had gone so far as to raise the possibility of a separate Franco-Italian pact for the security of their respective frontiers. The latter fell victim to irreconcilable Italo-Yugoslav relations, the amelioration of which was a prerequisite to any such accord between Paris and Rome. But the appeal of such a combination as a device to guarantee the territorial integrity of Austria remained. De Chambrun recalled in his memoirs the first interview he had with Monsignor Ignaz Seipel upon assuming his position as French minister in Vienna in 1926. The Austrian leader remarked: " 'Men are never dumfounded by events whose causes they are familiar with if they pay careful attention to the game of possible combinations. In order to avert the threat of [Anschluss], there is a means, but your country, as well-disposed toward us as it is, refuses to . . . put it into operation. What is it? An entente between France and Italy.' " The future French ambassador to Italy admitted that Seipel's observation "opened my eyes." A strong argument can therefore be made that the Austrian question held the key to relations between the Third Republic and the fascist regime. Given French unwillingness to sacrifice the principle of the territorial status quo or to make any sweeping concessions to Italy, cordiality between the two countries seemed to depend on whether Italy would consider waiving or postponing her ambitions in order to achieve French backing. According to Arnold Wolfers, "such support would be important to Italy only if she anticipated the need of assistance against Germany, a need likely to arise in connection with the problem of Austro-German *Anschluss.*"[17]

A case in point occurred with the 21 March 1931 announcement of the Austro-German customs union project. French reaction to the proposal was sharp. In a note to London, Paris denounced the customs union as a violation of the 1919 treaty pledges and maintained that it represented a prelude to *Anschluss* just as certainly as the *Zollverein* of 1834 had foreshadowed German unification. Foreign Minister Briand was furious and pledged to both the Chamber and the Senate that "we shall do everything possible to oppose the realization of this enterprise." Italian treaty revisionism, of course, did not extend to the Brenner. Thus a coalition of Paris, Rome, and Prague appealed the customs union proposal to the International Court of Justice at The Hague as a violation of treaties. The successful litigation, prepared scrupulously by Paul-Boncour, not only demonstrated the usefulness of this international organization but was remarkable in that France, Italy, and Czechoslovakia had cooperated on the same side. An interesting sidelight to this affair was the British reaction. Britain adopted an apparently neutral stance, seeing nothing patently objectionable about the customs union proposal, a stance which occasioned some tension between London and Paris.[18] In this particular instance Britain played a relatively small role in influencing French policy vis-à-vis Italy. But the divergence between the two western powers was symptomatic of the future, when British policy was to play a decisive and frequently deleterious role.

Diplomatic victories over a politically floundering, depression-ridden Weimar Republic were fairly cheaply won. Hitler's accession to power in January 1933, however, intensified the Austrian question. Although the French had some misgivings about Mussolini's support for the antiparliamentary policies of Chancellor Dollfuss, they were willing to acquiesce in some Italian predominance at Vienna in the belief that such policies would only serve to embitter the Duce's relations with Hitler. Paris recognized that Austrian independence remained a key to Mussolini's Danubian policy, and indeed Jouvenel's instructions for his special mission to Rome in the first half of 1933 had enjoined him "to use present conditions to bring forth by common accord a decisive coup to the *Anschluss*." One of France's major goals during Paul-Boncour's tenure at the Quai d'Orsay was to protect Austrian independence by assuring its economic links between France, Italy, and members of the Little Entente, reserving a large role for Italy in these different economic understandings. Jouvenel was instructed to call these perspectives to Mussolini's attention and to use the Austrian issue "to strive once more to convince him of our sincere desire for progress and for results in the search for all the avenues of understanding practicable for Franco-Italian collaboration in Europe."[19]

Although Paris consistently opposed Mussolini's suggestion of deflecting the German desire for *Anschluss* by providing an outlet for German expansion in the Polish Corridor—perhaps the establishment of autoroutes across it—Jouvenel argued that the plan ought to be given more careful consideration. Such a development, he believed, would strengthen the hands of moderates in Germany at the expense of radicals who wanted to push treaty revision in the direction of Austria. "It is necessary to recognize," he wrote to Paul-Boncour on 8 March 1933, "that German expansion by *Anschluss* constitutes a serious threat for France, while an adjustment of the Polish corridor on the contrary dispels a threat of European War." The special ambassador cautioned against the naive expectations that Germany and Italy could never find some ground for achieving *Anschluss*. He urged, therefore, that France pursue the question of an accord with Italy based primarily upon the maintenance of treaties, while at the same time working toward the reconstitution of the Locarno triplice between England, France, and Italy. "*Accord à deux* on Franco-Italian affairs, *accord à trois* on European affairs: such seem to me to be the necessary points of departure for the long-range negotiation toward the definitive effectuation of the [Four-Power Pact] treaties in which M. Mussolini is asking us to become involved." By April 1933, indications that German troops and materials were crossing the borders to strengthen the Austrian Heimwehr prompted concern in Vienna about the imminence of a Hitlerian coup de main. Emerich von Pflugl, Austrian delegate to the disarmament conference in Geneva, cornered René Massigli, chief of the French delegation to the League, to urge the French government to provoke a Franco-Italian conversation on the matter. A fruitful result would be more conveniently achieved now rather than after a fait accompli. Chancellor Dollfuss visited Rome in April to seek Mussolini's support against the policy of *Anschluss*. While there, he specifically asked Jouvenel to try to see that the parties of the left in France abstain from supporting the Austrian socialists against his clerical-corporativist policies.[20]

Dollfuss had placed his finger upon the issue of Austrian domestic politics that was hindering full-fledged French support for his opposition to Hitler. The chancellor had recently suspended constitutional government and was ruling by decree. Although he expressed an intention to restore parliamentary prerogatives as soon as the tension between socialists and the Heimwehr was resolved, he urged that France not make such a restoration a condition for a loan then under consideration. This would be viewed domestically as knuckling under to the socialists and would result in an increase in the strength of the Austrian Nazis. Paul-Boncour, however, instructed Gabriel Puaux, his minister in Vienna, to get some definite indications from Dollfuss about the return to parliamentary government before continuing discussions on the loan. Puaux openly disagreed with his foreign minister on several occasions, arguing that for France to make constitutional requirements a condition of the loan to Austria would be a serious error: "It does not seem to me that the refusal of the loan by France can, in any fashion whatsoever, reinforce the situation of the socialist party. If Italy substitutes herself for us [as lender], she will push Austria toward fascism and the monarchy. If Austria does not find money, the result will be bankruptcy, inflation and a disaster which will benefit only the Hitlerians." In further communications he pointed out that the Austrian socialists were not particularly strong, and in any case, before Hitler's advent to power, had themselves been "rattachistes." Given the political situation in the country, he saw no other viable alternative for France than to extend confidence and support for Chancellor Dollfuss.[21]

This little contretemps over Austrian domestic politics prompted some concern in Rome that France was weakening in its determination to maintain Austrian independence. Jouvenel vigorously reassured Suvich that such was not the case, but the latter's concern revealed a real uncertainty. Jouvenel pointed out to Paul-Boncour that the Italians were playing a very difficult game by maintaining a link with Germany while at the same time opposing one of her most fervent desires. He believed that France could take advantage of the Italian position in order to act against Germany, although substantial care would have to be taken to avoid the appearance of wanting to turn Rome against Berlin.[22] The realist must not ignore Mussolini's sense of himself as an arbiter among the European powers.

The conclusion of the Four-Power Pact negotiations in June 1933 finally permitted Jouvenel and Mussolini to explore how best the two powers might stand against *Anschluss*. The Duce unburdened himself in long conversations with Jouvenel on 13 and 14 June, decrying the fact that all Austria had to sustain itself was " 'a feeble Christian social bourgeois party . . . threatened on both Right and Left, and obliged to face up to a disastrous economic situation.' " This was a prelude to Mussolini's proposal to link up Austria and Hungary in some fashion—avoiding, of course, any Habsburg restoration—and thus forming " 'an Austro-Hungarian front against German pressure.' " Mussolini thereby provided the opening for Jouvenel to move toward the objectives outlined in his instructions of 17 March. Expressing doubt that Austria and Hungary together would be strong enough to resist German pressure, the French ambassador advanced the idea of an economic entente between Austria, Hungary, and the states of the Little Entente. Mussolini at first demurred, wondering whether such a combination more likely would be directed against Rome than against Berlin. But after Jouvenel's assurance that its main purpose would be to guard against *Anschluss,* the fascist leader agreed that the suggestion merited consideration. Jouvenel added a further dimension to the equation a couple of weeks later in order to avoid the possibility that an economic union among Austria, Hungary, and the Little Entente might encourage Germany and Italy to work together to share economic influence there. (Trade statistics cited by the French ambassador showed that Germany was the most active power in the area.) France attempted to prevent this eventuality by linking a resolution of Adriatic problems to that of central Europe. The question of Albania and the recurrent tension between Italy and Yugoslavia had become, according to Jouvenel, as important to

Italy as the Austrian question. His total proposal, therefore, encompassed the following: "A guarantee of Austrian independence, and economic entente among the Danubian countries and recognition of a special regime for Italy, an Italo-Yugoslav accord putting an end to all competition between the countries over Albania: such seem to be . . . the three conditions for strengthening the peace in Central Europe."[23]

The test of combined Franco-Italian determination on the Austrian question was soon to come. During the summer of 1933, Dollfuss complained repeatedly about subversive German Nazi activities emanating from Bavaria and clearly designed to destabilize his regime—radio propaganda and seditious pamphlets dropped from the air by planes taking off from and returning to Germany. The chancellor appealed for a concerted Anglo-Franco-Italian demarche in Berlin. Paul-Boncour supported such a gesture and, on 4 August 1933, proposed a text of representations to be presented to Germany. The proposed communication called attention to "subversive German activity in Austria" and pointed out that this was in violation of the principle of nonintervention in a neighboring country and also of Article 80 of the Treaty of Versailles. The note called upon the German government to investigate these activities and to use all means at its disposal to end them. The Italians, however, disapproved of the concerted three-power demarche in Berlin, fearing that such an action might be prejudicial to the recently signed Four-Power Pact. Instead, the Italian ambassador in Berlin was instructed unilaterally to have a "friendly conversation" with German authorities and to urge Germany to abandon anti-Austrian activities on German soil. The French ambassador in Rome was informed of the success of this initiative in that Germany pledged to interfere with seditious radio broadcasts and to interdict the flight of pamphlets. The Italian gesture can be viewed as yet another example of Italy's determination to stand firm against *Anschluss*. But it was also rather disconcerting to those who were working to build a pattern of collective security in the Danubian region. Austria had clearly stated its preference for concerted action in Berlin, hence Italy's unilateral activity, although successful for the short turn, raised questions about the future of cooperative ventures. The political director of the Ballplatz summarized his views on the matter to the French chargé d'affaires: " 'This little maneuver proves once more that M. Mussolini intends to secure the role of exclusive "protector" of central Europe and desires to eliminate all competition in this area.' " Paul-Boncour, however, was willing to accept Italy's propensity to look after certain "housekeeping details" in Germany, since "it is now established that her opposition to *Anschluss* is as irreducible as ours."[24]

The British position can be described as one of wait-and-see while applying pressure on both France and Italy to work out a common policy on the Austrian question. Sir Robert Vansittart, permanent undersecretary at the Foreign Office, foresaw a recrudescence of Austrian Nazi threats to the Dollfuss regime beginning in the fall and was anxious for France and Italy to reach a common understanding on the issue. Vansittart believed that geography destined Italy to play a large role in Austrian matters; he also had a reputation as a Francophile and thus was keen on developing a tripartite strategy for containing German expansion—especially in Austria. His immediate goal, therefore, was the narrow one of "holding Italy to her self-imposed task of keeping Hitler under control," while at the same time working toward a cooperative effort between Britain, France, and Italy as the "bulwark of peace" in Europe. Vansittart's strategy, however, was not expected to come cheaply. Its cost, apparently, would be borne largely by the French, which explains his desire to remain on the sidelines until after Franco-Italian policies had been coordinated. He believed that Italian support against Germany was so vital that the French "ought to be prepared to pay for it" and "to make concessions."[25] Whether public opinion in either Britain or France would be prepared to pay Italy's price was a matter as yet unresolved.

On this particular issue, British and French policies were squarely in line, although Paul-Boncour was not reluctant to pass on the price for Italy's cooperation to others. In a lengthy telegram on 17 August 1933 to his representatives in London, Rome, Belgrade, Prague, Bucharest, and Vienna, the French foreign minister pointed out that whereas Germany had made certain pledges to Italy concerning political threats to Austria, Berlin "has expressly refused to relieve its economic pressure. Such pressure can be fatal in the long run if it is not remedied in time." To meet the threat, Paul-Boncour advocated quick action on the British recommendation for Franco-Italian cooperation. In the preservation of Austrian independence, he said, Italy's cooperation was "indispensable," but Franco-Italian cooperation "will only be truly possible if . . . the Little Entente can practice a single policy in central Europe and show its good intentions by giving the necessary appeasements to Rome." He urged his representatives in Little Entente countries to impress the urgency of this situation in their capitals and encourage favorable economic policies toward Austria. At the same time, he instructed his ambassador in Rome to begin negotiations for a Franco-Italian accord.[26]

Whereas in August Mussolini had refused to join Britain and France in a demarche on the question of *Anschluss*—preferring to play a lone hand in his "special relationship" with Hitler—by September he was moving more toward the French view. In a conversation between de Chambrun and

Mussolini on 5 September 1933, the latter underscored the importance of a common stand against *Anschluss*. Furthermore, the Duce stressed that France and Italy must work toward economic collaboration. Mussolini suggested that France seek this goal in the capitals of the Little Entente, while Italy would pursue it in Vienna and Budapest. Paul-Boncour endorsed such a procedure five days later, pronouncing as his goal the achievement of a kind of Danubian "common market" based on preferential tariffs, relations with outside states and transportation rights.[27]

Mussolini's determination in the face of renewed Nazi activity in Austria also took military form. In early October, French diplomatic channels were informed that Italy was proceeding with troop concentrations south of the Brenner and that the Duce was "well-disposed to authorize the German military attaché [in Rome] to go to verify this *sur place.*" Mussolini confirmed this in an interview with Pierre Dupuy, editor of *Le Petit Parisien:* " 'If the *Anschluss* [the Duce said], as dangerous for Italy as it is for France, has not taken place, it is largely because I have vetoed it. The Germans know that I have sent troops to the frontier and that if they entered Austria, I would intervene with armed force.' " Whether these measures were meant to provoke military collaboration with the French or were simply an omen of yet another Italian "lone hand" was not clear at the time. Mussolini preferred to deal directly with the Austrian question, and on more than one occasion advised Dollfuss not to appeal Nazi activities in Austria to the League of Nations, the forum of first resort favored by the French. He told de Chambrun on 8 February 1934 that, if necessary, he was willing to defend Austrian independence at Geneva. But failing that, the Duce said in the presence of Suvich, " 'we shall together defend Austria, if need be in the trenches of Vienna.' "[28] A plausible interpretation of the long-range significance of these events and declarations is that France's failure to mobilize her armed forces in the wake of the Austrian Nazi coup of July 1934 was at least partially predicated on the conviction that Mussolini would do so.[29]

The factor that intensified the Duce's determination to seek common ground with the western powers on the *Anschluss* question was Hitler's withdrawal in October 1933 from the Disarmament Conference and from the League of Nations, which effectively wrecked the Four-Power Pact. With German rearmament continuing and with Nazi activities in Austria becoming more strident, France and Italy drew closer together. On 17 February 1934, Italy joined France and England in a declaration that the three governments took "a common view as to the necessity of maintaining Austria's independence and integrity in accordance with the relevant treaties."[30] There is some indication that the text, issued in Rome by Suvich, de Chambrun, and Sir Eric Drummond, the British ambassador, was somewhat watered down. The French had originally proposed to express the three nations' common "volonté" to maintain the integrity and independence of Austria, language endorsed also by the Italians. The British demurred, however, maintaining that this word was untranslatable into English. Further incidences of Mussolini's drift toward France in central European matters were the signing of Italo-Yugoslav and Italo-Romanian commercial treaties on 4 and 6 January respectively.[31] By the beginning of 1934, Italy and France were in essential agreement on the fundamentals of the Austrian question.

But if French and Italian policies appeared to converge, problems remained with regard to ancillary Danubian matters. In March 1934, following official state visits to Rome by Dollfuss and Hungarian leader Julius Gömbös, Italy signed the Rome Protocols, which included agreements to undertake political consultations and to develop economic relations between Italy, Austria, and Hungary. Although Suvich still claimed to be a partisan of a general Danubian accord, he believed that serious differences between Hungary and Czechoslovakia rendered such a development out of the question at that time. Barthou instructed his ambassador in Rome to submit a formal demarche to the Italian government expressing the deep disappointment of the French government about this most recent tendency of Italy to seek her own advantage in Austria and Hungary without consideration for the interests of the Little Entente states.[32]

That the Rome Protocols created grave difficulties for French policy in central Europe was illustrated graphically in the following communication from Émile Naggiar, the French minister in Belgrade. Naggiar explained to Barthou that Little Entente leaders were fearful that France and England were, by default, according a kind of mandate to Italy in Austria and Hungary. The Yugoslavian and Romanian foreign ministers told Naggiar that the Great Powers "must not put the Little Entente in the position of having to choose between the Charybdis of the *Anschluss* and the Scylla of an Italian-dominated Austria or Austria-Hungary, for the Little Entente would not hesitate to choose what in their eyes is the lesser of these two evils, that is the *Anschluss.*"[33] Although the Rome Protocols served to pull Hungary away from Germany, they also portended the failure of French efforts to achieve a vast Danube community through Franco-Italian cooperation. Henceforth the Italian system and the Little Entente formed separate and hostile blocs, which provided a constant irritant to all efforts at Franco-Italian conciliation.

Such was the situation when the Austrian question exploded to prominence with the attempted Nazi seizure of power and consequent assassination of Chancellor Dollfuss on 25 July 1934. The date was chosen with some calculation. Dollfuss had been scheduled to meet Mussolini at Riccione on that day. His wife was already there. Presumably there would be talk about a concrete Austro-Italian agreement to guard against *Anschluss*. It was to prevent the conclusion of such an accord, which no doubt would have fortified the chancellor's resistance to Nazism, that the date of 25 July had been selected. Mussolini was infuriated, and his action was immediate—mobilization of Italian troops on the Brenner frontier as a clear warning to Hitler that should Germany intervene further in the Vienna catastrophe, Italian troops would cross the border. Mussolini, in fact, felt doubly betrayed. Not only did he regard Dollfuss as a personal friend and political protégé, but Hitler solemnly had promised the Duce, during the Venice meeting between the two dictators in June, that Austrian independence would not be altered and that the two fascist states would work together to seek a solution for internal Austrian problems. The Duce's revulsion against Hitler was revealed starkly in the telegram he sent to Prince Starhemberg, the Austrian vice-chancellor, on 26 July: "The independence of Austria, for which M. Dollfuss fell, is a principle which was and which shall be defended by Italy even more relentlessly in these exceptionally difficult times. . . . The civilized world . . . by its moral condemnation, has already struck those who were directly or indirectly responsible."[34]

Italian mobilization, although it dissuaded further German involvement and may be credited with saving Austrian independence at this point, created other problems for French foreign policy directors. There was evidence to suggest, for example, that if Italy were forced to cross the Brenner to stop *Anschluss,* this would be the signal for armed Yugoslav intervention as well, perhaps even against the Italians in the Istrian Peninsula. French diplomats received instructions to maintain constant contact with Rome with an eye toward the development of a common policy in Austrian matters. The English suggested a method, through normal diplomatic channels in Rome, to keep the three governments quickly informed of each other's views on Austria with the aim of developing common policies to preserve Austrian independence. Although Paris preferred the institution of a separate Anglo-Franco-Italian commission based in Geneva, the Quai d'Orsay could not reject the English proposal outright, since it represented a rare manifestation of English concern for maintaining the treaties in central Europe. The upshot of all this, which in fact represented the limit of French and British willingness to support the Italian mobilization, occurred on 27 September, when the three powers issued a joint declaration, reaffirming their earlier declaration of 17 February, pledging mutual consultation on the development of policies designed to maintain Austrian independence and integrity. Although some in the British Foreign Office felt that the declaration gave Italy a special position in that it amounted to tacit approval of her unilateral mobilization of July, Vansittart felt that England had no choice but to go along.[35]

How can one assess the significance of the Vienna coup, indeed of the entire Austrian question? Conventionally it has been maintained that the assassination of Dollfuss opened Mussolini's eyes to the German danger, and his own isolated action hardened his determination to resolve traditional differences with France. There can be no doubt that some in the Quai d'Orsay took this view, and the French chargé in Rome argued that the post-July 25 period offered "exceptionally favorable conditions" for leading the Italian government toward an accord with France.[36] For the short run, this certainly proved to be the case.

But the Austrian interlude also had some rather more disturbing implications. France's eastern European allies took quite a different view of the Italian mobilization. Czech disapproval, coupled with the fact that Yugoslavia marched seven batallions up to the Yugoslav-Austrian frontier, indicated that Austrian independence was not considered a vital interest to those states if it meant strengthing Italy's influence in central Europe. France's security system proved worthless in this situation, as her allies simply rejected French leadership when they saw their immediate interests at threat. This also may have forced Barthou to look beyond his grand design for an "eastern Locarno" and toward the strengthening of France's security system via an accord with Mussolini, but the eastern European implications could not help but be disconcerting. François-Poncet, one of France's most prestigious diplomats, regarded French policy as a failure. The fact that it took from 25 July to 27 September for Britain, France, and Italy to issue a joint declaration on the Austrian question only served to encourage Hitler for the future. "Never [the ambassador wrote] had I been up to then associated with such a lamentable maneuver, crowned by so flagrant a check." For François-Poncet, the lack of support for Mussolini from both France and England weighed heavily in the future orientation of his attitude. Perhaps the most disturbing and prophetic assessment of the situation came from Charles-Roux, who was then ambassador at the Vatican and who became secretary general of the Quai d'Orsay. He remarked in his memoirs: "It thus seemed to me conceivable that Mussolini could let go of Austria, abandon it to Germany, withdraw from the [*Anschluss*] question, in exchange for some advantage or concession accorded by Berlin. This is why, in my correspondence, I expressed it this way; 'it is not certain that Austria will always be an apple of discord between Germany and Italy;

it can become a bond of union between the two.' "[37] Such gloomy assessments acquired considerable cogency four years later when Nazi forces marched into Vienna without overt Italian opposition. But European circumstances were markedly different by then. For the moment, the Austrian question provided the clear and present danger necessary for the rapid resolution of those differences that had divided Paris and Rome for over a decade.

CHAPTER 6

The Laval–Mussolini Accords of January 1935

Louis Barthou's grand design for an "eastern Locarno" supported by a direct Franco-Soviet alliance is often viewed as the last creative response of French diplomacy to the threat of Nazi expansion. Duroselle views Barthou's tenure at the Quai d'Orsay as "a brief period of incontestable rectification on the road to decadence."[1] Above all, Barthou was a realist and did not permit domestic political ideology to interfere with a realistic conception of French interests abroad. First and foremost for Barthou, the enemy was Germany.

In seeking security against Germany, Barthou considered England unreliable—not committed to eastern European security and suspicious of any French attempt to isolate Germany. The French foreign minister believed that the alliances with the small states were significant and he dutifully made the tour of the eastern capitals. The negative response of the Czechs and Yugoslavs to the Austrian crisis, however, coupled with the bombshell of the Polish-German nonaggression pact of 26 January 1934 gave him considerable concern about their potential reliability. Even though Barthou was anticommunist in domestic French policy, he recognized the value of a diplomatic link to Moscow. Current political realities persuaded him that an alliance with Italy was also desirable, provided that Italo-Yugoslav relations could be mollified as an essential precondition. Two events convinced Barthou to go forward, even without the English, toward alliances with the Union of Soviet Socialist Republics (USSR) and Italy—the "Night of the Long Knives" of 30 June 1934 and the Austrian Nazi coup of 25 July. Direct negotiations with the USSR began following the latter's admission to the League of Nations on 18 September.[2]

These events also served as a preamble to serious Franco-Italian negotiations. Barthou and Aloisi had worked together closely at Geneva on the USSR's entry to the League and on the joint declaration of respect for Austrian independence issued on 27 September. In France, the pan-Latin sentiments of figures like François Piétri, the minister of the Navy, and Henri Béranger, were also important. Both men went to Italy late in 1934 to attend ceremonies designed to increase Franco-Italian good will. Given these factors, Mussolini told the French ambassador in Rome that he looked forward to an official visit by Barthou and suggested the end of October as a good time for a meeting to resolve long-standing Franco-Italian problems—specifically those concerning Tunisia and Libya. De Chambrun's instructions arrived in telegrams from Barthou and Léger. The latter preferred to subordinate discussions about the status of Italians in Tunisia and Libyan frontier rectifications to the conclusion of a general treaty of friendship. Léger also noted the exclusion of the essential question of Italo-Yugoslav relations from de Chambrun's program of study. Barthou cautioned his ambassador to avoid the questions of armaments and Franco-Italian military policies; these would raise serious questions in Belgrade and might, therefore, offer Mussolini an exit should he choose to withdraw from any direct negotiations. Barthou preferred to concentrate on major North African colonial issues and the Austrian question—and leave the fixing of a precise date for his arrival in Rome until a complete unity of views had been reached. It would be very bad to schedule an official visit prematurely and risk the possibility of a public failure.[3]

FORMAL NEGOTIATIONS BEGIN

And so formal negotiations finally began. Although Barthou preferred to play-down the question of armaments, Mussolini was extremely interested in the issue and was anxious to place it at the top of the agenda, even ahead of Libyan and Tunisian matters. The Italians were interested in establishing a concrete formula for Franco-Italian armaments. By 11 September a working agenda had been hammered out by de Chambrun and Suvich. The issues to be fully discussed before Barthou's arrival in Rome were (1) armaments ("in conjunction with the present European situation"); (2) central Europe; (3) rectification of the Libyan frontier; (4) statute for Italians in Tunisia; and (5) an eventual treaty of friendship. With these preliminaries out of the way, negotiations became substantive but with an interesting shift of emphasis that betrayed wider Italian colonial ambitions in Africa. Agenda items three and four were clearly connected, and the de Chambrun-Suvich negotiations began with a familiar rehash of the claims and counterclaims of the 1920s. Suvich wanted France to live up to the pledges of article 13 of the 1915 Treaty of London, which had promised Italy colonial compensations at the end of World War I. This could be achieved, he said, by appropriate rectifications along the Libyan frontier. De Chambrun responded that article 13 had referred to compensation as the result of French gains from former German colonies. Since France only received from Germany those territories ceded to it in the Congo in 1911, the ambassador believed that the concession of 1919 (salients of Ghat and Ghadamès) fulfilled the conditions of the Treaty of London. Any further concessions to Libya, he argued, must be matched by Italy's abandonment of its demands for the continuation of the 1896 special status for the 100,000 Italians living in Tunisia. Within a few days, however, the thrust of the Italian negotiating stance on these issues shifted to Ethiopia. On 23 September, de Chambrun talked with both Suvich and Theodoli (whose secret and unofficial talks with de Caix from 1928-32 are discussed in chapter four). Both men indicated that Italy would be willing to modify Libyan and Tunisian ambitions "in exchange for the development of her influence in the region which presently separates her two east African colonies [Eritrea and Italian Somaliland] without prejudice to French interests in her possession of Jibuti." De Chambrun's reaction to the Italian proposal was completely reserved, but he closed his telegram by noting that in all Italian circles, "the wind is blowing toward Ethiopia."[4]

With the agenda established and concrete negotiations in progress, coupled with indications from Belgrade that the Yugoslavs had moderated their opposition to a Franco-Italian accord, Barthou formally proposed the dates 4-11 November 1934 for his projected visit to Rome. Barthou's concern for Yugoslav opinion was genuine enough. He recognized that historically tense Italo-Yugoslav relations constituted the principal roadblock to a genuine resolution of Franco-Italian difficulties. Yugoslavia was particularly concerned about the possibility of an Italian occupation of Albania, virtually an Italian puppet state since the Italo-Albanian treaty of

1927. The French foreign minister, therefore, sought a rapprochement between Italy and Yugoslavia as a necessary preliminary to the resolution of Franco-Italian problems. Although the Italians harbored certain reservations about the political success of such a wide-ranging vision, this was the sole purpose of Barthou's invitation to King Alexander to visit France on 9 October 1934.[5] It was expected that the two would sign a Franco-Yugoslav accord, designed to be the first leg of the "Mediterranean Locarno." The complexities of Balkan politics intervened, however, to truncate Barthou's grand design. Members of the Croatian terrorist organization, the Ustashi, assassinated both Alexander and the French foreign minister on the day of the king's arrival at Marseille.

Security for King Alexander's visit had been scandalously insufficient, even though the Yugoslav legation in Paris had warned the French government about the possibility of an assassination attempt. The director of the Sûreté générale resigned, as did the minister of the interior, Albert Sarraut. But these resignations, as well as official apologies, were not enough to assuage Yugoslav resentment. French prestige suffered a terrible blow in the eyes of the new government of Yugoslavia, where Prince Paul, Alexander's brother, assumed a regency in the name of the young new king. As indicated previously, France's aim—to be carried out in Barthou's personal diplomacy with both Alexander and Mussolini—had been to encourage Italo-Little Entente cooperation in the support of Austrian independence. British, French, and Italian evidence for this period indicate that Barthou was prepared to grant an extension of Italian influence in Ethiopia in order to achieve Italian cooperation with Yugoslavia against Germany.[6]

PIERRE LAVAL

Pierre Laval succeeded to the Quai d'Orsay on 9 October 1934. His policy differed from that of his martyred predecessor on a number of key points. He was not nearly so enthusiastic as Barthou had been about building a Franco-Soviet alliance. Laval, who was fundamentally a pacifist, took over the Foreign Ministry determined to ameliorate relations with Germany rather than to undertake fully Barthou's policy of surrounding Germany with alliances. His abandonment of all opposition to the scheduled plebiscite in the Saar, for example, was meant to symbolize a new orientation in French policy. It was hoped that this "little step toward Germany"—which virtually assured German success in the plebiscite in January 1935—would open the way to a direct improvement of Franco-German relations.[7] In the short run, it worked, but subsequent events were to force Laval and his successors to abandon this particular orientation.

Why was Laval appointed minister of foreign affairs, given his substantial differences with Barthou's policies? Surface matters were of some importance. Laval was quite popular in France and well known abroad because of his brief prime ministry in 1931-32 and his well-publicized trip to the Washington Naval Conference in 1931. Besides, Laval brought with him the support of wealthy business interests and of the Patenôtre press, which included four great regional dailies plus a number of local papers. The prime minister, Pierre Etienne Flandin, who appointed Laval, addressed the question of his foreign policy in his memoirs: "I was determined . . . to continue the foreign policy of Monsieur Barthou. It was not consistent with that of Monsieur Laval on a number of points. But I saw little inconvenience in this, for behind Monsieur Laval's policy of Franco-German rapprochement, which would guarantee one against the thunderings of the Germanophile Anglo-Saxon superpacifists, I could continue the policy of not encircling Germany, but of barring German ambitions." Besides all of this, Laval was an energetic supporter of the drive toward a rapprochement with Mussolini's Italy. Moreover, he was familiar with the details of Franco-Italian negotiations up to this point. He had approved of the secret Theodoli-de Caix conversations dealing with the fate of Ethiopia during his earlier premiership, and during 1934 he had served as minister of colonies and so would have been informed of Italy's East African proposals.[8] Thus, there was a good deal of logic in Flandin's selection of Laval.

Laval's pro-Italian bias was clearly evident in his handling of the Marseille assassination crisis. There were indications that the crime committed by the Ustashi had been planned in Italy. Indeed the Ustashi leader, Ante Pavelič, lived there. But Laval, as well as many others in both France and England, felt that it would be risky to implicate Italy. Rather, the crisis must be quickly resolved through a judicial investigation that would obfuscate any Italian involvement. The evidence gathered revealed that Ustashi terrorists had operated on both Hungarian and Italian territory. But the primary thrust of the investigation placed the lion's share of the blame upon indirect Hungarian complicity in the crime (i.e., terrorists operating from facilities in that country). It is not surprising that Laval's appointment to the Quai d'Orsay was warmly welcomed in Rome and, only slightly less enthusiastically, in Berlin. Aloisi wrote in his journal on 14 October 1934, "The nomination is good for us."[9]

The assassination at Marseille made it even more essential that an Italo-Yugoslav rapprochement take place in direct liaison with any Franco-Italian arrangement. Naggiar informed Laval on 19 October that, since information pointed to the fact that the Marseille terrorists had come from either Italy or Hungary, opinion in the Little Entente countries was currently running strongly against Italy. The feeling in these countries was that the Marseille plot represented a victory in fascist efforts to stimulate the disintegration of Yugoslavia—thus disrupting the Little Entente and paving the way for Italo-Austro-Hungarian domination of eastern Europe. Therefore, Naggiar advised the postponement of the foreign minister's scheduled trip to Rome on 4–11 November. To go ahead with the visit (without first encouraging the normalization of relations between Rome and Belgrade) would be viewed negatively by France's allies in eastern Europe. They would interpret this as an abandonment of their cause by France and an indirect endorsement of Italy's stance as a revisionist power. Based upon advice like this, Laval proposed to delay his visit to Rome, even though the Italians had expressed a desire to maintain the scheduled dates. Laval instructed de Chambrun to stress to the Duce that France was not dragging its feet. Time was necessary to manage public opinion in the wake of the assassination crisis and to prepare the ground for the best possible accord. Laval said further that he would be particularly happy to review with Mussolini the latter's thoughts on those questions the two men had discussed back in 1931: suspension of naval armaments, attachment of Tummo and the oasis of Ojado to Tripolitania; and the continuation for ten years of the conventions of 1896 guaranteeing the privileged status of Italians in Tunisia. The British government, although still anxious for a rapid Franco-Italian rapprochement, approved the delay of Laval's visit to Rome.[10]

Although a summit meeting had been postponed, the French were encouraged by information from Rome indicating that the Italians, motivated by growing distrust of Germany, were increasingly anxious to achieve an accord with the Third Republic. The French military attaché, for example, reported that Edmondo Rossoni, Mussolini's undersecretary-of-state and personal confidant, had told him that: " 'only one thing interests the Italian Government; that is the conclusion of an accord with France going well beyond an entente on specific points, but having the value of a true alliance.' " No doubt with optimistic intelligence like this in mind, Laval outlined his specific goals in a detailed dispatch to de Chambrun on 31 October 1934, in which he addressed all of the major problems existing between France and Italy. With regard to general European questions, Laval made these proposals:

1. *Armaments*—a Franco-Italian accord calling for mutual consultation and response in the likely event that Germany should unilaterally reject the disarmament provisions of the Versailles Treaty following the Saar plebiscite.

2. *Austria*—a Franco-Italo-Little Entente agreement pledging adherence to the independence of Austria and pledging no interference in its internal affairs. Laval would like to see Yugoslavia on equal footing here, but there must at least be a common Franco-Italian declaration on the matter.
3. *Italo-Yugoslav Relations*—an Italo-Yugoslav treaty of arbitration and conciliation renouncing the use of force in settling differences and an Italo-Yugoslav declaration respecting existing treaties.

Laval then went on to detail his recommendations for resolving the specifically Franco-Italian issues. With regard to crucial North Africa problems, the foreign minister established a four-part negotiating stance: (1) For Tunisia, he rejected the simple prolongation of the 1896 accords protecting Italians and their schools. He suggested the possibility of delaying French naturalization for five or even ten years, but, echoing the language of de Caix, he insisted that Italian acceptance of this principle constituted the *condition sine qua non* for any concession that France would make to Italy elsewhere in Africa. (2) France, he wrote, was prepared to make territorial concessions to Italy in Libya, but (3) not in Morocco or the Levant. (4) In Ethiopia and on the coast of French Somalia, Laval indicated that concessions to Italy were possible, but care must be taken to protect the French port of Jibuti and its access by railroad to Addis Ababa. He took note of Italy's desire to purchase railroad shares, thus acquiring representation on the directing board of the Jibuti–Addis Ababa Railway Company. Beyond these colonial matters, Laval instructed de Chambrun to work toward a Franco-Italian treaty mutually guaranteeing the rights of Italians in France and French citizens in Italy. Finally, he wanted a Franco-Italian declaration on mutual arbitration and conciliation—in conformity with the League of Nations.[11]

Laval worded his requirements very carefully and designed them to elicit similarly specific responses from the Italians. He assiduously avoided any phrasing that would suggest compromising the independence of Ethiopia and left himself room for maneuver on the ticklish Italo-Yugoslav problem. De Chambrun's first conversation with Mussolini based on his instructions of 31 October was quite favorable, with agreement in principle on most of the major issues concerning German rearmament, Austrian independence with the Little Entente as an equal partner in the guarantee, and Libyan frontiers. Regarding Yugoslavia, Mussolini felt that the current anti-Italian feeling there would have to dissipate before Rome could consider any sort of formal proposal for a treaty of arbitration and conciliation. In Tunisia, if France would agree to a sufficiently lengthy prolongation (i.e., ten years) of the 1896 conventions, the Duce was willing to go forward with working out new conventions for the future.¹² Mussolini recognized France's reluctance to make concessions in East Africa that would compromise the economic viability of French Somalia. He would be satisfied with a concession "sufficiently visible on the map." At the same time, however, the fascist leader did not hide his interest in encouraging the French to define their economic interests in Ethiopia more specifically. It was clear to Dampierre that this matter represented the key to any subsequent accord.¹³

Negotiations continued into December, with each side making proposals and slightly amended counterproposals on technicalities surrounding the Tunisian and Libyan issues. While these matters moved forward, however, the main sticking point was clearly the French requirement that an Italo-Yugoslav rapprochement precede any Franco-Italian accord. On 12 December, Mussolini told de Chambrun that it was not desirable for the Little Entente to share equally in an Italo-French guarantee of Austrian independence; Austria would resent a guarantee from states made up of former subject peoples. The following day, Aloisi repeated the same argument to Laval in Geneva. The Italians were reacting to the fact that their conciliatory gestures toward Yugoslavia (probably stimulated by the French requirement) had not received a particularly warm welcome in Belgrade. De Chambrun said that he would congratulate the Italians on their efforts toward Yugoslavia and encourage the continuation of such behavior, but he speculated the Italians might fear that Belgrade would interpret their overtures as signs of weakness or culpability in the Marseille assassination. As late as 14 December, despite strong pleas by Aloisi and Theodoli for him to accept the French view, Mussolini refused to budge. He maintained that opinion inside the Fascist Party would not permit him to go further in the conciliation of Yugoslavia.¹⁴

The concern that a rigid adherence to the requirement for a prior or simultaneous Italo-Yugoslav accord might prejudice all the progress made in recent months on Franco-Italian issues led Laval to modify his views on this issue. Following his conversation with Aloisi in Geneva, he referred in a telegram to de Chambrun to "a 'climate' favorable to the indispensable reestablishment of relations of confidence between the two countries." The message was clear enough; the existence of such a "favorable climate" (not defined) would be sufficient for France to go ahead with an accord with Italy. This change in direction was made explicit on 18 December, when Léger instructed his minister in Belgrade to inform the Yugoslav government that de Chambrun's efforts to achieve a quick amelioration of Italo-Yugoslav relations had reached a dead point. To continue to insist on this part of the program would throw into peril the entire series of Franco-

Italian accords, which in fact augured well for the security of Yugoslavia. Belgrade was assured that France's decision to continue negotiations with Italy did not betoken any abandonment of Yugoslavia by France.[15] Somewhat later Laval reaffirmed his conviction that an Italo-Yugoslav reconciliation was essential to the security of central Europe and that he would continue to work for this as a consequence of his negotiations in Rome.

The improvement in the Italo-Yugoslav climate that Laval had been looking for occurred during the last week of 1934. On Christmas Day Mussolini, expressing concern about the ripening Ethiopian question, told Aloisi that " 'it is now necessary to get things moving fast' " with France. But he apparently recognized that an agreement required a reversal of Italian policy with regard to her South Slav neighbor. And thus, whereas two weeks earlier Mussolini had resisted French pressure to reconcile historic differences with Yugoslavia, by 29 December he demonstrated his willingness to proceed with Franco-Italian negotiations by agreeing to cooperate with the Little Entente nations to defend Austrian independence in conjunction with the League of Nations. On the same day the Yugoslavs reluctantly gave their blessing to Laval's formula for a subsequent Italo-Yugoslav treaty of arbitration and conciliation,[16] and shortly thereafter the dates for the foreign minister's official visit to Rome were fixed for 4–7 January 1935.

Meanwhile the diplomatic lines between Rome and Paris hummed with activity as the fine points on armaments, Austria, Tunisia, Libya, and Italian participation in the administration of the Jibuti–Addis Ababa Railway Company were discussed in great detail prior to Laval's arrival in the Italian capital.[17] Dampierre, the French chargé in Rome, has described the difficult situation facing de Chambrun in the marathon negotiating sessions required to set the stage for Laval's visit. The Italians considered France's offers on African frontier rectifications insufficient and pressed hard for a formula specifying French disinterest in Ethiopia: "My boss [de Chambrun], whose vigorous optimism did not weaken for all of this, was submitted to ever greater pressure from the Italians and, on the other edge of the sword, he found in Paris a reluctant minister and a group of reticent functionaries, who desired the realization of the projected visit but who were determined not to pay too high a price for it." Of particular importance, however, is the impression that can be gleaned of the evolution of Laval's thinking on the matter of Ethiopia. At the end of a long telegram, dated 17 December, dealing primarily with the subtleties of the Tunisian and the Jibuti–Addis Ababa Railway questions, de Chambrun inserted the following admonition: "Finally, I believe it my duty to emphasize the capital interest which will be attached to our response to the question posed by

Monsieur Suvich concerning the form of our eventual economic disinterest in Abyssinia. In effect, this response can be, from our point of view, *the key to the negotiation.*" Ten days later Mussolini again insisted "in the most pressing manner" that Laval agree to grant Italy participation in the Jibuti–Addis Ababa Railway and to indicate to him *"secretly"* that the economic interests of France in Ethiopia were limited to the railway zone. "He did not conceal the fact that this point was essential for the success of the accord."[18]

Laval, however, made very little reference to Ethiopia in the official diplomatic correspondence. At one point he simply expressed his reluctance to give the Italians any general assertion on French economic disinterest in Ethiopia for fear that this would be viewed by Addis Ababa as an abandonment of it to Italian penetration. He in fact specifically instructed de Chambrun to decline any further negotiation on the matter of Ethiopia. The foreign minister's last official word on the issue prior to departure for Rome occurred on 3 January 1935. The Ethiopian minister in Paris expressed alarm that the French government was in the process of giving Italy "a free hand in Ethiopia." In response, Laval instructed his representative in Addis Ababa to assure Haile Selassie that French policy "remained bound in principle to respect the independence of a sovereign member state of the League of Nations and attached by tradition to friendship for Ethiopia."[19] French documents make it abundantly clear that Laval intended to play his Ethiopian cards close to the vest and that he would personally carry out negotiations on this matter with Mussolini.

THE LAVAL-MUSSOLINI ACCORDS

French public opinion was carefully prepared for Laval's trip and for the anticipated accord with Fascist Italy. Given the history of tension and the anti-Italian press campaigns of the 1920s and early 1930s, it was believed necessary to mount a favorable publicity venture to plant the idea of a Franco-Italian entente. The publicity effort virtually ignored the communist press, which vigorously opposed any dealing with Mussolini at all, and also the press of the antiparliamentary right, which greeted with unalloyed enthusiasm the prospect of a French rapprochement with Mussolini. Rather, the campaign focused on the press of the moderate right and center and also on the socialist and moderate left-of-center press. The former's readers were assured by articles presenting Mussolini's regime in a favorable light and by stressing such things as its Latin culture, the First World War, and a common religion. For the socialist and moderate left-of-center newspapers (which opposed the nature of the fascist regime on principle), an entente with Italy was portrayed as a political necessity to isolate

Germany—a tactic in foreign affairs designed to maintain European peace. Pierre Milza, a historian of French public opinion, sums up the press campaign by concluding that the problem of foreign policy dominated the debate. To achieve the encirclement of Germany by an entente with Fascist Italy was regarded as a considerable objective and, in fact, overrode the objections of those in certain sectors of public opinion who opposed Mussolini's dictatorship on ideological grounds.[20]

If French public opinion was assiduously cultivated, the record suggests that Laval was considerably more cavalier in preparing his own advisors at the Quai d'Orsay. On 2 January 1935, a Foreign Ministry official told a journalist, Geneviève Tabouis, who was foreign affairs writer for *L'Oeuvre,* that the trip to Rome had not been properly prepared. Mussolini was sure to have hard questions for Laval about Ethiopia and North Africa, and " 'we haven't even begun to discuss these questions at the Quai d'Orsay.' " Léger claimed to have nearly resigned as secretary general of the Foreign Ministry in protest at what he regarded as a premature venture in personal diplomacy. Léger believed Laval was more interested in a sensational diplomatic success than in the substance of an agreement. Perhaps Laval really believed the definition of diplomacy he gave to journalists gathered in Rome to cover the Laval-Mussolini discussions: " 'Diplomacy, what is that? You offer something; your opponent offers something else. And you end by making a deal; it's no more difficult than that!' " This seems to be the method employed by the French foreign minister in Rome to break the impasse that developed there. Intense negotiations among the diplomats (Suvich and Aloisi for Italy, de Chambrun and Léger for France) throughout 5 and 6 January did not result in agreement. Only the famous tête-à-tête between Laval and Mussolini at the Palazzo Farnese on the evening of 6 January finally broke the ice. The two men, closeted together for several hours without either advisors or translators, emerged with the historic agreement that would be signed the following day. Tabouis relates the following anecdote, told to her a few months after Laval and Mussolini emerged from their private conversation. "Looking at each other with the air of two conspirators . . . the Duce, telling us [journalists] to bear witness, first gave satisfaction to Laval on points of detail. The latter, solemnly declared: 'I look at your hands; they are powerful hands, and I hope that you will not make bad use of them against Ethiopia!' And the Italian answered melodramatically: 'These hands have only peaceful intentions.' "[21] A great deal of ink has been spilled in an effort to understand and analyze what actually transpired between the French and Italian statesmen as they met privately in the French Embassy in Rome. Yet another attempt will be made in these pages, but first it is necessary to describe in some detail the accords that were signed by Laval and Mussolini amid great fanfare on 7 January 1935.

The public portion of the Laval-Mussolini Accords contained the following items:

1. A general declaration of friendship and collaboration with ritual references to the League of Nations and the International Court of Justice.
2. A procès-verbal pledging joint adherence to the principle of Austrian independence and integrity along with a pledge of mutual consultation should Austrian independence be threatened.
3. A protocol declaring the two powers' opposition to unilateral German rearmament and a pledge to concert their actions should Germany rearm unilaterally. This protocol also committed the two powers to work together, if the international situation permitted it, to bring about a plan of international disarmament.
4. A three-part treaty between France and Italy regulating their interests in Africa: *Part I* called for a special convention to be established in the near future outlining the rights of Italians in Tunisia according to the protocol on Tunisia signed the same day. *Part II* called for French cession of some 44,000 square miles of territory to be added to the southern Libyan frontier. *Part III* called for French cession of some 309 square miles of territory (including 13.5 miles of coastline) to the Italian colony of Eritrea.
5. A protocol guaranteeing free passage of the Bab-el-Mandeb.
6. A special protocol defining the terms of Part I of the African treaty. It stated that Italians would maintain their rights and privileges in Tunisia, as guaranteed by the convention of 1896, until 28 March 1945, after which time their return to French common law would be made in stages. Naturalization would occur over a twenty-year period from 1945 to 1965, after which all individuals born of Italian parents in Tunisia would fall under French nationality legislation. Italian schools were to remain protected until 1955, after which they would fall under French educational legislation.[22]

Most observers found the Laval-Mussolini agreements of 1935 very perplexing. In one sudden blow the Tunisian problem, which had bedeviled Franco-Italian relations for over half a century, appeared to be resolved wholly in France's favor. The rest of the agreements were important but rather perfunctory by comparison. The keystone to the entire series of public agreements was the sweeping protocol in which Italy agreed to the progressive liquidation of the special rights of Italian citizens in Tunisia, guaranteed by France since 1896. What was published, therefore, was clearly a victory for the French foreign minister. Many were dumfounded that Mussolini would sacrifice the rights of 100,000 Italians in Tunisia for what amounted to a few palm trees in Libya. This explained Laval's jaunty attitude upon his return to France, where he told an American journalist that although the fascist leader was an extremely hard bargainer, the fact of the matter was that Mussolini could not raise a dozen bananas on the desert territory ceded to Libya and that by getting the Italian dictator to drop his support for Germany's arms demands and for Hungary's revisionist claims, he had really come away from Rome "with the Duce's shirt and studs."[23]

Mussolini's payoff, of course, appeared in several secret protocols. These called for Franco-Italian military collaboration (discussed in chapter seven) and a transfer to Italy of 2,500 shares in the Jibuti–Addis Ababa Railway Company, along with a French pledge to work toward proportional Italian representation on the company's board of directors. (The shares transferred to Italian investors constituted nearly seven percent of the total of 34,000 shares. France retained 20,000 shares, thus assuring majority interest.) The most important secret protocol, however, stipulated that France "does not look in Abyssinia for the satisfaction of any interests other than those economic interests relating to the traffic of the Jibuti–Addis Ababa railway."[24] Laval went to his grave denying that he had promised Mussolini anything more than French "economic disinterest" in Ethiopia. Nevertheless, it seems reasonably clear now that, whether through the wink of an eye or the shrug of a shoulder, Laval granted to Mussolini a considerably greater concession in Ethiopia than the literal text of the secret convention conveys. Otherwise it is inconceivable that the Italian dictator would have surrendered the rights of Italians in Tunisia so lightly. All of which demands a careful perusal of the scanty and circumspect evidence surrounding the concessions that Laval might or might not have made to Mussolini on the Ethiopian question during their private meeting on the night of 6–7 January 1935.[25] Did he, or did he not, offer Mussolini a "free hand" in Ethiopia?

A "FREE HAND" IN ETHIOPIA?

Laval most certainly did caution de Chambrun of the absolute necessity of keeping protocols VII and VIII rigorously secret. These were the instruments pledging French economic disinterest in Ethiopia and promising to sell 2,500 shares of Jibuti–Addis Ababa railway stock to Italian investors. Ethiopia had been informed about the stock sale but would have objected to the paragraph saying that France would use its good offices to enlarge Italian representation on the railroad's directing agencies. But did this conceal some nefarious purpose or was it simply a matter of practical politics? For a proper understanding of Laval's role in the matter, it is well to keep in mind the climate of both domestic and international opinion prevailing at the time the accords were signed. In Berlin, the Laval-Mussolini agreements were greeted with shock. The French ambassador, François-Poncet, reported that Hitler was considerably disturbed at what he regarded as betrayal on the part of an Italian government that bore so many political affinities to the regime in Berlin. Particularly unsettling to the Führer were those parts of the Rome accords dealing with the maintenance of Austrian independence and opposition to German rearmament. These were clearly defeats for Nazi foreign policy ambitions. In London the initial reaction was one of enthusiasm. British leaders had championed the idea of Franco-Italian rapprochement as a device that might redound well to British security in the Mediterranean. Sir John Simon was foreign minister at this time and was not one to make a point of international morality over such a matter as Ethiopia—at least so long as no immediate Italian military adventures were foreseen. That the French government was solidly behind Laval's achievement was dramatically illustrated by the overwhelming majorities achieved in the parliament to ratify the accords. After assuring the Chamber of Deputies that "nothing in the Rome agreements nor in the conversations carried on for their application affects the sovereignty, independence, or the territorial integrity of Ethiopia," that body delivered a vote of 555 to 9 in favor of ratification. In the Senate a few days later, the vote was unanimous. Even among those Frenchmen whose opposition to fascism was profound, there was a sense of exultation. Blum, the socialist leader, confided that although he felt shame that a French foreign minister hosted Matteotti's assassin in the Palazzo Farnese in Rome, and although he harbored considerable doubts about Mussolini's peaceful motivations, nevertheless: "The program announced with so much fanfare by the official press is so noble, so beautiful, so far-reaching that one would be happy even if only a part of it were realized."[26]

Contemporary accounts of the bargain struck by Laval with Mussolini on the night of 6–7 January frequently ignore the atmosphere of euphoria indicated above. Judgments about Laval's motivations became severely distorted by what happened afterward—particularly the Italian invasion of Ethiopia in October 1935 and Laval's subsequent morally barren, defeatist, and collaborationist behavior during the Vichy interregnum of 1940–44. In retrospect the foreign minister's political opponents, who were legion, saw in the Rome accords a blatant and cynical endorsement of Mussolini's expansionist ambitions in North Africa or, worse, an early indication of Laval's affinity for the political philosophy of fascism. In short, his behavior was either naive or traitorous from the outset. Reynaud, for example, considered it extremely likely that the scheming foreign minister had made sweeping oral promises to Mussolini about a free hand for Italy in Ethiopia. Maurice Thorez, the communist leader, spoke openly on the eve of the 1936 elections about Laval's "complicity with the aggressor" in Ethiopia and of his "hitlerophile and anti-soviet policies." On the other hand, the prolific English journalist, Alexander Werth, writing in 1942, saw Laval not as a conniving traitor but rather as a naive, inexperienced politician who had been "bam-boozled" by Mussolini's "Machiavellian diplomacy" into submitting to "blackmail" by endorsing the fascist leader's plans for an immediate conquest of Ethiopia. The latter view was echoed in a recent biography of Laval, where the author maintains that the Rome accords bore the germ of the Ethiopian War and the rupture of the London-Paris-Rome axis. "Without knowing it, and for having been too much in a hurry to conclude, Laval was duped by a cunning partner."[27]

The evidentiary record shows that these judgments are seriously flawed—motivated either by ignorance of the facts, by political opposition, or simply by personal dislike for a politician who did not hesitate to use public office for his own enrichment and whose penchant for the use of argot and the familiar voice in professional discourse was a constant source of annoyance even to his friends. But none of this constitutes naïveté or lack of vision, to say nothing of treason. Laval's words speak for themselves. He testified at the trial of Marshal Philippe-Henri Pétain on 3 August 1945 that, when he first came to the Quai d'Orsay, he found only the sketchiest of drafts of an entente or agreement to be brought to a head with Italy. He intended, however, to pursue this aspect of his predecessor's containment policy enthusiastically. It was his judgment at the time that a Franco-Italian alliance would form the natural corollary to France's other alliances in central and eastern Europe and would maximize the benefits to France of the military efforts of Yugoslavia, Czechoslovakia, Poland, and Romania. With regard to the question of Ethiopia, and in response to an interpellation on a vote of confidence in his government following the revelation of the Hoare-Laval plan, Laval told the Chamber of Deputies on 28 December 1935:

> By economic renunciation on the part of France I have conceded the right to Italy to request concessions in all parts of Abyssinia, respecting only acquired rights, and Italy conceded to us the same right for a zone sufficient for feeding the traffic from Jibuti to Addis Ababa. Thus Italy obtained advantages corresponding to those which England had conceded to her in 1925. It was for Italy to make the best of these by working towards collaboration with Abyssinia, which, although its evolution had proceeded at a slower pace, offered opportunities of collaboration that might have been as profitable to Abyssinia as to Italy. France did not intend to put any obstacles in the way of this

peaceful development of influence. It was entitled to think that Italy would utilize this freedom of action solely in a peaceful manner. There was nothing in the agreements or in the conversations which preceded or followed that could encourage Italy to have recourse to war.[28]

Laval was here speaking before a partisan political body that was entertaining a motion of confidence in his government, and for that reason a bit of dissembling might have been expected. Yet, if one examines the personal, secret correspondence that ensued from December 1935 to February 1936 between Laval and Mussolini following the demise of the Hoare-Laval Plan, nothing substantially different emerges. In these letters Laval mourned the Duce's decision to go to war with Ethiopia and insisted that he only promised Mussolini that France would observe "désistement économique" in Ethiopia. The expression "mains libres," used verbally in their conversation of 6–7 January 1935, was equivalent to "désistement," and further, Laval wrote, it was clear that France could consent to Italian economic penetration only so long as it was carried out peacefully. Mussolini responded that, although he too regretted the Italo-Ethiopian War, its prosecution was fully consistent with the accords of January 1935.[29]

Did Laval endorse an Italian conquest of Ethiopia? Although it is impossible to know exactly what words were spoken or gestures made during the Laval-Mussolini conversation, the only judicious answer to the question is "no."[30] That is not to say that Laval necessarily opposed substantial Italian increases in economic influence and territory. The record shows that he was perfectly amenable to that. Later at the Pétain trial in 1945, although insisting that the only concessions he made to the Duce in Ethiopia were economic, Laval admitted having said: "You have henceforth in Abyssinia a free hand, but do not abuse your free hand by using acts of force. Follow the example of Marshal Lyautey," the former successful resident general of Morocco. He claimed that when Mussolini later went to war, he did so "against my will and against my objections." Guariglia, an Italian official with access to Mussolini, later wrote that Laval did make verbal promises that went beyond economic disinterest, but he believed it quite possible that the Frenchman did not dream there would be an Italian military operation against Ethiopia less than a year after the signing of the accords. On 27 June 1935, in a conversation with Anthony Eden, then Britain's Minister for League of Nations Affairs, Laval acknowledged that he had verbally given the Duce a free hand. Eden noted: "In conversation M. Laval had said to Signor Mussolini that he left him a free hand, but begged him not to make a bad use of his freedom. . . . If Signor Mussolini thought that France had left Italy a free hand that was true, but it all depended on the use which Italy made of it. He only gave up what France had a right to give up. He had agreed not to obstruct." In short, there is little doubt that Laval used the expression "free hand" in regard to Italy's activities in Ethiopia. Nor, given the matter-of-fact tone of the Eden document cited above, is there much doubt that the English were not terribly concerned about hidden concessions. However, there is no concrete evidence whatsoever that Laval had sanctioned political conquest. Bonnet claims to have verified this conclusion himself in the files of the Quai d'Orsay when he subsequently became minister of foreign affairs. It is possible that Mussolini may have misunderstood Laval's French or one of his gestures (Denis Mack Smith, after all, has written that Mussolini was dangerously prone to overestimate his own linguistic capabilities), but if the Frenchman did in fact make such a sweeping concession, he apparently confided it to absolutely no one else. Moreover, it is simply wrong to suggest that Laval's effort to seek an alliance with Italy was no more than an early indication of his admiration for fascism. Rather, the Laval-Mussolini accords of January 1935 (including the secret French recognition of a "free hand" for Italy in Ethiopia) followed logically from a major thrust of French diplomacy for at least the previous seven years. Although little concrete progress had been made toward a Franco-Italian rapprochement before Laval came to the Quai d'Orsay, what seemed a dramatic breakthrough at the time would have been inconceivable without the initiatives undertaken in the Theodoli-de Caix conversations of 1928–32 and in the policies carried forward by Paul-Boncour and Jouvenel in 1933. It is also worth emphasizing that, at this point in time, the notion of a Franco-Italian entente was not one cherished exclusively by the French right wing. With the exception of the communist press, editorial support for an accord with Italy can be found in newspapers of virtually all other shades of political opinion during the fall and winter of 1934–35.[31]

The sacrifice of some measure of Ethiopian sovereignty, as reprehensible as that may have been to some sensibilities, simply was not regarded as too high a price to pay to enroll Italy in the French security system. Subsequent events in Europe and East Africa also suggest that those who, like Laval, continued to champion concerted efforts to maintain Franco-Italian cooperation, even after the onset of the Ethiopian War, had a clearer vision of what constituted French security than many of Laval's successors at the Quai d'Orsay.

In light of future misunderstanding and outright antagonism between Great Britain and France over the Italian question, it is worthwhile to record the former's immediate reaction to the Laval-Mussolini understandings. Drummond lauded the accords as a great forward step with an "almost incalculable" potential effect on the preservation of European peace. Perhaps more important, Drummond saw Laval's diplomacy as an indication that France was moving away from her earlier superiority complex vis-à-vis Italy—an attitude that had annoyed Mussolini enormously. However, not everyone at Whitehall shared the British ambassador's unalloyed enthusiasm. Minutes attached to his dispatches from Rome expressed the view that the Laval-Mussolini accords were "founded on necessity rather than sentiment" and were due, not to increased reasonableness on either side, but rather to the steady growth of a common fear of Germany. Nevertheless, Vansittart summed up the various assessments and underscored his own view of the significance of what had occurred in Rome.

> Do not look this gift horse too sternly in the mouth. (I know all about its teeth.) We have wanted it for long, and now we have got it, and it is a long stride in the right direction. . . . [L]ots of good *ménages* have not been founded on sentiment, and have survived without the spur of necessity so patent here. We must welcome the necessity, since we cannot have it otherwise—unfortunately. And we must do all we can to preserve this unromantic combination.

Vansittart's admonition to nurture the new Franco-Italian relationship was based largely on his recognition that it held out the possibility of a cooperative effort to maintain stability in central and eastern Europe, a part of the continent where Britain had steadfastly refused to assume any hard-and-fast commitments beyond her pledge of 17 February 1934 to consult with France and Italy should Austrian independence be breached.[32] The future, however, held precious little British support for French efforts to appease Mussolini's Italy and, thereby, to thwart the coalescence of Europe's two principal fascist powers.

CHAPTER 7

Military Preparations and the Stresa Front

The Laval-Mussolini Accords of January 1935 constituted the single most important effort made by the Western powers in the 1930s to reconstruct the entente of World War I. It did not matter that Laval originally viewed the accords as a device to pressure Germany into a rapprochement with France rather than as an anti-German implement of coercion or encirclement. The fact is that France's strategic position in 1935, once the Rome Accords were buttressed by the Franco-Soviet Treaty in May, was more favorable than at any time during the entire interwar period. The real importance of the Rome Accords became apparent only in their aftermath in the secret military collaboration that they engendered between January and June 1935.

General H. Parisot, France's military attaché in Rome, reported as early as October 1934 that Italian military personnel had become very cordial to their French colleagues, from which he concluded that the Italians desired to couple military with political rapprochement. A month later he reported that Italian Minister of Agriculture Edmondo Rossoni, said to be close to the Duce, had remarked: " 'Only one thing today interests the Italian government, and that is the conclusion with France of an accord surpassing in importance that of an entente on specific issues, but one having the value of a veritable alliance.' " Italy's desire for such an alliance was based on distrust of Hitler and his increased efforts to build up a clientele in Yugoslavia following King Alexander's assassination in Marseille.[1] The active clauses of the Laval-Mussolini agreements that presaged military collaboration were those pledging mutual consultation and concerted action in the event of unilateral German rearmament and/or a threat to the independence of Austria.

On 11 January 1935, Mussolini took the initiative for a military entente with France by instructing General Badoglio to open conversations with the military attaché of the French embassy. Badoglio, an open Francophile who had strongly advocated the coordination of French and Italian military resources since the mid-1920s, was only too happy to undertake such an assignment. He met with Parisot on 12 January and expressed his concern about increased Nazi activity in Austria and the Alto Adige, and he indicated his conviction that Germany intended to stir up trouble again as soon as the Saar question was regulated. Badoglio was prepared, therefore, to put into force the obligations spelled out in the Laval-Mussolini Accords and to coordinate policies with France should an occupation of Austria become necessary. He raised the following questions: (1) What military actions would France intend to take in the different situations concerning Austria including a general German mobilization? and (2) Would the French government consent, in such a situation, to exercise her influence in Yugoslavia to facilitate common military actions and to avoid the possibility of political and military friction between Rome and Belgrade? Badoglio argued that any efficacious action to preserve Austrian independence would require a quick response by France and Italy—therefore, the technical preparations should begin at once. He expressed some surprise that these issues had not been discussed when Laval was in Rome. In a note to Laval, General Joseph Maurin, the French minister of war, strongly endorsed the proposed military talks. "Given the position taken recently by Rome, it seems opportune to me not to refuse Italy a tangible sign of the frankness of our intentions. We can hope to obtain in exchange a favorable attitude from Italy on our behalf in the event of an eventual conflict with Germany. I cannot underline strongly enough the military advantages that would accrue to us." Maurin also pointed out how advantageous it would be to constitute a military front directly linking France with its Little Entente partners. He closed by urging Laval to react quickly to the Italian overtures.[2]

Responding to pressure from both de Chambrun and Maurin, Laval made his official—and very cautious—answer to the Badoglio initiative on 26 January. His instructions to de Chambrun indicated that the French government was willing to give the Rome Accords relative to Austria their full chance for development, and he endorsed the idea of a periodic exchange of information between the two general staffs. Acknowledging that military conversations were in order, Laval insisted, however, that France must first be informed of the various hypotheses envisioned by Italy and what the latter would propose to do in each case. It was clearly an invitation to the Italians to get down to specifics, but Laval also laid out some parameters within which the negotiations must operate. He insisted that the talks were of a political nature and, therefore, ought to be conducted along diplomatic rather than strictly military lines—with the full collaboration of Yugoslavia and Czechoslovakia. Furthermore, it was important that Italy give the Yugoslav government "all appeasements and reassurances" about the potential for Italian troop movements near the Italo-Yugoslav border should it become necessary to mobilize in defense of Austrian independence. Despite the hedging tone of Laval's instructions, Badoglio was delighted at the French response and told Parisot that the success of these military talks "will be the crown of his career."[3]

Badoglio set to work straight away to define the various hypotheses in central Europe that would require coordinated Franco-Italian military action. He proposed, in a long conversation with Parisot on 29 January, the initiation of General Staff talks to define terms for the following four situations:

1. *First Case:* German mobilization for whatever reason (define common Franco-Italian attitude);
2. *Second Case:* German aggression against France (Italian intervention);
3. *Third Case:* Internal disturbances in Austria without armed German intervention (define military measures to be taken by France and Italy with Austrian cooperation. Italy prepares to intervene);
4. *Fourth Case:* Internal disturbances in Austria with German military intervention (define common military measures. Italy will intervene).

Badoglio emphasized that in the last two cases, any military measures undertaken by France and Italy could occur only with the accord of the Austrian government. He also indicated the desirability of establishing a direct liaison between the two General Staffs for the regular exchange of information—an indication that he saw these talks going well beyond the Austrian situation.[4]

In his review of the Badoglio scenarios, General Maurin pointed out to

Laval that the first two cases called for "a proposal for accords, or even an alliance, with France," which would bring Italian troops onto French territory, thus guaranteeing Alpine security and permitting the concentration of French forces in the northeast. In addition, communications with North Africa would remain entirely open. The third and fourth cases implied the sending of a French expeditionary force to support the Italians in Austria. This had the advantage of establishing a southern front against Germany and securing communications with France's allies in the Little Entente. Maurin could hardly contain his enthusiasm for the prospects, and his cover letter to Laval on 8 February, accompanying the Deuxième Bureau's analysis of the Badoglio proposals, again urged a quick decision in favor of beginning General Staff conversations.[5]

Badoglio also revealed his enthusiasm for a military accord with France to his old friend General Maurice Gamelin, who had recently been named vice-president of the Conseil supérieur de la guerre. It was apparently Gamelin who devised the opening French negotiating strategy later recommended by Maurin and approved by the Haut comité militaire on 20 February 1935. Gamelin proposed the deployment of one French army corps on the Italian right flank near Yugoslavia. The purpose was to minimize friction between Italy and Yugoslavia and to give France a wedge in influencing Danubian and Little Entente policy. In exchange, the Italians would be invited to deploy one army corps on the French right flank between Belfort and the Swiss frontier. He also suggested the possibility of air cooperation—making French bases available to the Italians in the Saône Valley and at Doubs, "in view of an action on Southern Germany, without violating Swiss neutrality." In any case, working out the technical details of such a proposal would take time and require high-level decisions which were beyond the capacity of the military attaché in Rome. Parisot, therefore, was instructed on 8 February 1935 to inform the Italians that France would welcome direct talks between the Deuxième Bureaux of their General Staffs on developing common action in the event of a threat to Austria or of general German mobilization. These talks could take place in either Paris or Rome and could begin in March or April. The decision to conduct the General Staff negotiations in Rome was made shortly thereafter.[6]

At this point it is interesting to interpose Laval's own views with regard to Franco-Italian military negotiations. Geoffrey Warner has written that, in subsequent years, Laval portrayed the Rome Accords of January 1935 as simply preliminaries to the staff talks which achieved a veritable military alliance six months later. But actually, Warner cautions, the initiative for the talks came from Italy—an indication that Laval valued the Rome Ac-

MILITARY PREPARATIONS AND THE STRESA FRONT

cords only insofar as they bolstered the possibility of eventual Franco-German understanding. Although Laval had authorized French participation in the General Staff negotiations, Warner is probably correct in his analysis of Laval's motivations—at least up to the point of Germany's unilateral rearmament of March 1935. The latter completely altered any realistic potential for a Franco-German rapprochement and put the Franco-Italian military negotiations into an entirely new light. Other evidence also suggests that, up until Germany openly announced her rearmament program, the French foreign minister was not nearly as keen as his military comrades about plunging ahead with military commitments to Mussolini. On 20 February, Laval cautioned the Haut comité militaire: "It is best not to respond too quickly to advances from Rome. It is necessary to keep the conversations going and to leave Marshal Badoglio with the hope of seeing them lead to a result. . . . Our situation is excellent on the Italian side, which is prepared for all military, naval and economic arrangements; but one must not commit any imprudence on the side of Belgrade." As late as 22 March Laval again took the position before the Haut comité militaire that it was necessary to be prudent in dealing with Italy, because any prolonged war with Germany would make the aid of England absolutely essential. Duroselle views this excessive deference to England, pursued throughout the 1930s in spite of excellent opportunities, such as a Franco-Italian military alliance, as one of the chief components of the decadence which paralyzed French foreign policy in the face of the Hitlerian menace.[7] As a general overview made from a distance of forty years this is fair enough, but there was really no way of predicting, in the winter of 1934–35, the ruinous consequences for France of England's decision in June to sign a naval accord with Germany. This matter will be considered in detail later in this chapter.

THE STRESA FRONT

Military negotiations between the French and the Italians were abruptly interrupted on 16 March 1935 when Hitler undertook his first open breach of the 1919–20 treaty structure. In a striking coup de théâtre, Foreign Minister Constantin von Neurath announced to foreign diplomats and representatives of the world press gathered at the Wilhelmstrasse that, given the failure of all the conferences on disarmament, Germany, in the interests of her own security, was undertaking unilaterally a program of military, air, and naval rearmament. Hitler made a similar announcement simultaneously in the Reichstag. The German action was not entirely unanticipated; many observers expected some dramatic gesture in the wake of the striking Nazi success in the Saar plebiscite during the previous January. Few, however, guessed that the move would be so sweeping and so blatant. In any case, unilateral German rearmament constituted a clear violation of both the Versailles and Locarno Treaties. In addition, the recently concluded Laval-Mussolini Accords called for mutual consultation and action in such an eventuality. The German move was a challenge to the other three principal powers involved in these treaty structures. Mussolini again seized the initiative by inviting the leaders of France and England to the northern Italian city of Stresa to work out a common and coordinated response.

What happened during the days immediately preceding the Stresa summit meeting is important to an understanding both of the evolution of Laval's views and of the suspicions growing in both Paris and Rome about the stance that London was likely to adopt vis-à-vis collective action directed toward the Third Reich. On 30 March, the Italian government expressed its interest in seeing France and Italy work together "in a common effort to associate England with their views." Such a demonstration of solidarity and resistance would, Suvich argued, leave the very clear impression in Berlin that new steps similar to those taken by Germany on 16 March would result in the most serious consequences. The Italians, he suggested, would like to establish agreements on the following: a line of conduct to follow with regard to Germany's unilateral rearmament, the defense of Austrian independence, and a common stance toward the other states disarmed by the 1919-20 treaties. Several days later, Mussolini himself, in an interview with the editor of *Le Temps,* underscored his conviction that the western powers must demonstrate their solidarity in the near future, since it was likely that rearmament would encourage Hitler to other provocative diplomatic gestures. The Duce suggested that England, France, and Italy should strive for common policies in all areas of potential German disruption—Austria, Memel, Czechoslovakia, and the demilitarized zone of the Rhineland.[8]

Laval responded to these observations on 3 April. His instructions to de Chambrun adopted a tone quite different from that of several months before when he had seen the chief value of Franco-Italian reconciliation as leading toward an eventual rapprochement with Nazi Germany. He now was convinced that a direct Franco-Italian entente was the instrumental ingredient in bringing about a common accord among the three western powers in order to face German initiatives. "I fully share M. Suvich's views," he wrote, "on the necessity of giving the German government, by the firmness of our common attitude, the kind of clear warning that will prevent it from going further along the path opened up on 16 March." The French foreign minister went on to propose an agenda for the Stresa gathering. With regard to Germany, Laval suggested a five-part discussion among the three powers aimed at achieving agreement on: (1) a common position to be taken at Geneva; (2) the question of regional pacts to contain German treaty violations; (3) the question of a tripartite air pact; (4) the adoption of common action for future German treaty violations; and (5) a reaffirmation of Locarno pledges in the event of German action in the Rhineland. In addition, Laval wanted a three-power rededication of their resolve to maintain Austrian independence and a discussion of the potential limited rearmament of the other nations disarmed in 1919–20. That Laval's fundamental stance had shifted dramatically in the wake of German rearmament was affirmed by British observers as well. Sir George Clerk, British ambassador in Paris, informed his government on 5 April that France no longer recognized any basis for a settlement with Hitler; additional efforts in that direction would only encourage the Führer to go further in tearing up treaty engagements. Clerk believed that: "M. Laval will consequently show no inclination at Stresa to seek any fresh basis of a general settlement with Germany. He will urge that no time be wasted on so fruitless a quest, and that the three Powers proceed at once with the attempt to organize security on a collective basis. . . ."[9]

In these days prior to the convocation of Stresa, both the French and the Italians were at pains to emphasize the importance of bringing England into a three-power combination. Yet both harbored serious reservations about the extent to which the English could be persuaded to commit themselves to collective action in central Europe. Mussolini referred on 4 April to the "clearly equivocal" attitude of England. His sentiments were echoed a week later by Dino Grandi, the Italian ambassador in London, who complained to Charles Corbin, his French counterpart, that despite numerous requests, he had been unable to get any useful information from John Simon, the British foreign secretary, about the position England would take at Stresa. Grandi was therefore quite pessimistic about England's readiness to collaborate fully with France and Italy, and he told Corbin that in his personal opinion the English government had "morally broken with the principles of 3 February." The latter was a reference to an official communiqué following Anglo-French talks in London in which Britain welcomed the Laval-Mussolini Accords, and the two powers declared their intention to work together to limit armaments, support the League of Nations, and defend the integrity and independence of Austria.[10] Although Corbin was not quite so disenchanted with the English as his Italian colleague, he was concerned about the tone of the English press, whose articles on the upcoming Stresa meeting created "an impression of reticence and hesitation." Vansittart attempted to mitigate their impact, but Corbin's own reservations were apparent in what he told Grandi on the eve of Stresa: "What we must seek to do is to inculcate in this country [England] the sense of European solidarity and to help those who already feel this way to educate the public. But if our proposition were declined, we would then be entirely justified in organizing European security in our own best interests."[11]

French and Italian suspicion of English motives was heightened by the fact that a British negotiating team had carried through with Anglo-German conversations in Berlin even in the wake of unilateral rearmament. That no prior consultation with Paris and Rome took place was a matter of considerable irritation in those capitals. Had it been known that one of the subjects under discussion was a formal regulation of naval ratios between the two powers, the reaction in Paris and Rome certainly would have been more spectacular than simple irritation. Simon was even so insensitive as to consider inviting German negotiators to London to begin Anglo-German naval talks at the same time that he and the prime minister planned to be discussing collective action against German treaty violations in Stresa. Simon was advised hastily by his ambassadors that such a procedure would provoke a "disastrous reaction" in France and would be regarded in Italy "almost as a breach of faith on our part."[12] In the end the British delayed formal negotiations with Germany until after Stresa, but the British documents reveal that Whitehall intended to conclude an Anglo-German naval accord regardless of the outcome of the three-power conference. French and Italian concern about English reliability was entirely justified.

The Stresa meeting, which took place from 11–14 April 1935, was an important gathering, regardless of what has been written about its significance in retrospect. In attendance were Mussolini and Suvich for Italy, Flandin and Laval for France, and Simon and Prime Minister Ramsay MacDonald for England. After three days of frequently stormy discussion, the six statesmen issued a final communiqué composed of three parts. First, a joint resolution called for continued negotiations for security in eastern Europe and an air pact for the west. It reaffirmed the principle of Austrian independence and recommended an early meeting of central European governments to negotiate an agreement whereby they would join the Rome procès-verbal of 7 January on Austrian independence. The three powers also agreed to pursue a common line at Geneva with respect to German violations of peace, and they agreed to continue the search for a formula of disarmament. Second, an Anglo-Italian declaration reaffirmed the Locarno Pact of 1925. And third, the final declaration stipulated that the three powers were in agreement "in opposing, by all practicable means, any unilateral repudiation of treaties which may endanger the peace of

Europe."[13] Furthermore, the three powers ratified the French protest that was to be made in Geneva, which accused Germany of deliberately violating the clauses of the Versailles Treaty by introducing conscription and creating a military air force. The three powers submitted this protest to the League of Nations on 17 April 1935 and followed it with a resolution formally condemning Germany's unilateral repudiation of treaties.

Perhaps the most controversial aspect of the entire Stresa interlude concerned the apparent absence from the agenda of the question of Ethiopia, where Italian pressures were mounting on the regime of Haile Selassie and where the potential for friction among the three powers was most evident. The standard view of what occurred at Stresa is recorded in Flandin's memoirs. At the last session, as the European leaders worked on the wording of their final declaration, Mussolini anticipated some allusion to African issues. According to Flandin, Mussolini proposed rewording the final communiqué to say that the three powers would oppose any unilateral repudiation of treaties which might endanger the peace "of Europe," rather than "of the world" as the original draft had it. The revised wording, which was accepted, safeguarded the independence of Austria but left Mussolini's hands free in Ethiopia. Flandin speculated that the Duce's revision "was an apparent invitation to the British delegation to speak of Abyssinia. But neither M. MacDonald nor Sir John Simon blinked. M. Laval and I, and no doubt Mussolini as well, had the impression of a tacit acquiescence given by the British government to Italian ambitions in Abyssinia, if not by the means employed, which only became apparent after Stresa."[14]

There are others, however, who question Flandin's version of events. Léon Noël, who accompanied the French delegation to Stresa, denounced Flandin's account as entirely erroneous and self-serving. Far from there being any "tacit acquiescence" in Italian plans for Ethiopia, Noël maintained that nobody mentioned East Africa because nobody took seriously Italian preparations in regard to Ethiopia. It was an oversight to be sure— but not a planned one. If Flandin were correct, his version would condemn the French as much as the British. In his recent study of Mussolini's foreign and colonial policy, Robertson, who based his findings largely on the work of Italian historian Renzo de Felice, maintains that both the French and the British were anxious to avoid any discussion of Ethiopia at Stresa. The French feared that embarrassments over Ethiopia would prejudice a three-power united stand against Germany, whereas the British were concerned that the Ethiopian issue would destroy good relations between Britain and Italy. The latter were a necessary vehicle in the long-range British aspiration to nudge Germany back into a collective security scheme and back into League of Nations' disarmament discussions. "In fact," Robertson concludes, "the British had themselves drafted the communiqué [containing the words 'in Europe'] the night before it was signed, which perhaps deluded Mussolini all the more into thinking that they would not oppose him over Ethiopia. The next two months were to show that he had gravely miscalculated."[15]

Accuracy in the recording of events should always be the first duty of the historian. All too frequently, however, the road is strewn with contradictory evidence which is difficult to verify. The archives of the French Foreign Ministry, for example, contain little documentation of the Stresa Conference. Thus, one is left with contemporary accounts and the memoirs of participants whose views may be flawed and self-serving. Nevertheless, it seems reasonably clear that, however the final version of the communiqué was arrived at, the Ethiopian question was raised at Stresa—if not in the plenary sessions between Mussolini and the French and British prime ministers then certainly in the deliberations of the individual delegations and among lower-level diplomats. It was simply decided, either in ignorance of or in misinterpretation of Italian military preparations in Africa, that the Ethiopian question was not important enough to put at risk the opportunity of building a tripartite coalition against future German treaty violations. In addition, there is evidence to suggest that, just as Laval had been willing to countenance an Italian expansion of influence in Ethiopia, the British also were willing—so long as it was achieved peacefully. Perhaps then the chronic instability in Ethiopia would be corrected by Italy, thus facilitating some Italo-English accords granting pasturage rights to British Somalia.[16] In any case, it is quite conceivable that Mussolini may have interpreted Stresa as a "tacit acquiescence" in his plans for the conquest of Ethiopia.

Ethiopia aside, the "Stresa Front" was greeted warmly and enthusiastically in France, especially in conservative and right-wing circles. It is well to recall, it was between the time of the announcement of German rearmament and the convening of the Stresa meeting that both houses of the French parliament overwhelmingly ratified the Laval-Mussolini agreements (22 and 26 March 1935). The rightist press was enthusiastic about the possibilities of Stresa, viewing it as a refreshing bit of reality injected into the vapid arguments being advanced in Geneva. It represented Anglo-Franco-Italian solidarity. *Le Temps,* on 24 April, summed up the general attitude of the right. It said that Stresa insured peace in both eastern and western Europe and maintained that: "The permanent co-operation of France and Italy constitutes the new element that has entirely modified the international situation and has brought the first ray of light enabling the peoples to regain confidence." The emphasis here was obviously on

Franco-Italian solidarity. English participation was appreciated, but it was secondary to the hope for expanded military collaboration between France and Italy for mutual defense and for the defense of central Europe. François-Poncet reported on the eve of Stresa that the German press was not at all disturbed. Their feeling was that MacDonald and Mussolini would reject any anti-German French proposals. But the final communiqué overwhelmed and completely belied German expectations. "Stresa and [the unanimous condemnation of German actions at] Geneva were the high-water mark of European solidarity against the ambitions of the *Reich.* . . . Never did her leaders, her diplomats, and her official journalists seem to be more confused and discouraged." The French could also derive satisfaction from the generally favorable reaction to Stresa among her eastern European allies. Prince Paul of Yugoslavia, although he expressed some apprehension about an apparent contradiction in the Stresa agreements involving their condemnation of German rearmament coupled with the pledge to consider modifying disarmament requirements for countries like Hungary and Bulgaria, offered his general endorsement. In Prague the reaction was less ambiguous. Stresa's success produced a sigh of relief in Czech political circles, which welcomed enthusiastically the clear determination to preserve Austrian independence and to deal with the Danubian problem right away.[17]

Italian expectations may well have exceeded what the Stresa agreements actually yielded. The record shows that it was Mussolini who was most forceful in his denunciations of the German danger and in his appeals that Stresa not be a conference, like so many others, that ended only in platonic formulas. The Duce constantly had a map at hand and insisted on considering all areas of potential German expansion—Austria, the Sudetenland, Memel, the left bank of the Rhine—with the aim of defining concrete measures to be taken in each instance. He wanted to arm the Austrians, Hungarians, and Bulgarians and bring them together into an anti-German front, to be led of course by Italy. And yet, in spite of such exaggerated expectations, Aloisi recorded general satisfaction with the results of the Stresa meeting. His diary entry for 13 April 1935 reads: "Formulas have been found for the different conventions; we have finished our work in a sentiment of mutual comprehension. Tomorrow we shall reread the texts. Franco-Italian friendship emerges strongly consolidated, and along with that, English support of the two countries."[18] Others saw bitter irony in the new constellation of forces. Blum remarked that the two western democracies, whose inability to cooperate had projected an image of weakness, had permitted Mussolini to emerge as the man of peace. "What can I say? The fascist dictator who has ceaselessly breathed the spirit of war for the last fifteen years, today poses as the leader of the League of Peace." Blum had hoped that the first fruits of Stresa would be to reestablish strong lines between Britain and France.[19]

How illusory this turned out to be could be foreshadowed by looking at the way in which the major business at hand was dispensed. Mussolini's desire for a strong tripartite reaction against Germany with concrete plans for the future has already been noted. Noël has written that Flandin and Laval arrived at Stresa with the draft of a strong resolution condemning German rearmament already in their pockets. This resolution, if approved by English and Italian leaders, was to have been submitted to the Council of the League of Nations. Not only did it denounce Hitler's repudiation of 16 March, but it also called upon the League Council, in the event of any new unilateral violations of an existing treaty, to order sanctions against the guilty state. Mussolini was perfectly amenable to this formula and spoke out strongly on the need to guarantee Austria collectively. If Hitler once absorbed Austria, all of the Danube valley and eastern Europe would be open to German influence. MacDonald and Simon, however, argued that they could not undertake any formal obligations at Stresa without first consulting the House of Commons and that the most they could do with the French resolution was to offer British "moral support." Although desiring to go further, Laval and Flandin "in the name of unanimity which condemned to impotence almost all conferences of this kind," joined their English colleagues—and the result was the final communiqué which Noël felt did nothing to deter Hitler and only served to convince the Duce of the weakness of the western democracies.[20]

Noël, therefore, placed the lion's share of the blame for the ultimate failure of the Stresa Front on MacDonald and Simon for their "pacifist utopias." In all fairness, given the state of British public opinion at the time and its aversion to any potential military commitments, there was little else that the English leaders could do. But there was another dimension to British foreign policy which has come to light only more recently. In an excellent article, Michael Newman discusses the thinking of E. H. Carr, at the time deputy head of the southern section of the Foreign Office. Carr believed, after the Austrian coup of 1934, that it was probably inevitable that Hitler would eventually absorb Austria and then move toward the Sudetenland, ending Czech independence. Danubia would be transformed into a German economic and political sphere of influence. But Carr saw certain advantages in this: Central Europe would be given political and economic stability; German trade would be diverted to a market of only marginal importance to Britain; and Franco-Italian friendship would be " 'rapidly and securely cemented.' "On the eve of Stresa, Carr was arguing strongly —and apparently with some success—that Germany should have a free hand in central and eastern Europe if she agreed in turn to respect Britain's vital interests.[21] The fact that Britain, unbeknownst to her French and Italian Stresa partners, was preparing to negotiate a naval accord with the Third Reich, which was destined to doom even the benign unanimity of Stresa to oblivion, lends further credence to this analysis of British motivation.

In the long run, then, the so-called Stresa Front, although it contained the seeds of a viable tripartite diplomatic alliance, actually accomplished little more than to raise a few false hopes temporarily. But historical events need to be understood not only for their long-range significance or lack thereof, but also for what they meant at the time. Evidence cited earlier shows conclusively that substantial numbers of French observers, and not a few Italians, valued Stresa not primarily because it cemented a tripartite Anglo-Franco-Italian coalition but rather because it intensified the growing cordiality between Paris and Rome. Mussolini's tough talk at Stresa was welcomed joyously in Paris, and the emergency ignited by Hitler's coup of 16 March spurred on the intensity of the temporarily interrupted Franco-Italian negotiations for a military accord.

TOWARD THE FRANCO-ITALIAN MILITARY ACCORD

After the signing of the Stresa accord, Laval left immediately for Geneva to present the formal condemnation of Germany to the League of Nations. Flandin remained for a further conversation with Mussolini. The two men agreed that the Stresa guarantee to Austria meant nothing unless it were accompanied by specific military conventions. Flandin said that he was well disposed to authorizing General Staff talks on this point if the Duce would agree that the military implications of Italian commitments to France in the Locarno Treaties be made part of the same talks. Mussolini was amenable, and the two men made a verbal agreement that in case a threat of *Anschluss* forced an Italian mobilization, France would immediately send one or two divisions to reinforce the Italian army. In case the Rhineland were threatened by German military reoccupation, Italy would send several air squadrons to France's eastern frontier. Flandin, no doubt impressed by Mussolini's penchant for vastly inflating Italy's real military strength, noted that at this time the Italian air force was viewed as the best in Europe. Generals Gamelin and Denain were sent to Rome immediately upon the prime minister's return to Paris. Flandin also recorded that Laval was not enthusiastic about staff talks, since the latter did not want Germany to feel that there was a Franco-Italian military alliance in the works which would be directed against the Reich.[22]

In the meantime, talks between representatives of the Deuxième Bureaux had been continuing in Rome—concentrating on an Italian proposal for a comprehensive exchange of information on German remilitarization and mobilization procedures. The Italians had proposed that a direct liaison of the two would take place every three months, alternating between Paris and Rome, and furthermore that an Italian officer would be accredited, for renewable three-month periods, to the French Deuxième Bureau and vice versa. The French officer who was sent to Rome to receive the Italian proposals commented that "in the area of information on Germany, the Italian General Staff prefers genuine collaboration to a single exchange of information." At the same time the French minister of war had been preparing an initial response to the four cases outlined by General Badoglio in his original proposal of January 1935. General Maurin's recommendations were quite specific with regard to cases one and two (concerning German mobilization and aggression), right down to division strength and location. He instructed his military attaché in Rome to inquire about the length of time that would be required to get several Italian divisions up to the Franco-Italian border, thus allowing the transfer of French forces to the north. His response to cases three and four, involving threats to Austrian independence, was much less specific. Before any commitment of French forces in Italy could be made, France first needed a Yugoslav guarantee that French troops could operate on their territory. A similar guarantee from Czechoslovakia would also be desirable.[23]

The aftermath of the Stresa Conference brought to Paris the first intimation, in late April 1935, that the English had invited Germany to send a delegation to London to conclude a naval agreement. That prospect and the fear of Germany's reemergence as a naval power, accelerated the pace and the urgency of the Franco-Italian military conversations in Rome. On 13 May an air agreement between the General Staffs of the French and Italian Air Forces was signed. The agreement covered three areas of potential German aggression. In the case of German aggression against Italy, the accord established zones for air activity on both French and Italian territory and stipulated that each country would make landing fields available to the other. Total French air support would be available to Italy should the latter request it. In the case of German aggression against France, the accord provided for much the same thing in reverse. Should there be a simultaneous German attack on both France and Italy, full mutual air support from the designated air bases would be available. The accord further called for mutual cooperation in the coordination of strategy and transmission of personnel and materials, a comprehensive exchange of tactical and technical information, and for meetings between the two Air Force General Staffs at least twice a year. So far as the larger staff talks were concerned, General Parisot reported from Rome on 17 May that technical details involving the coordination of military strategy in Bavaria, Austria, and along the Italo-Yugoslav frontier still needed to be articulated. But aside from this, "virtually complete accord" had been reached between French and Italian negotiators on the exchange and positioning of military units with regard to each of the four "cases" developed originally by General Badoglio. The progress allowed Mussolini's enthusiasm for the future of Franco-Italian collaboration to reach almost lyrical heights in a major foreign policy speech to the Italian Chamber of Deputies.[24]

It would be excruciatingly tedious to catalog all the technical details of the General Staff negotiations that took place in Rome between April and June 1935.[25] Suffice it to say that enough progress had been made so that on 13 June the Italian military attaché in Paris brought General Gamelin, vice-president of the Conseil supérieur de la guerre, an invitation from General Badoglio to go to Rome to finalize "a definitive regulation of our military collaboration." The French minister of war notified Laval of the invitation on 17 June and was totally unambiguous in his recommendations to the foreign minister.

> From the military point of view, it [Gamelin's proposed trip to Rome] would have an incontestable value in clearly defining an eventual cooperation between the French and Italian armies. On the other hand, from a more general point of view, it would seem an opportune moment to profit by the initiative of the Italian government to reaffirm, in the form of an exclusively military conversation, our will to strengthen the Franco-Italian entente emerging from the accords signed on 7 January in Rome. A refusal would in effect risk delivering a telling blow to this entente, which is important to avoid in present circumstances.[26]

The Council of Ministers authorized Gamelin's trip to Rome on 18 June. The Franco-Italian military pact was signed a week later.

Given the significance of these military understandings, it is important to analyze their contents in some detail. The final accord took the form of General Badoglio's four-case construction of January 1935.

1. *First Case*—General German mobilization: No troop concentration would take place in the Alps, but France and Italy would exchange advanced infantry units "to affirm the solidarity between these two countries."
2. *Second Case*—German mobilization with an attack on France: Given assur-

ance of tranquility on its Yugoslav frontier, Italy would: a) send nine infantry divisions to the Nice area for transshipment north to the front between Mulhouse and Colmar and b) undertake an offensive in Bavaria by *"action brusqué"* on Salzburg, with the cooperation of two French divisions operating on the right flank in liaison with Yugoslav forces.
3. *Third Case*—Internal disturbances in Austria coupled with German mobilization but no intervention: A French batallion would be prepared and sent immediately to the region of Gorizia on the Italian northeastern flank.
4. *Fourth Case*—Internal disturbances in Austria with German intervention: A French expeditionary force of two divisions would be sent into the region of Gorizia in order to move, in coordination with Italian troops, into Klagenfurth basin. French troops would serve as liaison between Italian forces on the left flank and Yugoslav forces on the right.[27]

The plan was particularly attractive to the French General Staff. It obligated the Italians to assume a substantial offensive burden and also provided a striking example of the "front continu," linking the French Alps, through northern Italy, to Yugoslavia and Czechoslovakia. The French chief of general staff noted on 14 June that he had informed the chiefs of general staff of the Czech and Yugoslav armies about the possibilities for combined operations in central Europe outlined above, and "the latter made no objections."[28]

If Laval had been unenthusiastic about the scope and direction of the Gamelin-Badoglio military accords, this reluctance was not evident in testimony he gave before a secret session of the Senate in March 1940. At that time, no doubt irritated at the progressive erosion of France's strategic position in Europe, he described the Rome accords and the military agreements in glowing terms as "a veritable military alliance." That French security was immeasurably strengthened by these accords, that they symbolized Franco-Italian determination to maintain the European peace, and that Germany constituted the greatest danger to both of them could not be denied.[29]

Although the French chief of staff had notified his Czech and Yugoslav counterparts of the military accords and received no objections from them, Laval insisted that the staff agreements of May–June 1935 could not come fully into effect until after an Italo-Yugoslav political rapprochement. The latter became increasingly difficult to achieve, especially after Yugoslavia joined the sanctionist powers following Mussolini's invasion of Ethiopia in October. In fact, an Italo-Yugoslav agreement was not reached until March 1937, but by then Yugoslavia's continued adherence to the French security system was problematical. Thus, the French condition for confirming the staff agreements went unfilled. Gamelin later expressed perplexity at the timidity of the French government in this matter. But the military and air agreements nevertheless played an important and persuasive role in French foreign policy. Their existence, and the apparent military security they provided vis-à-vis Hitler's Germany, made the subsequent Ethiopian crisis a devilishly difficult dilemma for Laval. The League of Nations, with its Locarno corollary, had been the basis for French security since the end of World War I. To support Italian ambitions in Ethiopia would mean rejecting the League. But to support England and the League against Italy would be to squander all that had been achieved in Franco-Italian relations between January and June 1935. Warner has summed up the cruel situation that faced Laval in the fall of 1935: "This then was the real choice: the whole system of French security as it had evolved since 1919; or a new, perhaps more effective but as yet untried system."[30]

THE ANGLO-GERMAN NAVAL AGREEMENT

To have introduced the Ethiopian crisis in conjunction with the signature of the Franco-Italian military accords is perhaps to put the cart before the horse. The issue which really focused the dilemma for Laval and the French government was the signature on 18 June 1935, barely two months after the founding of the Stresa Front, of a naval accord between Great Britain and Germany. It is apparent that British diplomats, such as Carr and Simon—believing German territorial ambitions to be exclusively to the east—had little interest in pursuing further solidarity with the French and the Italians à la Stresa. Their preferred option was to achieve a bilateral deal with Germany on naval armaments. Why? Several reasons have been suggested. One, British concern about Japanese policy in the Far East made it seem essential to reach a naval understanding with Germany in order to limit Britain's naval obligations in western waters. Two, British leaders were concerned about Hitler's statements, later proved false, that the German *Luftwaffe* had reached parity with the Royal Air Force. They thought perhaps naval conversations might progress to the matter of limitations on air power as well. Three, Neville Chamberlain, then chancellor of the Exchequer, was anxious to balance the budget by avoiding a costly naval race with Germany.[31]

Other observers have suggested, with equal plausibility, that the primary motive for Britain's determination to seek a naval accord with the Third Reich was concern about the evolving political and military cooperation between France and Italy. A naval understanding with Germany would assure England's position in the North Sea, thus allowing England to augment its fleet in the Mediterranean to counteract any potential Franco-

Italian domination. An indication of the validity of this view is that, as early as 15 January, the British Admiralty announced that the annual British naval exercises in the Mediterranean for 1935 would be carried out by two squadrons rather than the usual one. After the exercises one squadron would remain at Gibraltar. An Italian troop build-up in Eritrea during the spring and early summer made it likely that the end of the rainy season in Ethiopia would bring about some sort of Italian military venture there. And thus the Admiralty felt it necessary to bring the Mediterranean fleet up to war strength.[32] It may well be that a combination of all of these factors was involved in the British decision to reorient her foreign policy. In any case, signatures were affixed to the Anglo-German Naval Pact on 18 June 1935. The pact allowed Germany to construct a war fleet with submarines up to thirty-five percent of the tonnage of the entire British navy.

It is well to remember that the British went ahead in spite of the expressed disapproval of both the Italian and French governments. Paris and Rome were informed of the impending accord only in mid-June. Mussolini responded on 15 June, refusing his approval and emphasizing that such things should be the subject of joint discussion. Léger drafted an identical response which Laval forwarded to London on the 17th. The official French response also added that the proposed Anglo-German accord would make it necessary for France to increase its own naval tonnage in order to balance the tremendous increases envisaged for the German navy. Herriot, minister of state without portfolio in the new Laval cabinet, expressed the concerns of many French people at the time. His papers contain a note in his own handwriting summarizing his impressions of the meeting of the Conseil on 18 June, when Laval read the official response. Herriot regarded it as "insufficient" and stressed the absolute "necessity of establishing that England has just broken not only with the Stresa accord and with the accord of 3 February 1935 [but also] with the policy of S.D.N. [League of Nations]. It constitutes a considerable historical fact." Even in retrospect, Herriot was able to confide in that section of his memoirs dealing with those days: "I have often defended England; this time I condemn her absolutely." Herriot's reference to the accord of 3 February refers to the agreement reached at the London Conference between Laval and Flandin and their British counterparts, whereby Britain praised the Laval-Mussolini Accords and announced its intention to consult with other nations if Austrian independence were threatened. The London communiqué also stipulated that neither France nor Great Britain would approach Germany separately on political matters—especially with regard to questions of rearmament. When the naval pact was formally announced, therefore, Laval summoned Clerk to the Quai d'Orsay to express his profound regret

MILITARY PREPARATIONS AND THE STRESA FRONT

and to point out that "this was directly contrary to the solemn pledge entered into on 4 [*sic*] February 1935."[33] It is well to emphasize at this point that the German Foreign Ministry shared Laval and Herriot's assessment of the larger meaning of the Anglo-German Naval Accord, but for that reason regarded it in a favorable light. An unsigned Wilhelmstrasse memorandum stated unequivocably:

> The success of the Agreement lies principally in the political sphere. In this respect its consequences should not be underrated. As a result of the Agreement the most powerful of our former enemies and of the signatories of the Versailles Treaty has formally invalidated an important part of this Treaty and formally recognized Germany's equality of rights. The danger of Germany's being isolated, which definitely threatened in March and April of this year, has been eliminated. A political understanding with Great Britain has been initiated by the naval settlement. The front recently formed against us by the Stresa Powers has been considerably weakened by the Agreement.[34]

It was quite apparent that French opposition to the naval accord between England and Germany did not carry much weight in London. Some evidence suggests that British policymakers believed it had been French intransigence at prior naval conferences which had prevented restrictions on submarine construction. They held France largely responsible for opposing modestly limited increases in German land and air forces, thus provoking Germany into full-scale rearmament in violation of treaties. All these things made it seem desirable in British circles to establish a ratio between Britain and Germany in naval construction—not so much as an indication that Britain sanctioned German rearmament but as a means of controlling and limiting what was now a fait accompli. That argument was advanced in Britain's offical response to French protests on 22 June, along with the gratuitous conclusion that "His Majesty's Government are convinced that in the long run the action they have taken will be found to constitute a real contribution to European, and especially French, security." That many in France, who believed the Anglo-German Naval Accord directed primarily against them, found British reasoning entirely specious needs no explanation. It has been pointed out, however, that some British policymakers feared that France, rather than Germany, was the big disturber of the balance of power on the continent—a fear exacerbated immeasurably by the Franco-Soviet Treaty of May 1935. Most British statesmen, with the notable exceptions of Winston Churchill, Robert Vansittart, Austen Chamberlain, and Anthony Eden, were pronouncedly anti-French and enthusiastically pro-German.[35] The Anglo-German naval agreement was overwhelmingly popular in England—as was the Munich agreement three years later; only Churchill openly questioned its wisdom, but even that not very vehemently, on the floor of the House of Commons.

Not surprisingly, old clichés about *l'Albion perfide* made their reappearance across the Channel. The Doumergue papers at the Quai d'Orsay contain a letter, dated 19 June 1935, which graphically expresses its author's contempt for "these dirty egoists, these pigs of Englishmen. . . . They are so jealous of seeing Italy and France united that they go off to make love to the Germans." The letter went on to point out the absolute necessity for France to become "very directly united" with Italy. On 16 July, in a telegram addressed to the French ambassador in London, Laval indicated quite clearly that German naval rearmament would oblige France to increase her own naval construction and perhaps to seek more extensive naval collaboration with Italy.[36] The naval accord, therefore, made continued good relations with Italy all the more necessary for France, since Italy was now France's only dependable ally in western Europe.

But there was another dimension to the French reaction to British policy, which directly links the Anglo-German naval affair to the subsequent contretemps over Ethiopia that would, in the final analysis, sever fascist Italy's relationship with the western powers. The pro-Italian, right-of-center press in France (i.e., *Le Temps, l'Echo de Paris, l'Intransigeant*) portrayed the Anglo-German Naval Accord as not only a betrayal of France but also "a betrayal of League principles," since the League of Nations traced its birthright to the peace treaties of 1919-20. They suggested further that Britain's action absolved France in the future from opposing Italian ambitions in Ethiopia in the name of the same League principles that England had so blatantly ignored when it suited her purpose to do so. Such sentiments were echoed at the diplomatic level by Noël, who wrote, "By this accord of 18 June 1935, it is permissible to say that they [the British] implicitly threw in the sponge on German land and air rearmament, formally contrary to the Treaty of Versailles. This same accord removed from Great Britain all moral authority to stand in opposition . . . to Italian ambitions in Ethiopia."[37] There is also evidence to suggest that, although Mussolini had protested against the naval accord, the Italians nevertheless came to view it as England's sanctioning of a violation of treaties. It is not too far-fetched to suggest that the Italians may well have come away from this affair with the impression that they could get away with the conquest of Ethiopia with impunity. It is difficult to avoid the judgment rendered by Donald C. Watt that the Anglo-German Naval Accord "is a sad comment on the order of priorities held by the Conservative government, on the failure and eclipse of the foreign office, and on the resulting lack of thought given to diplomatic considerations in the decade before the war."[38]

In an effort to short-circuit a potential breach in Anglo-Italian relations over the Ethiopian issue, Eden undertook a mission to Rome on 24–25 June 1935. On his way he made what he hoped would be a good-will visit to Laval at the Quai d'Orsay to assuage French anger over the Anglo-German naval agreement. Eden was authorized by his Cabinet colleagues to counter expected French arguments that the accord would oblige France to augment its own naval construction. Should that occur, Britain would be forced to consider naval increases also. The net result would lead to further escalation since Germany could then make proportional gains. Not unexpectedly, Eden found his conversation with Laval and Piétri "distinctly difficult." The French premier was under considerable pressure from some of his own Cabinet colleagues, especially Herriot, who regarded his note of protest to England "much too mild in tone." Since this part of his mission was ostensibly to calm the waters, Eden did not mention to Laval that he intended to raise before the Duce in Rome the so-called Zeila Plan. This was a British scheme designed to persuade Mussolini to abandon aggressive designs in Ethiopia. By it, Ethiopia would be accorded a corridor to the sea ending at the port of Zeila; the Italians would be compensated by substantial territorial concessions in the Ogaden. It goes without saying that Laval would have opposed such an arrangement, since an outlet for Ethiopia at Zeila would compete with the French port at Jibuti and destroy the commercial monopoly enjoyed by the French-dominated Jibuti–Addis Ababa railway. As it turned out, the Italians also rejected the Zeila Plan since it would have allowed Ethiopia a port and also a corridor for the supply of arms. The Italians were, in fact, much more favorably inclined to the Avenol Plan, named for Joseph Avenol who was then the secretary general of the League of Nations. It called for wheeling and dealing at Geneva to make it appear that Ethiopia was preparing aggressive action against Italian colonies. In the general confusion following the stormy Eden-Mussolini exchange, Italy turned more and more toward France. Confident of the Rome accords, the Italians "based their hopes on French friendship and on the clever policy of Laval."[39] Eden's mission to Rome was a total failure.

The Eden expedition did, however, serve to focus French attention once again on her relationship with Fascist Italy. The Italian ambassador in Paris reported to Rome on 22 June, shortly after Eden had left the Quai d'Orsay, that Léger had told him that the Briton had not so much as mentioned Ethiopia and that he [Léger] attributed his silence "to the fact that the Foreign Office has also had occasion during the past few days to realize that the Quai d'Orsay is not ready to follow it in its intransigence." Léger added that he had recently reiterated his opposition to the British point of view on Ethiopia in a conversation with the British ambassador. An even more important and decisive conversation, however, took place on the eve of Eden's arrival in Rome between the Italian undersecretary of foreign affairs, Suvich, and the French ambassador, de Chambrun, who had recently returned from consultations with Laval in Paris. De Chambrun began the interview by stressing his continued dedication to Franco-Italian friendship and then told Suvich that Laval had expressly instructed him to let Mussolini know "that he is remaining faithful to the political line fixed in the agreements in Rome. Neither England nor any other country will be able to disturb Italo-French friendship."[40]

Suvich then asked whether Geneva might disturb this friendship. De Chambrun responded that while it was clear that France could not oppose the League, nevertheless, Laval was confident that the Ethiopian question could be resolved without provoking too much trouble at Geneva and without the need for an Italian recourse to arms. Laval "will do everything he can," Suvich reported de Chambrun as saying, "to meet our demands and to help us obtain the results we want in a peaceful way." Suvich pointed out that it was likely that the Negus would be unable to accept Italian demands peacefully, to which the French ambassador affirmed that "in any case, France is with us in the Ethiopian question."[41] The importance of this conversation cannot be stressed strongly enough. It supports Laval's subsequent claim that he never endorsed a violent conquest of Ethiopia and it also underscores the continued importance France attached to the Italian link. Such full and open support for the Italian thesis undoubtedly made it much easier for Mussolini to reject categorically the Zeila Plan presented to him by Eden over the following two days.

Shortly after Eden's departure, on 27 June 1935, Generals Gamelin and Badoglio signed the text of the procès-verbal outlining the various contingencies for Franco-Italian military cooperation in the event of German aggression against either of them or against Austria. According to British sources, Gamelin also secured Mussolini's pledge to maintain the stipulated effectives and war matériel on his European front even in the event of a war in Africa,[42] a promise no doubt calculated to firm up Laval's resolve to obstruct British efforts to truncate Italian colonial ambitions. By late August those military arrangements began to take effect. The French started to transfer some ten to fourteen divisions from the Italian border in the Alps to the northeast. This enabled the Italians to remove their troops from the French frontier to the Istrian Peninsula and the Brenner.[43] The high-water mark of Franco-Italian rapprochement had been attained. All the negotiations leading up to the military agreements indicated that Mussolini was in favor of moving directly toward a Franco-Italian alliance.

There were those in France who strongly favored such a development, and subsequent events were to show that an alliance with Italy, even in opposition to England, would have been in France's interest. However, Laval was unwilling to go that far at this point. With Ethiopia looming in the background and with the legacy of the League of Nations as the cornerstone of French security, one can begin to recognize the dilemma that was to confront Laval for the remainder of his tenure at the Quai d'Orsay.

There were others who perceived the emerging dilemma more clearly perhaps than did Laval and who therefore looked with some concern at the European situation in the late summer of 1935. François-Poncet remarked to his military attaché that since Stresa, France had lost ground while Germany had gained. England, he believed, would do everything she could to avoid war and would continue to seek accords with Germany on air and naval matters while disinteresting herself in land army questions. What, then, should France's policy be, given growing German strength coupled with English neutrality? François-Poncet articulated the options:

> What is important for us to avoid is a German-Italian rapprochement which Italy no doubt will seek in order to have complete liberty of action in Ethiopia, play a trick on England, and even drop France if we don't frankly play the Italian game in the Ethiopian question.
>
> In this regard, we have the greatest interest in not harnessing ourselves to a sterile interpretation of a Treaty which still leaves the door open to an accord with Italy on the subject of arms traffic to Ethiopia.
>
> It would be desirable if the war were to expose the importance of the Franco-Italian accord and the serious military repercussions of a reversal in Italian policy.[44]

For François-Poncet, therefore, the events of June 1935, although disturbing in their potential for the future, still left room for maneuver with Italy on the Ethiopian question. Laval's reluctance to firm matters up with Mussolini may be partially explained in that he apparently saw in the more limited Franco-Italian relationship the shred of an opportunity for a Franco-German rapprochement. The latter would avoid the dangerous division of Europe into two camps, which he feared would be the logical consequence of English diplomacy. Laval also had received recently new assurances from Mussolini regarding Italy's respect for French interests in East Africa. Paul Baudouin, director general of the Banque d'Indochine, also had been in Italy in June, at the Quai d'Orsay's request, to negotiate the sale to Italian investors of shares in the Jibuti–Addis Ababa Railway Company according to the stipulations of the Rome Accords. While there, Mussolini gave Baudouin firm promises about respecting French interests and French property in Ethiopia—a message which he faithfully took back to Laval. Baudouin subsequently testified after the war that, at that point, officials at the Foreign Ministry seemed to be expecting an Italian military adventure in Ethiopia "but that they did not foresee such a thing in the near future."[45] It is clear that Laval miscalculated both the scope and immediacy of Mussolini's Ethiopian ambitions and his own ability to manage the Ethiopian crisis, whenever it occurred, in the League of Nations. Both errors of judgment were costly to French policy in the long run, but for reasons that cannot be blamed wholly on Laval.

CHAPTER 8

Ethiopia and the Fall of Laval

The Ethiopian question has hovered in the wings of this narrative through the last several chapters. It is now time to bring it center stage. An explosion of literature on the subject of the Italo-Ethiopian War and its origins has occurred in recent years—testimony to the importance diplomatic historians continue to attach to this tragic series of events.[1] Much of the literature is based on British and Italian sources. French archival materials for the 1930s were unavailable to these authors and, truth to tell, the primary documentary record for France remains remarkably thin. The inevitable result is that the French role in these events has been largely reconstructed through contemporary accounts and through British and Italian documentary evidence. It is not the purpose of this chapter to redo the work of earlier historians by reexamining the Ethiopian War in all its details. Rather, its purpose shall be the more modest, albeit important, one of articulating French policy toward Italy as it evolved during the second Laval ministry—illuminated wherever possible by reference to recently declassified documents and personal papers from the Foreign Ministry Archives and the Army Archives at Vincennes.

The Ethiopian crisis of the mid-1930s had been brewing for nearly a decade before the so-called Walwal incident of December 1934 brought the stormy relations between Italy and the East African kingdom to a head. A military clash with resultant casualties occurred at this isolated desert oasis in the ill-defined border region between Ethiopia and Italian Somaliland, an area under Italian occupation since 1930. When Ethiopia proposed arbitration of the dispute under the provisions of her 1928 treaty with Italy, the latter refused. Ethiopia responded with an appeal to the League of Nations. Unfortunately for Haile Selassie, this first appeal to Geneva coincided with Laval's visit to Rome in January 1935. In the wake of the Rome Accords, the French were understandably anxious to avoid any potentially embarrassing decisions in Ethiopia. The timing for Addis Ababa's second formal appeal to the League was equally unfortunate. It occurred on 17 March and thus coincided almost exactly with the announcement of Germany's unilateral rearmament.

Not surprisingly, the latter was regarded as the more pressing problem, and French diplomacy in the spring of 1935 concentrated heavily on building the Stresa Front against German treaty violations. However, the festering situation in Ethiopia presented a first-class dilemma for French foreign policymakers. To support Ethiopia in Geneva might add credibility to the League of Nations as a bulwark against aggression. To follow that line, however, would imperil the Stresa Front, the Rome Accords, and the buttressed security promised by the Franco-Italian military collaboration then in negotiation. On the other hand, Paris might offer unqualified support to Mussolini's ambitions in Ethiopia and thereby retain recently won Italian support in Europe. The price to be paid for pursuing that alternative, however, would be to erode further the prestige of the League and to prejudice France's relations with England, which suddenly had become more outspoken about strengthening collective security through the Genevan institution. Given the nascent divergence of views between the League's two principal members, it was not surprising that on 25 May 1935 the Council declined to take action on Haile Selassie's second appeal, suggesting instead that the Ethiopian dispute be left to the parties directly involved for a period of two months—a decision repeated in early August at the suggestion of Laval with Mussolini's concurrence.[2] The effort to shove responsibility for the resolution of the Ethiopian crisis out of Geneva lasted for some four and one-half months, until Mussolini initiated hostilities in October. This period preceding the outbreak of warfare, which also coincided with the signing of the Anglo-German Naval Accord, was the source of a great deal of bitterness and antagonism between Britain and France with regard to Italy.

THE FRENCH DILEMMA

The Ethiopian problem was to vex French foreign policy for the next few years and to destroy Laval's scheme for strengthening French security on the continent. It prompted the following comment from Colonel Fabry, minister of war in the Laval cabinet from 6 June 1935 to 24 January 1936: "These seven and a half months were sufficient to disrupt profoundly the conditions of French security. An exterior situation, which in June 1935 was the best that France had known since 1918, was turned inside-out like a glove; it had become by November 1935 the most disturbing." The exterior situation described by Fabry reflected a terribly divided state of public opinion on the emerging Ethiopian issue. Some, notably the antifascists, to the left of center in the French political spectrum, opposed Italian ambitions in East Africa and favored alignment with the English; they would not abandon Ethiopia, whose membership in the League of Nations had, after all, been sponsored by France. But others, notably the pro-Italians, to the right in the political arena, argued that since Ethiopia was such a marginally developed state, aggression against it would not really constitute a true war, but rather a simple colonial expedition. Italy, overpopulated and restricted by the Rome Accords in Tunisia, ought not to be prevented from doing what other colonial powers had done a generation earlier.[3]

The French position on Ethiopia was defined carefully over the summer of 1935. On 11 June came a direct Italian request for a clarification of French policy on the Ethiopian question. The undersecretary for European affairs at the Palazzo Chigi reminded the French embassy secretary, Hubert Guérin, that France's declaration of disinterestedness in Ethiopia constituted the key to all the African accords of 7 January, and that it was the only factor which enabled Mussolini to persuade Italian colonial circles to accept the accords. Now the Duce would like to demonstrate to Italian public opinion that the rapprochement between France and Italy would bear fruit and, therefore, he was awaiting "a gesture of friendship." The Italian diplomat went on to say that he understood and found legitimate France's concern not to break away completely from its general policy of collaboration with England, "but we hope no less that France will extend friendly aid in the realization of our aspirations in Ethiopia." Guérin recalled that Italy had categorically rejected a British suggestion in Geneva that all border disputes between Italy and Ethiopia be submitted to League arbitration. He said further that Germany was encouraging this division between Italy and England, and that the situation contained the further danger that Italy might be forced to turn toward Germany unless guarantees could be secured from France.[4]

Laval responded on 19 July with an unambiguous statement of French policy. He instructed de Chambrun to assure Mussolini of France's faithfulness to the Rome Accords and of her determination to further Franco-Italian friendship and collaboration. But Rome must neither encourage nor support an action that would be incompatible with the principles of the League of Nations. Laval pointed out that for the last fifteen years French security had been based squarely on the League and Locarno systems. Therefore, should Italy break with the League, it would create great difficulties for Franco-Italian cooperation and would leave Germany a much freer hand in central Europe. Laval promised to work hard at Geneva to encourage a climate of opinion favorable to Italian views on the Ethiopian question. He expressed confidence that England could be brought round to the French position. The French premier advised the Italian government to help its own cause by avoiding gestures or declarations in opposition to the fundamental principles of the League, and he concluded by urging Italy "not to create a situation in which our good will, as large as it is, would inevitably be paralyzed." The French position, moreover, was clearly understood in Rome. Aloisi, who was advised in advance of Laval's policy, remarked to his diary: "Laval wants to support us right down the line, so long as it is possible to avoid war and to carry the least possible prejudice to the League of Nations. It's not too much to ask." The Quai d'Orsay also made its stance quite plain to the British on a number of occasions. Léger, for example, showed the British ambassador in Paris a copy of Laval's instructions to de Chambrun. Clerk was impressed enough to inform the British foreign minister that this "would seem to dispose of the belief that Monsieur Laval has given Signor Mussolini a complete free hand to wreak his will on Abyssinia."[5]

France further clarified her position in response to a British initiative. Shortly after Eden's speech to the Council of the League in Geneva on 25 June, where he had denounced Italian policies and threatened to move the application of sanctions should war erupt, Britain tried formally to make common cause with France against Italy on the Ethiopian question. Paris was notified that any possible outcome of an Italo-Ethiopian war would be likely to hurt French interests. If Italy won a short war, her "opportunistic and incalculable" policies would become even more erratic. If the war should be long, the European consequences for Italy's determination to defend Austria would be brought into question. Should Italy be defeated, her foreign policy would be sold to whomever would help her. Financially, a war would be disastrous and would be extremely deleterious for the League. And finally, such a war would look bad among the colored peoples of Africa, and France had the greatest colonial holdings near Ethiopia.

British diplomats apparently continued to believe that France could be brought around to the British view of sanctions by appealing to a realistic assessment of Italian military realities. Orme Sargent, secretary of state at the British Foreign Office, maintained that Mussolini's decision to embark on his Ethiopian adventure dated from the moment he felt assured of French military support on the Brenner, that is from the signing of the Badoglio-Gamelin military accords in June. But, since Gamelin returned from Rome unimpressed with the condition of the Italian army and convinced that a short, victorious war over Ethiopia was unlikely, Laval surely must have thought about the effects that would be produced in central Europe if Italy got bogged down in a long, costly war in East Africa. "Once this alternative is admitted," Sargent concluded, "it surely ought to be in accordance with French realistic policy for M. Laval to do all he could to save Italy from her own folly, seeing that Italy, strong and efficient in Europe, is now held to be a *sine qua non* of French security."[6]

If these dire predictions were meant to sway France over to Britain's side at Geneva, they failed entirely. Laval immediately conveyed the British warnings to Aloisi. He later explained to Eden that so long as Italy maintained troops on the Brenner and remained faithful to the military arrangements just concluded—while Britain continued to refuse to enter any commitment on the continent—France had no choice but to support the power holding Germany in check. It is worth mentioning that during the summer of 1935 the Germans were acutely aware of the threat of a Franco-Italian front in central Europe implicitly directed against them and supported by Czechoslovakia and Russia, and they were understandably anxious to block its consolidation. Laval indicated to London that if the latter were willing to change its policies, if "it would give him assurance that Britain would be as firm in upholding the covenant, to the extent of sanctions, in the future in Europe as she appeared to be today in Abyssinia," then his government might be able to modify its staunchly pro-Italian stance in regard to Ethiopia.[7]

Such a change in the direction of English policy never materialized, and the acrimonious debates over the Ethiopian impasse continued. In mid-August, Aloisi arrived in Paris to negotiate with Laval and Eden some acceptable formula for a peaceful settlement of the crisis. Actually, Aloisi's instructions from Mussolini were quite unspecific, and he was there mostly to delay any concrete action. Laval proved helpful and supportive, but Eden would approve only those Italian actions which would accord Italy an economic free hand in Ethiopia—not political advantages. The three outlined a document for a solution along these lines, and Aloisi dutifully sent it on to Rome, knowing in advance that the Duce would reject it. In fact the rejection was categorical, saying that further tripartite talks would be useless. Mussolini concluded, however, by instructing Aloisi to thank Laval for his efforts and to assure the French premier that Italy remained faithful to the January 1935 protocols and to "frank and concrete friendship for France."[8] That the Italians were counting on Laval's efforts to control or at least buffer English intransigence can be inferred from the fact that, after Aloisi's return to Rome with his favorable assessment of Laval's efforts on behalf of Italy, Suvich addressed a personal letter to the French premier saying that Italy would do everything to cooperate on this matter. Suvich promised to remain at Geneva, to rein in the current anti-English press campaign in Italy, and to reinforce the Franco-Italian entente—"all things that will prove useful to Laval in his efforts to pressure the English." Why did the Italians reject British suggestions for a compromise settlement? Vansittart believed it was because Italian leaders had developed a strong contempt for Britain's military weakness. This was a common theme in the permanent undersecretary's view of the world, but he felt fervently that if Britain were stronger militarily, "the Italians would have jumped at the suggestion we have made to them and we would have got a very quick deal." Moreover, the French similarly would have had no misgivings about whether to support England and the League on the one hand or Italy on the other. Italian reticence could also be attributed to the conviction that France, fearful of driving Rome into Hitler's arms, would never countenance a policy of sanctions in the Ethiopian affair.[9]

The divisions among French statesmen and within French society as a whole surfaced dramatically at a stormy meeting of the Council of Ministers at the Elysée Palace on 28 August 1935. Laval opened the meeting with a pessimistic description of the Ethiopian situation, stressing the likelihood that Italy would resort to force to achieve her goals there. It was also likely, he said, that should war erupt, England would press the League Council to invoke sanctions against Italy. The prime minister stated his resolve to maintain peace; he was convinced that sanctions against Italy would intensify the war and that he was not inclined to go that route. Fabry strongly supported Laval, saying that sanctions would cost France Italy's friendship and would necessitate a complete revision of security plans. France would no longer be able to manipulate freely its army in the Alps or its army in Africa. Mediterranean tranquility would be disrupted. It would weaken France's position in Europe where decisive events would be likely to occur quickly should a European war break out. The British army could offer no substantial or sustained support in these contingencies. Therefore, Fabry opposed supporting sanctions against Italy, a position endorsed by other key military personnel—François Piétri, General Denain, General Gamelin, and General George, who was Gamelin's second in command.[10]

This view was immediately challenged by Herriot, minister of state and the leading Radical in Laval's coalition cabinet. He voiced approval for continuing to work as hard as possible for a negotiated settlement and suggested that violent (i.e., military) sanctions against Italy should be avoided. But, he added in sharp distinction to his anti-British remarks following the Anglo-German Naval Accord, if the Ethiopian issue ever boiled down to a choice between England and Italy, "I would not hesitate 10 seconds; I stand with G[reat] B[ritain]. Nor do I want to abandon the S.D.N. [League of Nations], the keystone of our security." Herriot recorded that never before had the fundamental conflict between his own views and those of Laval been revealed so sharply. Apparently, however, the president of the Conseil was unmoved. "I shall never vote for sanctions," he replied.[11]

The Laval-Herriot contretemps at the Elysée Palace served only to underscore the terrible dilemma facing French policymakers. It is well to recall that those who spoke out so affirmatively in the heat of Council debate were quite capable of modifying their stances in less emotional circumstances. For example, Piétri, who had opposed sanctions on 28 August, wrote Laval a personal letter in September reminding him of the absolute necessity of English naval support should a Franco-German war erupt. "It is always the sea that determines the outcome of conflicts," wrote the minister, who went on to affirm that "the least risky solution is that which will not separate us from England." With such contradictory advice, it is no wonder that Laval hesitated to adopt a single strategy. Instead, Laval instructed de Chambrun to inform Mussolini on 30 August that it was unlikely France could turn her back on the League and that, therefore, it would be wise for Italy to accept a compromise. Meanwhile, Laval and Avenol continued to polish the plan designed to turn the tables on Ethiopia at Geneva. Italy would assume the role of accuser, placing emphasis on Ethiopia's unfitness for League membership because of ill-treatment of minority populations. Laval also worked with Hoare and Eden to develop as benign a system of sanctions as possible should all efforts at a negotiated settlement fail. Laval in fact got along rather better with Hoare than with Eden, and the two were in fundamental agreement in September 1935 that should sanctions be invoked, they would be only limited economic sanctions, applied cautiously and in stages. Furthermore, no blockade of Italy or closure of the Suez Canal would be considered.[12]

During these discussions in Geneva, Laval again asked Eden whether the British government would be as firm in upholding the Covenant in Europe, especially in the case of a violation of Locarno or a German thrust toward *Anschluss,* as it was with regard to the emerging situation in Ethiopia. Eden replied that it would be "impossible" for Britain to pledge unconditional support for France in Europe. He said, however, that Britain's determination to uphold the Covenant anywhere would be diminished if Italy were allowed to violate it with impunity in East Africa.[13] Facing such obdurateness from Eden, Laval made one final effort to seek an unambiguous statement of British policy in Europe.

On 6 September, Hoare told the French ambassador in London that if Italy should attack Ethiopia, it was his judgment that Article 16 on sanctions should be invoked immediately. He inquired what France's reaction would be. Laval used this formal inquiry as the vehicle for a long telegram to London, with instructions that its contents be conveyed in their entirety to the British foreign secretary. Laval wrote that before he could make any categorical response to Hoare's question, France had every right to understand England's position clearly. More specifically, "in what measure and under what guarantees can we be assured, for the future, of English engagement of immediate and effective solidarity in case of a violation of the Pact [of the League of Nations] and of recourse to force in Europe?" England's answer to this question was essential in order to permit France to assess her situation in the complex Ethiopian situation. Laval went on to say that Hoare was quite right; if Italy attacked Ethiopia, then Article 16 on sanctions was applicable, and the premier himself had recently affirmed France's devotion to the principle of the Pact. "However," Laval continued, "when it is a question of a State which weighs so heavily in European politics as Italy, the French Government has the duty to be concerned about the situation of fact that the recourse to sanctions would create— that is, an aggravation and extension of the armed conflict which it would be important to the contrary to limit, in both space and time, should it prove impossible to prevent it." Warming to his task, Laval noted that England had not always adhered rigorously to the principles it was now espousing so insistently in the Ethiopian matter. Ever since 1921, all French efforts to strengthen the League had met with English opposition, and the recent Anglo-German Naval Accord was hardly consistent with the principle of collective security. Given all of this, Laval wanted to know if Britain would be prepared to invoke sanctions immediately if any European state (whether a member of the League or not) were to have recourse to unprovoked aggression. More specifically, what would Britain's reaction be if Germany took advantage of the Ethiopian situation to realize her Austrian ambitions?[14] Corbin raised these questions on 10 September with Vansittart, who promised to discuss them with Hoare; the latter was to prepare a detailed response.[15]

This is a very important document. Some have interpreted Laval's efforts to seek clarification of British policy as an indication that the Frenchman would have modified his pro-Italian stance at Geneva had continental guarantees from England been forthcoming—even to the point of swinging France over to the English position on sanctions.[16] There is, however, no solid evidence to sustain that interpretation and, therefore, no reason to doubt Laval's sincere and often-repeated support for Mussolini's goals in Ethiopia so long as they could be achieved peacefully. It is more likely that Laval was seeking assurances from England that would allow him to play his adopted role as mediator in Geneva with much greater confidence and conviction. Continental guarantees from England would have enabled him to push the Duce harder toward a negotiated settlement in Ethiopia. In their absence there was absolutely no reason for Mussolini to believe that Laval would sacrifice the solid security afforded by the Rome Accords and their military corollaries simply to deny him the fruits of a colonial adventure in East Africa.

While awaiting Hoare's official response to this detailed telegram of 7 September, Laval continued his rather tenuous tightrope act in Geneva, mixing his messages of support and good will to both the English and the Italians. On 13 September he spoke to the League Assembly and stressed France's loyalty to the Covenant and her determination to defend it if attempts at conciliation failed. He made a veiled reference to "close collaboration" between England and France "for the safeguarding of Europe," thereby distorting the degree of Anglo-French solidarity. The speech caused some concern in Italy and even prompted a cynical editorial in the semiofficial *Gazzetta del Popolo*. At the same time, the French foreign minister urged Mussolini to agree to negotiate on a compromise solution proposed by the League of Nations' Council of Five. The latter proposed that Ethiopia cede territories to Italy and then be compensated by territories ceded to her in frontier regions of Somaliland and French Somalia. At roughly the same time, Laval told Aloisi that France could not detach herself completely from England, but " 'my task remains the same: to minimize the measures that the English now want to adopt against Italy, while seeking at the same time to satisfy your demands to the greatest extent possible.' "[17] It was a timorous foreign policy, to be sure, but absolutely consistent. Such was the situation when the official English response to Laval's inquiries of 7 September arrived at the French Embassy in London.

Hoare's letter to Corbin, dated 26 September, was the product of substantial discussion and redrafting within the British Cabinet. On 11 September Hoare delivered a famous speech to the Assembly of the League of Nations in which he affirmed Britain's support of the League and emphatically asserted his country's determination to maintain the Covenant in its entirety. The speech received wide press coverage throughout Europe, and the ringingly delivered, albeit ambiguous, words were no doubt intended to serve a dual purpose—to allay French fears about British commitments in central Europe and to scare Mussolini into moderating his Ethiopian policy. The latter objective was pure bluff, since one day earlier Hoare and Laval, meeting secretly, had ruled out military sanctions and agreed only to the cautious application of economic sanctions. On 14 September, Hoare wrote to King George V that his conversation with "the cunning peasant from the Auvergne" ran certain risks since the French "invariably let everything out in the press." Nevertheless, this was worthwhile because "there is now no danger of finding ourselves in an isolated position without French support." Britain's concern about isolation at Geneva was genuine enough; it was discussed in the Cabinet and in numerous Whitehall communications. Hoare was also concerned to get some assurance from France concerning military and naval support should Mussolini unleash a "mad-dog act" against British ships in the Mediterranean.[18] These were the concerns that shaped Britain's official response to Laval's inquiry about her policy.

Taking the form of a personal letter from Hoare to Corbin, the document reiterated at great length the substance of the foreign secretary's 11 September speech proclaiming Britain's loyalty to the principles of the League of Nations. With regard to Laval's specific questions about Britain's adherence to collective security in Europe and especially in Austria, the foreign secretary wrote: "In conformity with her precise and explicit obligations, I have said before, and I repeat it again, the League defends, along with this country, the collective maintenance of the Covenant in its entirety *and particularly the steady and collective resistance to all acts of unprovoked aggression.*" Hoare went on to say that all of those emphasized words were crucial. He concluded, therefore, that it was "impossible" for any government to say in advance how it would react to a specific act of aggression without first examining the existence or lack thereof of any provocation. Furthermore, Hoare stressed the fact that this response had the full endorsement of the British Cabinet and—calling attention to the results of the so-called "Peace Ballot"—the overwhelming support of the British people as well.[19] The letter was released to the press and published in French translation by the Havas Agency on 29 September 1935.

One can imagine Laval's disappointment, not to say bitterness, at such a categorical and public refusal on the part of England to commit herself to solidarity with the Third Republic on the continent of Europe. Laval's specific request for a policy on Austria was ignored. Hoare's response had some interesting repercussions both in France and abroad. François-Poncet reported from Berlin that German officials at Wilhelmstrasse were preoccupied with the firmness with which the British foreign secretary had pronounced his loyalty to League principles in the 11 September speech. But following the release of Hoare's letter, some of the state-controlled newspapers in Germany (most notably *Deutsche Allgemeine Zeitung*) noted that England had not responded specifically to Laval's request for information on England's reaction to aggression on the continent and thereby concluded that, "England affirms herself hostile to the thesis of the status quo, favorable to revisionist doctrines and she pronounces herself in favor of a supple and elastic conception of existing accords." In France itself, the English response fueled the anti-English and anti-League bias of the extreme right. The Italian-subsidized Parisian press (i.e., *L'Echo de Paris, Le Matin)* multiplied the number of articles dealing with the danger of throwing Italy into the arms of Hitler if League sanctions were voted against her and the hypocrisy of England in supporting sanctions on Italy when she had not done so six months earlier in the case of German rearmament. Léon Daudet, in *L'Action française,* argued that it was not worth risking Italian friendship for the sake of an institution, the League, which he referred to as "that detestable saliva-slinging society." He continued: "It is this collection of gabblers and half-wits who have transformed a simple colonial expedition into the threat of world war. This bloody Tower of Babel, bristling with vanity and ignorance, this Tower of Babel with its Cecils and Hoares and Herriots and Paul-Boncours, should be destroyed as the Romans destroyed Carthage." Such overheated rhetoric, however, was characteristic only of the extremist factions of the French right. Charles Micaud has pointed out that the largest faction on the right, the *modérés,* reluctantly admitted the necessity of maintaining good relations with England and of supporting League sanctions against Italy if necessary.[20] Many moderates saw the connection—certainly clear enough to Laval—between the application of sanctions in Ethiopia and their potential application against a future aggressor in Europe.

Laval could have stepped boldly forward to side fully with Italy in the Ethiopian matter and thus carry out his threat never to vote for sanctions. A retrospective look at the events of the late 1930s suggests that French security would not have been any more compromised than it became, and might well have been strengthened, had he adopted such a course. To do so, however, would have risked the whole candle on a new and as yet untested commodity—Franco-Italian solidarity—and would certainly have destabilized the internal French political scene even more than it was already. General Gamelin, a strong advocate of Franco-Italian collaboration, looking back at the origins of the Italo-Ethiopian War, wrote the following: "The great error was having accepted the launching of the Abyssinian affair without having reached any precise understanding with the country which must be the basis of our combinations, that is Great Britain."[21] The record cited above demonstrates that Laval strove mightily to avoid the "error" mentioned by Gamelin. It was English policy which forced the French foreign minister to continue to pursue his apparently vacillating posture at Geneva after the Ethiopian War broke out in October 1935. He played virtually a lone hand but, thanks to London, with precious few high cards to distribute.

THE ITALO-ETHIOPIAN WAR

The Italian invasion of Ethiopia began on 3 October 1935. The Council of the League of Nations met on 5 October, and by the 11th the General Assembly voted that Italy had violated the Covenant and that, therefore, economic sanctions were in order. For Laval, as was indicated earlier, Ethiopia was purely an African matter. It was preferable to have the Italians occupied there than to have them stirring up trouble in the Adriatic. So long as French interests in the Jibuti–Addis Ababa Railway were protected, the Ethiopian operation should not be allowed to become a matter of great European significance. It appeared early on in the struggle that both Britain and France, for basically different reasons, were resolved to follow what George W. Baer has called a "double policy" of sanctions and negotiations designed to halt the Italian invasion without antagonizing Italy and without breaking its fragile links to the League of Nations. The thinking was that carefully applied economic sanctions would contribute to domestic dislocation in Italy, forcing Mussolini to accept a negotiated settlement rather than run the risk of losing control at home.[22] Critics have suggested that this double policy destroyed both the League and the Stresa Front. They are probably correct. But, at least for French statesmen, it seemed the best and least costly means of avoiding both war and the humiliation that would have derived from a failure to support the League on a matter of Covenant violation. Moreover, throughout the crisis, both London and Paris received hints that the strategy would work. There seemed to be no more viable alternative.

The decision finally to support Britain and the League on the issue of sanctions was a difficult one for Laval. It placed him in a very awkward situation vis-à-vis his own public in France. The extreme right was incensed; it wanted to pull back from Geneva and continue to pursue a solid working relationship with Italy. For them, the real villain was an imperialistically aggressive Great Britain. Moreover, although there was nothing similar in France to the British "Peace Ballot" of 17 June 1935, there were indications of a similar sentiment toward pacifism. A rightist group of French intellectuals issued a "Manifesto for the Defense of the West and Peace in Europe" on 4 October, while protesting in advance the application of sanctions against Italy. The next day a more moderate group of intellectuals issued a "Manifesto for Respect of International Law," which stated that it was the duty of the French government "to join in the efforts of all those governments which fight for peace and respect of international law." Some have viewed this as an endorsement of League sanctions, but the language was circumspect. And finally on 19 October, yet another association of French intellectuals proclaimed their "Manifesto for Justice and Peace," which condemned Mussolini's adventure in Ethiopia but which also said that they were prepared to accept an Italian conquest. A general conflict resulting from the Ethiopian crisis "would be a calamity for civilization and for the entire world; it would also be another crime against the peoples who would be involved in this tragedy." Only the political left in France was solidly behind a pro-League, sanctionist policy. Within the government itself, Laval was tied to the center. Radical Party leader Herriot was a member of the governing coalition and he was enthusiastically pro-League and pro-British. The president of the Conseil was also concerned how his government's reaction to the Ethiopian crisis would affect the prospect of civil conflict growing out of the activities of the right-wing leagues. It was within this complex and unsettled climate of opinion that the government made its decision to support sanctions against Italy at Geneva. It was an extremely reluctant decision to be sure, conveyed to English diplomats by Laval and Flandin on 7 October 1935. Both Frenchmen indicated that France would support an English motion to invoke limited economic sanctions but cautioned that cooperation should not be expected beyond that point. Given the state of political realities in the Third Republic, such reticence was not unanticipated. Ralph Wigram, head of the southern section of the Foreign Office, minuted that no French government, "either that of M. Laval, or of M. Herriot, or M. Blum or anyone else," would be willing to offer active and vigorous help against Italy. Vansittart, echoing a familiar theme, noted on 12 October that even half-hearted French support was better than nothing, because "we can never again be strong enough to stand alone." It was clear that Laval would work diligently to minimize the impact of sanctions and to make them as palatable as possible. As he told the foreign affairs committee of the Chamber of Deputies on 23 October: "It will be another ministry than mine that would propose military sanctions."[23]

Another factor which may well have undergirded French thinking on the matter of sanctions was the effort to put the best face possible on Hoare's letter of 26 September. On 3 October a long analytical dispatch arrived at the Quai d'Orsay from Corbin. The latter went through the document paragraph by paragraph, pointing out that the emphasized words had the effect of considerably diminishing the impact of those earlier sections of the letter which had so forthrightly stated England's adherence to the League. The whole crux of Hoare's message seemed to be that unless France went along with England on the sanctions issue, there was absolutely no assurance that England would be favorably disposed to support France in case of German aggression in Austria. Nevertheless, Corbin went on in great detail to outline the evolution of British policy since 1933, the proper context, he stressed, for understanding Hoare's note. In 1933 British policy had been isolationist and absorbed with internal problems. But by 1935 the British appeared to be coming around to a more expansive view of their world and European role. Given the results of the Peace Ballot, British leaders now seemed more willing genuinely to support the idea of collective security—even if they would not make specific promises about policies in the future. "In spite of everything," Corbin concluded, ". . . if in the wake of the movement of opinion launched by M. Mussolini's colonial ambitions, England recovers a clearer awareness of her world and above all her European mission, France . . . will be able only to congratulate herself on it."[24] Thus, when the British Cabinet declared on 2 October that England would not ask for military sanctions against Italy—largely because the French refused to go along with them—the decision was taken in Paris to support modest economic and financial sanctions should these be proposed by the British. Even this compromise solution met vociferous opposition from former French premier Flandin at the Cabinet meeting of 3 October. He remained a staunch partisan of the Franco-Italian entente and had less confidence than Laval in the latter's ability to play a successful role as mediator between London and Rome. In any case, keeping in step with the British on a scheme of diluted sanctions would allow France to moderate any potential British adventurism in the Mediterranean in the hope that, eventually, London would recognize that secure European frontiers were of far greater importance than African colonialism. In the meantime, Laval could assure Rome of his continued adherence to the Laval-Mussolini accords of the previous January along with their military extensions.

    The principal diplomatic question of the Ethiopian War, before the Hoare-Laval plan was articulated, concerned the question of French military support for Britain should the latter's ships be attacked by Italy while carrying out League sanctions. The issue first came to the surface at Geneva in a conversation between Eden, Massigli, and Robert Coulondre, who was the French Foreign Ministry's associate director of political affairs. They were discussing the concerns expressed by some nations, notably Greece, about measures that Italy might take against their commercial ships should they be involved in League sanctions. Eden's response was clear and immediate. The terms of the League Pact stipulated that member nations must comply with sanctions if they were voted by the entire body. Britain's League of Nations representative went on, in much more pointed fashion, to add: "However, for reasons I shall not go into . . . it would be desirable to have confirmation at the Foreign Office that the French Government interprets the obligations of the Pact in exactly the same way." Massigli replied that the answer to that question lay beyond his competence and would have to be raised through regular diplomatic channels. He added that an English demarche on this subject would be expected shortly.[25]

The following day, British officials raised the issue directly with Laval at Geneva. Would France be with them should an armed conflict with Italy result from the imposition of sanctions? Laval's response was the same as Massigli's—raise the question through channels. Some have argued that Laval, by brushing the matter aside, missed an excellent opportunity for a deal with the English. In exchange for his affirmative answer, he might have been able to get from the British those assurances regarding German aggression in the Rhineland and Austria that he had been unable to obtain earlier.[26] It seems rather more likely, however, that Laval saw British concern about such military questions as a device whereby he could rein in any danger of the overexuberant application of sanctions on Britain's part. He could thus magnify his importance as a mediator between London and Rome. Besides, Laval always could have floated the idea of a deal with the British at a later date. There were plenty of opportunities to have done so. But the documents contain no evidence that this was in Laval's line of thinking. It is also quite conceivable, given the premier's enigmatic personality, that he was not above giving the British a dose of the same kind of medicine he had been forced to swallow a month earlier.

The evidence also suggests that Britain believed French cooperation necessary to the success of League policy. French docking facilities would be essential in the event of an Italian attack in the Mediterranean. But during October and November Laval proved reluctant to give firm promises of French support. Whitehall raised the matter through normal channels on 14 October. Hoare instructed Clerk to secure from the Quai d'Orsay "a quite explicit assurance" that France would come to England's aid should the latter's ships be attacked by Italy while carrying out sanctions. He added that "We expect an immediate and spontaneous affirmative." Laval's informal response was immediate but hardly unqualified. He indicated on the 15th that France could guarantee military support only if an Italian attack "has been clearly brought about by application of provisions of [Article 16]," adding that British naval strength in the Mediterranean was so pervasive that the Italians might well regard it as provocative quite apart from the issue of sanctions.[27] Anger at Laval's attitude was evident in the British Cabinet meeting of 15 October, where it was suggested that a failure of French support in enforcing the Covenant might result in the breakdown of Locarno obligations: "If it was arguable that our reinforcement of the Mediterranean Fleet was so provocative as to enable Italy to attack us without bringing paragraph 3 of Article XVI into operation, it might be argued that in the event of a German attack on France the French fortifications and other defensive preparations were equally provocative to a German attack." In any case, Laval's ambiguity about French military assistance in the event of an Italian attack mirrored the French admiralty's reluctance to discuss cooperation with the British or use of Mediterranean sea ports, causing Prime Minister Stanley Baldwin to wonder whether France could be relied on at all. Both Laval and Gamelin seemed to regard the impasse as tantamount to a veto over any decisive British move against Italy.[29]

In fact there were some rather serious and practical explanations for France's delay in making specific military and naval commitments to Britain. Some seriously regarded the notion that an attack on British shipping by Italian forces might conceivably be motivated by fear of an imperialist rival who had amassed unprecedented sea power in what Mussolini regarded as mare nostrum. The British must understand that France would not go to war for the British Empire. There was also a further ironic dimension to the French dilemma, which was pointed out by Corbin. He noted that if Hitler decided to use the diversion caused by the Ethiopian crisis as the opportunity to thrust forth his ambitions toward *Anschluss,* France would be bound by previous accords to cooperate with Italy against Germany. Hence, should France guarantee England naval support in the matter of sanctions, France could end up supporting Italy on land against Germany while at the same time fighting Italy on the Mediterranean alongside England.[30] This was a rather farfetched scenario but not totally beyond the realm of possibility. In any case, the general expectation was that France could not delay indefinitely a formal response to British overtures for clarification of her policy.

On 18 October 1935 France reluctantly pledged military support in the event of "the possible attack by Italy upon Great Britain by reason of the latter's collaboration in the international action undertaken by the League of Nations and pursued in concert with France." This declaration was again far from the unrestricted guarantee sought by the British. It prompted Clerk to ask Laval a month later if Mussolini understood that, if he attacked a British battleship, he would be committing an act of aggression against the entire League of Nations. He requested that Laval make it known in Rome that France was *not* a benevolent neutral. Laval said he would do so and informed Vittorio Cerruti, the Italian ambassador in Paris, that there could be no isolated attack on the British. Hoare, concerned that Cerruti would tone down the message before transmitting it to Mussolini, asked Laval on 28 November to have de Chambrun repeat the message directly to the Duce. But a week later de Chambrun had received no such instruction. Officials at the British Foreign Office were furious. Vansittart said: "This is another instance where Laval is playing fast and loose with us. . . . This is in fact intolerable. . . . This is one of the points on which I think we must have it out with him in Paris." A major reason for British impatience was the Admiralty's insistence about the indispensability of French cooperation in the Mediterranean. Since Malta could not be used in the sanctions operation because of its vulnerability to Italian air attacks, and since the docking and repair facilities for capital ships at Gibraltar and Alexandria were deemed inadequate, access to French naval bases at Toulon and Bizerta was essential. The Admiralty also pressured the Foreign Office to secure a pledge from France, in the event of an Italian attack, to initiate air operations against targets in northern Italy in order to divert the Italian air threat to Malta and the Mediterranean Fleet.[31] Given Laval's doubts about the wisdom of the sanctions policy, the latter prospect was little more than a fantasy.

After some diplomatic feeling out, the French and British Foreign Ministries agreed to initiate staff talks to work out common policies of cooperation should either be attacked in the Mediterranean as a result of applying the Covenant in the Ethiopian crisis. Staff conversations between the two admiralties were initiated on 9 November and, in an effort to assuage British pique at French dilatoriness, were extended to army and air staffs on 9 and 10 December. While these procedures were being elaborated, Laval made every effort to assure Mussolini of their harmlessness. The fact that he kept the Italians informed about the nature of France's relationship to Britain is important. On 9 November, the Quai d'Orsay received an aide-mémoire from the Italian Embassy. The document acknowledged receipt of the French assurance that no military sanctions would be applied by either France or Britain—there would be no blockade, ship inspections, or closure of the Suez Canal. The Italians then went on to request more specific information from France on the nature of Franco-British commitments, and they requested an early exchange of views with France aimed at defining how the political and military engagements between France and

England "can coexist with the Rome Accords and the related Italo-French military agreements, as well as with the Treaty of Locarno and the Stresa Accords." At roughly the same time General Badoglio asked the French military attaché in Rome to assure him that the conventions he had signed with General Gamelin in June were still in effect.[32]

The French response was immediate, delivered in person to the Italian Embassy in Paris on 14 November by Léger. It stipulated the nature of the Franco-British military commitments under the auspices of the League of Nations, and Léger reminded the Italian ambassador that all this had been communicated to Grandi in London, and had been discussed with Italian naval experts during their last visit to Paris. But the French aide-mémoire went on to inform the Italians that "it must be noted that, practically, between France and Great Britain, the obligations indicated above could only be applied if Great Britain were attacked in the act of carrying out her collaboration with the S.D.N. [League]. *On the faith of the reiterated assurances of the Italian Government,* the French Government must insist that it is depending on Italy to avoid this eventuality and to maintain herself entirely within the law." The aide-mémoire maintained that France had fulfilled the obligations of Stresa and the Laval-Mussolini accords by keeping Italy fully informed of the Franco-British negotiations on the application of sanctions. While this document was being prepared, Laval instructed de Chambrun to remind Mussolini of France's continued efforts at good will ever since the Rome Accords of 7 January. France had done everything to seek a peaceful solution in Ethiopia, to delay the application of sanctions, and to moderate English demands at Geneva. Laval pledged to continue to work for a peaceful solution to the Ethiopian crisis in a sense favorable to Italy. In exchange he requested that something be done to ameliorate the anti-French tone adopted by the Italian press in the wake of sanctions.[33] Both of these documents, but particularly the emphasized part of the former, indicated that France had received assurances from Italy that the latter had no intention of attacking the British fleet. With these in hand, Laval could be reasonably sanguine about the limited military commitments made to the British in the event of an Italian attack.

THE HOARE-LAVAL PLAN

If sanctions by themselves were to prove ineffectual in deterring Italian expansionism, then Laval was left to play the other card in his "double policy" on Ethiopia. On 2 November he had told the coordination committee of the League of Nations that "we must endeavor to seek, as speedily as possible, an amicable settlement of the dispute. . . . I shall therefore stubbornly pursue my attempts—from which nothing will deter me—to seek elements that might serve as a basis for negotiations." These elements of possible negotiation were not difficult to come by. The fact that the Italians took initiatives along these lines only served to convince Laval that his Ethiopian policies were sound and that they stood a reasonable chance of breaking through the impasse without severely damaging Franco-Italian relations. On 16 October, for example, shortly after limited sanctions had been invoked, Italy submitted a compromise plan to the British and the French. Italy claimed: (1) a mandate or other form of administration over the peripheral zone of Ethiopia; (2) the outright cession to Italy of those regions that had been Italian before the humiliation of Adowa in 1896; and (3) control of Ethiopian armaments. In return Italy would cede the port of Assab as a commercial outlet for Ethiopia and would agree to respect the sovereignty of the Negus. Mussolini believed that in order for Britain to accept this plan, and then to coerce Haile Selassie, it would have to be actively championed by Laval.[34] Here then, on Italian initiative, was the basis of what became the Hoare-Laval Plan.

Two events combined to push Laval into a more energetic pursuit of this aspect of his policy. On 18 November the French military attaché in Rome reported that, because of the application of sanctions, Franco-Italian military conversations had been adjourned, although plans were still on the drawing board for General Mario Roatta's projected visit to Paris. When Laval revealed this information at a meeting of the Haut comité militaire at the Quai d'Orsay on 21 November, General Gamelin expressed his bewilderment at the government's lack of willingness to make concessions to Italy in Ethiopia and even along the Jibuti–Addis Ababa Railway. He saw the whole thrust of his pro-Italian policy being eroded away, and he feared that the ratification of the Franco-Soviet pact would alienate Italy even more and further disrupt France's already tenuous relations with the succession states of eastern Europe. Secondly, on 19 November the Quai d'Orsay received word that General Badoglio had been nominated to replace General Emilio De Bono in charge of the Ethiopian campaign. In his analysis, Parisot pointed out that Badoglio's presence in Africa would make it difficult for him to get back to Rome in time to deal with potential European complications. And perhaps even more important, "a sure and sincere friend of France . . . will no longer be present in the councils of the Government or the Crown to raise a voice in our favor if need be. Finally, it is he who represents so well here such things as balance, consistency and loyalty, primordial qualities which the French mind values above all others."[35]

These events were decisive. Laval began to push the British harder to work with him on the articulation of an acceptable compromise solution to the Ethiopian crisis before the issue of oil sanctions—certain to divide the two western powers—could be raised at Geneva. Thus, it is apparent that what came to be called the Hoare-Laval Plan was as much a device to relieve Franco-British tension as it was to resolve the Ethiopian War. Under constant French pressure, the main lines of the compromise proposal were worked out in advance between Vansittart and Grandi in London, and Laval and Cerruti in Paris, during the first week of December. While these were taking place, the Italians sent signals of their own through Poland as a third party. The Poles were requested to extend their support to Laval. Giuseppe Bastianini, the Italian ambassador in Warsaw, declared the matter extremely urgent and indicated that "Italy will accept any rational and reasonable entente." He also suggested that Poland contact England on this matter to stress the necessity for a compromise solution, pointing out that the Duce represented a bulwark against communism in Italy.[36]

Such was the background for the meetings that took place between the French and British foreign ministers in Paris on 7–8 December 1935, meetings which produced "the proposals which the Duce could not refuse."[37] The plan, presented by Laval to Hoare, offered Mussolini many advantages. It provided for nearly doubling the area of Italian Somaliland and increasing the size of Eritrea by the amount of land recently conquered by the Italian expeditionary corps in Tigré. In addition, a large zone in south and southwest Ethiopia would be offered to Italy in which the latter, acting under the League, would enjoy a monopoly of economic development. In exchange the Negus would retain sovereignty over territories not ceded outright to Italy and, as the Italians had themselves proposed two months earlier, Ethiopia would be compensated by an outlet on the Red Sea at Assab. Vansittart and Hoare agreed to the scheme on 8 December. The plan would be sent immediately to Ethiopia, to Italy, and to the Committee of Five in Geneva, which would be responsible for overseeing its implementation. Mussolini would then be notified that a failure to accept these proposals as the basis for an armistice and negotiations would certainly result in the application of oil sanctions. During the course of discussions, Laval argued forcefully against using the threat of oil sanctions, fearing this would increase the chance of a Mussolinian "mad-dog act." In the end, however, he acquiesced. Hoare noted, in his summary of the discussions, that should France be forced into military support for England in the Mediterranean, it would in all likelihood cause a political crisis in France.[38]

The British certainly were led along the road to cooperation with France because of their own feelings of vulnerability in the Mediterranean, due in part to Laval's vacillation in the matter of military guarantees. The First

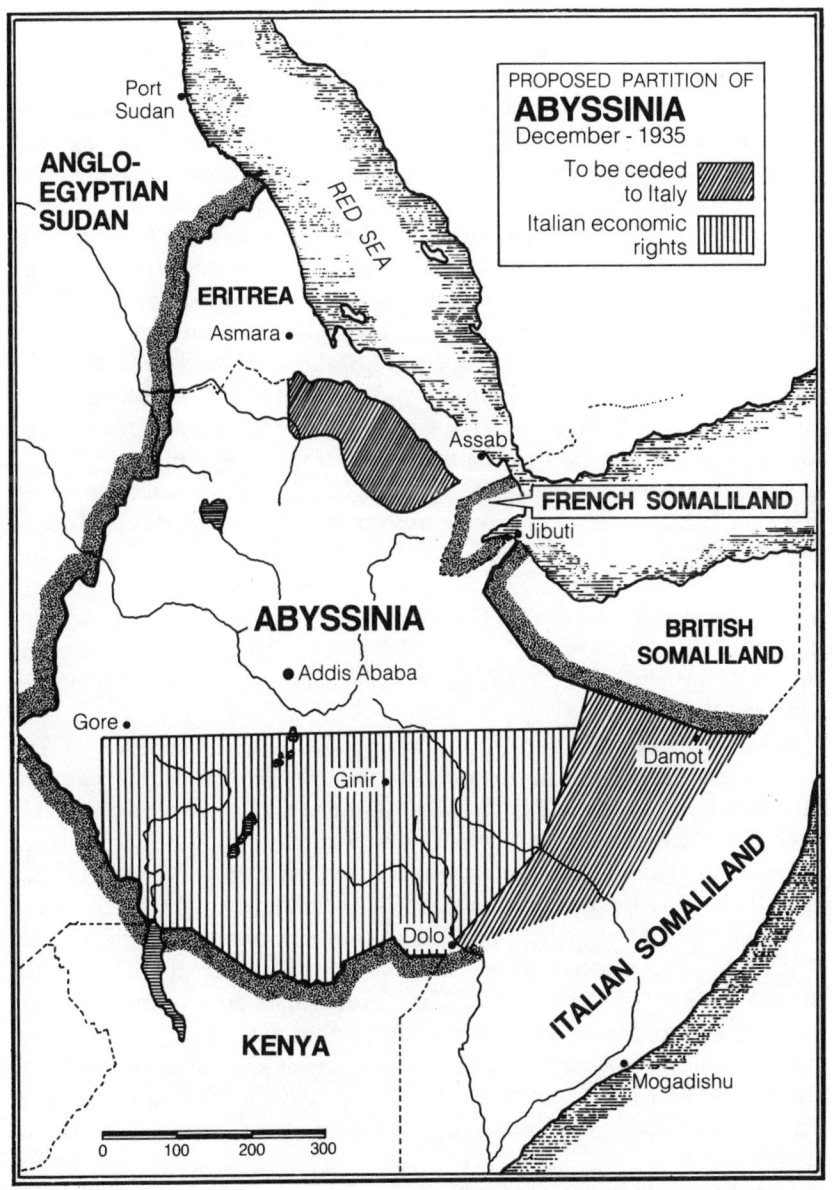

The Hoare-Laval Plan, 1935

Lord of the Admiralty, Eyres Monsell, spoke out strongly against sanctions precisely because he deemed a nonhostile Mediterranean essential to all strategic planning in the Far East, which depended upon reinforcement via the Suez Canal. At the same time he feared that a sanctions policy might unite the two fascist dictators.[39] If it had been Laval's purpose to rein in the English on the sanctions issue, then that part of his scheme was successful. On 10 December the British Cabinet met and agreed that if Italy accepted and Ethiopia refused to consider the proposals, the British government would neither propose nor support further sanctions "at once nor before it is clear that no chance remains of settlement by agreements." Rulings such as this certainly took the wind out of the sails of sanctionist proponents in both England and France. For these reasons, Laval thought the Paris proposals of 7–8 December a huge success.[40] He believed they would be acceptable to Italy and that France and Britain could then force Ethiopia and the League to go along. In the French Council of Ministers meeting of 10 December, only Herriot voiced opposition. He doubted that either Ethiopia or the League would find Hoare-Laval acceptable, and he demanded to know what France's reaction would be if Italy agreed to begin talks but Ethiopia refused. Laval's answer was simple and direct. Such a situation would create a possible way out of the dilemma the French had been in since the beginning of the Ethiopian War. France was under no obligation to Ethiopia should the latter refuse to cooperate on a plan endorsed by England, France, and Italy, and it certainly would absolve France from further participation in League sanctions, especially an oil embargo.[41]

Laval then played his trump card in Rome. On 10 December he instructed de Chambrun, in conjunction with his English counterpart, to present the Hoare-Laval Plan to Mussolini. Once this had been done, the French ambassador should talk frankly with the Duce in Laval's own name, emphasizing how hard the French premier had worked to get England to modify her position and underscoring the necessity for a quick, favorable decision. Furthermore, Laval continued, "after having led the British Government to the furthest extent possible, I have myself reached the extreme limit of my own effort. If this proposal for an amicable arrangement should fall through in spite of the substantial advantages offered to Italy, I don't see how my conciliatory actions could continue to be exercised." The Frenchman claimed the right to expect Mussolini to accept a proposition which would serve both the interests of peace and those of Italy.[42]

The immediate Italian reaction was to record only relatively minor objections. Aloisi noted on 11 December that Mussolini was prepared to "interrupt" the war, annex the territory promised in the Hoare-Laval Plan, and then wait for an opportunity to finish the job. The only apparent snag at this point was the oil embargo. If that could be postponed, then the Duce would accept the principle of opening talks. The first secretary of the Italian embassy in Berlin termed the Hoare-Laval Plan "an extraordinary success for Italy."[43]

So far, so good; Laval's policy seemed well on the way toward a costly but acceptable liquidation of the Ethiopian imbroglio. Then on 13 December, before the Italians had an opportunity to respond, the details of the Hoare-Laval Plan were published dramatically in two Parisian and one London newspaper. François Quilici, diplomatic editor for the Havas Agency, had received a copy of the plan from an unsympathetic secretary at the Quai d'Orsay and turned it over to André Géraud who, under the pseudonym of Pertinax, published the details in *L'Echo de Paris* and *The Daily Telegraph*. Geneviève Tabouis also ferreted out and published, in *L'Oeuvre,* the essence of the plan. The premature publicity and the resultant outcries of indignant public opinion, in both England and France, against the "moral outrage" of rewarding Italian aggression delivered a fatal blow to the Hoare-Laval Plan. This was not apparent immediately, however. In spite of the untimely disclosure, the evidence suggests that the Italians were inclined to accept the plan. De Chambrun asked Aloisi on 17 December if the Italians would accept the project, and Mussolini's chief of staff responded that the answer was probably yes. The French air attaché in Rome reported that at first the Franco-British proposals had been welcomed by Italian diplomats with "unconcealed satisfaction." The fact that they had been presented as the basis for negotiations left open the possibility that through pourparlers, Italy would be able to reach an even more favorable settlement.[44]

As late as 18 December Mussolini was inclined to accept Hoare-Laval as the basis for a negotiated settlement of the Ethiopian crisis. He had planned to make that recommendation to the Fascist Grand Council at its meeting on 20 December. On the night of 18–19 December, however, came the shattering news of the resignation under pressure of Sir Samuel Hoare.[45] Tantamount to a repudiation of the policy that had given birth to the Hoare-Laval Plan, Parliament's acceptance of the foreign secretary's resignation effectively killed it as a viable diplomatic option. "What a pity," Aloisi remarked to his diary.[46] Laval made one final desperate attempt, through direct communication with Mussolini, to save the essentials of his policy. In a secret letter to the Duce, dated 22 December, the president of the Conseil regretted the fact that Mussolini's delay in responding had undercut his efforts to reach a compromise solution, but the day might yet be saved by "an immediate adhesion" to the details of the proposal. The Duce penned his response on Christmas Day. He explained that a matter of such importance required deliberation and careful consideration, and then he added (in a phrase that must have rankled at the time but which Laval later cited to justify his foreign policy) that had it not been for the premature publicity and the consequent political turmoil, "the [Italian] response would not have been unfavorable."[47] It is also worth noting that Hitler, upon being informed of the details of the Hoare-Laval Plan, remarked to the French ambassador in Berlin, "I don't understand Mussolini's attitude. He should have accepted these propositions right away. It was an unhoped for opportunity."[48]

The full impact of the way in which the Hoare-Laval Plan failed can be illustrated in an interesting counterpoint of clashing perspectives—one English and one French. Lord Robert Cecil, an ardent spokesman for the League of Nations, told the House of Commons:

> I am deeply grieved at the attitude of France. If we are to be asked to defend France in the event of treaties being broken, France must realize . . . that what applies to the German goose applies equally to the Abyssinian gander. The half-hearted action of France about the Italian-Abyssinian war has gravely chilled our friendship. We do not like the way the French treat the League as a sort of particular umbrella, valuable for keeping France out of the wet, but when not so needed to be rolled up and used only for gesticulation. . . . We shall keep our word to France; yet keeping faith is something different from friendship.

A corresponding bitterness surfaced among French policymakers who held Britain largely to blame for the failure of a scheme that might have foreshortened the war. Jules Blondel, the French embassy counsellor in Rome, wrote in his memoirs:

> Under pressure from "Leaguist" elements in the Cabinet and from parliamentarians in Westminster, who reflect the opinion of old women and pastors so powerful in Albion, the leader of the Foreign Office, Sir Samuel Hoare, surrenders his portfolio to the minister until then charged with the affairs of the League of Nations, Anthony Eden, who does not approve of his attitude in the Ethiopian matter. Thus, the bitter-sweet solution . . . is turned aside, the path remains open, conquest beckons the aggressor.[49]

The domestic fallout over the Hoare-Laval Plan reached a crescendo in stormy sessions of the Chamber of Deputies on 27 and 28 December 1935. Yvon Delbos, a leading member of the Radical Party and a stalwart proponent of the Popular Front coalition, introduced a motion of censure against Laval and followed it with a ringing speech denouncing the foreign minister's policies as having led France into a "dead end," upsetting everyone without satisfying Italy. He urged a "return to the spirit of the Covenant by preserving the agreement with nations gathered at Geneva." Delbos's stand may have been a significant factor in Blum's decision six months later to offer him the Quai d'Orsay. Other leading political lights from the center and left joined the fray. Reynaud, then president of the Center Republican Party, excoriated Laval in a lengthy anti-Italian and antifascist speech. He pointed out that Hoare had accepted the Hoare-Laval Plan not to reward the Italian aggressor but primarily to save the League of Nations. The latter had been put in peril because of France's refusal to guarantee military support to the British fleet in the Mediterranean should the latter be attacked by Italy while carrying out its sanctionist mission. Reynaud applauded the good sense of the English people for forcing the withdrawal of Hoare-Laval, and he urged the French people and French leaders to abandon the wooing of Italy and seek collective security with England in a common determination to "halt the aggressor." Blum, leader of the Socialist Party, also vented his disgust with the fruits of Laval's efforts, decrying the fact that they had resulted in an almost complete isolation of France in world opinion. The socialist leader also predicted that in the long run, Laval's policies would generate in Italy "more resentment against France than against those powers which took the lead in the movement for sanctions."[50] All these statements were applauded energetically from the left side of the Chamber.

Laval responded to his critics with a ringing defense of his foreign policy. He made no apology for the Hoare-Laval Plan, the essence of which he still regarded as crucial to ending the Italo-Ethiopian War and thus safeguarding the Rome Accords of January 1935 and their military corollaries. These, he insisted, were vital to French security in Europe, given England's evident lack of interest in such continental matters. Laval also stressed that there had been no secret bargains with Mussolini about a carte blanche in Ethiopia. He had pledged only a French "désistement économique" in that country. "Nothing in the records nor in the conversations that preceded and followed them could have encouraged Italy to have recourse to war." The foreign minister's rhetoric proved decisive. Delbos's motion of censure went down to defeat by a vote of 297 to 276, a count which found nearly one-third of the Radicals in support of the government. Shortly thereafter a motion of support for Laval's policies passed the Chamber by the relatively more comfortable majority of 304 to 261.[51] In the end, of course, votes are more conclusive and convincing than overheated rhetoric. The vote of 28 December demonstrated that there was still substantial support in France for a pro-Italian foreign policy which promised a great deal in the way of military security for France in Europe.

Moreover, there is evidence that Laval's policies enjoyed the support of one of France's most important allies in eastern Europe. On 3 January Dr. Milan Stojadinovich, the Yugoslavian minister of foreign affairs, informed the French minister in Belgrade that England had recently raised three questions with the Yugoslav government: (1) Was Yugoslavia disposed to come to England's aid (under paragraph 3 of Article 16 of the League Pact) should the English fleet be attacked by the Italians? (2) Was Yugoslavia prepared to inform the Italian government of its affirmative response to the first question? and (3) In case of war, would Yugoslavia put at the disposal of the British Admiralty its coasts, docks, and ports? Stojadinovich told the French minister, Dampierre, that Belgrade had given an affirmative response to England to the first question; Yugoslavia was a member of the League of Nations and thus accepted full responsibilities of membership. But Belgrade could not respond affirmatively to the second and third. Yugoslavia, with French support, had worked too hard to establish its March 1935 agreement with Italy to put it in peril by agreeing to number two. Number three would be viewed by Italy as an act of aggression and, since Yugoslavia shared a border with Italy, it would put this small country at the mercy of the Italian army. The Yugoslav foreign minister concluded by saying: "'You can tell M. Laval that I shall undertake no unilateral engagement with England, and that I shall follow France in this entire affair. In addition, the French Government will be very precisely informed of the result of any conversations embarked upon between the English and Yugoslav Governments.'" On the anniversary of the signing of the Laval-Mussolini Accords, the French military attaché in Rome reviewed the general tone of the Italian press. The latter was still inclined to look favorably upon the Italo-French relationship despite the inevitable tensions raised by the sanctions issue. "'It is also necessary to pay homage to the efforts made by M. Laval, and sustained by a portion of French public opinion, to ward off the crisis.'"[52]

All of these indications lead to the conclusion that dissatisfaction with Laval's foreign policy was not a principal factor in the demise of his Cabinet on 23 January 1936, as Blum claimed later. Laval's coalition government depended upon support from the large faction of Radicals in the Chamber of Deputies. His Council of Ministers contained six Radicals, including Herriot. When the latter resigned from that party's chairmanship on 18 December, he was succeeded by Daladier, then an enthusiastic champion of the Popular Front. With national elections scheduled for May 1936, pressure mounted upon the Radical ministers to resign in order for the party to position itself for an electoral coalition with left-of-center forces. That strategy became apparent when the Popular Front program condemning the government's domestic and foreign policies, drafted with Radical participation, was published in January. On the 22nd four of the six Radical ministers, including Herriot, submitted their resignations to the prime minister. Rather than face the humiliation of losing a vote of confidence in the Chamber, Laval resigned the following day.[53]

ASSESSMENT OF LAVAL'S ETHIOPIAN POLICY

How can one assess Laval's foreign policy? He issued a personal statement to the press the day after his resignation. Reviewing his government's foreign policy accomplishments, Laval concluded: "Peace has been maintained. Our obligations toward the League of Nations have been kept. Our friendships and our alliances are intact. The independence of our foreign policy is assured and strengthened. . . . France remains mistress of her destiny."[54] One need not accept such statements at face value in order to understand, and even tolerate, a politician's need to defend his record. Yet most scholarly assessments conclude that Laval's diplomacy was an utter failure. It has been blamed for weakening the League of Nations and for unnecessarily provoking British irritation and thus impeding effective cooperation between the two western democracies in the face of fascist provocations. He has been accused of making public statements to the effect that French military forces should only be used to defend French borders, thereby virtually declaring France's abandonment of her eastern European allies.[55] Some have gone so far as to suggest that France's failure to support England energetically in the matter of sanctions had the effect of determining the direction of British foreign policy for the future. Thus Laval's policies led inexorably to England's lackadaisical response to the *Anschluss* and to the problem of the Sudeten Germans. The latter is an astonishing judgment. Laval, who languished in the political wilderness for two and one-half years prior to September 1938, is blamed for the Munich fiasco! More recently some eminent French scholars have moderated, if ever so modestly, such totally negative assessments.[56] Yet such is the unrelieved blackness of his historical reputation that he is still regarded as something of a nonperson at the Quai d'Orsay. The corridors of the French Foreign Ministry display the portraits or photographs of nearly all those individuals who held the position of foreign minister since the inception of the modern diplomatic service in the Renaissance. Even the likeness of such a nonentity as Edmond Lefebvre du Prey, who held the portfolio for a grand total of three days in 1924, can be found. One will search in vain, however, for Laval—not even a blank space on the wall is evident. It is as though his tenure at the Quai d'Orsay had been thrust into an Orwellian memory hole.

From the evidence cited in this and the previous two chapters, together with the analysis of the immediate aftermath discussed in the next, it must be apparent that the judgments of Laval's severest critics are unwarranted, that they were, perhaps, influenced by the undeniable moral failings of Laval the collaborator during World War II.[57] It may well be true that Laval hoped his policies would result in an eventual rapprochement with Germany, but one based on a position of strength rather than craven submission. To be sure there were weaknesses. French diplomacy in the Laval era was guided by the need to keep Italy separate from Nazi Germany—a not unlaudable objective. It is evident that Mussolini sincerely sought an alliance with France, even during the early months of sanctions, and the German ambassador in Rome reported to Berlin well after the failure of Hoare-Laval that Laval's initial victory in the Chamber was received by Italian leaders with "keen satisfaction. . . . Although France is one of the sanctions powers, she is being courted, especially in the press, in an unworthily seductive way," thus illustrating the "indomitable hopes" Italy continued to place on France. Given this state of affairs, perhaps Laval should have made it absolutely clear to the British in the spring of 1935, when they were still vacillating, that Franco-Italian solidarity would not be breached because of a colonial expedition in East Africa. Had that line been taken early, it might have been able to prevent Franco-Italian relations from sliding into intransigence. Then, instead of voting for sanctions according to Article 16 of the Covenant, it would have been preferable to insist on applying the less stringent requirements of Article 15, as had been the case in the Sino-Japanese conflict of 1931. This probably would have satisfied Mussolini and, to a certain degree, saved the face of the League. Laval, unfortunately, did neither of these things. He voted for sanctions and then hindered their effectiveness, even permitting the Italian expeditionary corps to use the railroad linking the French Somaliland coast to Addis Ababa.[58] But it was precisely because Laval had deep and well-founded doubts about Britain's willingness to defend French security on the continent that he was led to pursue the course he did. Subsequent events were to show that the loss of the pro-Italians' influence at the Quai d'Orsay, following the resignation of Laval, was to cost France very dearly indeed.

Shortly before he resigned, Laval penned a personal letter to Mussolini. In it he reviewed the events of the previous year and acknowledged that Italy had legitimate claims in Ethiopia. He repeated, however, that his use of the expression "mains libres" at their meeting of 6 January 1935 did not mean that he countenanced war and conquest. He had used that common expression simply to confirm the view that Ethiopia was reserved for Italian economic exploitation. Laval closed as follows:

> I do not want to leave the Quai d'Orsay without repeating to you the deep satisfaction I experienced in signing the Rome accords with you. If, because of circumstances, they have not yet been able to bear all their fruit, I remain convinced that they represent the solid and durable basis of Franco-Italian friendship, and at the same time an essential factor of European peace.
>
> French opinion interprets them this way as well, and I express my fervent desire that nothing ever alter this mutual confidence that we both place in this completed foundation.[59]

There is no reason to doubt Laval's sincerity. Subsequent events, moreover, suggest that continued loyalty to the Italian conection—even in open opposition to England—would have served French interests rather better than the course ultimately adopted by Laval's successors.

CHAPTER 9

Sanctions, the Rhineland Crisis, and the Inception of the Popular Front

Laval's fall from power complicated the Franco-Italian situation considerably. There can be no doubt that with Laval's resignation the pro-Italians at the Quai d'Orsay lost their most ardent and effective spokesman, and relations with Fascist Italy subsequently deteriorated—to the detriment of both countries. The installation of a new government, however, did not betoken any sudden alteration in French foreign policy, an indication that the reversal of the Laval cabinet had little to do with general dissatisfaction with his diplomacy. The great change would occur only after the electoral victory of the Popular Front in May 1936. For the moment Sarraut formed a new government and immediately appointed Flandin to the Quai d'Orsay. Flandin had been president of the Conseil for some seven months following Barthou's assassination and had worked closely with Laval in charting the course which led to the Rome Accords and their related military understandings. He has been described as a pompous and pretentious version of Laval, who, primarily because he had not been directly associated with the discredited Hoare-Laval Plan, could afford to be even more outspokenly conciliatory toward Mussolini than his predecessor had been.[1]

At best the Sarraut ministry could be regarded only as a caretaker government, which would maintain a pretense of political unity until the scheduled elections in May. The rising political fortunes of the left in France, particularly the socialists with their pronounced antifascist ideology, could not but be a source of concern to Mussolini. The latter's foreign policy appeared to veer erratically between France and Germany during the first half of 1936. The Ethiopian War and the failure of the Hoare-Laval Plan had placed a heavy burden upon the spirit of the Rome Accords, and it was perhaps only natural that Italy would seek to avoid isolation by tilting toward Berlin. Yet, at the same time, some Italians continued to regard close relations with the western powers as essential to Italian security. Suvich feared that Italy's distraction in Ethiopia might encourage Germany to seize Austria. Should that occur, Italy would have no choice but to become aligned with Germany's enemies. Suvich believed that once Germany installed herself on the Brenner, barely 100 kilometers from the Adriatic, she would aim to become a Mediterranean power.[2] The concern for security on Italy's northern frontier, coupled with the desire for recognition of its imperial conquests in Ethiopia, help to explain the apparently bewildering oscillations of Italian foreign policy during this period. It was against this scenario that French policy, weakened by the uncertainties of the domestic political situation and the lack of support from England, lost its best opportunity to capitalize on Mussolini's fundamental distrust of Hitler to resurrect the Rome Accords and the Stresa Front.

During the first two months of 1936, French diplomats increasingly became concerned about an apparent orientation of Italian policy toward Germany. On 26 January, in an unsigned article in *Popolo d'Italia,* the Duce expressed his indignation at the publication of the Anglo-French Declaration of Mutual Assistance in the Mediterranean by hinting at a redefinition of Italy's obligations under the Treaty of Locarno. He regarded the Declaration as directed against Italy and maintained that it was not permissible for a guaranteed power (France) to conclude military agreements with a guarantor (England) to the detriment of a second guarantor (Italy). Such actions jeopardized the whole structure of Locarno. Mussolini's views were reflected further in an inspired article by Virginio Gayda in *Giornale d'Italia.* He regarded the Franco-British Declaration of Mutual Assistance as a major shift in French policy, perhaps concealing a full-scale secret military accord involving French support to England in the Mediterranean against Italy in exchange for a British pledge to support France in the event of German aggression. Gayda's broadside, coupled with Mussolini's article, prompted an immediate reaction from Léger. The French secretary general instructed de Chambrun to deny such allegations and to remind the Italian government that it had been kept fully and precisely informed of all Anglo-French negotiations dealing with the application of paragraph 3 of Article 16 of the League pact on sanctions. France remained loyal to Italy; no further secret agreements existed. These Italian journalistic manifestations were confusing in that, just two days earlier, Mussolini had told the French ambassador that he was prepared to work closely with France to rebuild the Stresa Front as soon as circumstances permitted and that, with regard to the continuation of friendly relations between France and Italy, *"his will had never varied."* [3]

A month later, Mussolini told the German ambassador in Rome that France was passing more and more into the hands of the left, and consequently relations between France and Italy were deteriorating steadily. Stresa, he said, was dead, and Locarno, as an appendage of the League of Nations, would wither of its own accord the moment Italy withdrew from Geneva. During this period, French officials in Rome warned their superiors in Paris that France's policy on sanctions was driving Italy toward Germany. Although Suvich and Aloisi assured the French ambassador that such was not the case, de Chambrun nevertheless reported to the Quai d'Orsay on 20 February 1936 that "one thing appears certain. M. Mussolini, who just a short while ago expressed to me his desire to rejuvenate the policy of Stresa, today seems inclined toward a return to the spirit of the Four-Power Pact."[4]

Italian policy was ambivalent. No doubt Mussolini's hints about a possible breakup of Locarno played well in Berlin, but his critique of the 1925 agreements had been expressed in such a way as to imply that he would continue to cooperate with France provided the latter would use her influence to deflect the League of Nations from extending sanctions. Clearly, France's ability to influence England on the issue of an oil embargo held the key to future Franco-Italian relations. Aloisi told de Chambrun on 24 February that Italy would denounce the military accords with France if the latter adhered to oil sanctions. Furthermore, the Italians explained that "the application of oil sanctions at this point in time would be not only an odious gesture but also a useless one since, given the march of events, they would not hinder our advance in Ethiopia while they would risk ruining Franco-Italian friendship." De Chambrun reported this conversation to the Quai d'Orsay, and he added his personal conviction that French support for oil sanctions would prejudice the Franco-Italian military accords and would force Italy to withdraw from the League of Nations and frankly orient herself toward Germany.[5]

Mussolini reinforced earlier warnings in a conversation with the French ambassador on 27 February. The Duce assured de Chambrun that, although sanctions had been burdensome for Italy, he had not wavered in his support for the policy of Stresa. But, the fascist leader continued, the voting of oil sanctions would occasion a radical change in Italian policy and force Italy's withdrawal from the League of Nations. The real problem at Geneva, as he saw it, lay with the small nations. He suggested that France use her influence among them to dissipate their apprehensions about Italy and to persuade them that their security depended on Italy's remaining in the League. The Duce indicated further that if the oil embargo could be avoided, Italy would then be in a position to negotiate a settlement of the Ethiopian War with Haile Selassie, which would protect a portion of his sovereignty. "Everything is possible," he concluded, "if new sanctions are not applied." De Chambrun's telegrams and dispatches show that he supported an end to sanctions, and that he believed Mussolini a partisan of closer Franco-Italian relations. The ambassador's views were shared by the military attaché in Rome. The latter, in reporting the Mussolini-de Chambrun conversation to the Deuxième Bureau, said that France must act quickly to control rising German influence in Rome and concluded, "I persist in my personal impression that Mussolini continues to lean clearly toward France, and that he will play the German card only as a last resort if he considers it impossible to do otherwise. But I also know that Germanophile elements in this country are redoubling their activities, even in the General Staff where our influence over them is more difficult now that Marshal Badoglio is in East Africa."[6]

The impressions of French representatives in Rome only served to confirm Flandin's own views on the Italian question. Although not an advocate of encircling Germany and unenthusiastic about risking war to defend Austria, Poland, Czechoslovakia, and the Soviet Union, the foreign minister was sensitive about maintaining French defensive capabilities. The loss of the Franco-Italian military accords would make it necessary for France to defend her frontier with Italy, thus weakening the watch on the Rhine. The issue of the continued validity of the Locarno treaties was especially acute for France at this moment, as indications pointed toward some Hitlerian coup de théâtre in the Rhineland. On 3 March 1936, reacting to the British government's announcement that it favored an oil embargo on Italy, Flandin retaliated by using Laval's old device of undermining British support for collective security in Africa by calling for it in Europe. Eden's announcement, Flandin told the British foreign secretary at Geneva, lessened the chance for peace in Ethiopia and raised "a more serious question." The application of oil sanctions was likely to result in Italy's withdrawal from the League and an Italo-German rapprochement. Such an eventuality might encourage Germany to take action in the demilitarized zone of the Rhineland. Should this occur, Flandin explained, it was unlikely that Italy would fulfill her Locarno responsibilities as a guarantor power. For this reason, Flandin asked for reassurance from England that the latter was prepared to support France, even if Italy defaulted, in the maintenance of the demilitarized zone. Such reassurances were necessary before the French government could make a decision about supporting England at Geneva on the extension of sanctions. Flandin's aide-mémoire put considerable pressure on the British, but it outlined the French dilemma clearly. Without unambiguous British support against Germany in the Rhineland, it would be difficult for France to alienate Italy by supporting oil sanctions at Geneva. Eden's indirect response came in a ringing speech at Geneva denouncing Italian policies in Ethiopia and championing an oil embargo. The speech won almost unanimous press approval in England, causing the French ambassador there to wonder whether or not Eden was a prisoner of the hopes placed in him by "an electorate blindly faithful to principles the consequences of which it is not fully prepared to accept." Corbin concluded with the hope that eventually the British government will open its eyes "to all aspects of the Abyssinian problem, among which it would be too convenient to turn aside those which interest France above all."[7] The connection between continental and African politics was more clearly understood in Paris than in London.

THE RHINELAND CRISIS

Germany's dramatic remilitarization of the Rhineland on 6–7 March 1936, in violation of both Locarno and Versailles, placed an entirely new complexion on the issue of sanctions, momentarily removing them from the forefront of concern at Geneva. The intrusion of the Rhineland crisis forced postponement of a meeting of the Committee of Thirteen (League Council minus Italy), which had been called to consider a negotiated solution to the Italo-Ethiopian War. On French initiative, designed in part to defer a decision on the proposed oil embargo, the Council was scheduled to meet in London to consider the possible adoption of sanctions against Germany in light of the latter's violation of Locarno. The Italians, very suspicious of Hitler and concerned that a success in the Rhineland would encourage Germany once again to look toward the *Anschluss,* supported the French initiative, "for despite her differences with Britain, she might influence Britain in Italy's favor over Ethiopia."[8] Italian support, which in any case was not authorized to go beyond a moral note of censure against Germany, served to allay suspicions in both London and Paris of collusion between the two fascist dictators. Some had feared that Rome was prepared to support Germany in the Rhineland in return for German support in Ethiopia.

These rumors were formally denied on a number of occasions. Aloisi went so far as to tell the French ambassador in Rome that he remained "a staunch partisan of strengthening the existing links between France and Italy even to the point of a military alliance." Similar indications of noncollaboration between Hitler and Mussolini arrived at the Quai d'Orsay from Berlin. Moreover, Mussolini had previously expressed his fear that a German success in the Rhineland might tempt Hitler to revive efforts aimed at *Anschluss*. The Duce told the Polish ambassador in Rome that he was determined to prevent it and was prepared, if necessary, to act militarily to safeguard the independence of Austria.[9]

The thrust of events, therefore, appeared to strengthen Flandin's hand in his efforts to moderate England's posture on sanctions and thus to rebuild the Stresa Front against German treaty violations. In the wake of Rhineland remilitarization, Anglo-French negotiations resulted in an agreement on 19 March 1936. As a result the British Cabinet joined in a mutual guarantee with Belgium and France against unprovoked aggression. The French had tried in vain ever since 1919 to secure a formal British pledge to defend French security on the Rhine. Now that instrument was a reality. Flandin had succeeded where Laval and his predecessors had failed. But by this time it was a hollow victory. Britain could contribute little to a continental land war—perhaps no more than two inadequately equipped divisions. It is likely that the French realization of Britain's military limitations encouraged policymakers at the Quai d'Orsay to continue to pursue a rapprochement with Italy. On 27 March, Mussolini spoke directly with de Chambrun about the advantages of collaboration between France and Italy. Reluctant to give any anti-English character to such collaboration so soon after the 19 March aggreement, de Chambrun saw "its true meaning only in a common opposition to any drive for German hegemony." The French ambassador derived the impression that the Duce's words were motivated by more than a simple concern to get French aid in lifting sanctions. When de Chambrun spoke of reconstituting the Stresa Front, Mussolini responded that he was anxious to move in that direction, but he doubted that England was so inclined at the present time "except if a Franco-Italian bloc were constituted in a manner sufficiently strong to exercise an attraction apart from which the British Government would find it difficult to stand." Based on statements like these, the French military attaché in Rome also concluded that the fascist leader, fearful of potential German expansion, was prepared to orient Italian-policy toward France in spite of growing popular hostility against sanctions.[10]

There are indications that German diplomats were concerned about the potential diplomatic ramifications of the Rhineland coup. The German chargé in Paris reported that the Italian ambassador there had been making distinctly anti-German noises in interviews with government leaders and the press. Moreover, since 7 March French public opinion had moved "increasingly in favour of the lifting of sanctions and [is] counting upon Italian support against Germany." In his statement to the Chamber of Deputies on 20 March, Flandin spoke "in markedly optimistic terms of the prospect of reestablishing the Stresa Front." The vision of a rejuvenated Stresa coalition received an added fillip from the French air attaché in Rome in two communications on 20 and 30 March 1936, both heavily underlined and bracketed in blue pencil by officials at the Ministry of Air and the Deuxième Bureau. The latter maintained that a favorable attitude toward Stresa was evident in Rome and that Italy could easily be lured back into conjunction with the western powers if they would take the lead in suppressing sanctions. The French air attaché concluded that Italians "would gladly see such an initiative undertaken even by France alone, if it could not take place otherwise, for . . . a sincere Franco-Italian rapprochement would have the effect of overriding English resistance."[11]

Buoyed by optimistic reports from de Chambrun and Parisot about Mussolini's readiness to pursue a western orientation and motivated by news from Ethiopia about the likelihood of a complete Italian victory there, Flandin was encouraged to argue strongly with the British for a moderation of policies toward Italy, bilateral peace negotiations, and no extension of sanctions. De Chambrun pointed out that such a program should be advanced quickly because military intelligence reports suggested that Italy was on the verge of important victories which would only increase the Duce's demands for a peace settlement—thus making England's adhesion much more difficult. On 3 April 1936, the French ambassador reported that Mussolini wanted "absolutely to reconstruct the Stresa Front" and was prepared immediately to negotiate an end to the Ethiopian War as soon as sanctions were lifted.[12]

Approaching Eden at Geneva at the beginning of April, Flandin proposed to the English statesman a scheme for joint Anglo-French mediation of the Italo-Ethiopian War. He argued that only weeks separated Italy from an invasion of Addis Ababa. Should that be allowed to occur, "it will no longer be possible to reconstruct anything with [Mussolini] in Europe to check German ambitions, which the reoccupation of the Rhineland hereafter prevents France alone from stopping." Flandin proposed to end hostilities based on a treaty concluded directly between Italy and Ethiopia under Anglo-French mediation; the final document would be registered with the League of Nations. The proposed treaty would require Ethiopia to cede to Italy all the non-Amharic provinces of the Empire, including the Tigré (where Adowa was located). In exchange, the independence and sovereignty of the Negus would be recognized in the territory of the old Ethiopian Empire, such as it existed before the conquests of Menelik. Flandin's proposal, strongly reminiscent of the Hoare-Laval Plan, was based on a realistic assessment of Mussolini's mood and military realities. The Italians had moved much more rapidly in Ethiopia than anyone had anticipated when the war began seven months earlier. Nevertheless, Eden flatly rejected the French foreign minister's proposal, arguing that the approaching rainy season would allow Haile Selassie a chance to reconstruct his forces for a more prolonged resistance to Italian advances. By September, he predicted, Mussolini's demands for a negotiated settlement would be much more moderate. Furthermore, Eden was unconvinced by Flandin's warnings about the possible conjunction of Italo-German interests; Austria, he said, still stood in the way of any Italo-German understanding.[13]

To be sure, Eden's freedom of maneuver was restricted by the state of British public opinion in the spring of 1936, outraged by the Italian bombing of civilian populations in Ethiopia and the use of poison gas. Nevertheless, yet another opportunity to negotiate an end to the Ethiopian War had been squandered—a victim of British moral outrage and the inability of the Third Republic, weakened by domestic political uncertainty, to coerce her erstwhile English ally. The English view of events was considerably different, captured most effectively by H. Lloyd Thomas, the English minister in Paris. He described a conversation with Flandin on 24 April, shortly before the elections of 26 April–3 May swept the French foreign minister from office. Flandin expressed concern about an Austrian coup and his uncertainty regarding what England would do if that should occur. He also commented on his horror at the depth of anti-French and anti-Italian feeling in England. Thomas concluded that Flandin was like many other French people in his overwhelming preoccupation with the potential German threat. The French, he wrote, "in their heart of hearts. . . feel they have not been very clever about Abyssinia; once more these mingled feelings of panic and frustration vent themselves in blind recriminations against us and our alleged failure to fulfill our Locarno pledges. Unreasonable and exasperating as they are, this seems to me to be the frame of mind prevalent in France to-day, and we shall have to reckon with it in laying our plans for the [League of Nations] meeting at Geneva on the 11th May."[14] That Eden read Thomas's assessment at the British Cabinet meeting of 27 April 1936 indicates that he had effectively captured his government's point of view.

Meanwhile Italian military advances in Ethiopia continued apace, as French intelligence had predicted they would. Somewhat surprisingly, although the controlled Italian press continued its denunciations of English diplomacy, its tone in the wake of military success in Ethiopia became decidedly more friendly to France. Italian newspapers commented favorably upon the moderating role that French statesmen had attempted to play at Geneva—especially the work of Paul-Boncour in limiting denunciations and sanctions. On 17 April, Mussolini personally assured de Chambrun that the Gamelin-Badoglio military accords were still in effect and that he was prepared to move forward on implementing other aspects of the Laval-Mussolini agreements once the question of sanctions had been definitively resolved. De Chambrun, buoyed by these assurances, concluded on 20 April that, from the point of view of Franco-Italian relations, "the situation is no longer very remote from where it stood before the crisis. . . . [V]arious paths are open for us, depending upon whether we want to confine ourselves to perpetuating relations of friendship and good neighborliness or whether we desire to go further and orient ourselves toward a closer collaboration for the political action of the two countries."[15] Even in the wake of continued sanctions and the inability of France to alter the fundamental course of England's anti-Italian orientation, there remained strong indications that Italy was prepared for a reconciliation with France—a reconciliation which could not but strengthen the Republic's diplomatic position on the continent.

By the end of the first week in May, the war in Ethiopia was over and Haile Selassie had fled into exile. Mussolini told de Chambrun that he had never intended to take over all of Ethiopia or to deny the Emperor his throne. But since the latter had sought exile and no native administration remained, Italy had no choice but to claim the entire country. The Duce added that the 1925 and 1935 accords, linking Italy respectively with England and France, would continue to be scrupulously maintained, but he hoped that now that the war was over, sanctions would be lifted. If such an action were not forthcoming at the League of Nations meeting scheduled for 11 May, Italy would have no choice but to abandon the Genevan institution. Although Flandin feared that an Italian decision to annex Ethiopia pure and simple would make it impossible for the League to lift sanctions, the Italian course was irrevocable. On 9 May, Mussolini announced the establishment of the Fascist Empire. All the territory and people of Ethiopia were to be placed under full Italian sovereignty, and King Victor Emmanuel III would assume the title King of Italy and Emperor of Ethiopia. May 11 passed without the lifting of sanctions, and the Italian delegation left Geneva the following day.[16]

The withdrawal of the Italian delegation from Geneva undeniably complicated the French postion. It seemed clear to the Sarraut ministry that the conclusion of the Italo-Ethiopian War rendered the restoration of friendly Franco-Italian relations both possible and desirable. Yet it was correspondingly aware that too direct an approach to Rome might irretrievably compromise the League of Nations and the Anglo-French relationship. Massigli prepared a briefing paper for the Council of Ministers in which he noted all the arguments, pro and con, in connection with the question of lifting sanctions on Italy. He repeated de Chambrun's observation that if sanctions were not lifted, Italy would quit the League definitively and gravitate toward Germany, a situation which would inevitably compromise the independence of Austria. But simply to lift sanctions without any guarantees from Italy would just as surely prejudice the League. France must consider the following points in any decision to raise sanctions: (1) If the sanctions based on Article 16 were revised, would Italy agree to recognize their applicability "sur le plan européen"? (2) Would Italy be prepared to join a mutual assistance agreement with all countries bordering the Mediterranean guaranteeing these countries against nonprovoked attack and assuring their free communication in the sea? (3) In central Europe, is Italy prepared to collaborate on a defensive policy for Austria and Czechoslovakia in collaboration with France and the Little Entente?[17]

Massigli's questions were well formulated, but when de Chambrun posed them to Suvich, the latter declared in no uncertain terms that, although Rome still considered the Laval-Mussolini accords and their military corollaries in force and no political entente whatsoever had been concluded or even envisaged with the Reich, the failure of the League to lift sanctions (described by Suvich as "vexatious and gratuitously punitive," given the conclusion of the war) could lead to a revision of Italy's political stance in Europe. Similar warnings had been articulated by Suvich and Mussolini a few days earlier, but it is interesting to note that in all these cases the possibility of an Italian turn toward Germany was described by the Italians as a distasteful last resort. All the documents emphasize that Mussolini preferred to reestablish "a frank and active collaboration between France and Italy."[18]

Substantially the same message came from Marshal Badoglio, who had been recalled to the capital because of the gravity of the European situation. This well-known Francophile wrote, in a personal letter to France's military attaché in Rome, that sanctions were now pointless, and their maintenance would put the future of good Franco-Italian relations at risk. "The time has come to decide," Badoglio wrote. He urged the French to take the initiative at Geneva for the suppression of sanctions, a gesture "which would not be forgotten by Italy."[19] Complete military victory in East Africa had emboldened the Italian negotiating stance, a judgment confirmed by the French ambassador. The latter reported on 30 May that, whereas earlier it would have been possible to secure a pledge from Mussolini on Austrian independence in exchange for the lifting of sanctions, now the Duce would want the lifting of sanctions first. Only afterward would he be willing to negotiate with England and France on schemes for guaranteeing the status quo in central Europe.[20]

Italy's triumph in Ethiopia in May coincided with the massive electoral victory of the Popular Front in the French spring elections. Given Blum's ideological hostility to fascism, it seemed clear enough to Flandin that, if Franco-Italian reconciliation were to be salvaged, the effort would have to be initiated prior to the Popular Front's installation in power on 4 June. Writing of this crucial juncture in his memoirs, Paul-Boncour noted that, "it appeared to M. Sarraut, M. Flandin and me that the situation contained the elements of a negotiation; the Abyssinian affair was closed; sooner or later it would be necessary to move toward the recognition [of the Italian empire]; it was worthwhile to try to make the best of it." The three men, accompanied by Léger, called upon Blum, whose government would inherit responsibility for following up any diplomatic initiatives. They proposed sending instructions to Corbin in London asking England to associate herself with a comprehensive initiative to Rome. Their plan called for the raising of sanctions, already inoperative, and the recognition of the Italian conquest of Ethiopia, which was in any case a fait accompli. In exchange Italy would be requested to return to collective security in Europe by participating with England, France, and other interested states in a series of accords concerning the Mediterranean, central Europe, and the Balkans.[21]

It may be that such an all-embracing initiative, launched by an outgoing government, stood little chance of success. But the weight of evidence suggests that Flandin was either disingenuous or just plain wrong when he blamed the failure of his proposals on the refusal of Blum to accept them or to bind his government to follow them up. In his first foreign policy speech, delivered shortly after the Popular Front's electoral victory but prior to the installation of his government, Blum addressed in general terms the question of France's future relations with the fascist countries: "With all nations of the world whatever may be their internal policy, we wish to cooperate in eliminating the causes of conflict which might, some day, lead to war. We wish to work with all nations and for all nations, provided they sincerely desire to work with us in building up peace." These words may well reflect post election euphoria rather than concrete policy planning, but it seems likely that at the beginning Blum was prepared to entertain ideologically unpalatable but realistic policy alternatives. John Dreifort has speculated that one of the reasons for Blum's selection of Delbos over Herriot for the Quai d'Orsay was that Delbos was not so strongly identified as a partisan of sanctions against Italy. It was likely that the issue of lifting sanctions would come early on the Popular Front agenda, and Delbos would be in a better position than Herriot to carry the matter through. Blum's antifascism was not always stubbornly doctrinaire, and the general outlines of the Sarraut ministry proposals were in fact sent to London on 23 May 1936.[22]

Rather, the principal roadblock to French policy came once again from across the Channel. The English response was decidedly cool, and the matter was, therefore, not pursued further once the Popular Front government assumed power on 4 June. An excellent opportunity for a creative appeasement of Italy, at comparatively little cost, had been lost because of the irresponsibility and shortsightedness of British policy. What makes this series of events all the more inexplicable and ironic is that it was Eden who appeared before the League of Nations just a month later to appeal for the lifting of sanctions, when it had been France which had argued against their application all along. Half a year later, on 2 January 1937, England unilaterally negotiated a "Gentleman's Agreement" with Italy regulating the status quo in the Mediterranean. But in the spring of 1936, when Paris advanced a proposal for a combined Anglo-French appeasement of Italy, no such conciliatory spirit existed in London. Among British statesmen, only Vansittart believed that, in spite of Ethiopia, Mussolini could still be kept as an ally through the extension of timely concessions, most particularly the ending of sanctions. But his advice, hindered by the unwillingness of British public opinion to abandon a lost policy in time to have some effect on Mussolini, was ignored. And so disappeared an opportunity to find out whether the Duce was sincere in his statements that an end to sanctions would restore good relations.[23] One cannot escape the conclusion that at this crucial juncture—before the outbreak of the Spanish Civil War and the onset of the Popular Front era obscured political issues with ideological fervor—it was British diplomacy, not French, that was characterized by immobility and lack of vision.

THE POPULAR FRONT AND ETHIOPIA

Blum's government was installed on 4 June 1936. The inauguration of the Popular Front era in France left a cloud of uncertainty over the future direction of French foreign policy. Whereas the new prime minister had expressed a degree of ideological flexibility before actually assuming office, once in power he proved unwilling to assume any initiatives toward a rapprochement with Italy. Those at the Quai d'Orsay who favored a continuation of the Barthou-Laval-Flandin efforts to separate Italy from Germany were particularly perplexed and concerned. On 5 June Bertrand de Jouvenel, Henry's son and diplomatic correspondent for *Paris-Soir,* found the prospects for future collaboration between France and Italy "hardly encouraging." Although Mussolini reiterated, in a private conversation with the French publicist, his conviction that in principle a Franco-Italian entente represented "the best policy for Italy," he doubted that this would come to pass in the near future because "the new French government is composed of men who are his adversaries." Jouvenel feared that Mussolini would be led little by little toward an entente with Germany.[24] It was, no doubt, concerns such as these that led Massigli to prepare a long briefing paper on Franco-Italian relations for the incoming foreign minister, Yvon Delbos. Massigli's essay reviewed the entire orientation of Italian policy in light of the Ethiopian question, referring to Mussolini's speech and especially to key telegrams from de Chambrun in May indicating that Italy was still convinced of the need for Franco-Italian collaboration. He also reviewed the question of sanctions and concluded by posing the danger clearly and succinctly. His words are worth quoting at some length.

> If no precise conclusion may be derived, at least [these events] compel the statement that one no longer has the right to rely on the fact that Italian policy will, in all hypotheses, remain faithful to conceptions which prevailed in Rome last year. The decisions, whatever they may be, which will be taken at the next meetings in Geneva [on sanctions] appear, from that point on, as susceptible to singularly widespread repercussions which will flow beyond the general framework of theoretical problems concerning the organization or authority of the League of Nations and which risk affecting directly the equilibrum of forces in Europe.[25]

The record is abundantly clear that, even after the installation of the Popular Front regime, Italy made several direct appeals to France for some sort of conciliatory gesture that would facilitate the normalization of Franco-Italian relations. Through Jean-Louis Malvy, a French senator visiting Rome, Mussolini hinted that if France would support the lifting of sanctions once the issue was raised at Geneva, he would be "disposed to collaborate closely with France on all problems." Several days later the Duce requested Hubert de Lagardelle, a French socialist journalist, to tell Blum that he remained faithful to the accords and military conventions of 1935, and that he was prepared to consider the possibility of a Mediterranean pact once the Franco-British naval agreements directed against Italy (instituted in the wake of the adoption of sanctions) were removed. These two verbal approaches were unceremoniously brushed aside by Popular Front leaders. When Malvy returned from Rome, he quickly sought out Delbos to relay the substance of his conversation with Mussolini and to suggest that a French gesture was necessary to avoid a coalescence of Italy with Germany. The foreign minister shunted him off to Blum, who explained to Malvy: "I understand. . . . But it is a policy I cannot take upon myself. I am the leader of the Popular Front. . . . For this action, you need another Prime Minister and another majority." Blum refused even to receive Lagardelle, and thus the Duce's message came to the Quai d'Orsay only at second hand through the French chargé d'affaires in Rome, whom Lagardelle had contacted immediately after his interview with the fascist leader.[26]

During the last week of June, the French ambassador met twice with Mussolini's son-in-law, Count Galeazzo Ciano, whose recent appointment as Italian minister of foreign affairs was viewed widely as an anti-French and pro-German gesture. On both occasions Ciano stressed that Italy wished to cooperate with France and the League if only the sanctions were lifted. In exchange, Italy would abolish slavery in Ethiopia and would make periodic reports to the League on its "civilizing" activities there. Moreover, Ciano emphasized, Italy would not request official recognition of her conquest from France, although he hoped that it might come in the not-too-distant future. The new foreign minister also stated that no political or military entente of any sort existed between his country and Germany, and that Italy regarded the continued independence of Austria as "a vital interest."[27]

Despite these diplomatic advances from Rome, there is no indication that either Delbos or Blum took them seriously, a result perhaps of their mutual hatred for Mussolini as the assassin of Matteotti, coupled with an unsubstantiated ideological conviction that it was not possible to keep Fascist Italy and Nazi Germany apart in any case. Delbos mentions in his memoirs that both he and Blum "loathed Mussolini intensely." It would have cost France little to have tested Mussolini's sincerity since sanctions, for all practical purposes, were a dead issue anyway, and France's eastern allies had been arguing for some months that their continued application was harder on their own economies than Italy's.[28] The Popular Front was willing to consider lifting sanctions if some other nation took the lead at Geneva, as subsequent events revealed, but it refused to assume any initiative in the matter.

The price paid for such shortsighted neglect of French interest was soon made clear. In June reports began to arrive in Paris about Italian troop movements from Bolzano and Bologna up to Turin and Cuneo—that is, toward the French frontier. Even Badoglio, for so long the symbol of Francophilia in Italy, explained that these moves were undertaken to redress a military situation that had been allowed "to fall into desuetude." In addition, the French ambassador in Berlin reported on 6 June that the Italians had dramatically increased their efforts to seek good relations with Germany—an indication to François-Poncet that Mussolini was finally prepared to play the "German card" if he could not obtain satisfaction from England, France, and the League of Nations. Rumors of an emerging Italo-German military collaboration were alarming enough, but some in France could still maintain their equanimity by suggesting that Austria remained as an unbreachable barrier between Rome and Berlin. Such complacency was shattered beyond recall on 11 July 1936 with the publication of an agreement between Austria and Germany which normalized relations between the two neighbors. They agreed to relax discriminatory restrictions, particularly in the field of cultural activity, to seek a solution to the Austrian émigré problem, to expand economic relations, and to pursue coordinated foreign policies. Vienna agreed to work toward the association of members of the national opposition (i.e., Nazis) with the Austrian government. In short, Germany pledged not to interfere in Austria's internal policies, and Austria pledged to behave like a German state. Thus one of the strongest ties between France and Italy—the concern to preserve Austrian independence—had at least temporarily disappeared. By removing the fear of *Anschluss,* Hitler correspondingly reduced the attractiveness of a French connection for Italian leaders. The German ambassador in Rome remarked that, although it would be wrong to conclude that Italy would finally and conclusively turn against Paris, "France is today estimated [in Rome] as a considerably less important factor than formerly."[29]

The matter of sanctions also came home to roost. On 18 June Eden informed the House of Commons that the British government no longer saw any useful purpose in sanctions and would support their removal at the next meeting of the League of Nations Assembly. The French Cabinet followed suit a day later, and early in July both the League Assembly and the Sanctions Coordination Committee voted overwhelmingly (only the Ethiopian delegate cast a dissenting ballot) to lift sanctions against Italy effective on 15 July. As early as 20 June 1936, Ciano expressed to Lagardelle his astonishment that England, rather than France, had taken the lead at Geneva in moving toward the abolition of sanctions. He accused the French of "deceit" and "deception." Three weeks later he indicated to the French ambassador that, given the current state of Franco-Italian relations, the

Italian government would find grave difficulties in participating in the next conference of Locarno powers scheduled to meet in Brussels.[30] The connection between sanctions and French security on the Rhine could not have been expressed more starkly.

The Italian gesture obviously impressed Popular Front leaders. Delbos vehemently denied Italian allegations that the assurances made to each other by naval powers in the Mediterranean the previous autumn, in light of the Ethiopian crisis, amounted to a multilateral pact directed against Italy, which could continue into the future. He urged the English on 8 July to clarify their position on the Mediterranean guarantees (i.e., that they applied only in connection with enforcing Article 16 on sanctions) in order to assure Italy's participation at the Brussels conference of Locarno powers. The French foreign minister evinced for the first time a modicum of panic about the international situation: "With regard to the general situation on the continent, the Italian abstention could have extremely serious consequences. Both in London and here [in Paris] we must take every possible precaution to facilitate the Rome government's adhesion [to the conference] by appeasing without delay the sensitivities and anxieties which can result for Italy from the uncertainty to which she feels herself exposed. A day later the Quai d'Orsay informed London and Rome that, as soon as sanctions were lifted (15 July), France would consider the accords on assistance to the British fleet in the Mediterranean in case of an Italian attack as null and void. The suddenness of the French announcement was interpreted as an effort to assure Italian participation in the Brussels conference and a maneuver designed to win Italy back into the camp of the western powers.[31]

If so, it was a miserable failure—a case of too little too late. Even with British assurance that its fleet in the Mediterranean would be substantially reduced following the formal lifting of sanctions (the main body of the British fleet departed from Alexandria on 18 July), the Italians could not be persuaded to withdraw their threat to absent themselves from the Brussels conference. Italy's nonparticipation at Brussels presented serious impediments to France's security arrangements on the continent. Delbos outlined these in a telegram to Rome on 18 July, with copies to French representatives in London, Berlin, and Brussels. "That the Italian government, assured of the raising of sanctions, believed it necessary to refuse to participate in an upcoming meeting of powers faithful to the Treaty of Locarno, should raise doubts about the position M. Mussolini might subsequently adopt with regard to a situation created by the violation of the Treaty of Locano.[32] Delbos instructed de Chambrun tactfully to request clarification from Ciano on how Italy now viewed her responsibilities vis-à-vis Locarno, but it was abundantly clear that the continental security system hammered together by Barthou and Laval had collapsed almost entirely.

THE SPANISH CIVIL WAR

The tragically belated decision to lift economic sanctions on Italy coincided with the outbreak of the civil war in Spain. The latter, with all of its emotional and ideological overtones, cast a long shadow over Franco-Italian relations for the next three years. The initial weeks of that struggle presented the new Popular Front government in Paris with a foreign policy challenge and a moral dilemma of the first magnitude. On 13 July 1936, José Calvo Sotelo, an opposition leader in the Spanish Cortes and former minister of the deposed Spanish dictator Miguel Primo de Rivera, was murdered in Madrid. Four days later General Francisco Franco declared a military revolt in Morocco against the Spanish *Frente Popular,* which spread the next day to the mainland and within forty-eight hours engulfed the entire country. It is well known now that Franco's derring-do, which stood little chance of success without foreign intervention in his behalf, had been reinforced by prior assurances of support from Mussolini's Italy. While the Italians had cultivated favorable relations with Spain during the dictatorship of Primo de Rivera in the 1920s, Italo-Spanish relations had deteriorated following his dismissal and the inception of the Republic in 1931. But Hitler's rise to power and the Japanese success in Manchuria rekindled Mussolini's dreams of mare nostrum. In March 1934 the Duce and Marshal Italo Balbo had met with Spanish monarchist leaders and declared Italy's readiness to assist them to overthrow the Spanish government with money and war materiel. They also indicated that undefined "greater support" would materialize later as circumstances made it necessary. The first physical evidence of Italian commitments occurred as early as 30 July 1936, when two Savoia-Marchetti S 81 Italian air force bombers crash-landed in French Morocco. Their Italian crews were arrested by French authorities who also captured papers linking them to the Italian air force. The two planes had been painted clumsily in a vain effort to blot out Italian military markings. They formed part of a squadron of twelve Italian aircraft ordered to Spanish Morocco for service to General Franco.[33]

Within a few days of the uprising in Morocco, the Spanish government in Madrid approached Paris with a request to purchase first-class war materiel. Money was available, and Spain was entitled under international law to purchase war materiel. The French government did not intend initially to abstain from aiding the Spanish Republic. There were, in fact, solid reasons for Paris to come to the support of Madrid. In addition to the ideological affinities of the two Popular Front regimes, Paris was painfully aware that the spring 1936 events had weakened France's strategic position on both the Italian and German frontiers. A Franco success might well introduce a potentially hostile Spain along her southern border, thus further weakening France by necessitating the deployment of forces along the Pyrenees. Futhermore, a Franco regime indebted to Italy might be vulnerable to Italian demands for access to naval bases in the Balearic Islands, thereby putting Italy in a position to hinder the movement of French colonial troops from North Africa to her Mediterranean ports in the event of a European war.[34] All of these factors contributed to Paris's initial decision of 23 July to honor the Spanish government's request for assistance in the form of aircraft. Yet within two days, on 25 July, it was announced that France had decided for the moment not to sell the aircraft. Following the crash of the Italian bombers in French Morocco, Pierre Cot, the aviation minister, received instructions to go ahead with the secret delivery of the French planes, some seventy of which reached the Spanish government during the first five months of the civil war. At the same time, however, the Chamber of Deputies instructed the government to request the other major European powers to abstain from intervention in Spain, and an appeal along these lines was sent by the Quai d'Orsay to London and Rome on 1 August. It was later extended to Germany, the Soviet Union, Portugal, and other nations.[36] On 8 August the French government announced that in order to facilitate an international understanding on the principle of nonintervention, it would close its Pyrenean frontier and prohibit the exportation of all further war materiel to Spain.[37]

Why this sudden shift in French policy from an initial inclination to aid the Spanish Republic on 21–23 July to a firm decision to withhold support and stump actively for nonintervention between 25 July and 8 August? Many factors may have been brought to bear—the pacifism of the French people;[38] the weakness of Blum, Delbos, and War Minister Daladier; the opposition of conservative and Catholic circles to the Spanish Republic; the social disarray of strikes and demonstrations; and the preoccupation of the French people with domestic matters. Two schools of thought on the issue have emerged. One argues that the principle factor in changing Blum's mind was pressure from England. The British were concerned acutely about the potential international ramifications should France become embroiled in Spain. These concerns were presented starkly to Blum by Baldwin and Eden between 21 and 25 July. Elizabeth Cameron has argued that it was Léger who persuaded Blum to go to London to talk with British leaders and then urged him to propose the nonintervention plan for fear that unless France remained neutral, Britain might support Franco. Léger feared that British concern about "Red" influences in the French Popular Front might lead London to align with White Spain, Germany, and Italy. He therefore got Blum to assure British neutrality by foregoing the shipment of arms and materiel to Spain.[39]

More recently scholars have argued that the emphasis on English pressure as the determinant of French policy is unwarranted. They stress divisions within the Popular Front coalition itself, particularly between the overt interventionism of Air Minister Cot and the more cautious Radicals in the Blum government, led by Daladier and Delbos. The latter feared that aid to Spain might lead to open conflict with Germany and Italy. Given the adamant opposition of French conservatives and the right wing, there was some concern that aid to the Madrid government might well intensify the domestic crisis in France and lead perhaps to civil war. Therefore, Blum's reluctant decision to adopt a stance of nonintervention was dictated fundamentally by the French domestic situation.[40]

There is much to be said for both points of view, but the record suggests that the latter school dismisses the impact of British pressure much too readily. Although prior to 25 July 1936 the British view remained largely undefined, on 8 August 1936 the British government "delivered a virtual ultimatum that if France did not promptly ban the export of war materiel to Spain, and a war with Germany ensued, Britain would consider herself absolved of her obligations, under the Locarno treaty, to aid France. . . ."[41] It was the same threat that British leaders had used to thwart French policy in the past. Given the furor of opposition in the right-wing press to continued aid to Spain and the reluctance of Radical leaders within his own government to support military intervention, Blum pursued the alternative aim of a nonintervention agreement among the powers to prohibit the export of arms to either side. Delbos, who originally had supported the sending of aid to Spain, spoke out strongly in the 8 August Cabinet meeting against the continuation, even covertly, of such a policy. The Radical foreign minister evidently had been persuaded that the French nonintervention proposals of 1 August had been greeted in Italy, Germany, and Russia as "favorable in principle," and that France must hold scrupulously to nonintervention if its proposal was to have any chance of isolating the Spanish conflict. Delbos's main concern was to act in concert with England on this matter. He believed that Laval's reluctance to impose effective sanctions on Italy had alienated the British—a breach that France must repair in the interests of her own security.[42] This analysis makes it clear that Blum's choice in July–August 1936 was not between intervention and nonintervention, but between nonintervention and the collapse of the

Popular Front coalition. When he realized his dilemma, Blum's initial inclination was to resign; to do so, however, would have doomed the Popular Front social program which was yet to be launched. The tension between domestic political goals and foreign policy was compelling. In Spain Blum was prepared neither to stand alone nor to alienate British opinion.

The French nonintervention initiative also may have been stimulated by reports from Rome and Berlin about the potential the Spanish conflict offered for direct cooperation between the two fascist powers. De Chambrun indicated on 30 July that Italian policy was becoming increasingly anticommunist and less inclined to pursue any effort at strengthening Franco-Italian links. A week later, François-Poncet submitted a much more alarmist report suggesting that the Wilhelmstrasse's initial actions in Spain "leave scarcely any doubt about the existence of an accord of mutual consultation and concerted diplomatic action between Germany and Italy." In fact no such clearly articulated understanding existed, but concern about it affected French diplomacy. On several occasions both Mussolini and Ciano, while agreeing to adhere to the principle of nonintervention, pointed out the difference between "direct" and "indirect" intervention and couched their reservations about the French proposal in terms of its vagueness about the latter. The prohibition of direct intervention in the Spanish struggle was clear enough—no government-supplied guns, aircraft, munitions, or soldiers. But indirect intervention involved such matters as moral solidarity with one of the sides in the struggle expressed in the form of demonstrations, press campaigns, and the like, and the private enrollment of "volunteers" to fight in Spain. De Chambrun argued that the latter was the main stumbling block to Italian adherence to nonintervention and urged the adoption of some means to control these activities in France.[43]

On 21 August Italy officially adhered to the French nonintervention plan and agreed to forbid all commerce (including reexportation) of arms and war materiel to Spain or its possessions and to concert with other powers in carrying out a policy of nonintervention. Within a week Great Britain, the Soviet Union, Germany, and several smaller nations also accepted the French plan, and shortly thereafter a formal Nonintervention Committee, composed of representatives from all the participating nations, set up shop in London to oversee compliance with the accord. The sorry three-year history of the Nonintervention Committee has been told many times before, and there is no need to repeat it here. It served as a screen of public propaganda behind which Germany, Italy, and the Soviet Union flagrantly violated both the letter and the spirit of the agreement. Soviet support for the Madrid government gradually faded out in 1937 as chances for ultimate victory diminished. Italian and German support for the Nationalists in the form of substantial supplies of war materiel and "volunteers" eventually proved instrumental in Franco's triumph. Between 1936 and 1939 France remained relatively steadfast in enforcing her own compliance to nonintervention. It has already been mentioned that between July and December 1936 France surreptitiously supplied Spanish republican forces with some seventy aircraft—important in the successful initial defense of Madrid. But seventy aircraft in five months represented scant support when compared to the hundreds of planes and crews sent to Franco's forces during the same time period by Italy and Germany. In terms of indirect aid, some Spanish pilots were trained in France during 1936, and French authorities occasionally permitted Catalan reinforcements and supplies to reach the Biscayan region by way of southern France until the collapse of the Basque front. War materiel and volunteers from third parties also on occasion crossed the Pyrenees into Catalonia. This kind of support, however, was intermittent and small scale, usually occurring from time to time to placate leftist opinion in France. At no time were there any official Italian or German protests on this point in the Nonintervention Committee. After 8 March 1937, when the frontier patrol was reinforced by officers from the London committee, the Franco-Spanish border effectively was closed.[44]

It frequently is asserted that the Italo-German comradeship in arms in behalf of General Franco formed the seedbed of the Axis of World War II. But John Coverdale has demonstrated rather convincingly that such was not the case. His book suggests that Franco-Italian hostility on a host of matters between 1936 and 1939, certainly embittered by their opposition over Spain, was more decisive in pushing Mussolini into Hitler's arms than Italo-German collaboration in the Spanish Civil War. The two fascist dictators had quite different goals in the Iberian conflict. De Chambrun seemed to recognize this fact in his immediate response to Italy's acceptance of the nonintervention formula on 21 August 1936. Italy adhered only to direct nonintervention but maintained its "observations" regarding indirect nonintervention, apparently planning to keep its options open in that category. Nevertheless, de Chambrun told the American chargé d'affaires in Rome that he was "well-satisfied" with the Italian note and pleased that Italy had expressed only "observations" and not "reservations" concerning indirect nonintervention. Simultaneously he stressed to the Quai d'Orsay that one of the main reasons for Italy's coming around to accept the French proposal was that the Italian government "scarcely desired to see a power as redoubtable as Germany appear as an active factor in the Mediterranean." The French ambassador, ever conscious of Italian sensibilities and anxious to forestall any potential Italo-German commonality of interest, advised Delbos that, "We have every interest in seeing that our press does not concentrate on Italian concessions and abstains from representing them as a retreat of the fascist government. Rather it should make the most of the substantial results obtained in the course of long and delicate negotiations where proofs of a comprehensive good will have been evident on all sides."[45]

Two weeks later Count Ciano told de Chambrun that Italy was prepared to discuss the possibility of returning its delegation to the League of Nations in Geneva. The Italian foreign minister also said that Mussolini was anxious in the near future "to reestablish an active and efficacious collaboration" between Italy and France. Such observations might be written off as simply the Pollyanna fantasies of an Italophile ambassador. But even so pro-English and anti-Italian an observer as Reynaud, reporting in *Paris-Soir* on a conversation he had had with Ciano in October 1936, concluded that Italy's deepest interest is to rejoin her wartime allies."[46] These indications that Italy was prepared to welcome French gestures of what de Chambrun had called "comprehensive good will" had no hearing within the councils of the Popular Front. The Blum regime's intransigence on the matter became quickly apparent with regard to the retirement of the French ambassador.

A SEMI-BREAK WITH ROME

De Chambrun's formal retirement at age 60 was not initially at issue. He had been scheduled to leave Italy on vacation in the fall of 1936 but had informed the Quai d'Orsay that it might be a good idea for him to remain in Rome since, upon his return, Italy would most likely demand new letters of accreditation addressed to the "king of Italy, emperor of Ethiopia." Such a designation implied de facto recognition of the Italian conquest of the East African kingdom, a gesture which the ideological proclivities of the Popular Front prevented France from making. The issue could have been sidestepped simply by leaving de Chambrun at his post in Rome, and Ciano in fact advised the French to avoid embarrassment by doing precisely that. The immediate response from Paris was the testy observation that if the Italians really intended to extort such a backhanded recognition of the conquest, then the embassy might best be left in the hands of the chargé d'affaires. De Chambrun was instructed to inform Ciano that, if new letters of accreditation would be required, he would leave Rome definitively at the end of October. Ciano confirmed Italian policy, but fascist leaders made every effort to prevent the departure of the pro-Italian ambassador and the downgrading of Franco-Italian relations that inevitably would follow. Mussolini himself told de Chambrun on 16 October that, even if his assignment were prolonged for ten years, Italy would not demand recognition of the empire in Ethiopia, but a new ambassador would have to fulfill that requirement. "'Your recall,'" the Duce said, "'is an error, I would say even a serious error.'"[47] It was all to no avail; Mussolini and Ciano's advice, and all good sense, were ignored. De Chambrun returned to Paris, and for two crucial years Franco-Italian relations were allowed to drift with nobody of ambassadorial rank in Rome.

Such a gesture could only have been calculated to impress upon Italy the scant regard held for her weight in European affairs by the current French regime. Once taken, however, the action could be redressed only with difficulty. It was a very serious blunder. Noël, at the time France's ambassador in Warsaw, noted the silliness of his government's refusal to address credentials to the "king of Italy, emperor of Ethiopia" for fear that this would connote an indirect recognition of the Ethiopian conquest. Louis XIV and his successors had not been so fastidious; up until 1801 the kings of England had insisted on carrying the title "king of France," yet this had not caused grave difficulties of protocol between the courts of Versailles and St. James. Thus, for a technicality, France deprived itself of official representation in Rome. De Chambrun's own analysis was much more blunt and perhaps more to the point: "I got the sense of [the totally political nature of my recall] in speaking to M. Blum, who responded to my heavy pleas to remain on good terms with Mussolini with these words, astonishing in the mouth of one responsible for French policy: 'you forget that I was Matteotti's friend.'"[48] It seems likely, therefore, that the recall of an ambassador who had actively championed the Rome Accords of January 1935, and who had been a consistent advocate of Franco-Italian friendship, was meant as a signal to Rome that the foreign policy of Pierre Laval was dead and gone.

Raymond Sontag has argued that no fundamental shift in French foreign policy occurred when Blum became premier. "Even in relations with Germany and Italy he made no break with the past."[49] In a very broad sense, Sontag may be right; Blum occasionally verbalized a desire to regain Italian friendship. But the tone of French foreign policy had altered dramatically since the fall of Laval and Flandin, and errors of both commission and omission prejudiced Franco-Italian relations virtually beyond recall, thus leaving French continental security to the inadequate English guarantees in the west and the uncertainties of the newly ratified Franco-Russo-Czech arrangement in the east—the latter having provided the immediate excuse for Hitler's Rhineland gamble in March 1936.

The Franco-Soviet accord only served to increase Italian fears about the "bolshevization" of France and to magnify the Duce's determination to deal carefully with leaders of the Popular Front. Ironically, French military leaders maintained virtually no confidence in the Soviet connection. Opposed to it on ideological grounds—a reticence shared by many of the Republic's conservative and right-wing politicians—the French army staff also harbored a persistent skepticism about Russia's political motives and military capacity.[50] These attitudes preempted any sustained effort to meet the German challenge through direct collaboration with the Soviet Union. The Franco-Soviet accord also prejudiced France's relations with Great Britain. Much conservative, anti-French feeling derived from France's apparent unwillingnesss to allow events in eastern Europe to take their "natural" course. French efforts to encircle Germany threatened to drag Britain into a war to maintain the very status quo she wished to see altered. For this reason, Sir Austen Chamberlain reported that many conservatives regarded the Franco-Soviet pact as " 'almost a betrayal of Western Civilization,' "[51] and, therefore, furthered the tendency in London to view every French move with suspicion.

Given the background of Eden's heavy-handed insistence on the application of sanctions against Italy and then their extension to an oil embargo—policies which undermined French efforts in 1935 and 1936 to align Mussolini with the western powers—it may seem ironic that it was he who took the initiative to end sanctions in June and then moved toward the normalization of Anglo-Italian relations with the "Gentleman's Agreement" on preserving the status quo in the Mediterranean in January 1937. Why this sudden shift in policy? It seems likely that the British Foreign Office was responding to pressure from the Admiralty Office and the Naval Chiefs of Staff. The latter two had opposed sanctions openly from the start, the application of which had overextended dangerously British naval resources in the Mediterranean. The Rhineland crisis, raising the threat of war with Germany, served to convince naval leaders of the need to repair relations with Italy and thereby tranquilize the Mediterranean situation. That would allow Britain to bring the Home Fleet back up to strength and permit the defense of vital British interests in the Far East against Japan.[52]

Eden's shift in policy after the Rhineland may be seen as a realistic effort to achieve these goals. It also must be realized, however, that corollary to the Admiralty's insistence on ending sanctions was its conviction that a peaceful Mediterranean also depended on the restoration of friendly relations between France and Italy. In this respect Britain's record of undermining French efforts to achieve a rapprochement proved virtually impossible to undo. The damage to Franco-Italian relations was further abetted by the shortsightedness of the Popular Front government. The evidence cited shows that Mussolini and Ciano made repeated overtures to Paris in the summer and fall of 1936—well after the Popular Front had been installed in office. These either were ignored or treated with thinly veiled condescension. The failure of the Brussels conference of Locarno powers offered a pointed warning, which was echoed several months later by the fiasco of de Chambrun's recall from Rome.

The uncertain status of Franco-Italian relations at this juncture was captured dramatically in two interesting documents. The first was a personal letter over an indecipherable signature addressed to Gaston Doumergue. It informed the former president and prime minister of the Italian state of mind in the summer of 1936, when Doumergue's correspondent had visited Italy. Government officials repeatedly told the Frenchman of Mussolini's chagrin and frustration at the condescending way in which his overtures had been received by the Quai d'Orsay since the fall of Laval. He quoted an official in the Italian Ministry of Industry: "'The duce is not at all germanophile but he has been well obliged to seek a rapprochement with Germany since all other nations and above all your Popular Front—to say nothing of England—opposed Italy. Not a single Italian is germanophile at heart, and the great majority ask nothing more than to be francophile. But, . . . '" Doumergue passed the letter on to the Quai d'Orsay. Heavily bracketed in blue pencil by officials there, this passage accurately reflected the dilemma faced by Italian leaders in these circumstances. The final uncompleted sentence bespoke the heavy price exacted by clumsy French and English diplomacy. Its message reverberated again in one of de Chambrun's last dispatches from Rome. Assessing the lamentable state of Franco-Italian relations, the outgoing ambassador remarked on Italy's increasing anti-communism and her tendency to view French policy as "dangerously linked to that of Moscow." Moreover Italian leaders viewed the prolonged social malaise following the election of the Popular Front as a sign of serious weakness. Following the outbreak of the Spanish Civil War, de Chambrun believed that Italy's moves toward a rapprochement with Germany constituted but a first step in a new effort to realize the Four-Power pact, ever more attractive to Mussolini since the demise of the Stresa Front. In regard to Franco-Italian relations, de Chambrun concluded, "Without by any means despairing . . . of future sudden changes [in policy] which Italy has so many reasons to adopt, it would nevertheless be folly to conceal the fact that our situation, in the eyes of public opinion and of the government of this country, is gravely diminished at the present moment."[53] The ambassador's generally somber assessment was not barren of any glimmer of hope that wise and careful diplomacy would be able to effect a "future sudden change" in Italian policy vis-à-vis France. But the absence of official representation in Rome, continued tension over the Spanish question and the recognition of the Ethiopian conquest, and lack of coordination between London and Paris all combined to belie even this faint-hearted vision.

CHAPTER 10

From the Spanish Crisis to the *Anschluss,* October 1936– March 1938

The two years between the recall of de Chambrun from Rome to his replacement by François-Poncet in November 1938 represented a period of drift and disarray in Franco-Italian relations. Official contacts between the two nations at this decisive juncture in the development of European relationships was diminished still further by the departure of the Italian ambassador from Paris in October 1937 and the definitive withdrawal of Italy from the League of Nations in December. The only ostensible reason for this nearly total collapse of communication between Paris and Rome was the Ethiopian question. Although sanctions had been dropped in July 1936, the matter of recognizing the Italian conquest remained unresolved. Until the League could agree to recognize the Italian conquest—or until an acceptable face-saving formula could be developed which would allow member nations to deal with the Ethiopian question individually—the rule of unanimity prevailed. The issue, totally symbolic after the Italian military victory, would not go away. In addition, French policy vis-à-vis Italy suffered assaults in Spain, eastern Europe, and with regard to the

Republic's strategic military situation. All of these vulnerabilities magnified the role of Great Britain as the determining factor in relations between Rome and Paris.

ETHIOPIA, EASTERN EUROPE, AND SPAIN

In his last dispatch from Rome, de Chambrun returned to the thorny matter of Ethiopia, identifying it as "a major factor poisoning relations" between France and Italy. He also commented on the blatantly anti-Bolshevik policies of the Italian government, which viewed the Franco-Soviet alliance, the victory of the Popular Front, and the subsequent social upheaval in France as factors signifying a decided weakening of the Third Republic in European affairs. Mussolini, he observed, was not anxious to associate himself with weak powers. Moreover, the Duce's drive to strengthen ties to Germany in the fall of 1936 did not necessarily betoken any desire to build an Italo-German alliance, in which Italy could expect to play only a subservient role. Rather, the Italian was most likely paving the way for a future proposal along the lines of the Four-Power Pact.[1] The latter arrangement, ideal for the weakest, materially, of the major European powers, would magnify the importance of the Duce's desired role as a mediator between Germany and the western democracies.

Perhaps it was thinking along these lines that led Delbos to make a modest gesture toward Rome by ordering the transformation of France's legation in Addis Ababa into a consulate general accredited to Rome. The move, Delbos insisted in instructions to Blondel, was designed solely to facilitate services to French interests in Ethiopia and did not carry "the sense of de jure recognition." Ciano accepted the French demarche and pledged to respect French diplomatic rights in Ethiopia. Blondel stressed that the Italian foreign minister "fully appreciated" this turn of events, but he pointed out that the Italians would certainly view it as de facto recognition of the Empire and trumpet it as a diplomatic victory in the press. "Nevertheless," he concluded, "this gesture clarified the atmosphere in Franco-Italian relations"—but only slightly and for a short period of time. After an initially mild and favorable Italian press treatment, the Italians quickly became impatient at what they regarded as insufficient French determination to follow up this gesture with other moves "to eliminate the paradoxical situation in which the French embassy in Rome finds itself." By February 1937 the Italian press was openly hostile to Delbos's apparent foot-dragging.[2]

The persistence of the Ethiopian roadblock prompted Mussolini to approach Lagardelle. He suggested that at the next meeting of the Council of the League, France might take the lead in overcoming the collective policies of the Genevan institution by moving to let each member state decide for itself on recognizing the Italian conquest, rather than relying on a unanimous League decision. France and England could then lead the way by recognizing the conquest, after which Italy could retake its seat at Geneva. Although the Duce's hints about reestablishing good Franco-Italian relations, in April 1937, were never very precise, the French military attaché in Rome believed that Mussolini sincerely desired to collaborate with France and suggested that dividends might be earned by making a concerted and good-faith effort to smoke the Italian out through negotiating "the price of our intervention in favor of the recognition of the Empire." Other counsels were not so optimistic. Dampierre interpreted Mussolini's reluctance to be specific about Franco-Italian relations as another indication that the persistence of the Ethiopian affair had contributed greatly to the Italo-German rapprochement. Even the final regulation of the matter in the sense indicated by Mussolini to Lagardelle "would not by any means determine a brusque clearing of the air by an [Italian] return toward previously charted directions."[3] Dampierre's doubts about resurrecting the Rome Accords and Stresa were clear, but Mussolini's formula for overcoming the roadblock on recognition of the Italian Empire was in fact adopted some eighteen months later. By then the Axis was decidedly more solid than it had been in the spring of 1937 and the chances of deflecting Italian policy correspondingly slimmer. One is tempted to conclude that Dampierre's doubts and Delbos's suspicions became a kind of self-fulfilling prophecy.

The inability, or unwillingness, to break through the Ethiopian impasse had other deleterious consequences for Franco-Italian relations. In August 1936 General Parisot reported that France, largely because of its policies on sanctions and recognition, had not been invited to send a military mission to Italy to observe the annual army maneuvers in Irpinia. Since the French had participated in 1934 and 1935, their absence in 1936 dramatically illustrated "the ground that we have lost here. . . ." A month later the military attaché notified the Ministry of Defense that the personal collaboration and exchange of documentation between the French and Italian Deuxième Bureaux, established by the Gamelin-Badoglio accords of June 1935, were "rendered somnolent" by the general political situation. At the end of the year, Parisot forwarded to the Ministry of War a French Embassy report drawing the logical conclusions from this collapse in Franco-Italian military collaboration. After a lengthy examination of Italy's economy, finance, army, navy, air power, and colonial activities, the report concluded that Italy had no hard and fast military commitments to any other power and in the event of a European war would probably adopt an initial stance of neutrality. But should Italy eventually enter a war on the side of Germany, France would need to maintain a strong military presence in the Alps, thus depleting its troop strength in the northeast. Such a development would also hinder communication with North Africa and the Little Entente. The report concluded: "'It is therefore important to appreciate the Italian factor at its proper value, without either exaggerating or minimizing its importance and without leaving the impression that we consider that there is nothing definitely to be expected from this side.'"[4] The embassy appeal to give appropriate weight to "the Italian factor," endorsed by France's military attaché, apparently counted for little at Delbos's Quai d'Orsay.

The Third Republic's weakening diplomatic position in Europe suffered another blow with regard to Yugoslavia, its staunchest ally in eastern Europe. On 26 September 1936 Belgrade signed a commercial accord with Rome, which gave rise to rumors that the Little Entente intended to imitate Belgium by withdrawing from their alliances with France into a state of neutrality. Dampierre regarded all such rumors as greatly exaggerated, but he did not conceal Yugoslavia's concern about what it viewed as the growing influence of communism in France and the apparent domestic weakness of the Popular Front regime. He also noted Belgrade's anxiety about the tepid French response to the Rhineland remilitarization, and he suggested that further French guarantees of the integrity of the Little Entente states would be welcomed. In addition, Yugoslavia assured the French that, although eager to further its normalization of relations with Italy, its commitment to friendship with France and the other members of the Little Entente remained intact.[5]

Nevertheless, the Quai d'Orsay evinced considerable discomfort at the prospect of a general Italo-Yugoslav accord in the spring of 1937. On 23 March Dampierre informed Delbos that Ciano himself was coming to Belgrade to conclude and sign a general accord with Yugoslavia in which the two powers would pledge, among other things, not to resort to war to resolve difficulties between them, to develop further commercial relations, and to respect the independence of Albania. Apparently Italy had initiated matters by proposing a formal alliance, but Belgrade rejected that in favor of this more modest accord. Dampierre requested instructions on how to respond to Ciano.[6] Not to congratulate the Italian foreign minister would create the impression that the French government disapproved of an accord that had been a principal objective of French diplomacy since 1924.

Delbos hardly could avoid acknowledging that he favored such an Italo-

Yugoslav agreement "in principle." But he reminded Dampierre that the Franco-Yugoslav treaty of 1927 required prior consultation before concluding accords with third powers, and so far France had not received official notification of the terms of the accord from Belgrade. Beyond this technicality, the French foreign minister deplored its timing. Italy would no doubt take propaganda advantage by portraying the accord as a diminishment of French influence in eastern Europe and by touting it as a Yugoslav endorsement of Italian policies in Spain. For these reasons, Delbos instructed Dampierre to suggest to the Yugoslav government that the proposed agreement be simply initialed at the present time, with formal signature to await more favorable circumstances. Furthermore the signing, whenever it occurred, should be accompanied by a public declaration from Belgrade affirming its loyalty to France and to its Little Entente partners.[7] The Yugoslavs accepted neither of Delbos's suggestions; Ciano and Stojadinovich signed the agreement on 25 March 1937 amid great fanfare in both countries.

Why did Italy seek an accord with Yugoslavia at this time, especially given the dearth of prior preparation and her apparent concessions with regard to Albania? Kamil Krofta, the Czech foreign minister, advanced the optimistic view that Italy was seeking a general rapprochement with the Little Entente in order to counter German influence in central Europe and the Balkans—a view echoed in the Italian press. Dampierre offered a more negative assessment of Italian motivations by speculating that Ciano sought a quick success for Italy's prestige by signing an accord with a country considered a staunch ally of France. By sending Ciano to Belgrade, Mussolini hoped to impress the other Little Entente states, thus making the Italo-Yugoslav accord a first thrust toward the future expansion of Italian influence in the Balkans at French expense. Regarding Yugoslav motivation, Dampierre felt the accord simply represented the fulfillment of Belgrade's long-standing desire to negotiate with Italy independent of any third-party mediation and did not signal a hostile attitude toward France.[8] Nevertheless the timing of the accord and the way in which it came about could not help but magnify the impression of a diminishing French stature in European affairs.

In addition to this litany of relatively minor irritants in Franco-Italian relations, there was also Spain and the question of security in the Mediterranean. The first six months of the Spanish struggle saw the British and the Italians fortify their positions in the Mediterranean Sea—the British in Cyprus and Malta and the Italians on the island of Majorca in the Balearics. The situation was regarded in Paris as prejudicial to France's vital access to and communication with her colonies in North Africa. The growing collusion of the two fascist dictatorships was also evident. In late October 1936 Ciano visited Berlin and Berchtesgaden for conversations with German Foreign Minister von Neurath and Hitler, securing German recognition of the Ethiopian conquest. On 1 November in Milan Mussolini delivered the famous, theatrical speech in which he characterized recent developments in Italo-German relations as constituting an "Axis" around which European diplomacy must revolve in the future. A week after its delivery, Mussolini clarified the Italian position by declaring his desire for "a gentleman's agreement [with Great Britain]. That is what I want . . . a solution as simple and clear in form as possible. . . . Anglo-Italian interests in the Mediterranean are not antagonistic but complementary. Neither nation can afford the luxury of being hostile to the other in that sea." The Duce wanted to establish good relations with Germany for purposes of intervention in Spain and to secure the northern frontier, but to do so without sacrificing relations with Great Britain. Ciano's visit to Berlin and Berchtesgaden in late October accomplished the first objective, and Mussolini's proposals for an Anglo-Italian Mediterranean agreement left the door open for negotiations with Britain—offering the further prospect of isolating the French. By 18 November Rome and Berlin simultaneously announced their recognition of the Nationalists as the official government in Spain.[9]

Moderate and right-wing opinion in France viewed Mussolini's Milan speech as an invitation to reopen the idea of a Franco-Italian rapprochement or to rebuild the Stresa Front as a counterweight to dependence upon Germany. In a debate on the floor of the Chamber of Deputies on 5 December 1936, Jean Ybarnégaray, Felix Grat, Ernest Pezet, Louis Marin, and Pierre Taittinger all argued at length that continued Italian resistance to *Anschluss* indicated her receptivity to a revival of the Stresa Front, which should form the thrust of French policy. At the very least France could work toward a four-power pact arrangement with Italy acting as a useful go-between. Similar attitudes appeared in the conservative Parisian press. The Spanish Civil War presented an obvious dilemma for the right. To them there seemed only a choice of either strengthening the Franco-Soviet alliance by intervening in Spain, abhorrent on ideological grounds, or seeking a Franco-German rapprochement at the expense of eastern Europe, unacceptable on treaty-revisionist grounds. The "out" lay in advocating a revival of the Stresa Front. Regardless of motive or practicality, the hope-in-Stresa policy remained a staple of French right-wing politicians until the outbreak of World War II and dominated the moderate and centrist press as well.[10]

Such a position could hardly be said to correspond to the realities of the

European political situation in the fall of 1936. Blondel summed up the gloomy prospects in a hard-headed dispatch on 20 November. He pointed out that the Ethiopian affair and the Spanish Civil War had driven Italy toward Germany. Reading Mussolini's speech of 1 November correctly, Blondel informed the Quai d'Orsay that Rome sought to reestablish amicable relations with England in order to balance its connection to Germany. He also indicated that "if one wants to describe the present position of Italy and the wild fluctuations of her policy, he must not hide from the fact that, with regard to France, ideological factors are currently of maximum importance in pushing Italy in a direction unfavorable to our country. Developments in official fascist circles dictate a growing antipathy vis-à-vis the French Popular Front government."[11] Implicit in Blondel's analysis—and also among those who held to the hope-in-Stresa formula— was the conclusion that any future moderation in Franco-Italian tensions depended upon the maintenance of Anglo-French solidarity. French statesmen pursued this line consistently from 1936 to 1940, but events were to reveal precious little cooperation from London. The way in which the English concluded the "gentleman's agreement" to which Mussolini had referred offered a disturbing harbinger for the future.

On 5 November in a speech to the House of Commons, Eden concurred with Mussolini's interest in an Anglo-Italian agreement. The following day the two countries signed a trade agreement which prepared the way for the transformation of the British legation in Addis Ababa into a consulate general accredited to Rome. Despite claims in Rome to the contrary, London stressed that this move did not constitute recognition of the Italian conquest and bore no relation whatsoever to any potential Mediterranean agreement. By 25 November Grandi informed Eden that Mussolini was prepared to conclude an agreement, acknowledging that British recognition of the conquest of Ethiopia could not be made a condition. These events unfolded amid increasing apprehensions of isolation among French diplomats. Corbin approached Eden on 24 November and exposed to him "in the most dramatic fashion" the fears that a bilateral Anglo-Italian accord on the Mediterranean would awaken among the French people. He expressed the same sentiment to Sargent who politely thanked Corbin for his observations but suggested that a détente between England and Italy might well pave the way for a similar agreement between Paris and Rome. The French view, articulated most succinctly by René Massigli, was quite the opposite. The associate director of political affairs at the Quai d'Orsay believed that Italy and Germany would certainly exploit the fact of France's nonparticipation by depicting it as a weakening of her general position in Europe and a loosening of her links to England. The result was more likely to increase rather than diminish Italian antipathy toward France.[12]

Twice, on 26 November and again on 18 December, France lodged official demarches at the Foreign Office requesting an English initiative to expand negotiations on the Mediterranean to include the Third Republic. In each case these were brushed aside with curt observations that this would only complicate and therefore delay an accord. The French had to be satisfied by vague assurances from Eden that the interests of all riparian powers would be protected. It is clear that Delbos had few illusions about persuading the English to seek a trilateral negotiation; his instructions to Corbin for the second demarche included the fall-back position to adopt in the event of failure. That is, the British government "must seize the first opportunity to indicate publicly that the French government has been kept au courant of the negotiation and its conclusion."[13]

French diplomacy exercised little if any suasion on the British Foreign Office. Acting on instructions from Whitehall, Drummond asked Ciano on 31 December for a guarantee that Italy had no permanent designs on the Balearics or any other Spanish territory. The Italian foreign minister responded immediately that "so far as Italy is concerned the integrity of the present territories of Spain shall in all circumstances remain intact and unmodified." Ciano's assurance cleared the way, and the Anglo-Italian Gentleman's Agreement was signed in Rome on 2 January 1937. In the document, considered at the time to be a milestone in the development of good will between the two powers, London and Rome recognized that the freedom of entry into, exit from, and transit through the Mediterranean was a vital interest to both; furthermore, they agreed to respect each other's rights and interests and disclaimed any desire to modify the status quo in the Mediterranean area.[14]

The Gentleman's Agreement produced none of the hoped-for ameliorations in the western democracies' relations with Italy. It said nothing specifically about Spain, the immediate source of tensions in the Mediterranean, and even Ciano's pledge of 31 December 1936 contained no assurance that Italy would refrain from intervention on behalf of General Franco. Indeed the Italians had chosen to land some 5,000 soldiers at Cadiz the day after the signing of the accord. The British government was quite concerned about the organized flow of volunteers into Spain, and in a note of 24 December 1936 Whitehall instructed its representatives in Berlin, Rome, and Moscow to stress the urgent need for putting an end to it. London announced that it would take legislative measures to halt the flow of volunteers out of England and requested that similar programs be undertaken by other governments.[15] Britain in fact invoked the Foreign Enlistments Act early in January 1937, forbidding her citizens to fight in Spain, and France adopted similar legislation.

The note of 24 December seemed to indicate that Britain was prepared to take a firm stand on the question of volunteers. Yet she signed the Gentleman's Agreement on 2 January 1937 before receiving a reply from Italy. Diplomatic moves such as this could only convince Mussolini that London would not prevent him from continuing to send reinforcements to Spain. The initial Italian and German replies to the British note were generally discouraging, expressing dissatisfaction that Britain had acted outside the Nonintervention Committee. But after meetings in Rome from 20 to 23 January, where Marshal Goering conferred directly with Mussolini and Ciano, the two fascist states agreed that since Franco by then had been adequately supplied with men and war materiel, Germany and Italy should support the British proposal to prohibit the entry of further volunteers into Spain. They communicated this decision to London but insisted that measures to stem the flow of volunteers could not be put into effect until the general outlines of an adequate system of control had been agreed upon in the Nonintervention Committee. Western diplomats in the London Committee sought to capitalize on this obvious delaying tactic by linking the establishment of a control plan to a provision calling for the withdrawal of volunteers already fighting in Spain. The Italians, with troop strength in Spain estimated at sixty to seventy thousand men in March 1937, were understandably unenthusiastic about a withdrawal provision. In any case, that subject terminated abruptly on 23 March when, following the defeat of 38,000 fascist troops at Guadalajara, Grandi informed the Nonintervention Committee of Italy's categorical refusal to withdraw a single Italian volunteer until the complete victory of the Nationalists was assured. Since no headway could be made on the withdrawal issue, the London Committee proceeded rather quickly to establish a volunteer control scheme, which called for the patrolling of Spanish coasts and ports by the participating powers and the assignment of neutral observers to merchant vessels destined for Spain. The observers were empowered to examine all persons and goods to be off-loaded in Spain.[16] The control scheme, weakened by the absence of any provision calling for the control of air traffic and the lack of legal procedures to be imposed on those caught smuggling, became effective on 19 April 1937.

Anglo-Italian diplomacy in late 1936 and early 1937, therefore, ranged from one end of the Mediterranean to the other, but the stated British objective of establishing a firm understanding with Rome remained unfulfilled. The Gentleman's Agreement dealt in moral obligations rather than concrete commitments, and its applicability to Spain was only implied.

Italy, on the other hand, had established a treaty recognizing the Franco regime in November 1936, and the Italo-Yugoslav agreement of March 1937 strengthened her position in the central Mediterranean. Moreover, evidence suggests that British diplomacy had achieved little in the way of thwarting a growing cohesion between Rome and Berlin—a matter of increasing concern to both Whitehall and the Quai d'Orsay.

Events of fall and winter 1936 stripped virtually all initiative from French hands with regard to her relations with Fascist Italy, and French documents betray the decidedly uncomfortable role of a passive observer of events. Nevertheless, several significant trends are discernible from an examination of French archives for the first half of 1937. First, French diplomats were made aware, both by their own observation and through informants, that the Gentleman's Agreement had not led to a moderation of relations between London and Rome. In fact, there were a number of indications that the Rome-Berlin Axis was becoming the cornerstone of Italian foreign policy and might even result in the near future in an alliance between the two fascist powers. Second, many of the writers of these same documents took heart from the fact that Mussolini had not definitively slammed the door on his relations with the western powers. While acknowledging the growing cohesion of the Axis, these observers viewed it only as a "tactical necessity" for Rome, which would last only so long as Mussolini was unable to find a formula for entente with France and England on the subject of Ethiopia. But third, such sanguine assessments were balanced by disturbing indications that, so far as Italy was concerned, France counted for little in the international constellation of power. With regard to this last point, Delbos forwarded to Blondel the assessment of Boris Stein, the Soviet ambassador to Rome, who indicated that, "France is at once detested and scorned in official Roman circles. Detested because of its government, scorned because one is convinced in these circles that France is only a satellite of England. We shall arrange our affairs with Great Britain, one hears in these milieux, and France will follow. We don't have to concern ourselves with her." The Deuxième Bureau of the Army echoed Stein's judgment in an assessment of Italian public opinion on 22 July 1937. The report found little animosity toward France among the Italian people, or at least a great deal less than during the period of sanctions. But "it is believed that London directs the foreign policy of France, which follows along like some sort of Dominion."[17]

The above summary of French archival materials for the first half of 1937 indicates that a pattern had emerged from the episode of the Gentleman's Agreement and its aftermath. Following the hasty and foolhardy withdrawal of the French ambassador from Rome in October 1936, England was clearly in the driver's seat with regard to policy between the two western democracies and Italy. France could do little to chart an independent course of action, and events were to demonstrate that her efforts to exert pressure to alter British diplomacy met with only limited success. Thus, the situation that French foreign ministers from Poincaré to Flandin had sought to avoid, that is, exclusive reliance upon England, was a fundamental reality by the summer of 1937. The French military attaché in Rome penetrated to the nub of the matter in April 1937 when he reported that Italy's defensive measures were still very general and not directed against any particular adversary. Italy's policy was to wait, not to designate in advance of any general European conflict what her "definitive preferences" were likely to be. The report concluded, however, that "it is beyond doubt that the attitude of England will weigh very heavily on the decision of the fascist government."[18]

IN ENGLAND'S WAKE

The continuing crisis in the Mediterranean provided the theater in which Anglo-French relations with Italy would be tested. It would also demonstrate the limits to which the French could influence British policy. The atmosphere was particularly complicated in that neither the British nor the French cabinets were united on how to deal with the Italian question. In England the split between Eden, who was increasingly inclined toward a hard-line stance vis-à-vis Italy in cooperation with France, and Prime Minister Neville Chamberlain, an equally ardent spokesman for appeasement, led to a major cabinet crisis and the former's resignation in February 1938.[19] A similar split divided the French Council of Ministers. Delbos, in alliance with Léger at the Quai d'Orsay, championed a more assertive role, whereas the new Radical Socialist premier, Camille Chautemps, and his Minister of Finance, Georges Bonnet, advocated a softer line toward Rome.[20] In any case, the initiative fell to England.

On 19 July 1937 Eden delivered a speech in the House of Commons expressing disappointment that the Gentleman's Agreement of January had not achieved the anticipated degree of Anglo-Italian cooperation in the Mediterranean. He repeated Britain's determination to defend its interests in the sea but closed by emphasizing that there was room enough for all powers. The speech received good press in Italy, and Grandi indicated to Whitehall that the Duce was prepared to discuss closer relations between Great Britain and Italy. Chamberlain seized the opportunity to write directly to Mussolini on 27 July. The prime minister regretted the strained relations between the two countries and suggested two-power talks to alleviate differences. The Duce couched his reply, which arrived in London on 2 August, in friendly terms and reciprocated the sentiments of the British leader. France's role in these matters was predictably passive. Delbos complained to American ambassador William Bullitt about England's typical lack of prior consultation with France and said that "he was furious with Eden and Chamberlain for having inaugurated a rapprochement with Italy . . . [which] should be treated with contempt and disdain as a relatively unimportant jackel." But the diplomatic correspondence for the summer of 1937 revealed a perceptible moderation in the violently anti-French tone of Italian diplomacy, especially following the Chamberlain-Mussolini exchange of notes. The Italians evinced some urgency, given the slowness of their military progress in Spain and renewed suspicions of their Axis partner's ambitions in Austria, to repair the breach with England. They apparently recognized that French support for bilateral Anglo-Italian negotiations would carry some weight in London and, therefore, hinted on a number of occasions that such a détente might well lead to an amelioration of Italo-French relations as well.[21]

The Italian ambassador in Paris delivered a similar message in a rare conversation with Chautemps on 6 August. The French premier, obviously elated at the message delivered by Cerruti, concluded that "this very friendly meeting . . . was characterized by the reciprocal demonstration of a desire for appeasement in international relations, and most particularly in the atmosphere between our two countries."[22]

Although it was recognized that Italy's price for a rapprochement in Franco-Italian relations would certainly be recognition of the Ethiopian conquest, nevertheless the improved atmosphere demonstrated by these documents led the French to give their blessing to the proposed Anglo-Italian negotiations. On 29 July 1937, Delbos instructed Corbin to inform Eden that France would not oppose the talks. That the French foreign minister was not quite so sanguine as Chautemps about their potential outcome was revealed in his request that France be much more fully informed about developments than she had been prior to the Gentleman's Agreement of 2 January. Delbos also expected that England would take steps to assure that any eventual Anglo-Italian détente would not lead the Italian government to reaccentuate the anti-French tone of its foreign policy.[23] With the French endorsement in hand, the British Foreign Office made plans to open conversations with Italy in September. These arrangements may be regarded as the seedbed from which emerged some six months later the famous Anglo-Italian Easter Accord. But a new crisis, involving open hostilities in the Mediterranean, interrupted bilateral pourparlers and provided Delbos an opportunity to assert forcefully a rare French initiative.

MEDITERRANEAN "PIRACY" AND THE NYON CONFERENCE

During the month of August 1937, eight British ships and eighteen other neutral ships were either sunk or attacked in the Mediterranean by "unknown" submarines and, in a few cases, by airplanes. Although no concrete evidence as to the identity of the unknowns was available at the time, a great deal of circumstantial evidence pointed in the Italian direction. Demonstrators in Paris, armed with paint cans, rechristened the Boulevard des Italiens as the Boulevard des Inconnues. It is now known beyond question that Italy was behind the lawless destruction in the Mediterranean.²⁴ The crowning blow, so far as Great Britain was concerned came on 27 August when the Italian press published the texts of telegrams exchanged by Mussolini and Franco after the Nationalist victory in the Battle of Santander. The telegrams referred to Italian casualties, and Mussolini praised the contributions of his soldiers to the Nationalist victory. The Duce also stated that: "This comradeship of arms—now so close—is a guarantee of the final victory which will liberate Spain and the Mediterranean from all threats to the civilization we share."²⁵ Once Italy threw off the mask in this way, it became extraordinarily difficult for other governments to defend the policy of nonintervention against its critics. Mussolini's telegram to Franco momentarily derailed the possibility of bilateral Anglo-Italian talks.

The breach afforded Delbos his opportunity. On 26 August Roger Cambon, the French chargé d'affaires in London, approached the Foreign Office with a rather ill-defined proposal for diplomatic conversations among the Mediterranean powers to deal with the upsurge of piracy. Invited by the British to develop the proposal more fully, Cambon delivered a more detailed communiqué on the 30th. It called for the British and French delegations to the League of Nations to arrange a meeting of the Mediterranean powers to consider measures to protect their shipping in the Mediterranean Sea. The note stressed that this proposal represented the consensus view of the Council of Ministers and insisted that "only common action by France and England would serve to bring about a modification in the Italian attitude." In the absence of such common resolve, "the French government would examine the basis on which the Nonintervention Agreement rests and redeem its right of complete freedom of action."²⁶

As Eden later acknowledged in his memoirs, "this was the germ of the Nyon Conference."²⁷ The French proposal fitted well with the British foreign secretary's predilections, and after some discussion about which nations ought to be invited to such a discussion, the British Cabinet forwarded its adhesion on 2 September. On the 5th Paris and London dispatched notes to Albania, Bulgaria, Egypt, Germany, Greece, Italy, Romania, the USSR, Turkey, and Yugoslavia inviting them to attend a conference at the small Swiss city of Nyon on 10 September to "end the present state of insecurity in the Mediterranean and to ensure that the rules of international law regarding shipping at sea shall be strictly enforced."[28] The Italians and Germans found an excuse to absent themselves from Nyon, arguing that the proper venue for such a discussion was the London Nonintervention Committee.

This clumsy attempt to undermine the conference failed; it opened as scheduled on 10 September with Delbos as presiding officer. Both Delbos and Eden agreed that the major aim of the conference should lie in the organization and disposition of naval forces in the Mediterranean so that unlawful attacks could be dealt with promptly. They reached full accord by 12 September, a remarkably short time for an agreement of such scope and potential significance. Among other things the Nyon Agreement divided the Mediterranean into zones to be patrolled by ships of the participating powers, which would have orders to counterattack and sink aggressive submarines or any submarines in the vicinity of an attack. In the western Mediterranean and the Malta Channel, exclusive of the Tyrrhenian and Aegean Seas, the British and French fleets were to enforce the Nyon decision. In the eastern Mediterranean the territorial waters were to be entrusted to the riparian powers and the high seas to Britain and France. The Black Sea was reserved for Soviet patrol. On 17 September the powers signed a supplementary agreement at Geneva, extending the terms of the Nyon Agreement to include attacks on shipping by surface vessels and aircraft.[29]

The brunt of enforcing the Nyon decisions thus fell to Britain and France. Their navies were assigned to patrol the main trade routes from Suez and the Dardanelles to Gilbraltar, and from the North African ports to Marseille. As for the Tyrrhenian and Aegean Seas, it was hoped that Italy could be induced to join the patrol scheme in those areas—as they were unimportant commercially, Italy could chase her own submarines where it mattered least. The decisions reached at Nyon were rapidly put into effect. As Eden pointed out in a speech to the House of Commons, members of the conference agreed to all plans and details within forty-eight hours, and in less than two weeks the decisions of the conference, including the patrolling of trade routes in the Mediterranean by an Anglo-French force of some eighty destroyers, had been put into effect.[30] The Nyon

Agreement did curtail piracy. The naval blockade was effectively applied, and attacks on merchant ships subsided quickly—an indication that whenever England and France acted with unity of purpose, their rights and interests would not be taken lightly by other powers.

Eden, of course, was delighted. In letters to Winston Churchill he pointed with pride to the efficacies of Anglo-French cooperation and characterized the Nyon Agreement as a "counterattack" against Britain's continued retreat before Germany, Italy, and Japan. The foreign secretary uttered similar judgments publicly in a speech at Llandudno on 15 October 1937. The initial French public response was equally enthusiastic. Newspapers across the political spectrum praised the fact that France had taken the lead in developing a policy of Franco-British cooperation. The left was gratified by the apparent assertion of collective security, while the right expressed satisfaction that Soviet warships would be restricted to patrols in the Black Sea. Subsequent analysts have described the Nyon Conference as one of the rare successes for western diplomacy in the 1930s, an assertion of strength indicating that the Axis could be checked and the relationship between Mussolini and Hitler weakened by pursuing such common action in lieu of ill-coordinated acts of appeasement.[31]

There can be little doubt that coordinated policies in London and Paris—whether of defiance or of appeasement—would have had a salutary effect in Rome. But the fact of the matter is that the Nyon episode represented but a momentary coalescence between the two western countries. The strain it placed on Anglo-Italian relations allowed Chamberlain to reassert the thread of the Gentleman's Agreement by moving back to the negotiations of July and August, temporarily interrupted by the piracy issue. A footnote to the Nyon Conference made this direction clear. It had been hoped originally that Italy could be induced to participate in the patrol scheme in a subsidiary fashion. But the Italians balked, demanding parity with Britain and France as the price for their adhesion. Under substantial British pressure, the principle of equality was accepted as a basis for negotiation, and on 21 September Mussolini sent representatives to Paris to discuss Italian association with the Nyon arrangement. Negotiations continued throughout the month, and on the last day naval experts from Britain, France, and Italy reached an understanding whereby Italian participation in piracy control would begin in November. Italy acquired patrol zones in the central and eastern Mediterranean and between the Balearic Islands and Sardinia, as well as in the Tyrrhenian Sea, areas which would enable the Italians to continue sending supplies to the Spanish Nationalists at Majorca without fear of detection. Rome, in exchange, repeated shopworn promises about the eventual withdrawal of volunteer troops and denied territorial ambitions in Spain. Ciano bragged to his diary on 21 September 1937: "We agree to a technical conference to modify the Nyon clauses in accordance with our wishes to enter the Arrangement. It is a fine victory. From suspected pirates to policemen of the Mediterranean—and the Russians, whose ships we were sinking, excluded." The German consul at Geneva described the conversations in Paris "as a marked political victory for Italy."[32]

Such contemptuous sentiments were, of course, not communicated to the western democracies, although their tone was clear enough. Delbos could rightly claim credit for promoting and ensuring the initial success of the Nyon Conference, as he did some years later in an article for the London *Sunday Times*.[33] But the French foreign minister and the Popular Front coalition lacked both the strength and the will to push the British further along this path. After September 1937, Chamberlain's plan for a bilateral rapprochement with Mussolini moved once more to the fore.

FRANCE AND THE ANGLO-ITALIAN RAPPROCHEMENT

The Nyon interlude, for all that it impressed analysts in retrospect, produced confusing signals to participants at the time. The foregoing discussion shows that for some (Eden and the French communists to be sure and, to a more limited degree, Delbos and Léger as well), Nyon represented a policy of assertiveness and solidarity—just the ticket to counter the illegal and unpredictable attitudes of the fascist dictatorships. But for others the pursuit of the Nyon attitude carried the risk of totally alienating Italy from the western powers, an alarming prospect that flew in the face of over a decade of careful French diplomacy. These traditional concerns reasserted themselves in the fall of 1937 when, in the wake of a particularly violent anti-French press campaign in Italy, intelligence reports indicated substantial Italian military concentrations in Libya and Spain. The French regarded the latter as particularly dangerous to their maritime communications with North Africa.[34]

Some French diplomats tended to interpret these developments as a bluff designed by Mussolini to impress Hitler and pro-Germans in his own cabinet, such as Ciano and Dino Alfieri, of his loyalty to the Axis. Behind the smokescreen, Charles-Roux suggested from the Vatican, Mussolini was inclined to live on good terms with France. At the moment Italy felt the Axis was absolutely essential as a safeguard against an England dominated by Eden's policies. But Franco-Italian relations were likely to improve once the necessity for the Rome-Berlin link became less urgent. More realistic and influential was Blondel's analysis of the situation. The French chargé in Rome submitted a long factual and analytical dispatch on 30 November 1937, beginning with a detailed discussion of Italian military capabilities and ending with a Kennanesque essay on how to deal with Italy in the future. His various essays on the Italian army, navy, air force, explosive devices, economics, and finances reached the conclusion that Italy possessed substantial military power which constituted a real danger for France. After reviewing the growth of Italo-German solidarity in the wake of sanctions, he asserted that the chances of breaking the Axis apart by alternating pressures in Rome and Berlin were slim. This would assume French and British willingness to make substantial concessions to one or the other fascist power—not a likely possibility. How, then, to respond to the Italian question? Of first importance, Blondel insisted, was to maintain a solid tie to England, for the Franco-English entente was a matter of concern in Rome. But such a policy should not include the corollary of abandoning all hope of resolving Franco-Italian differences: "On the contrary, by employing patience vis-à-vis the Italian government and by demonstrating toward it sentiments of apparent understanding or at the minimum a serene indifference, we should doubtless be able to ameliorate our position here considerably and gradually recover an influence that we have, at present, completely lost." Now that the Ethiopian conflict was over and the Spanish Civil War appeared to be winding down, Blondel believed that the future held the possibility of a genuine rapprochement.[35]

These kinds of views no doubt exercised some influence on French leaders when they travelled to London for full-scale talks with their British counterparts on 29–30 November 1937. The discussions were wide-ranging, encompassing Germany, Italy, colonial issues, and central Europe. The French ministers displayed great irritation on the subject of relations with Italy, especially when it was announced that England intended in the near future to seek bilateral negotiations with Mussolini aimed at the achievement of an accord on Mediterranean issues far more comprehensive and explicit than the Gentleman's Agreement of the previous January. Delbos complained bitterly that the timing for such an initiative was awkward in light of continued Italian press polemics and that Italy was likely to use the negotiations to divide France and Great Britain. But in the end Premier Chautemps accepted the British proposal for conversations with Italy on three conditions: (1) that Italy renounce her "violent propaganda" against France and England; (2) that the French government be kept fully informed of the progress of negotiations; and (3) that the eventual Anglo-Italian accord be open to the adhesion of France. Eden carried the French conditions to the Cabinet meeting of 1 December, where British ministers authorized the initiation of Anglo-Italian conversations. It was agreed that the French government would be kept informed and that no Anglo-Italian bilateral agreement would be concluded on matters of concern to France. Furthermore, the Cabinet instructed British negotiators to insist on the modification of anti-French and anti-British propaganda in Italy. Interestingly enough, however, and a harbinger of future hard feelings between the two western democracies, the following phrase was striken out of the typewritten record of the Cabinet Conclusions for the meeting of 1 December: "and that at the appropriate stage the French Government would have to be brought into the negotiations." On this basis, Eden invited Grandi to his office on 5 December and, assuring him of the "complete solidarity" between England and France, informed the Italian ambassador of England's interest in launching Anglo-Italian conversations.[36]

Four days later Mussolini complicated the situation with a sensational speech in Palermo announcing his intention to put the issue of Italy's withdrawal from the League of Nations before the Fascist Grand Council. The latter endorsed the move, and on 11 December the Duce proclaimed his official break with Geneva, citing the League's refusal to recognize the Italian conquest of Ethiopia. The gesture could be viewed as a strengthening of Italy's links to Germany, since it occurred shortly after Rome's adherence to the Anti-Comintern Pact. But Blondel suggested that it was meant primarily as a signal to England that Mussolini would not countenance the use of the proposed Anglo-Italian negotiations as a device to "chloroform" him and thus to delay England's recognition of the Italian Empire. Evidence suggests that there was a good deal to this interpretation. An Italian diplomat at the Vatican told his French colleague, "Today what we want is the official recognition of our empire; it is in order to obtain it from France and Great Britain that we are playing the *trump card,* that we are exposing ourselves to this present *bluff.*" The Italian went on to say that Ethiopia represented Mussolini's only territorial ambition. "Recognize the conquest of Ethiopia and within two months, relations between Italy and France will be relaxed, the tone of our press appeased."[37]

The evidence also suggests that the French took Mussolini's "bluff" more seriously than the British. Officials in the British War Office told the French military attaché in London that they were not inclined to lose sleep over Italy's withdrawal from the League or its troop buildup in Libya. These moves were probably designed to intensify British anxiety about the security of Egypt and, therefore, to render her more readily disposed to buy off Italy via the recognition of the Ethiopian conquest. Given the fragility of the Italian economy and Italy's still-delicate military position in Ethiopia, the War Office considered recent Italian gestures as bluff—allowing time for the execution of the British rearmament program. Implicit in this analysis was the impression that gaining time represented a major objective of Anglo-Italian negotiations. Blondel, however, was considerably less blasé. Noting that a number of smaller nations had already made the decision to recognize the Italian conquest, Blondel insisted that it would be unfortunate if recognition were granted by a majority of European states in such a way that it would appear that Anglo-French objections had been ineffective or motivated by bad will toward Italy. "Don't we have a greater interest . . . in permitting and even approving early recognition by the small states of Europe, while reserving the right to imitate them ourselves at the moment when it would finally be considered by us as opportune?"[38] This telegram represents Blondel's first formal effort to push the Quai d'Orsay toward recognition of the Italian conquest. In any case, Mussolini's withdrawal from the League, coupled with the intensification of the Austrian question in the winter of 1938, removed the matter of Anglo-Italian negotiations from the forefront of the diplomatic calendar.

ANSCHLUSS

Italy's formal withdrawal from Geneva, a symbol for many of the coalescence of Italian and German foreign policy, once again focused attention on the question of Austria's continued independence—an issue whose importance receded after the Italian mobilization on the Brenner in July 1934 and the Austro-German Treaty of 1934. In the interim the possibility of *Anschluss* had received scant but contradictory analysis from French diplomatic correspondents. On the one hand came reports suggesting that Austria no longer weighed heavily in Italian calculations and that Ciano, given the Mediterranean orientation of Italian policies from 1935 to 1937, was prepared to accept with equanimity the inevitability of Germany's eventual appearance on the Brenner.[39] These were offset, however, by other communications indicating that Italian resolve remained solid and that Rome's tendency to neglect Austria was more apparent than real—a reflection of Mussolini's need to maintain good relations with Hitler while tensions with Paris and London ran high. The clearest expression of the latter point of view came from Hugues Barthon de Montbas, the French chargé in Vienna, on 26 May 1937. He advanced the view that Italy had not abandoned her Austrian interests as thoroughly as some others had speculated. Rather, the Duce's deepest desire was to detach himself from Germany, but that could occur only after two prior conditions had been met: (1) the western recognition of the Italian Empire in Ethiopia, and (2) a military victory for Italians in Spain to efface the disgrace of Guadalajara. Montbas concluded that Mussolini would reassume "his position on the Danube on the day when the amelioration of his relations with Paris and London will permit him to escape from under the thumb of Berlin. The question is to know if the dictators of the Third Reich will allow him, as he hopes, time to receive the first western 'signal.' "[40]

Implicit in Montbas's analysis was the conviction that the key to bringing Italy back into line on the Austrian question was a common Anglo-French determination to resolve differences with the Italian dictator. It was a refrain echoed time and again in French diplomatic correspondence following Italy's withdrawal from the League and Hitler's now-famous "conversation" with Austrian Chancellor Kurt von Schuschnigg on 12 February 1938. The Austrian minister of foreign affairs, Guido Schmidt, put the matter quite succinctly in a conversation with the French minister in Vienna on 26 December 1937. "I have never ceased to think," he said, "that only an accord among France, England and Italy can guarantee the independence of Austria."[41]

But once again the Quai d'Orsay's stubborn refusal to communicate directly with Rome undercut the best advice of its field representatives. In addition, the *Anschluss* crisis revealed the cross-purposes at which Paris and London approached the Italian question. This conundrum emerged clearly in the events of February and March 1938. On two occasions following Hitler's tumultuous interview with Schuschnigg at Berchtesgaden, Gabriel Puaux insisted, quite correctly, that Austria's only hope for survival lay with Italian determination to defend its independence. But Mussolini's policy would be conditioned by the state of his relations with England and France. Puaux, therefore, urged it as "the duty" of the French and British governments to approach Mussolini "before it's too late." While the French diplomat called for concerted Anglo-French action in Rome, the British ambassador in the Italian capital advised a more limited approach. Perth apparently saw the impending Austrian crisis as an opportunity to force Eden's hand on the truncated proposal for Anglo-Italian negotiations on the Mediterranean. He therefore telegraphed the British foreign secretary on 16 February with the advice that "the only thing which could prevent further German encroachments on Austrian independence would be the early conclusion of a general agreement between Italy and ourselves." His communication omitted any mention of French participation other than the disingenuous suggestion that the French chargé d'affaires shared his views on the essentiality of an Anglo-Italian accord.[42]

It was in this situation that, on 17 February 1938, Delbos launched a new set of instructions to the French ambassador in London. Ignoring Blondel's and Puaux's judgments that Rome represented the appropriate target for concerted action on behalf of Austria, the French foreign minister instructed Corbin to seek a combined Franco-British demarche to Berlin declaring the two western powers' unalterable opposition to any sort of *Anschluss*. Delbos suggested a combined effort along these lines: first, a statement that Schuschnigg had made enough concessions already in the interests of European peace; second, that Britain and France could not remain indifferent in the face of new German initiatives; and finally, that any act of force to alter the territorial status quo in central Europe would meet with the "resolute opposition" of the western powers. He went on to say that Italian collaboration, while desirable, was very unlikely since Mussolini seemed inclined to sacrifice Italy's position in central Europe "to her Mediterranean ambition." He concluded that, "It is by underscoring this measure of our resolution and by freely demonstrating that we do not intend to suffer events passively that we in fact shall establish the best chance of one day leading the Italian government back among us." Delbos's scant regard for the importance of Italy was scarcely concealed here. However, as Robert J. Young has suggested, apparently the French initiative was not serious, given the military's dismal assessment of the prospects of defending Austrian independence by force. Rather, the gesture was prompted by domestic political exigencies to make it seem as though something were being done. Premier Chautemps later told the Austrian ambassador in Paris that he had been under no illusion that Britain would go along with such a proposal.[43]

The French proposal for concerted Anglo-French diplomacy in Berlin arrived in London shortly after Lord Perth's missive indicating the moment opportune to move forward on the conclusion of a bilateral Anglo-Italian accord. The conjunction of the two brought the fundamental divergence of views between Chamberlain and Eden into the open. At a stormy meeting between the two British statesmen and Grandi on 19 February, the prime minister inquired directly if Italy had in fact written off Austria. Avoiding a forthright response, the Italian ambassador proceeded to establish a link between the Austrian question and Italian expansion, indicating obliquely that Italy might be inclined to oppose *Anschluss* if Britain first would recognize the annexation of Ethiopia and agree to examine other Mediterranean questions bilaterally. Eden refused to foresee any Anglo-Italian accord if the Italians did not first agree to a satisfactory resolution of the Spanish question (i.e., the withdrawal of volunteers). Chamberlain, however, overrode his foreign minister's objections and indicated that he was prepared to open conversations with Italy. Eden announced his resignation the following day. In the wake of these events, it came as no surprise that Britain formally rejected Delbos's proposal for an Anglo-French demarche in Berlin. Noting that Britain shared France's concern about the

Austrian situation, the British memorandum deemed it inadvisable to take common action against German activities, preferring instead to observe the situation closely through normal diplomatic channels. Delbos's response indicated that Britain's lack of willingness to establish a common policy against German aggressiveness would be interpreted in Berlin as a sign of weakness among the western powers which would most likely whet Hitler's appetite for further adventures—probably in the Sudetenland.[44] Once again Delbos's communication failed to mention Italy.

The Cabinet crisis in England, coupled with increasing concern over the fate of Austria, prompted a major foreign policy debate in the French Chamber of Deputies on 25–26 February 1938. Speaker after speaker, representing primarily opinions to the right of the political spectrum, mounted the rostrum to denounce Delbos's foreign policy. Flandin, Marin, Ybarnégaray, Pezet, and Marcel Boucher, among others, all denounced what they regarded as the government's outworn notions of collective security based on the League of Nations. They suggested, quite correctly as it turned out, that *Anschluss* could be stopped only with the aid of Italy and that therefore a rapprochement should be initiated at once. If Britain could not be induced to work with France to reconstruct the Stresa Front, then France should deal directly with Rome. Delbos, supported in this instance by Reynaud, deplored the situation that left Austria standing alone but argued that without British cooperation, there was little that France could do.[45]

Fiery speeches delivered in the political arena by a regime's opponents might easily be dismissed as ideological fulmination designed to elicit partisan advantage, but numerous communications from France's diplomatic representatives in the field lent credence to the arguments simultaneously being enunciated on the floor of the Chamber. Between 19 February and 5 March, Delbos was literally bombarded by dispatches and telegrams from Blondel in Rome, Puaux in Vienna, and Charles-Roux at the Vatican urging him to undertake some sort of initiative with the Italian government. The tenor of this flurry of correspondence was that the benign "public face" Italy had adopted in the Austrian situation actually concealed substantial fears and concerns among Italian officials as to the real nature of German intentions. All three suggested that France should capitalize upon this uncertainty by making direct overtures to the Palazzo Chigi. Should France be willing to consider recognizing the Ethiopian conquest, then a more resolute Italian stance vis-à-vis Germany over the Austrian issue could be expected. In the absence of any positive response from the Quai d'Orsay, Puaux made one final attempt to persuade Delbos of the wisdom of approaching Mussolini. On 7 March he telegraphed Delbos that only a revival of the Badoglio-Gamelin accords could safeguard Austrian independence. But, "soon it will be too late. I believe it is my duty to warn Your Excellency [of the situation], because for want of considering a military measure, the threat of which alone can make the adversary draw back, the government of the Republic will risk finding itself in a very short period of time confronted, as was the case on 7 March 1936, with the irreparable." The French minister stuck his neck out even further the following day in a desperate attempt to persuade Massigli to intercede with Delbos. His personal letter warned that it was necessary for the government to recognize clearly the consequences "of refusing to chat with Mussolini. Why not send him an unofficial emissary in the person of [Anatole] de Monzie, [Jean] de Mistler or Henri Béranger?" All to no avail. Puaux received a curt reproach from Paris, informing him that his suggestions were "inadmissable" and even "improper." On 11 March, shortly before the 5:00 P.M. deadline for Germany's ultimatum demanding the resignation of Schuschnigg was to expire, Blondel received telephone instructions from Paris not to seek any further intercessions with Ciano on the matter.[46]

The *Anschluss,* therefore, unfolded amid no more than token verbal objections from London and Paris against this further violation of the treaties of 1919–20. The foregoing demonstrates more clearly than any other series of events Delbos's absolute distaste for dealing directly with Italy, even in spite of repeated assurances from agents in the field that a French gesture stood at least an even chance of galvanizing some form of Italian resistance to the Austrian coup. As far as the British were concerned, it seems equally clear that Italy's previous role as a guarantor of Austrian independence, or as a barrier to the expansion of German influence in Danubia, mattered not at all in their calculations. What did matter in London was the scope of Italian Mediterranean ambitions. Consequently, Whitehall proved decidedly unsympathetic to any common policy with France, toward either Berlin or Rome, for fear of complicating and thus delaying completion of an Anglo-Italian accord designed to regulate the two powers' potentially dangerous relations in the Mediterranean area.[47]

The denouement of the *Anschluss* crisis seemed a vindication, albeit bitter, for those who saw it as yet another lost opportunity to salvage the semblance of a working relationship with Italy. From all over the Peninsula came reports about the consternation of the Italian people at seeing Hitler install German troops on the Brenner, barely 100 kilometers from Trieste and in immediate contact with the German-speaking peoples of Trentino and the Alto Adige. Blondel felt strongly that Mussolini and the Italian government were taken completely by surprise at the speed and totality of the German takeover. Although Hitler solemnly hastened to guarantee the Brenner frontier, there could be no denying that henceforth Germany would exercise a strong and perhaps decisive influence on the Balkans. The Duce's embarrassment made him all the more receptive to blandishments from London with regard to an Anglo-Italian accord. France, Blondel advised, had no recourse now but to support such an arrangement and then to use it as a springboard for the normalization of Franco-Italian relations as well.[48] It can be argued that such a policy stood virtually no chance of success since an independent Austria was a thing of the past. But the collapse of the Popular Front, following a prolonged ministerial crisis in the spring of 1938, assured that Blondel's strategy at least would be given a try.

CHAPTER 11

France and the Anglo-Italian Easter Accord of 1938

Prior to Eden's resignation and Germany's absorption of Austria, French officials mounted an effort to discourage separate Anglo-Italian negotiations. In Geneva on 28 January 1938, Delbos and Massigli told Lord Cranborne, the British secretary of state, that whereas France was prepared to contemplate a general settlement with Italy, including de jure recognition of Italian sovereignty in Ethiopia, a sine qua non for such an understanding was the prior withdrawal of all foreign troops from Spain and the implementation of the Laval-Mussolini agreements of January 1935. Delbos did not disguise his contempt for Mussolini and insisted that it would be a grave mistake to embark on conversations with Rome until a serious beginning on Anglo-French approaches to Berlin had been undertaken. Such efforts met with predictable resistance from British representatives in the field and at Whitehall. Lord Perth, regarded by his French colleague in Rome as oversolicitous of the Duce's sensibilities, warned on several occasions that the French conditions were totally unacceptable to Mussolini and would certainly doom any prospect of a direct Anglo-Italian rapprochement. Delbos's formal demarche urging joint Anglo-French action in Berlin to defuse the Austrian question elicited the following scornful minute by William Strang: "This is a rather typical French production. They put up proposals which go well beyond what they themselves are willing (or in a position) to perform, and will place the responsibility for inaction upon us." Sargent and Alexander Cadogan added observations of a similar nature.[1] Quite obviously the British resented what they regarded as French meddling in a private affair, an attitude that was to appear in even more pronounced fashion following Eden's resignation.

The announcement of the foreign secretary's resignation was accompanied by a simultaneous notice that negotiations aimed at an Anglo-Italian accord would open soon in Rome. The latter's success, according to Corbin, had become a matter of prestige for Chamberlain, who was now likely to abandon "certain of the conditions and guarantees with which M. Eden wanted to hem in the negotiations with Italy." Delbos immediately instructed the French ambassador in London to secure clarification from the new British foreign secretary, Viscount Halifax, on the details of the proposed Anglo-Italian talks and to express regret that the British had not sought prior consultation with Paris, a condition that left him vulnerable to a predictable storm of indignation in the Chamber of Deputies.[2]

That the British government sympathized neither with Delbos's antipathy toward Italy nor his delicate parliamentary situation can be inferred from Halifax's curt riposte to French objections. Observing that the French had been and would continue to be advised in a general sense on Anglo-Italian relations, the foreign secretary instructed Phipps to "convey a hint to Monsieur Delbos that, since it is His Majesty's Government who are conducting these negotiations, they must be the sole judges as to the procedure and tactics to be followed, and since moreover most of the questions to be discussed will primarily be matters affecting only Great Britain and Italy, we cannot be expected to discuss them in detail with the French Government." He promised only to keep in touch with Paris on questions affecting "the common interests of Great Britain and France, such as Spain, the Mediterranean, and de jure recognition." Halifax's claim that the French had been kept up to date on British intentions was based on conversations that Eden had had with various French statesmen and diplomats on 29-30 November 1937, 25 and 28 January, and 5 February 1938. Most of these meetings, however, had been initiated by the French in their search for information. Subsequently, officials at Whitehall advised that the French should be given only "purely general indications" of the details involved in the Anglo-Italian negotiation, a strategy endorsed by Halifax on 2 March.[3]

Just prior to *Anschluss,* the French made one final effort to circumscribe unilateral British action in Rome. After being informed in general terms on 4 March of the topics the British intended to raise in Rome, the Quai d'Orsay responded with a lengthy list of specifications designed to protect French interests. The British were requested to safeguard French interests in the Red Sea and to seek a cessation of anti-French propaganda in Italy. Any decisions on Spain should be subordinated to the Nonintervention Committee. Furthermore, Paris insisted that any discussions with regard to Tunis, the Balearic Islands, Corsica, status quo in the Mediterranean, and Ethiopia should be conducted à trois with France as a participant. Perth advised rejection of the proposal out of hand, saying that such an approach would wreck the conversations, and that was essentially the response handed by Halifax to the French ambassador in London on 10 March. The British foreign secretary refused for tactical reasons to raise with Italy the prospect of any eventual tripartite negotiations involving the French. The furthest he would go was to assure Paris that England would work to include, in the eventual Anglo-Italian accord, a provision calling for third-party adherence to clauses relating to the maintenance of the status quo in the Mediterranean. He concluded by observing that the amelioration in Anglo-Italian relations would create a climate in Rome receptive to French initiatives for a bilateral accord similar to the one currently in progress between England and Italy.[4]

The above exchanges of communications between Paris and London during the winter of 1938 show clearly that the British resented French intrusions and were determined to achieve an accord with Italy, if necessary, over and above French objections. But Halifax's suggestion that Mussolini would be receptive to a French proposal for détente was not entirely without foundation. On 9 March Blondel bruited the same possibility but indicated that it would be a very complex operation. He repeated Mussolini's well-known reservations about the Popular Front and the Franco-Soviet treaty, but he stressed that recent German activities in Austria might make it possible to draw Italy back to the policies of 1934–35. France, however, must appease the Duce if it expected to come to terms with him; for Italy the recognition of Ethiopia was an absolute condition and must not be held out as a bargaining chip. These observations involved what Blondel called the "psychological factor" in dealing with Mussolini: "What I mean by that is that, in my opinion, we stand an infinitely greater chance of obtaining substantial advantages in the course of an open negotiation conducted in a 'climate' already appeased. However, it is certain that in such a circumstance appeasement can occur only if the recognition of the Italian Empire is, if not accorded outright, at least presented as possible and even probable."⁵ Blondel had advanced such judgments before, but so long as Delbos remained at the Quai d'Orsay, they stood little chance of being acted upon.

The Chautemps government fell on 13 March, replaced by what could only be regarded as a caretaker regime headed once again by Blum, with Paul-Boncour at the Quai d'Orsay. The obvious weakness of the French government made the British even more reluctant to respond favorably to appeals from Paris for support in securing French adherence to the Anglo-Italian accord. In fact, British sources betray a pronounced distaste for the Blum-Paul-Boncour tandem and frank impatience with repeated French intrusions into the Anglo-Italian negotiations. Consequently, once the Italians had definitively rejected the idea of French adherence even to selected portions of an eventual Anglo-Italian accord, the British dropped the matter entirely, fearing that to pursue it further would prejudice the whole framework of negotiations, and advised the French once again to initiate their own conversations with Rome.⁶

Italy's rejection of any tripartite Mediterranean settlement represented its repugnance for an arrangement with the western powers smacking of a recrudescence of the Stresa Front. This was clearly an illusion by the spring of 1938. But French diplomatic correspondence in the wake of *Anschluss* indicates that the Italians were prepared to repair the breach in their relations with France and to supplement the Anglo-Italian accord with separate bilateral Franco-Italian understanding. Moreover, important figures in the French military intelligence community advocated the revival of close Franco-Italian military collaboration in the wake of *Anschluss*. Colonel Buisson, one of the premier's chief military advisors and former chief of operations in the Army General Staff, prepared a long memorandum on 13 March 1938. He pointed out that the breach with Italy had made it necessary for France to redeploy up to one-third of her armed forces in the Alps and North Africa, and that it also had destroyed direct contact with her Little Entente allies in central Europe. Given the fact that France was insufficiently prepared to face Germany alone, Buisson concluded, "There is only one way to stop [Germany] militarily and that is to reform, as in 1935, the circle of our Friendships from England to Poland, including Italy. . . . IT IS NECESSARY TO RECREATE THE PARIS-ROME AXIS. . . . Whatever the price of our accord with Rome may be, it will never be too high."⁷ The problem was to find a satisfactory formula for the advancement of a French initiative.

The altered situation encouraged Blondel to renew his appeals for a dramatic gesture designed to appease the Franco-Italian situation. The French chargé literally deluged Paul-Boncour with lengthy dispatches advising that the psychological moment was at hand to break out of the impasse that had blocked all progress in Franco-Italian relations for the previous eighteen months. A breakthrough, he argued, would not be easy; it would require considerable concessions from France—most particularly a willingness to concede outright the recognition of the Italian Empire in Ethiopia. He pointed out that "we would gain absolutely nothing by holding our recognition in suspense after the conquest of Ethiopia will have been morally accepted by England" in the projected Anglo-Italian accord. In exchange for recognition, France would likely be able to get a pact on Mediterranean security, similar to the one in negotiation with England, with special provisions for maintaining the status quo in the Syrian mandate. Not to seize this opportunity to complement British diplomacy would risk leaving Italy insufficiently secure in the Mediterranean, thus leaving her no choice but to move closer to Berlin.[8]

Blondel's urgent appeals finally brought forth some movement at the Quai d'Orsay during the final days of the Popular Front. Paul-Boncour maintained in his memoirs that "contrary to everything that has been said, Blum and I were in full agreement to seek ways to bring this prolonged deficiency to an end."[9] Nevertheless, the burden of previous legalisms was a heavy one, and the situation was extraordinarily complex for two reasons. First of all, the League of Nations had yet to pronounce on the matter of recognizing the Ethiopian conquest. During the first week of April 1938, the French and British Foreign Ministries agreed to cosponsor a resolution at the League Council meeting in May aimed at removing this roadblock.[10] Second was the fact that France had no ambassador with plenipotentiary powers to negotiate in Rome, and the Italian government had made it abundantly clear that it would interpret letters of accreditation addressed to "the king of Italy, emperor of Ethiopia" as de jure recognition of the conquest—even if these words were used only as a gesture of courtesy. On 7 April 1938, Massigli wrote a personal letter to Blondel reviewing these difficulties but assuring the chargé that the Quai d'Orsay was convinced of "the necessity to renew contact with Rome." To that end, Paul-Boncour met the day before with Italian Senator Puricelli and proposed that France send an unofficial "negotiator" to Rome, empowered only to negotiate a Franco-Italian accord similar to the soon-to-be-completed Anglo-Italian accord. Once an agreement or understanding had been reached, the negotiator would be named ambassador and be supplied with the appropriate letters of accreditation. Since this procedure could only go forward if the Italian government approved it in advance, Paul-Boncour asked Puricelli to investigate its feasibility with Mussolini. Massigli instructed Blondel to sound out his contacts as well.[11]

It was at this point that the Popular Front period came officially to a close with the resignation of the Blum government on 10 April 1938. Daladier formed a new, more broadly based administration with Bonnet in charge of the foreign affairs portfolio. Bonnet's appointment could not but be regarded with some enthusiasm in Rome; in the past he had applauded Mussolini's Four-Power Pact scheme in 1933 and offered vocal support for the Rome Accords of January 1935. The resolution of the prolonged French ministerial crisis coincided with the announcement that the Anglo-Italian accord would be signed on Easter Sunday, 16 April 1938. This accord was a wide-ranging understanding on a variety of Mediterranean issues. Among its most important provisions were: an Italian pledge to begin a program of evacuation of volunteers from Spain and to remove all men and war materiel at the end of the civil war; Britain's assurance to sponsor legislation in Geneva that would free the League's member nations to recognize the Italian conquest of Ethiopia; a reaffirmation of the Gentleman's Agreement of January 1937; and an agreement to exchange information on military movements in the Mediterranean Sea, Gulf of Aden, and other areas in the Middle East.[12] Although the conclusion of the Easter Accord provided the occasion for fanfare and celebration, its signature did not mean its immediate implementation. The latter was contingent upon two factors: the "settlement of the Spanish question" and British recognition of the Ethiopian conquest.

The successful conclusion of Anglo-Italian negotiations allowed the matter of Franco-Italian relations to come to the forefront. Blondel reported from Rome that commentaries in the Italian press on the new French government were favorable and that recent tendencies toward a rapprochement between France and Italy were receiving extensive coverage. But the Italians were confused about Paul-Boncour's earlier proposal to send a negotiator to Rome rather than a full-fledged accredited ambassador. Blondel believed it was important to work quickly to get some sort of negotiation in the works before Hitler's scheduled visit to Italy in May.[13] The new foreign minister obviously shared these views. On 15 April Bonnet instructed Blondel to express to Ciano France's congratulations on the successful outcome of Anglo-Italian talks and to assure the Italians that the question of Ethiopia would be high on the agenda of items before the League Council in May. That being the case, the French government "would be favorable to the early opening, either in Paris or Rome, of a Franco-Italian negotiation." If the Duce preferred to talk in Rome, France was prepared "to give full instructions and full powers to her diplomatic representative in Rome" and to supply him with the necessary technical experts to permit a full discussion of all the issues. Bonnet concluded his instructions by repeating his desire for "a frank and cordial Franco-Italian collaboration," which would hasten "the possibility for France officially to accredit an ambassador to Rome."[14] Blondel carried out his instructions immediately; Ciano assured him, unofficially, that he was confident Mussolini's response would be affirmative and that he would prefer to negotiate in Rome.[15]

Buoyed by the recent turn of events, Blondel reported on 29 April that the Anglo-Italian accord enjoyed an excellent press in Italy and that public opinion in the Peninsula had turned decidedly more favorable to France. He cited several factors to explain this salutary situation. First of all, Italian participation in victories on the Ebro heightened the impression that the Spanish Civil War would end soon in a Franco victory. Secondly, the change of government in France had begun to resolve the "psychological atmosphere" so worrisome to Ciano. And finally, the sudden appearance of Germany on the Brenner was the source of substantial public discontent. Blondel stressed that all of this did not mean that Mussolini was prepared to abandon the Axis and move back to the Stresa Front. What he hoped would evolve was some sort of four-power arrangement where Italy could magnify her role in European affairs by acting as middleman between Germany and the western powers. Nevertheless, conditions were ripe for a resolution of Franco-Italian difficulties, and Blondel urged the quick preparation of substantive proposals along with an effort to flatter fascist egos with a favorable press campaign in France.[16] Ciano let it be known in Paris that if a new ambassador were appointed and some hint given that France was disposed to recognize the Empire, a Franco-Italian agreement was within reach.[17]

Bonnet's instructions arrived the following day. They authorized Blondel to present to Ciano a complex, twelve-item agenda of French desiderata for an accord with Italy, the goal of which was to make it possible for France to support a British resolution on Ethiopian recognition at Geneva and to set the stage for implementing the Rome Accords of 1935. Amid a flurry of relatively minor provisions calling for mutual agreement on such things as the status quo in the Mediterranean, the Syrian mandate, the Suez Canal, Libya, the cessation of propaganda, and protection of French interests in the Middle East and the Red Sea, Bonnet also included two matters of fundamental concern. First, the French wanted an Italian declaration of disinterest in Spain, along with reciprocal agreements on nonintervention in the civil conflict and on the withdrawal of volunteers and war materiel. Second, Bonnet requested a reciprocal commitment to negotiate, once normal relations were reestablished, a new convention on Tunisia, "on the bases defined in the accord of 7 January 1935."[18] It seems clear now that, of this laundry list of French requirements for an accord with Italy, only those regarding Spain and Tunisia were essential. Why, then, were these matters buried in a lengthy agenda of items of lesser moment—especially if progress on an accord were to be achieved before the League Council meeting and Hitler's visit to Italy in early May? Noël maintained that this obfuscation ran counter to Bonnet's inclinations and attributed it to the deliberate doings of Léger and his "anti-Italian clan" at the Quai d'Orsay, who placed little value on an Italian connection. Noël's judgments are buttressed by contemporary British sources. Ambassador Phipps reported that Léger "takes the usual Quai d'Orsay view that no agreement with Italy is worth the paper it is written on as she will violate it whenever it suits her book." Even after Phipps had insisted on the importance of providing Italy with alternatives to Germany and suggested the value in convincing British and French public opinion that at least everything had been done to improve relations, "M. Léger only very grudgingly admitted that there might be something in this."[19]

In any case, the length and complexity of the French proposal served to cool whatever ardor Italy may have felt for an understanding. Ciano told Blondel on 22 April that the twelve-point program would have to be studied carefully and that, as a result, even an accord in principle stipulating mutual good will and the intent to resolve differences could not be taken up immediately. No detailed Italian response could be expected until after the Italian foreign minister's state visit to Albania and Hitler's visit to Italy had been concluded. However, Ciano's initial reaction to French proposals was mildly encouraging. Upon his return from Tirana, Ciano called Blondel to the Palazzo Chigi for an hour's conversation in which the foreign minister expressed basic agreement on all but two matters. The Italians flatly rejected the point dealing with Spain. For reasons of national dignity, Rome would not repeat in any Franco-Italian accord the same "formula of repentance" that she had already granted to England in the Easter Accord. Furthermore, Ciano reported that Mussolini had a number of reservations regarding the French request to adhere to the Red Sea and Levantine clauses of the Anglo-Italian accord. Ciano promised a more detailed Italian response on these and other matters once the Hitler visit was concluded.[20] All in all, Blondel was struck by the good will evinced by the Italian. He believed that French concerns about Spain might be taken care of by a simple French declaration endorsing the revelant portions of the Anglo-Italian accord on Spain. Beyond that he did not anticipate, at this point, any serious future difficulties provided a solution could be found for the issues of the Red Sea and the Levant.[21]

Meanwhile, during the hiatus in Franco-Italian talks occasioned by Ciano's visit to Albania and Hitler's sojourn in Italy, the Quai d'Orsay pursued its concern about Spain and the Levant in London. Daladier and Bonnet met with Chamberlain and Halifax on 28 and 29 April. The primary result of these meetings involved the establishment of military staff talks between France and England, about which more will be said later. But the French ministers also sought and received British support for France's adherence to the Red Sea and Levantine clauses of the Easter Accord. Given the scope of French interests in the region, they believed it essential to maintain a position of parity with the other two powers. In addition, before moving formally on any blanket endorsement of the Easter Accord on Spain, Daladier and Bonnet wanted a definition of what was meant by a "settlement of the Spanish question" as a condition for bringing the Anglo-Italian accord into force. The British ministers responded that progress in the Nonintervention Committee and a substantial withdrawal of Italian volunteers was what they had in mind. More than a little cynicism was evident among members of the British Cabinet on 4 May when Chamberlain and Halifax reported the results of their conversations with the French ministers. Regarding Spain it was noted that "enormous quantities" of arms and munitions were pouring across the French frontier to Spanish government forces, and the general impression was that France intended to stuff as much war materiel as possible into Spain before agreeing again to close the border.[22] This state of affairs encouraged permanent officials at the Foreign Office to caution extreme prudence with regard to any assurances that Great Britain might make to France about Spain. Their minutes, recorded on 12 May 1938, cited the extent of French infractions of the Nonintervention Agreement and, in light of these, they saw no reason for Italy to make any pledges to France. Furthermore, they advised that England should not intercede on France's behalf in Rome.[23] It seems clear that France's decision to reopen the Spanish border to traffic in war materiel was designed to delay implementation of the Easter Accord and to pressure England into supporting French adhesion to portions of it.

This background is of some importance in understanding the "decidedly less conciliatory" attitude evinced by Ciano toward the French proposal for an accord following the conclusion of Hitler's visit. On 11 May he threw up a number of additional objections and counterproposals that could only have the effect of delaying the matter. No doubt the German Führer had exercised his suasion with Mussolini, but the recent exacerbation of the Spanish crisis could hardly be viewed as an example of France's desire to seek a definitive resolution of the protracted break in relations with Rome. Even the League Council's decision to clear the way for British and French recognition of the Italian Empire was not enough to thaw the refreeze in

Franco-Italian relations that set in after 9 May. Given the hopeful atmosphere for Franco-Italian rapprochement following *Anschluss* and the generally favorable initial Italian reaction to French proposals for an accord, it is hard to disagree with the judgment advanced by the president of the Italian Aeronautical Association that the League's decision was perhaps too late. If, he told the French military attaché in Geneva, "this question had been regulated two years ago as the logical corollary of the suppression of sanctions, Italy would still be in the League of Nations, the Rome-Berlin Axis would not exist and the *Anschluss* would not have occurred."[24]

Be that as it may, Hitler's visit to Italy served to reverse the entire tone of Franco-Italian relations that had seemed so promising prior to his arrival. Lowe and Marzari have argued that French leaders totally misperceived Mussolini's initially benign response to their twelve-point program. He was, in fact, simply trying to show Hitler, on the eve of the latter's visit, that he had other irons in the fire. After the Führer's departure, Mussolini abruptly rang down the curtain on further conversations with France. In a stingingly bellicose speech delivered at Genoa on 14 May, the Duce declared the Stresa formula "dead and buried" and indicated that negotiations with France could not succeed because the two countries supported opposite sides in the Spanish Civil War. In striking contrast, he had only favorable things to say about the recently concluded Anglo-Italian accord. Speculation over the causes of Mussolini's outburst ranged from his presumed pique at French newspaper editorials depicting the Hitler visit as a failure symbolic of the weakening of the Rome-Berlin Axis, to frustration at Franco's lack of progress in Spain, which was checked by the reopening of the Pyrenean frontier and which thus delayed implementation of the Easter Accord with England. Whatever, the speech acted as a cold shower in Paris, where pro-Italians had been buoyed by the prospects for successful Franco-Italian talks. The German ambassador reported its aftermath to the Wilhelmstrasse: "Astonishment and disappointment, in some cases even bordering on consternation and dejection, prevail among Frenchmen friendly to Italy, that is from the Right and Center. Among Leftist circles the failure of the so-called realistic politicians, Daladier and Bonnet, is emphasized; the malignant joy that is expressed over this cannot, however, hide the feeling of disappointment that undoubtedly exists even in the parties of the Left over the rebuff given France by Mussolini." The British ambassador in Paris, noting the marked difference in Mussolini's attitude when speaking of Great Britain and France, summed up the situation with some perspicacity. "It is to be feared," he wrote to Halifax, "that Italy, having obtained what she wanted from England, will now make very hard conditions to France over Spain, Tunis, and Morocco. The era of true 'realism' has commenced."[25]

"True realism" apparently dictated a three-pronged approach to the Italian question on the part of the Quai d'Orsay in the wake of the Genoa discourse. First, Bonnet instructed Blondel to persevere in his efforts to rejuvenate Franco-Italian conversations in Rome, insisting that any accord must include clauses dealing with the Spanish question and providing for French adherence to those portions of the 16 April agreement concerning Saudi Arabia, Yemen, and the Red Sea islands. Ciano's refusal to receive the French chargé d'affaires led the Quai d'Orsay to pursue a second avenue via London. Corbin called at the Foreign Office on 17 May to inquire whether Britain could make any representations in Rome on France's behalf. Cadogan informed the French ambassador that Perth had already been instructed to protest the tone of Mussolini's Genoa speech and to express Britain's interest in the success of Franco-Italian negotiations. But Cadogan also made it clear that Britain was reluctant to assist actively the Franco-Italian talks due to the awkward situation created by the vast quantities of war materiel flowing over the French frontier to Barcelona. If this reinforcement continued, the Briton warned, any real Franco-Italian rapprochement would be extremely difficult to bring about. Moreover, it might also induce Mussolini to intensify his own intervention in Spain, thus prejudicing implementation of the Anglo-Italian accord. The lukewarm Foreign Office response to the French appeal for support was echoed in Rome. Ciano told Perth that Mussolini was opposed unalterably to any mention of Spain in a Franco-Italian agreement, since assurance had already been given to England on this matter; he also vetoed French adherence to the relevant clauses of the Easter Accord dealing with the Middle East.[26]

Given this apparent check to his initiatives in both Paris and London, Bonnet sought a third avenue to break through the impasse and save the Franco-Italian negotiations. Arguing that the tone of Mussolini's Genoa speech made it absolutely essential for France to have some guarantees from Italy on the Spanish question, Bonnet turned as a last resort to the Nonintervention Committee in London. If some sort of general entente in the committee concerning the withdrawal of volunteers, or at least the registration there of an understanding between the French and Italian delegations, could be realized, it would facilitate—in the eyes of French public opinion—the removal of the Spanish question from any direct Franco-Italian negotiations. Corbin was instructed to sound out Lord Plymouth, chairman of the Nonintervention Committee, on this issue. Simultaneously, the French foreign minister summoned Renato Prunas, the Italian chargé d'affaires, to his private residence in Paris. He told Prunas of his initiative to the London Committee, assured him that France was still interested in an accord and that such an accord was not designed to disrupt the Axis, expressed surprise that Ciano had not yet agreed to receive Blondel, and suggested that France would be receptive to detailed Italian objections to his twelve-point proposal.[27]

Ciano's indirect response to all of these various French soundings came through a speech he gave in Milan on 2 June 1938. In a tour d'horizon of Italian foreign policy, the foreign minister expressed fulsome praise for the Anglo-Italian accord of 16 April and for Prime Minister Chamberlain but did not so much as mention France. Blondel viewed the speech with unaccustomed pessimism. It indicated to him that Ciano had slammed the door on further Franco-Italian conversations. Now that the Anglo-Italian accord had been signed and the League of Nations had voted to allow member states individually to decide on recognition of the Italian Empire, Blondel believed that the Italian game plan "of separating France from England by creating a disparity of treatment to the detriment of our country, appears more clearly than ever." He predicted that Rome would place increasing pressure on London to put the Easter Accord into force "which would result in leaving us completely isolated in the Franco-Italian affair." Even Bonnet's patience seemed to be exhausted by the latest turn of events. On 3 June he repeated Blondel's analysis to the British ambassador in Paris and urged that the western democracies not fall into the Italian trap. Britain, he said, must "impress upon Italian Government that Anglo-Italian agreement can never come into operation until conclusion of their agreement with France."[28]

Apparently reverting to the "Nyon tactic" of the previous fall, Paris proceeded over the next several weeks to apply considerable pressure in London to link ratification of the Easter Accord to the reestablishment of normal relations between France and Italy. Failure to do so, warned Bonnet on 20 June, would have a distressing effect on French public opinion and would, in effect, be regarded as a betrayal of France, which had supported British efforts to achieve an accord with Italy and which recently had sealed off her Spanish frontier to the transshipment of war materiel. On other occasions the French foreign minister threatened that unless England cooperated on this matter, France would be compelled once again to throw open the Pyrenean frontier, thus preventing the conclusion of the Spanish Civil War, and to draw closer to the Soviet Union. Bonnet's campaign at least served to convince the British ambassador in Paris that Italy was seeking to separate Britain from France. Phipps observed that if the Anglo-Italian agreement came into force before any improvement in Franco-

Italian relations, the result would most likely be an even more serious rift in the latter: "The French Government realize perfectly well that we cannot in so many words make the coming into force of our Agreement with Italy conditional upon the conclusion of a Franco-Italian Agreement, but they are absolutely convinced that once the former materializes any chance of the latter vanishes into thin air." But the European political atmosphere had altered considerably since September 1937, and French blandishments were not nearly so persuasive as they had been when English ships were under attack in the Mediterranean. Halifax did indeed resist Italian efforts in June to implement the Easter Accord, saying that the necessary preconditions (armistice in Spain followed by a substantial unilateral Italian troop withdrawal) had not yet been met. He also instructed his ambassador in Rome to tell Ciano that France had demonstrated good will by closing the Pyrenean border to military supplies, and that Great Britain regarded a Franco-Italian accord as a "logical complement" to that negotiated between London and Rome. But the British foreign secretary also made it clear that neither a Franco-Italian accord, nor even the resumption of negotiations for such an understanding, could be regarded as a precondition for the eventual implementation of the Anglo-Italian accord of 16 April.[29]

Obviously emboldened by this declaration, Ciano told Perth on 28 June that "'it is perfectly all right with me if there is no French ambassador in Rome for eighteen months or eighteen years.'" Mussolini followed four days later with a memo to the British ambassador insisting that "the resumption of the Italo-French conversation will be able eventually to take place after the application of the Agreements of 16 April, but never before that. . . ." Perth attributed Ciano and Mussolini's uncompromising, almost insulting, attitude largely to temper or temperament. Vansittart was more realistic. The permanent undersecretary of state for foreign affairs saw Mussolini's memo as a deliberate policy of separating England from France and warned that "he is beginning to succeed pretty well." Should the stalemate continue the Easter Accord would indeed become a dead letter, and that would only serve German interests. "If it does happen," Vansittart concluded, "it will be largely because we are being outmanoeuvred." His judgment can be confirmed by German sources. Gleefully reporting the latest developments in the deterioration of Franco-Italian relations, Count Johannes Von Welczeck, the German ambassador in Paris, reported that "the changed attitude now openly encountered indicates that even in England they have given up hope for an early Franco-Italian settlement. As a result, the anti-Italian circles in France are receiving a new encouragement, so that, unless there are new developments, it can hardly be expected in the near future that the French will do much for the improvement of relations with Italy."[30] His predictions were amply confirmed by French diplomatic correspondence during the remainder of the summer of 1938. It was a virtual catalog of increasing Italo-French rancor, in which even the faintest glimmer of post-*Anschluss* euphoria was buried in reports of extravagantly anti-French propaganda in the Italian press.[31]

THE CZECH CRISIS AND ITS AFTERMATH

The Munich crisis of September 1938 occurred while Franco-Italian relations were at their nadir. It served to catalyze a final effort in Paris to resuscitate an understanding with Rome prior to the outbreak of World War II. Hitler's escalating pressure on Prague to "relieve" the situation of the Sudeten *Volksdeutsche,* culminating in his demand for the incorporation of the Sudetenland into the Reich, once again raised the threat of general war in Europe. Britain's reluctance to risk military engagement for the sake of central Europe was well known. But France's alliance commitments to Prague offered the unwelcome prospect that should war erupt between France and Germany over the Czech question, Britain might well be dragged into the conflict, all of which magnified the importance of the bargain struck between French and British leaders at their summit meeting back on 28–29 April 1938. The principal significance of the meeting involved Britain's acceptance of the principle of joint Anglo-French staff talks in all three military services and her pledge to establish "confidential informal contact" with France for the common purchase of strategic materials. In return Daladier had agreed to support a joint demarche in Prague in favor of Czech concessions to the Sudetens.

That arrangement went some distance to defuse the "May crisis" over Czechoslovakia. However, neither side was particularly pleased about the staff conversations. For England they went too far; for France not far enough. And Daladier was none too happy about applying pressure to Prague rather than to Berlin. But at least the British had established a wedge for themselves in the eventual peaceful resolution of the German-Czech crisis. Young has viewed the April 1938 conference as a major shift in responsibility. Prior to that time, French commitments to Czechoslovakia made her the arbiter of European peace. But Daladier was justifiably doubtful about English support in the event of war over the Sudeten question, and his service chiefs left no doubt that France was in no condition to stand alone against Germany. By accepting the bargain of late April, Daladier "tied France to a country whose own military advisers were even more adamant than their French counterparts about the need to avoid war. . . . Whether to shirk its responsibilities [by abandoning Czechoslovakia], or whether to honor them more effectively [by solidifying the Anglo-French relationship], the Daladier government had hitched its wagon to a British star."[32] The April bargain gave the British the upper hand at Munich and thus lessened the likelihood that France would stand by her military commitments to Prague.

The mounting crisis served once again to magnify the importance of Italy as a potential lynchpin for peace in Europe. French military intelligence reports for September warned repeatedly that, although German policy vis-à-vis Czechoslovakia was not popular among the Italian people, it was not likely that the outbreak of a general war would find Italy repeating its performance of 1914-18. Its options clearly appeared to be either neutrality or overt intervention on the side of Germany. It was equally clear that the Italians did not believe the French could do much about the Czech situation. An unidentified "high fascist official" outlined the hopelessness of the French position in a conversation with Jean-Paul Garnier, the secretary to the French Embassy at the Vatican. Blondel believed the conversation was meant to convey the position of the Italian government. France, the official said, could do nothing but mount a futile symbolic protest if Germany moved against Czechoslovakia. Yugoslavia had been immobilized by her 1937 accord with Italy; Poland and Hungary were covetous of Czech territory in Teschen and Slovakia respectively; and England would be reluctant to back a French military gesture since her interests were not directly affected by central European crises. The Italian official continued, "There is nothing that France can do. You have no policy with Italy. You continue to persist with old formulas which no longer correspond to anything. You continue to play your cards close to the vest with us by withholding recognition of the Empire, the sending of an ambassador, and who knows what else. It's ridiculous!" France might rather contribute to defusing the world situation, he suggested, by accepting the inevitability of Franco's victory in Spain, allowing Germany to regulate the Sudeten matter, recognizing the Italian Empire in Ethiopia, and providing tangible proof of good will toward Italy by sending a fully accredited ambassador "without prior negotiations." These steps, the Italian insisted, could avoid a major catastrophe by contributing to the establishment of a four-power directorate in Europe.[33]

All of these factors assured the immobility of the French government. His hands tied, Daladier played only a minor role at Munich, where the Sudeten crisis was resolved wholly in Hitler's favor. Mussolini's pivotal role at the conference no doubt fueled his illusions about the evolution of a four-power directorate with Italy in the position of arbiter between Germany and the western democracies. The Duce's apparent success also impressed key French officials and set the stage for diplomatic moves that might have been very significant had they occurred a year or two earlier. François-Poncet later wrote that the Munich conference convinced him that "Mussolini was, decidedly, the only one capable, as he had just proved, of restraining Hitler from the bent toward war and that as a result, the key to peace no longer lay in Berlin, but in Rome."[34]

Munich shattered French credibility in eastern Europe and underscored the need to cultivate other allies. General Gamelin confided to his staff officers that France must now turn toward the Mediterranean, toward an entente with Spain, Italy, and Turkey, in an effort to consolidate her position in the Balkans, the Levant, and North Africa.[35] In short, the shock of Munich forced the Quai d'Orsay off the dime with regard to Italy. But once again French efforts to repair the lengthy breach in Franco-Italian relations were blunted by faulty coordination between Paris and London.

Blondel averred that the post-Munich euphoria in Italy provided the perfect "psychological moment" for France to send a new ambassador. The following day Bonnet telephoned the Italian chargé in Paris to inform him that the French government had decided to recognize formally the conquest of Ethiopia and to send a fully accredited ambassador to Rome. Upon inquiring who the Italians would like to see at the the Palazzo Farnese, Bonnet was quickly informed, "We don't want Laval. Send us a career person." Italian desires coincided with François-Poncet's request to be transferred from Berlin to Rome. Bonnet appointed him immediately and charged him with the mission of "reestablishing confident relations between France and Italy." The French gesture was warmly received by both the Italian press and by government officials.[36]

This reversal of French policy coincided with an Italian effort to bring about the long-delayed implementation of the Easter Accord with England. On the same day that Bonnet announced France's intention to send an ambassador to Rome, Ciano informed the British ambassador there that Italy was withdrawing 10,000 soldiers from Spain. The foreign minister characterized this as half of the Italian contingent, and he suggested that it met the British terms for ratification of the Anglo-Italian accord. The latter, therefore, ought to come into effect immediately. Ciano further indicated that if the accords were implemented "we would be able to reopen conversations with France and a general détente would finally result." The Italian proposal caught the British off guard. Ratification of the 16 April accord could only occur by Parliamentary consent, and the House of Commons was not scheduled to meet until 1 November. In the meantime, however, the Cabinet met on 26 October and approved the methods by which the Anglo-Italian accord would be brought into force. Halifax argued successfully that, although Italy's announcement of her intention to withdraw 10,000 men did not formally constitute a "settlement" of the Spanish question, further delay would risk the entire agreement. The date for bringing the accord into force was set for 16 November. Whitehall instructed representatives in Paris, Rome, and elsewhere to notify their governments "in strictest confidence" that the British government "today decided to bring the Anglo-Italian Agreement into force. As soon as there has been a discussion in the House of Commons next week on the subject new credentials will be issued to His Majesty's Ambassador at Rome accrediting him to the King of Italy and Emperor of Ethiopia."[37]

British pique at France's sudden recognition of the Ethiopian conquest was barely concealed. In a telegram informing the French government that a discussion of the implementation of the Easter Accord was scheduled in Commons for the following week, Halifax requested to be authorized by Bonnet to say that British action in the matter was welcomed by the French government. "Our decision has been influenced in no small measure," he wrote, "by action already taken by the French Government and by our desire to coordinate our actions with theirs." The Quai d'Orsay hardly could refuse to welcome the British decision to recognize the Italian king as Emperor of Ethiopia, and both Daladier and Bonnet authorized Halifax to say as much in Parliament. But the question of implementing the Anglo-Italian agreement was decidedly more delicate. Bonnet in fact refused to indicate any support for this aspect of British policy and authorized Halifax to say only that the French government had been informed.[38]

The House of Commons dutifully ratified the Easter Accord on 1 November by a vote of 345 to 138. Among Conservative members who abstained were Churchill and Eden. They argued that, since no armistice in Spain had been signed and all volunteer elements had yet to be withdrawn, the conditions for effectuating the accord had not been met. On 16 November Ciano and Perth signed the various declarations bringing the Anglo-Italian accord of 16 April into full force. Thus, after some seven months, Italy finally achieved what it had wanted all along: an accord with Great Britain *alone*. After having maintained solidarity with France on this issue since July, the English Cabinet ended by abandoning that position. British impatience with the French, in light of the evidence cited here, is understandable enough. Yet, Britain's reversal of policy could only magnify Italian hopes of separating France from England. Although Whitehall argued that the implementation of the Easter Accord would be likely to hasten the desired Franco-Italian rapprochement, it in fact rendered François-Poncet's task of restoring confident relations between Paris and Rome ever more delicate.

CHAPTER 12

From the Recognition of Empire to the Pact of Steel

The historical debate about the nature and efficacy of appeasement continues unabated. Most recently, Anthony Adamthwaite has challenged the views of men like J. W. Wheeler-Bennett, Coulondre, Duroselle, and others, who found the British to be the main architects of the numerous policies of appeasement while the French were dragged along unwillingly. Adamthwaite argues that French leaders went along willingly and even encouraged Britain to take the lead, thereby providing a pretext for disengagement from central and eastern Europe. His thesis is developed almost exclusively with regard to Germany, but concerning Italy he maintains that "after Munich the search for agreement with the fascist dictators quickened. Despite the acrimony which had soured Franco-Italian relations since the Ethiopian War, the Daladier government strove to reach a *modus vivendi.*"[1] Adamthwaite oversimplifies the complexity of the situation in two respects: first by suggesting that French policy toward Italy and Germany was the same, and second by implying that the Daladier government was united on the Italian question. It most assuredly was not; the fundamental tension between Foreign Minister Bonnet and Prime Minister Daladier colored the entire panorama of Franco-Italian relations in the post-Munich era.

Unlike Daladier, Bonnet tended to see Munich as a positive point of departure for eventual Franco-German and Franco-Italian rapprochements. For that reason he removed some of his most prominent critics from the Quai d'Orsay; Massigli, the political director, and Pierre Comert, chief of press services, were swept away, the former to an ambassadorship in Ankara. Léger, however, remained.[2] Bonnet had emerged during the 1930s as a champion of four-power diplomacy and viewed Munich as an example of its efficacy. In this, Bonnet stood closer to Chamberlain than to his own prime minister. Daladier, on the other hand, saw Munich as a dirty business and resented what he regarded as the third-rate role he was forced to play there. Consequently he refused to court Mussolini as Bonnet and Chamberlain subsequently urged him to do. In addition, Daladier sought to assuage the shame of Munich by reviving the importance of the French Empire to balance the strategic loss of Czechoslovakia. This new imperial emphasis was bound to clash with increased Italian colonial claims, which were soon to be made plain.[3] It was within the context of this division in the French government that François-Poncet took up his new task as ambassador to Rome on 7 November 1938, after eight tumultuous years of duty in Berlin.

Although the new ambassador received an enthusiastic welcome from the French community in the Italian capital, Mussolini stipulated that his arrival was not to be accorded any special fanfare. The Duce had already expressed his antipathy for François-Poncet personally, telling Ciano that " 'I shall do everything to help him to break his head. I don't like the man.' "The German ambassador reported that the French gesture of sending a new ambassador "leaves the Duce cold, as it comes 1 or 2 years too late and is now obviously intended to give the appearance of a Paris-Rome rapprochement at the expense of the Axis." In his memoirs François-Poncet noted that the inspired fascist press warned that if he expected to renew the tradition of Camille Barrère, he might as well keep his bags packed and return home. Mussolini reinforced this initial *douche froide* by systematically ostracizing the French emissary at social and official functions, pointedly turning his back on François-Poncet while ostentatiously greeting his British counterpart. It seemed clear that Mussolini—far from pursuing the expected Franco-Italian reconciliation—was in fact aiming to weaken the Franco-English entente vis-à-vis the central European totalitarian camp.[4] It is hard to escape the conclusion that England's ill-timed effectuation of the Easter Accord with Italy only served to catalyze this Italian reaction. It is also worth mentioning here that François-Poncet's opposite number in Paris, the newly appointed ambassador to France, was Raffaele Guariglia. The choice appeared flattering at first blush; Guariglia was a well-known Francophile with a long and distinguished record in the Italian diplomatic service. But when he went to see Ciano to pick up his instructions before leaving for Paris, the conversation went like this:

ME [Guariglia] —'What ought I to do in Paris?'
CIANO —'Nothing.'
ME —'That's fairly difficult, but I shall do my best.'[5]

Despite such inauspicious beginnings, François-Poncet had not yet entirely despaired of reaching a rapprochement with Rome. In fact, his first meeting with Ciano went rather well. The latter stressed the importance of the Spanish question, rehashed the history of French Popular Front support for the Spanish "Reds," and insisted that Franco-Italian relations would remain problematical so long as the French attitude on Spain remained in doubt. François-Poncet pointed out that the Spanish frontier was then closed and that France was adhering rigorously to the nonintervention agreement, to which Ciano responded that Rome was still concerned that a new political crisis in France might enable Popular Front leaders to send more aid to Barcelona. He emphasized, however, that since June 1938, Italy had sent to Spain "not one man, not one rifle."[6] Mussolini considered Spain the touchstone upon which the future of Franco-Italian relations would depend. In these conditions, Ciano stressed, if France would completely renounce her support for Barcelona, the atmosphere would be purified and friendship would be reborn, " 'for there is scarcely anything between us . . . but mosquitoes.' "[7]

François-Poncet presented his letters of accreditation to Victor Emmanuel III on 19 November 1938, thus officially recognizing the Italian monarch as Emperor of Ethiopia. The end to this lengthy impasse, however, did not result in the desired appeasement. The French ambassador's first conversation with Mussolini on 26 November proceeded in much the same tenor as the earlier talk with Ciano. He found the Duce could be courteous and correct, above all concerned about Spain and the future orientation of the French government. All these events of his first three weeks in Rome left François-Poncet in rather an ambivalent frame of mind. It was obvious that conditions had changed drastically since 1935. With the conquest of Ethiopia, the Italians had achieved much of what they wanted from the 1935 accords and would, therefore, be reluctant to resume work quickly on negotiating separate conventions for effectuating the 1935 deal on Tunisia. British sources indicate that, despite the cordiality of the French ambassador's first meetings with the fascist leaders, Italy's price for a rapprochement was likely to be quite high, requiring French concessions with regard to Tunisia, the Jibuti–Addis Ababa Railway, and the Suez Canal. Reconciliation with France, François-Poncet believed, was chiefly valuable to Italy as a device to procure for her a greater liberty of maneuver vis-à-vis Germany. It was this bedrock of mutual distrust between Rome and Berlin that might be advantageous to France in the long run. Given this situation, only one thing seemed absolutely clear to François-Poncet at the end of November 1938. Generalizing from the concerns expressed by Italian officials about the uncertainties of France's internal political situation, he wrote to Bonnet: "Mussolini, like Hitler, is waiting for us, watching us carefully, and it is clear that he will be influenced by the spectacle that we ourselves will give him before orienting his present uncertainty in one direction or the other. It is either the affirmation of French strength or its decline, both domestically and abroad, which will have a decisive effect upon the Franco-Italian problem."[8]

François-Poncet's apprehensions were confirmed by the infamous incident in the Italian Chamber of Fasces and Corporations on 30 November 1938. The French ambassador had been invited to attend a major foreign policy address by Ciano. This proved to be a long paean of praise for Italian victories in Ethiopia and Spain, a judgment the Italian foreign minister believed was endorsed by the English when they effectuated the accord of 16 April. Ciano closed his remarks by saying that the Italian government intended in the future "to defend the legitimate interests and aspirations of the Italian people"—a conclusion which sparked off a major demonstration in the assembly hall, coordinated with a popular manifestation in the streets outside. Deputies jumped to their feet to demand the annexation of Tunisia and Corsica. One even cried out "Savoy." The outburst brought no reaction from Ciano. Mussolini, also in attendance, sat passively. The absence of any official attempt to moderate the demonstration lent credence to François-Poncet's conclusion that the whole episode had been orchestrated in advance, designed to derail any Franco-Italian rapprochement based upon existing agreements or to encourage further French concessions. In retrospect this incident has appeared crucial in determining the future course of Franco-Italian policies. Some have concluded that the irreconcilability of rival imperial interests emerged clearly on 30 November, and that no French government, especially in the wake of Munich, could entertain the notion of surrendering to such extensive Italian demands. After this point, Italophobes in France gained the upper hand, and the major organs of public opinion turned generally anti-Italian as well.[9] Such conclusions, although superficially persuasive, undervalue the dynamics of subsequent diplomatic developments which only a detailed examination can reveal.

The French reaction to the events of 30 November was immediate and expected. Bonnet went before the French Chamber of Deputies to announce that France would never cede an acre of her territory to Italy. He ordered François-Poncet to seek clarification from Ciano and to make it clear to him that if he did not repudiate the exaggerated claims of 30 November, France would be forced to reexamine the general orientation of its political position in regard to Italy. The French foreign minister stressed that France still adhered to the accords of 1935 and regarded their application as "the surest step in the amelioration of Franco-Italian relations." François-Poncet complained officially to Ciano on 3 December, remarking ironically that Franco-Italian problems which only two weeks earlier had been brushed aside by Ciano as "mosquitoes" appeared in reality to be "elephants." Ciano, of course, denied any government complicity in the demonstration of 30 November, explaining it away as an isolated incident involving a few overheated deputies. He offered, however, no substantive suggestions for the future.[10]

The French ambassador's immediate interpretation of events was decidedly pessimistic. In a series of telegrams to Paris, he outlined several possible scenarios gathered from informers in Rome. One speculated that the accords of 1935 were dead and buried, and that the only hope for a future accord lay in returning to the 1896 conventions on Tunisia coupled with a favorable settlement for Italy in Jibuti. Another anonymous Italian source interpreted the events of 30 November as an example of Italy's effort to begin realizing some concrete gains from the Axis relationship with Germany. Up to this point, the Axis had benefited only Hitler. Now, Mussolini was anxious to stimulate German support for Italian gains in the Mediterranean and North Africa. The French military attaché in Rome developed a similar view, even suggesting that Ciano's speech and the subsequent demonstration indicated that a German-Italian deal had already been worked out—to the effect that Italy would support German claims to the Sudetenland in exchange for German support for Italian ambitions in Tunisia, Corsica, and Savoy. That the Italians were dissatisfied by the meager return on their commitment to the Axis may be inferred from a letter Ciano wrote to Joachim von Ribbentrop, German foreign minister, at the beginning of 1939. In it he explained that Italy's demands on France were of two kinds. The first involved residues from the accords of 1935 (Tunisia, Jibuti and the Jibuti–Addis Ababa Railway, the Suez Canal) and could be dealt with through normal diplomatic channels if France would seize the initiative. "The other demands," Ciano noted, "are of a historical nature and refer to territory which belongs to Italy from a geographic, ethnographic, and strategic point of view and which we have no intention of renouncing finally. This, however, is a problem of a different calibre requiring quite other methods for its solution, and we do not wish to bring it up at the moment."[11] It is likely that this statement represented an effort to bring forth a German commitment to support Italian imperial aspirations. This did not occur, however, and Italy was left to deal with Mediterranean questions on her own.

François-Poncet speculated that Italian policy might very well be aimed at separating England from France by making it seem dangerous for England to maintain close ties to France. In this situation, the French envoy advised the maintenance of sangfroid and returned to his earlier theme of the importance of reestablishing French domestic order and discipline. This would help to dissipate any Italian illusions about wringing easy Munich-like concessions from a domestically weakened Third Republic. "One must hope," he added, "that the language of England will also contribute [to dispelling Italian illusions]."[12] It is clear that London's role, brought decisively into question by the sudden effectuation of the Easter Accord, was viewed as an important one in both Rome and Paris.

The two-week period between the presentation of the French demarche in Rome and the formal Italian denunciation of the Laval-Mussolini accords on 17 December well may have been decisive in determining the future course of events. It was a time of great confusion and blurred diplomatic signals in London, which left the French little room for the creative maneuvers advocated by François-Poncet. The situation was complicated by the fact that on 6 December 1938, Ribbentrop arrived in Paris to sign with Bonnet a Franco-German declaration of peaceful intent. The rather anodyne document bound the two nations to pursue good neighborly relations, solemnly recognized existing Franco-German frontiers, and called for joint consultation on future political difficulties. The timing of this mission suggested to some that Germany was less than solidly in support of her Axis partner's Mediterranean ambitions.[13]

In fact, the Ribbentrop gesture probably served as a warning to Italy that the Führer was not about to risk for the Italians of Tunisia what he was, at that point, unwilling to risk for the Germans of Alsace. This may explain the tone of subsequent French diplomatic communications, which posited that the 30 November program was a maximalist agenda designed to stimulate a French diplomatic initiative that would result in much more modest gains for Italy. According to this record, references to Nice, Savoy, and Corsica were merely smokescreens; Italy's real objective was the redefinition of the situation of Italians in Tunisia. Perhaps Italy sought to portray

Italians in the Regency as equivalent to the Sudeten Germans in Czechoslovakia and to seek a solution similar to the one of Munich—with England again playing the role of arbiter. These views also corresponded with those of Lord Perth. The British ambassador did not take the 30 November demonstration seriously, brushing aside clamor for Corsica, Nice, and Savoy as an awkward Italian bluff designed to make the French more malleable on the real issues of Tunisia, Jibuti, and Suez. The British also pointed out that such extravagant Italian claims ran completely counter to the recently implemented Easter Accord which reaffirmed the principle of maintaining the status quo in the Mediterranean. François-Poncet noted that the Italian press reflected a perceptible moderation of the Italian position. He cited an article in *Giornale d'Italia* by Virginio Gayda, a well-known spokesman for the regime. Gayda, although declaring the 1935 accords defunct, made no reference to Corsica, Nice, or Savoy, emphasizing instead the need to negotiate new understandings on Tunisia, Suez, and Jibuti. The fact that he referred to a negotiation rather than a recourse to force led François-Poncet to view his article as: "a bit of a deflation, which seems to authorize one to believe that the purpose of all the uproar we have witnessed since 30 November is to try . . . to initiate a conversation which would make a *tabula rasa* of the accords of 1935 and establish new bases of negotiation."[14]

What, therefore, did the French ambassador advise in terms of strategy? His recommendations were detailed in two lengthy communications on 13 and 14 December 1938. François-Poncet identified Italy's attitude as based primarily upon an inferiority complex vis-à-vis its Axis partner. He stressed that France must abandon all policies which could convey an impression of Italy as a minor power to be treated like a little daughter. To the contrary, although Mussolini's position had slipped in recent years due to the poor economic condition of the country and the impression that Italy was playing the junior partner to Hitler, his situation was not critical and one would be poorly advised to anticipate the collapse of fascism in the near future. This analysis explained Italy's intransigent attitude toward France; the Duce, painfully aware that Germany had been the only beneficiary of the Axis relationship, must persuade Italian public opinion that the time had come for the payoff to Italy, whose major goals were in the Mediterranean and in North Africa and whose major adversary was obviously France. How far Italy would go with her demands depended heavily on the extent of support she could find in Berlin and also upon the attitude of England. At this moment, François-Poncet warned, the pro-German faction in Italy was strong; the extremist Roberto Farinacci was very influential, and the anti-Semitic program was being emphasized. Mussolini had indeed won a propaganda victory with his intervention at Munich, but many Italians interpreted that as yet another service Rome had rendered to Berlin.

In this situation, the French ambassador stressed the futility of France's clinging to the Laval-Mussolini accords of 1935. He suggested instead a three-pronged approach: (1) great care must be exercised to avoid all incidents, especially in Tunisia, which would allow Italy to portray the 120,000 Italians there as a persecuted minority similar to the Sudeten Germans in Czechoslovakia; (2) France must make it absolutely clear that she would maintain the integrity of *all* her territories and that Italy must expect no concession on this point; (3) at the same time, however, France must not remain intransigently opposed to those Italian claims that did not involve issues of sovereignty. For example, France might consider the following: establishment of a free port for Italy at Jibuti; granting to Italy of supplementary facilities by the Jibuti–Addis Ababa Railway Company; lowering of tariffs for use of the Suez Canal; entry of Italians to the administrative council of the Suez Canal Company; acceptance in *lire* of a portion of the freight costs for use of the Canal. With regard to Tunisia, obviously the most serious bone of contention, François-Poncet proposed a three- to five-year prolongation of the 1896 statutes—after which a more relaxed international atmosphere might permit the reexamination of the entire Tunisian issue. All of these possibilities might be suggested to the Italians in exchange for a reversal of the intolerable and incessant press campaigns and street demonstrations against France.[15]

The strategy thus posited, if pursued from a position of strength, was a wise and prudent one designed to protect France's southern flank in the event of an eruption of the potentially more serious problem across the Rhine. The success of François-Poncet's program depended, however (as he himself emphasized), upon energetic support from England, which was lacking entirely. The confused signals from London, in fact, more than likely convinced Italian leaders that France was diplomatically isolated and that it was safe to abandon the accords of 1935—thereby forcing Paris to pursue its Italian policy from a position of weakness and setting in motion the events that would lead Mussolini to the Pact of Steel six months later.

Throughout the period immediately following the events of 30 November, François-Poncet underscored his conviction that the attitude adopted by the British government would be crucial in either encouraging or restricting Italian appetites.[16] Although Lord Perth presented a demarche to Ciano on 4 December requesting clarification of the 30 November demonstration, he chose the same day to announce that Chamberlain and Halifax had scheduled a state visit to Rome for 11–14 January

1939. Such enormously bad timing led François-Poncet to doubt that Perth had put across the desired message of Franco-British solidarity. In fact, Perth had been at some pains to convince François-Poncet that Mussolini was " 'a wise, moderate and prudent man, hostile to war.' According to him, the Duce and Count Ciano would be models of rectitude and frankness. Recent events have left me with exactly the opposite impression."[17] The French ambassador noted that the Italian press completely ignored the British demarche, focusing instead on the announcement of the British officials' visit to Rome. Italians thus interpreted the British response as "proof that Great Britain has not been deflected from her policy and remains faithful to the recently activated Italo-British accord. The English government has not been influenced by the excitations of the French press nor by the emotion that France would like to have excited in England by exploiting the incidents of 30 November." François-Poncet was convinced that unless the British attitude were clearly and energetically redressed, it would "yet another time" be the cause for serious complications.[18]

French concerns were indeed expressed in London, where Cadogan assured Corbin that he would suggest that instructions be sent to Perth to cut short any false interpretations of British policy. Such assurances, however, did not convince François-Poncet, who considered Perth incapable of articulating a strong British position on this matter. The fact that Perth did not take the incident of 30 November seriously, and even said as much to François-Poncet, led the latter to conclude that Italy expected England to play some sort of mediating role. He thought the Italians would one day ask England "to confide a new mission to Lord [Walter] Runciman." François-Poncet cautioned Perth about the dangers inherent in the western powers' remaining too long in an equivocal position—as had been the case in Czechoslovakia. "But of course I was not able to change his mind." England's lackadaisical attitude prompted a similar interpretation of events among French military aides. A General Staff memo on the state of Franco-Italian relations, dated 6 December 1938, concluded in this manner: "It seems that . . . Italian diplomacy, sheltered by the accords with England, is seeking to aggravate tensions with France and to follow, with the support of the Reich, a maneuver destined to impress the British ministers prior to their visit, and thus to extort important concessions from France."[19]

The British position in all of this became even more muddled on 12 December when Chamberlain, in response to a question in the House of Commons, declared that Britain had no specific military obligation to go to France's aid in case of an Italian attack on French territory or possessions. Such obligations, he said, did not exist in any treaty, pact, or accord between Britain and France. The statement was literally true but failed to stress other commitments that Britain had under Article 12 of the Kellogg-Briand Pact or more informal pledges of support to France articulated by Eden in 1936 and confirmed by Chamberlain as late as 24 November 1938. Bonnet, concerned about how the prime minister's statement would be interpreted by the Italians, demanded an immediate and public clarification of his remarks. Chamberlain responded through his ambassador that such an action was unnecessary since, in response to another question in Commons, the prime minister had said that Britain intended to conserve the status quo in the Mediterranean.[20]

Britain's failure to clarify its position had a number of important and unfortunate consequences. There is no reason to doubt London's official position that it considered the visit of Chamberlain and Halifax to Rome as the most effective means of guiding the Italians toward reasonable views and of convincing them of the necessity of arriving at an accord with France.[21] But that quite reasonable objective appeared almost totally belied by Chamberlain's bold assertion in Commons. The Italian press seized upon it as a rebuke for France. François-Poncet reported that the overwhelming impression disseminated in the fascist press was that Chamberlain would play the same role of mediator between France and Italy as he had done at Berchtesgaden and Godesberg in the Czech crisis. He was convinced that most Italians believed this to be true, and that London had done nothing to deflate these illusions or to defuse a press campaign "which every day is giving the public of the Peninsula an altered and systematically tendencious image of the British state of mind." Responding to a number of appeals to put the French position vis-à-vis England in unequivocal terms, Daladier stated categorically in the Chamber of Deputies on 13 December, and echoed the message in the Senate six days later, that "France will not cede an acre of her territories to Italy, even if maintaining such a policy results in armed conflict."[22] To underscore his message Daladier scheduled an official trip to Corsica, Algeria, and Tunisia to precede and thus to blunt the impact of the voyage of British ministers to Rome.

This bizarre series of events reached its logical conclusion on 17 December 1938, when Ciano formally denounced the Franco-Italian agreements of 7 January 1935. In a letter to François-Poncet, the Italian foreign minister argued that the accords had never been officially ratified, nor had any steps been taken to draft a document altering the status of Italians in Tunisia. Ciano declared the accords "historically *dépassés*" and therefore no longer valid. It seems reasonably clear, however, that Ciano did not intend to close the door entirely; the final sentence of his letter said that, although the 1935 accords no longer constituted the basis of Franco-Italian relations, "if one wants to ameliorate them, it is evident that relations must be examined again in common accord between the two governments."[23]

François-Poncet regarded Ciano's letter as a pure and simple denunciation of the 1935 accords. Even though the final paragraph made an oblique reference to a new accord, it contained no suggestions on what such a new understanding would contain. François-Poncet, therefore, advised against any French initiative in proposing terms for an accord, for fear of being placed in the eyes of the world as the supplicant. In the end, France did nothing more than simply acknowledge receipt of Ciano's denunciation. Bonnet's letter to Ciano on Christmas Day argued that France indeed had lived up to the Laval-Mussolini accords. The latter were ratified by the French parliament almost unanimously on 22 and 26 March 1935, but the ratification was not exchanged because of the adjournment of the commission on Tunisia, at Italian request. The French sold 2,500 shares in the Jibuti–Addis Ababa Railway to an Italian group. And in October 1938, the new ambassador was accredited to the "King of Italy and Emperor of Ethiopia." This lengthy preamble concluded by simply acknowledging receipt of the Italian denunciation.[24] There was no mention of a new accord and no request for Italian suggestions.

This total impasse magnified the importance of third powers. Germany's role was, for the most part, discounted by the French, who believed quite rightly that Berlin had little interest in encouraging its Axis partner in policies which might lead to a major conflagration in the Mediterranean. At worst it was expected that Germany might seek to prolong the Franco-Italian diplomatic imbroglio in order to distract the western powers' attention from the Reich's ambitions in eastern Europe.[25] All of which placed increased importance on the role of Great Britain, especially in light of the scheduled Chamberlain-Halifax visit to Rome in January 1939.

It is quite clear that the French were suspicious of the role that the British might attempt to play. Given Ciano's denunciation of the Laval-Mussolini accords, it appeared to François-Poncet that the Italian strategy was to maneuver England into the role of mediator by portraying France as totally intransigent on the issue of renegotiating the points agreed to initially in January 1935. His concerns about English policy are worth quoting at some length.

> By all evidence the Italian effort in London is aimed at leading M. Chamberlain to play at Rome, this time at our expense, the same role that he played at Godesberg. I don't know what the British prime minister's present state of mind is on this matter, but the optimistic remarks and the exhortations toward conciliation being uttered by members of the British Embassy in Rome,

in their conversations with French colleagues, do not constitute a reassuring indication that they would foresee their country supporting a legitimate intransigence on our part in the face of exaggerated Italian pretensions.

François-Poncet reiterated his immediate concerns about Tunisia and Jibuti in particular. France must exercise great prudence in those areas and adopt a line of conduct designed to avoid any possibility of a violent confrontation between France and Italy which would encourage the British to intervene as mediators, "in order to impose upon us, as at Munich, the obligation to make concessions which must then be carried out by us in singularly unfavorable conditions."[26]

François-Poncet's fundamental distrust of the English could not have been more abundantly expressed. He further underscored his pessimism several days later, reporting that Perth had expressed his astonishment at France's blunt reaction to Ciano's "moderate and reasonable" appeal of 17 December for an exchange of views with France on subjects in dispute. François-Poncet wondered to what extent Chamberlain was influenced by Perth's reports on the basic good will and honesty of Mussolini and Ciano, and he urged that France's position be forcefully and unambiguously advanced in London prior to the Chamberlain-Halifax visit to Rome. Based on information and advice such as this, Bonnet moved quickly to undercut the possibility of any English intervention in the Franco-Italian quarrel that might prove detrimental to French interests. In a long telegram to his chargé d'affaires in London on 27 December, Bonnet reviewed his interpretation of Italian strategy. Italy's tactic, he said, was apparently to intensify international tension over its claims against France even to the threat of war. Italy's expectation was that the threat of war would encourage English intervention to exercise a moral suasion on France to make territorial cessions to Italy in the name of peace. Given this potential scenario, Bonnet instructed Roger Cambon to make it clear to Chamberlain that France categorically rejected the surrender of any of its rights and that "the accords of 1935 represent the limit of concessions which can be granted to Italy. . . ." Furthermore, Cambon was instructed to make it plain that France "rejects in advance all intervention or arbitration by third powers, even that of its friend England." Rather, it would be most useful in undercutting unrealistic Italian expectations, for the British ministers to tell Mussolini frankly that they would not accept the role of intermediary, and that they understood and approved the French attitude in the matter. In strictest confidence, however, Bonnet hinted to the British ambassador in Paris that France might "after a decent interval had elapsed" be ready to consider discussing such subjects as: representation for Italy on the Suez

Canal Board, lowering of Canal dues, a free port at Jibuti, and reduced charges on the Jibuti–Addis Ababa Railway.[27] Although there is some evidence to suggest that the British intended to exercise a mediating role in Rome,[28] this strategy was abandoned quickly following Ciano's 17 December denunciation of the Laval-Mussolini agreements. In light of the latter, E. M. B. Ingram, head of the Southern Department of the British Foreign Office, believed it wise for England to stay out of the Franco-Italian squabble—at least for the moment.

> We do not want to be forced during the Rome visit to act as intermediaries for the French and we shall be in a better position to offer unbiassed [*sic*] and even effective comment on any Italian claims against the French (if the Italians can be induced to divulge them to us) should we be in a position to say to the Italians that we have refrained entirely up to that moment from intervening in the Franco-Italian wrangle or offering advice to Paris. After the Rome visit, we may be in a better position to offer advice in Paris. Our hand will, I think, be stronger in Rome if we studiously refrain from doing so now.

Halifax fully endorsed this point of view on 25 December.[29]

As a gesture to underscore French determination, Daladier followed through with his hastily arranged and heavily publicized official visit to Corsica, Tunisia, and Algeria between 2 and 6 January 1939. Everywhere he went he was welcomed by enthusiastic crowds which demonstrated the attachment to France of these territories claimed by the Italian press and the demonstrators of 30 November. Italian newspapers interpreted the timing of Daladier's visit as a provocation and an effort to undermine the talks between Chamberlain and the Duce.[30] Although that view is open to question it is quite clear that the premier's gesture was meant to impress the English of France's determination to reject any mediation.

François-Poncet, however, maintained his extremely pessimistic attitude toward the British and continued to insist that, in spite of the French demarche of 27 December, the French position must be strongly reaffirmed to the British ministers on 10 January when they stopped in Paris on their way to Rome. The French ambassador's concerns were magnified by a perceptible increase in the anti-French tone of the Italian press and by an officially inspired article by Giovanni Ansaldo in the *Gazetta del Popolo*, inviting Chamberlain to become involved in the Franco-Italian problem. Only British mediation, Ciano's mouthpiece argued, could head off potential conflict between the two Mediterranean powers. It is interesting to note that although Ansaldo mentioned Tunisia, Corsica, and Jibuti as areas of potential conflict, he did not articulate any concrete Italian goals in any of the three areas.[31]

With all this as background it is not surprising that the Chamberlain-Halifax visit to Rome was nearly barren of concrete results. The French demarche of 27 December was indeed reinforced personally to the British ministers when they stopped in Paris on 10 January. The discussion at the Quai d'Orsay proved stiff and desultory. According to Cadogan, the French and British ministers sat around in chairs, without proper secretariat or interpreters, while Chamberlain and Halifax "tried to talk French." Nevertheless, Daladier made it quite clear that the French government would make no concessions to Italy; Italian actions since 30 November had produced an "union sacrée," and any French government attempting in these circumstances to make concessions would be swept away. So far as the Italians were concerned, the mission had lost much of its meaning. In fact, the record shows that Mussolini never raised the question of British mediation or intervention in the Franco-Italian dispute. Nor did he articulate Italian demands in any of the major points at issue, specifically rejecting any Italian initiative. The Duce, according to Halifax, presented his list of general grievances against the French and underscored his disappointment that France had totally ignored the invitation for an exchange of views contained in the last lines of Ciano's denunciation of the Rome Accords. It was not likely, therefore, that any direct Franco-Italian discussion of these issues could be foreseen until after General Franco had won a complete victory in Spain. Nevertheless, Halifax was mildly buoyed by his visit to Rome. He believed that "Mussolini's attitude towards the French questions was much more restrained than I had ever expected, and I am left with the pretty clear feeling that . . . he does not want to embark upon any policy of adventures endangering peace. . . ." De Monzie, the pro-Italian minister of public works in the Daladier cabinet, remained cynical about British motives. He remarked to his diary that, "Chamberlain and Halifax are cooing in Rome. England, who hinders us with Italy and prevents us from putting together a reconciliation, shows no scruples about trying for itself what its diplomatic prudery forbids to us."[32]

Even François-Poncet had to admit, however, that although the British visit did not modify the Italian position vis-à-vis France, at least it served a useful purpose in finally getting the British to specify their solidarity with France directly to Italian leaders and thereby write finis to idle speculations about another Munich-like mediation. His assessment was strongly echoed by France's ambassador in London. Although regretting the delay in the articulation of British solidarity with France, Corbin believed that the relationship between the two countries had been strengthened since 30 November, and that few in the Foreign Office currently shared the optimistic views of Lord Perth in Rome. The strengthened ties between London and Paris made war in the Mediterranean less likely, given Italian military and economic exhaustion due to Italy's adventures in Ethiopia and Spain. The thinking in London was, therefore, that the Duce's continued provocations were designed either to intimidate France into giving partial satisfaction to his demands or to provoke an imprudent action, which could be represented as a hostile act and thus bring in German assistance. Corbin concluded his lengthy analysis with the following observations: "If we can maintain our sang-froid and our firmness, the fascist rodomontades need not cause us great fear. In reality everything depends upon the support Italy can expect from the Reich, but here the commitments of England have been publicly expressed frequently and clearly enough to leave no doubt about the attitude that the British government would take [in case of war]."[33]

Corbin's analysis was buttressed by Prime Minister Chamberlain's speech to the House of Commons on 6 February 1939, in which he made it explicit that should France be the victim of aggression, it could count on immediate military assistance from England. Ever since the signing of the Anglo-Italian accord of 16 April 1938, Italy's goal had been to separate England from France. By February 1939 that possibility seemed finally to be foreclosed, but nearly a year had been lost. Chamberlain's speech caused considerable consternation among Italian officials, who had assumed for a long time that Britain would play the role of mediator in the Franco-Italian dispute. But Chamberlain coupled his remarks with a proposal to France for the formal establishment of full staff conversations based on the presumption of war against Germany and Italy. Why this sudden British determination to dramatize a set of commitments that France had sought in vain since 1919? Young has argued convincingly that after Munich, British faith in appeasement waned precipitously and that, therefore, French passivity—an objective of British policy before Munich—was no longer seen to be in their best interests. It became important to have a French ally fully determined to resist fascist pretentions in Europe, the Mediterranean, and overseas. Yet the French were very slow in responding. In fact, conversations at the staff level were delayed for two months and only came into being after Hitler's coup in Czechoslovakia in March.[34] It seems clear that the French, having been deceived by the British in the past, feared duplicity again in the British offers of 4–6 February. They did not want to be tricked into a war to defend the British Empire and wanted to assure themselves that any joint military planning was to be for the mutual benefit of both countries.

THE BAUDOUIN MISSION

The foregoing reveals an interesting—and in the long run a possibly self-defeating—concatenation of public postures. Ciano's denunciation of the Rome Accords and Mussolini's subsequent reluctance to define a specific list of Italian modifications were couched in such a way as to indicate that Italy wished to reach some sort of modus vivendi with France, but without being placed in the position of supplicant. The same reluctance may be read into France's reaction to Italian policy, especially in the rejection of any third-power mediation. Paris, likewise, was unwilling to be seen in the eyes of world opinion as the initiator of concessions apparently wrung from her by threat of force. All of which magnified the importance of the secret mission to Rome undertaken by Paul Baudouin, then director-general of the Banque d'Indochine, in the winter of 1939. The details of the Baudouin mission have been mooted in memoir literature and in parliamentary testimony for forty years, but they have only recently seen the light of day in published French diplomatic correspondence.

The Baudouin mission to Rome must be assessed against the backdrop of events in Spain, since the continuation of the civil war there has been cited frequently as the major obstacle to a move toward Franco-Italian reconciliation. General Franco's splitting of the loyalist forces by his capture of Barcelona in late January 1939 assured the ultimate victory of the Nationalists. The Italian press played up the event as a major victory for Italian prestige. Although there is some indication that the British believed Franco's victory would make the Duce more moderate toward France, François-Poncet was decidedly more pessimistic. He felt that, given the renewed intensity of anti-French press campaigns in Italy, recent events in Spain were much more likely to whet Mussolini's appetite and make him more determined than ever to use the Rome-Berlin Axis (and the possibility of German mediation) to realize some concrete gains at the expense of France. It was clear by this point that any conflict resulting from the tensions would bring France diplomatic support from Britain, but most Italian officials believed that any serious British military support was unlikely.[35] What, then, could one expect the Italian stance vis-à-vis France to be?

François-Poncet believed that Mussolini would delay any specific claims on France until the conclusion of the Spanish Civil War. But he felt that the Duce, capitalizing on Franco's victory, would try to claim enough to humiliate France but not be so severe as to alienate British and German opinion. France, he said, should be prepared to respond to a variety of Italian claims. These would be likely to include the demilitarization of Corsica and the cession or sale of additional shares in the Suez Canal Company coupled with increased representation on the company's administrative board. In addition, François-Poncet believed that Italy would no longer be satisfied with a free port at Jibuti and participation in the Jibuti–Addis Ababa Railway; France must be prepared for a demand for the cession of substantial portions of the Somali coast to Italy. With regard to Tunisia, Mussolini's immediate demands were likely to include southern border rectifications granting territories to Cyrenaica, the right to send a massive contingent of Italian agricultural workers to the Regency, and extension of the conventions of 1896.[36] Such was the situation when Daladier and Bonnet approved Baudouin's unofficial mission to Rome.

Baudouin, who was to become minister of foreign affairs under Marshal Pétain at Vichy, had negotiated the sale to Italy of shares in the Jibuti–Addis Ababa Railway following the Laval-Mussolini accords of 1935, and he had maintained important contacts with the banking community in Rome. Despite subsequent allegations in the press and in parliamentary testimony, Baudouin claimed never to have met Ciano prior to 2 February 1939. Shortly before a scheduled visit to Rome for an administrative council meeting of a Franco-Italian consortium of which he was a member, Baudouin received a telegram from an Italian banker and business contact, Vincenzo Fagiuoli. The latter said that Ciano, disturbed about the potential warlike actions of Germany and believing the moment ripe for clarifying relations with France, would like to talk with him. Baudouin relayed this contact immediately to Bonnet and Daladier. The three met together several times, and the French leaders decided to charge Baudouin with a secret mission to collect information that might be useful in dealing with Italy.[37] Pressed subsequently for details as to why Baudouin's project was secret, bypassing François-Poncet, Bonnet explained that the bank director's task was merely to listen and to acquire whatever information he could. The foreign minister stressed that there was nothing official about Baudouin's mission. He was simply to find out whether Italian claims extended beyond the possibility of negotiation or whether they were realistic. In the latter case, François-Poncet would be charged with undertaking an official negotiation. By avoiding any connection with the French Embassy at this point, Bonnet felt that he was sidestepping any impression that France was asking anything from the Italians. He did not want "at any price" to appear as a petitioner. It has been suggested by at least one eminent French diplomat that the strategy of secrecy backfired disastrously. Noël, then French ambassador to Warsaw, maintained that Baudouin's reputation as an intriguer and a hypocrite made him a bad choice for such a delicate mission. Furthermore, by not informing François-Poncet in advance, Daladier and Bonnet discredited their own ambassador and undercut his authority in any future negotiations.38

Baudouin met twice with Ciano for a total of about two hours on 2 and 3 February 1938. During the first meeting the two discussed a wide range of issues, which Baudouin boiled down as follows: (1) Italy wanted a largely conceived free zone in Jibuti with dock facilities linking up to the Jibuti–Addis Ababa Railway. (2) Italy wanted the cession of French-owned shares of that portion of the railway located in Ethiopia. Baudouin indicated that cession was unlikely since it was a private company, but that it might be possible for Italy to purchase shares at a fair price. (3) Italy wanted several seats on the council of administration of the Suez Canal Company. (4) Italy wanted Italians in Tunisia to have the right to remain Italian rather than being subject, after whatever length of time, to forced naturalization. Pressed further on this point, Ciano acknowledged that Italy would not ask for French concessions in any other matter but that of naturalization. The question of Italian schools, for example, would not be raised. (5) Ciano indicated that Italy would make no separate declaration to France regarding withdrawal of volunteers from Spain, having already done so to England. The following day, Ciano notified Baudouin that he and Mussolini were in accord on the above program and that if France were willing to discuss these issues, then " 'the Italian government sees no obstacles to the rapid materialization of negotiations it ardently desires.' " He stressed, however, that official conversations must be initiated by the French rather than by Italy. Baudouin ended the discussion by emphasizing the unofficial nature of his mission and promising to carry the Italian claims back to Paris.39

Although the French government continued to insist that Baudouin's mission had no official standing whatever, there are indications that its character was misunderstood both in Paris and in Rome. Pertinax exposed the mission in the French press in mid-February, arguing in the face of the Quai d'Orsay's denials that the banker had carried proposals to Rome calling for French concessions on Suez, the Jibuti–Addis Ababa Railway, Jibuti, and Tunisia. Moreover, he pointed out, Fernand de Brinon, a prominent member of the right-wing, pro-Nazi Comité France-Allemagne, had been sent concurrently to Berlin to inform the German government of the concessions and to request that Germany use her good offices to encourage Italy to accept. Vigorously repudiating the Pertinax exposé, Bonnet wrote to François-Poncet on 21 February 1939 denying that there had ever been any such mission, and he affirmed that any Franco-Italian negotiation, official or unofficial, could only be undertaken through the auspices of the French Embassy. He indicated that François-Poncet himself had shaped the French policy, which had been expressed in the 26 December response to the Italian denunciation of the Laval-Mussolini accords. Bonnet's only reference to Baudouin was the oblique note that: "We had taken care to learn what the Italian claims were before knowing if one could engage in an official discussion."[40]

The French ambassador in Rome, who had in fact witnessed Baudouin's arrival at the train station, was not appeased by such verbiage. Two very cold telegrams informed the Quai d'Orsay that the Italian press was full of stories about the mission in the wake of Pertinax's exposé and that, far from having a salutary effect upon Italy's anti-French press campaign, the mission seemed to have exacerbated it. The fact that Baudouin had avoided all contact with the embassy was also the source of considerable speculation throughout the Peninsula. François-Poncet concluded that this sort of behavior would only encourage the fascists to persevere in their demands. Whatever the character of Baudouin's assignment, François-Poncet said that it "has excited, rather than calmed, appetites which are going well beyond their primary aims; and if tomorrow we deviate, after having accepted the ignominious treatment inflicted upon us, it is clear that we shall be exposed in the future to the risk of being consumed like an artichoke, leaf by leaf." François-Poncet's position remained intransigently firm through the middle of March, and the French government, in fact, abandoned the Baudouin flirtation following its revelation in the French press. On 9 February Daladier told Baudouin that he was unable to authorize any further action, citing the internal political situation as the constraining factor. "One must not," he said, "weaken France by actions which could be interpreted as acts of weakness. Moreover, a negotiation with Italy would profoundly divide the Radical Party." Bonnet, also present at this meeting, remained conspicuously silent.[41]

If the Baudouin mission had been designed to provoke a direct negotiation between Paris and Rome, then it must be judged a failure. Once again, as in the Hoare-Laval Plan of December 1935, premature publicity torpedoed a potentially promising initiative. In a more limited sense, however, the effort had provided concrete indications of the scope of Italian ambitions vis-à-vis France. Moreover, the mission also revealed that Mussolini had not yet committed himself fully to Nazi Germany. Even François-Poncet, once he recovered from his initial pique, eventually came to champion a more responsive French policy toward Italy in the wake of Hitler's Czechoslovakian coup in March 1939.

THE PRAGUE COUP AND ITS AFTERMATH

The record shows that the British remained steadfastly loyal to Prime Minister Chamberlain's 6 February pronouncement of Franco-British solidarity, going so far as to present an official demarche in Rome against a rumored Italian troop buildup in Libya.[42] French documents indicate that Rome was receiving little, if any, support from its Axis partner in Berlin, the latter in fact urging Mussolini to adopt a more conciliatory stance vis-à-vis Paris.[43] Germany's interest in minimizing her potential obligations in the Mediterranean became starkly apparent on 15 March 1939, when her troops marched into Prague. The move, ostensibly a peacekeeping effort initiated at Czech request, was Germany's most provocative expansionist endeavor to date, with no possibility of justification via the national self-determination rhetoric attendant upon previous adventures in the Rhineland and Austria. Hitler's gesture came as a surprise to Rome and presented an opportunity for completely altering the configuration of European politics—especially as they affected relations between Italy and France.

Some important politicians, such as Reynaud, Mandel, and Jean Zay, tended to believe that Italian and German policies, in the Mediterranean and central Europe respectively, were coordinated. But reports from Rome suggest that people in various fascist milieux were nonplussed by recent events in Czechoslovakia, regarding them as yet another example of Hitler's reaping benefits from the Axis, while leaving Mussolini empty-handed. François-Poncet reported that those Italians who contacted the French Embassy in the wake of the Prague coup were nearly unanimous in suggesting that the time was ripe for France to adopt a more accommodating posture toward Italy's Mediterranean claims. The message was that Mussolini was uncomfortable with the Axis arrangement; if he could present to the Italian people some gain from France, it would restore his freedom of movement toward Nazi Germany. "For want of that, the government of Rome would have no other recourse than to play the German card to the end and would see itself, perhaps soon, led to adopt an aggressive position, with all the risks that such an attitude implies."[44] At this point, however, François-Poncet was reluctant to evaluate the validity of intelligence gathered so close to the event; he passed it along to Paris as simple information.

Other sources tend to validate the ambassador's information. Ciano noted in his diary on 19 March 1939 that: "The events of the last few days have reversed my opinion of the Führer and Germany; he, too, is unfaithful and treacherous and we cannot carry on any policy with him. I have also worked today with the Duce for an understanding with the Western Powers. But will they have at least a minimum of good sense in Paris, or will the possibility of an understanding be compromised once more due to unwillingness to make any concession?" Two days earlier an article by Gayda appeared in the *Giornale d'Italia* which excited the diplomatic community in Rome. His piece declared in quite straightforward fashion that Italy's claims in the Mediterranean were linked neither to any pact with Germany nor to any current or foreseeable event in another part of Europe. Although François-Poncet still advised caution in his analysis of this article and an analogous piece by Ansaldo in *Popolo d'Italia*, his telegram to Bonnet concluded: "I ask myself if it is not possible to see in these formulations the veiled expression of a secret desire to leave open the possibility of negotiation."[45]

In Paris on 16 March, Laval broke his long political silence at a secret meeting of the Senate Committee on Foreign Affairs. He deplored that France was doing nothing to prevent German expansion in central Europe. He pointed out the irony of the fact that Germany, a defeated power in World War I, now possessed more extensive territories in Europe than it had before 1914. Turning to the theme of his tenure as foreign minister in the mid-1930s, Laval argued that there was only one way to prevent Hitler from seizing Europe—" 'to strengthen the chain from London to Paris with links to Rome, Belgrade, Budapest, Warsaw, Bucharest, and Moscow; otherwise it is Germany who will win.' " This speech was to be the source of future political problems for Laval because he continued on to suggest that because the current Chamber of Deputies was unlikely to approve a conciliatory policy toward Italy, it was advisable for Daladier to adopt more authoritarian measures and, in fact, to govern without the Chamber. The former prime minister assured his successor that the French people " 'will be with you, when they are persuaded that your only concern is defending the interests of the country. . . .' " In spite of the doubtful constitutionality of his final advice to Daladier, Laval's statement was leaked to Italian press correspondents in Paris, whose communiqués to Rome discussed the incident in a "highly favorable light." *Popolo d'Italia*, for example, published an article with a Paris dateline suggesting that plans were afoot to appoint Laval to carry out "an extraordinary mission to M. Mussolini."[46]

Laval had indicated to Bonnet in the Senate Committee on Foreign Affairs that he was convinced a settlement with Italy on reasonable terms was possible, and that he was prepared personally to undertake a special assignment to Rome in order to help bring it about. Léger vehemently quashed such rumors, formally denying to the British ambassador that

France was entertaining any plan to grant concessions to Italy—by Laval or anyone else—in the hope of splitting the Axis. That the British had some doubts about the wisdom of Léger's intransigence was made clear in a minute on this information by Sir Andrew Noble, a Foreign Office counsellor. "I don't altogether agree with M. Léger's conclusion," he wrote. "Italy certainly cannot afford to abandon Germany at this moment; but all our information goes to show that Signor Mussolini is far from happy and I believe that he would like to settle his dispute with France in order to regain some freedom of maneuver." The British official believed that it was in the interests of both Britain and France to try to see how reasonable Italian claims could safely be met; blind obstinacy on this issue would only bind Mussolini closer to Hitler.[47]

The rumors of a special Laval mission to Rome coincided with a second unofficial Italian approach to Baudouin. Working again through Fagiuoli, Ciano instructed the Italian banker to try to reinitiate negotiations with his French counterpart. Baudouin saw Daladier immediately on 20 March, but the French premier maintained that negotiations with Rome were impossible so long as the Italian press attacks against France continued. In a private letter to Baudouin, he expressed serious doubts about the efficacy of secret, select missions which were then revealed inopportunely to public scrutiny in the press. He feared, quite justifiably, that such a pattern weakened rather than strengthened the country's morale. The president of the Council of Ministers, however, expressed willingness to withhold a final judgment until after the scheduled major public addresses of King Victor Emmanuel III and Mussolini. He wrote to Baudouin: "It is evident to me that no negotiation can take place while the Franco-Italian climate remains unameliorated. Everything depends upon the upcoming speeches of the King and Mussolini. If they open up a serious and serene possibility of negotiations and contact, I shall seize it with pleasure. But I shall do nothing until then which would force such a result."[48]

Not everyone felt that the correct strategy was to await the public pronouncements of Italian leaders. *Le Temps*'s correspondent in Rome, Paul Gentizon, a specialist in eastern European affairs, wrote to François-Poncet that the Prague coup had altered the entire situation; Italians did not view Germany's success in central Europe with equanimity; it was yet another example of Italy's vassaldom to the Reich. For precisely this reason, Gentizon did not expect the Duce's speech of 26 March to be the conciliatory gesture anticipated by Daladier. Therefore, he urged the French ambassador, *now* was the time to offer Mussolini a face-saving way to begin his disengagement from the Axis. The French journalist suggested that it must be a substantial gesture, including readjustments in Suez, Jibuti, and Tunisia, in order to defuse whatever charges the Duce might be preparing against France in his 26 March address. Furthermore, Cardinal Maglione, the well-informed secretary of state at the Vatican, told Charles-Roux that his recent conversation with Ciano had revealed the latter's doubts about the wisdom of maintaining a close relationship with Germany. Charles-Roux reported to Bonnet that "even on the question of Franco-Italian relations, the Italian minister of foreign affairs had indicated discreetly [to Signor Maglione], by way of allusion, that at the present moment France and Italy needed each other."[49]

Whether or not the decisive moment would be seized seemed to depend heavily on the content of and reaction to major public pronouncements from the Italian king and, especially, from Mussolini scheduled for 23 and 26 March respectively. Victor Emmanuel's speech was moderate in tone; his references to Ciano's note of 17 December seemed to offer to France an opportunity honorably to reopen discussions with Italy. Mussolini's address to the Chamber of Fasces and Corporations, however, was considerably more violent and polemical. Concentrating almost exclusively on the inviolability of the Axis, the Duce did no more than mention the issues currently dividing France and Italy, articulating neither precise claims nor a potential method of resolution. According to Baudouin, Ciano was horrified. Mussolini had changed the text, approved several days earlier by the Fascist Grand Council, calling for negotiations. The Italian foreign minister hastily dispatched his unofficial emissary, Fagiuoli, to Paris to reassure French leaders (through Baudouin) that the Duce, "mobile and easily impressed," had been worked over shortly before the speech by the Prince of Hesse, who had brought him a letter from the Führer. Ciano wanted Daladier to know that he should not interpret Mussolini's speech literally; he hoped that the premier's own radio discourse, scheduled for 29 May, would hold open the possibility of negotiations.[50]

Apparently François-Poncet shared these views. In spite of the habitual and shocking rudenesses of style evident in Mussolini's speech, the French ambassador judged it as in fact "relatively moderate and prudent." The Duce did not insist that the war in Spain represented an irrevocable barricade to Franco-Italian reconciliation. François-Poncet regarded the Duce's vagueness on such key issues as Tunisia, Jibuti, and Suez as intentionally calculated to encourage France to initiate a discussion, "which he clearly desires." In short, the fascist leader's speech carefully avoided closing the door on the possibility of negotiations.[51]

Such judgments represented a 180-degree turn for François-Poncet, who had remained steadfast in his hard-line opposition to appeasing Rome since the unfortunate events of 30 November 1938. In a series of communications to Paris, the French ambassador insisted that Mussolini's speech represented a turning point and that it would be ill-advised to let it go unanswered. Mussolini should be given an opportunity to specify his demands on France and to outline a minimum program. To make no initiative toward Italy at this point would in effect simplify matters for the Duce, since he could then show that Italy had no choice, regardless of popular feeling for France, but to side irreversibly with Germany.[52]

The diplomatic record abounds with confirmation of François-Poncet's new point of view. Maglione told Charles-Roux that, apart from certain violences of language that unfortunately marked Mussolini's style, the passages in his speech relating to Franco-Italian litigation "seemed inspired by the desire to negotiate and seemed to him to render a negotiation possible." Maglione also said that he had been informed, should a negotiation take place, the Italian government had no plans to ask for any territorial cessions in Tunisia. Count Szembeck, the Polish undersecretary of state for foreign affairs, told Noël in Warsaw that his recent visit to Rome had revealed a Mussolini absolutely furious over German duplicity and fearful that, unless the dispute with France were resolved, Italy might be dragged into war on the side of Germany. " 'Profit by it,' he told me several times, 'and do so quickly.' He even added that, given the state of mind he noticed [in Rome], it did not seem to him impossible that in the event of general war, Italy might once again place herself in the camp opposed to Germany." Noël emphasized that Szembeck was an experienced and careful diplomat and that his expressions were couched in the most categorical tone.[53]

In order to test the waters, Bonnet asked the Romanian minister of foreign affairs, Grégoire Gafenco (who had been urging a Franco-Italian détente), to tell Mussolini during his scheduled visit to Rome that France was prepared to put an end to Franco-Italian tension and to suggest to the Duce that he join the western powers in a general accord on Mediterranean security. Gafenco then reported Mussolini's response to François-Poncet: " 'The difficulties that exist between Italy and France are *sérieuses;* but they are not *graves*. These difficulties are of a colonial order but not of a territorial nature. It is not the sort of thing over which we will go to war.' He placed strong emphasis on the phrase *'they are not of a territorial nature.'* I believe to have understood that he wanted an accord and that he judged it possible." There is also evidence gathered by "Monsieur Nac," an informer for the Quai d'Orsay, who met with Guariglia, the Italian ambassador in Paris, and his legal advisor at the Italian Embassy on 29 March 1939. In his summary to the Quai d'Orsay, "M. Nac" said that the two Italian officials stressed Mussolini's discomfiture with the Axis relationship and his corresponding interest in settling Franco-Italian differences. The two Italians maintained that a settlement could be reached that would not prejudice any French territory or rights so long as France was prepared to recognize new realities attendant upon Italy's conquest of Ethiopia. In other words, Italy must have concessions at Suez and Jibuti of such a magnitude as to enable her to exploit her conquest economically. Intelligence gathered by the French military attaché in Rome corroborated many of the above indications.[54]

This apparently positive atmosphere was reflected in decidedly more affirmative advice from France's diplomatic corps in Rome. It will be recalled that just one year earlier, Blondel had despaired of any possibility of a Franco-Italian alliance against Germany. Simply to preserve an armed and threatening neutrality on Italy's part vis-à-vis France would, he had speculated, have required substantial and immediate French territorial concessions in Jibuti, French Somaliland, and Tunisia. Exactly one year later, however, François-Poncet, obviously influenced by the favorable reaction to Mussolini's speech, advised the Quai d'Orsay that he was convinced that the Duce "was relatively sincere when he expressed, in his way, his desire to negotiate with us." The ambassador continued at length to report a conversation with "an important personality of the regime." The latter had said that now was the time for France to make a conciliatory gesture, but that it must be done quickly to capitalize on Mussolini's irritation with Hitler. The fascist official had suggested that two-pronged negotiations could be set up: in Rome, between Ciano and François-Poncet, and in Paris, between Bonnet and Guariglia. Although still vague on the specifics of an accord that might come from such pourparlers, he indicated that they might include: Italian purchase of additional shares in the Suez Canal Company and the Jibuti–Addis Ababa Railway; the conversion of Jibuti into a free port; modest French territorial concessions in Somalia; and the extension for ten years of the conventions of 1896 on Tunisia, with French consent to an unspecified annual level of Italian immigration. The fascist official concluded by saying: " 'I hope that M. Daladier's speech [scheduled for 29 March 1939] will permit the opening of negotiations which, if well-conducted, will be advantageous for both our countries and for Europe.' "[55] The tone of François-Poncet's reporting of this conversation is evidence that he endorsed the indicated procedure.

Why did specific suggestions, such as those outlined above, come only from unidentified "important personalities" of the fascist regime rather than through official channels via the Italian Foreign Office or from Mussolini himself? Repeated references are made in the French documents for 1938 and 1939 to a certain psychological state of mind at work in Italy that hindered direct negotiation with France. It was said that many in Italy were bewildered by the apparently totally different ways in which the western powers reacted to Germany and Italy. When Hitler made demands or took aggressive action (Rhineland, *Anschluss,* Munich, Prague), the western powers either conceded or did nothing but make speeches. Conversely, Britain and France were unwilling to make even small concessions to Italy. The impression created among many Italians was that, whereas the west feared the strength of Germany, it considered Italian power comparatively inconsequential and so could afford to ignore Italian aspirations.[56] It seems quite plausible that this Italian inferiority complex may well have been reflected in the bombast of the Italian press and in the histrionics of Mussolini. It may also explain Rome's reluctance to adopt the initiative in officially putting forth conditions for a détente with France.

The reverse psychological state of mind may have been operating among the French leadership. That is, so many concessions had been granted to Germany that French leaders were reluctant to appear weaker by taking the initiative in proposing even modest concessions to the Italians. Despite François-Poncet's repeated assurances of the genuineness of the various indirect Italian approaches, he was unable to persuade Daladier to undertake an initiative. On 29 March 1939, the president of the Conseil delivered a radio speech specifically designed to scotch all rumors of such a good will gesture toward Italy. To launch new initiatives at this point, Daladier argued, would be "to weaken the juridical position of France" based on the accords of 1919 and 1935 and tacitly to admit that these no longer were valid. Despite the Italian denunciation of the Rome Accords of 1935, Daladier stressed that France considered them still in effect and that he stood ready to pursue their execution. In the spirit of those accords, France was prepared to examine any specific proposals the Italians might wish to make, although the premier dramatically repeated his earlier refrain that "we shall cede neither an acre of our territories, nor a single one of our rights."[57] Although Daladier was critical of Italy for not defining its position clearly, he too refused to indicate how far France would be willing to go to resolve differences. The impasse remained.

Reaction to the speech was predictably mixed. Corbin reported from London that the British response was quite favorable. Daladier had calmly but vigorously enunciated the French thesis without closing the door to future "reasonable" Italian claims that might be advanced via the normal diplomatic route. The speech was perceived differently, however, in Rome. The Italian press analyzed it in decidedly negative fashion. Gayda wrote a typically strident editorial in *Giornale d'Italia* denouncing Daladier for rudely slamming the door on all further Franco-Italian negotiations.[58]

Diplomacy is always a double-edged sword. It seems clear now that Gayda's diatribe was intended for domestic consumption, while the Italian government continued with other off-the-record and indirect appeals to France. On 4 April 1939, for example, the Italian ambassador in Berlin, Bernardo Attolico, approached Saint-Cyr, the French chargé d'affaires, to express his grave disappointment in Daladier's speech. The French premier, Attolico said, did not understand that Mussolini actually desired a settlement based upon the following conditions: Italian participation in the administration of the Suez Canal; Italian control of the Jibuti–Addis Ababa Railway in Ethiopia, with guaranteed access to the sea at Jibuti; an extension of the 1896 statutes on Italian nationality rights in Tunisia; plus some minor territorial adjustments in Libya to fulfill the promises of the 1915 Treaty of London. Saint-Cyr regretted that Mussolini himself had not been this specific in his speech of 26 March, but he emphasized that it was likely that Attolico had been instructed to make this inquiry in Berlin, knowing that it would be transmitted to the Quai d'Orsay. In short it represented a serious, albeit indirect, Italian gesture designed to stimulate a specific French response. British sources corroborate this impression. Perth reported on 4 April, quoting Ciano directly: " 'If France were prepared to take the initiative Italy would not refuse discussion.' " Two days later, Perth informed London that François-Poncet believed that the Italians were ready and anxious to begin direct talks but that, while Bonnet was in agreement with such an approach, Daladier maintained his adamant opposition. The information in Perth's telegram was transferred to the Quai d'Orsay. For his part François-Poncet dramatically altered his impression of Perth; he notified Paris on 5 April—without the customary unflattering asides—that the British ambassador in Rome was convinced that the Italians truly desired direct Franco-Italian conversations and that these would prove fruitful. "Count Ciano assured him that Italy would make her suggestions known once France asked for them."[59]

The French ambassador continued this line even after the Italian attack on Albania in April 1939. François-Poncet reported, "I don't believe that Italy has resolved to play the card of war nor that she considers the door definitely closed to all possibility of a negotiated regulation of the Mediterranean problem." He regretted that no direct contact had been established with the Italian government and complained that, despite all of the favorable indications, he had been given no authorization from the Quai d'Orsay to proceed. His frustration was reflected in the observation that, since neither Paris nor Rome was willing to undertake the first step, the ambassadors in both capitals had been reduced "to simple observers—[a situation] equivalent to a suspension of normal diplomatic relations."[60]

Despite the Daladier speech and the Italian invasion of Albania, several behind-the-scenes maneuvers indicated that there was still time to save the Franco-Italian situation if only the will to do so could be found in Paris and Rome. On 4 April, Ciano sent a secret telegram to the Italian embassies in London and Paris, instructing them what to do in the event of Italy's military occupation of Albania: " . . . you are urged, through third parties, to spread the information that the Italian action is designed to block further German expansion in the Balkans. It will be useful if a newspaper made reference to this hypothesis. I repeat that this step must be taken with the utmost discretion in order to make it absolutely impossible to identify the origin of this interpretation of our eventual move."[61] Ciano was no doubt concerned about how such a message, if revealed, would be perceived in Berlin. It is a clear indication that even as late as 4 April, Mussolini had made no irrevocable commitment to the Axis. On 18 April, Victor Emmanuel III spoke to the Chamber of Fasces and Corporations. He articulated again the familiar Italian complaint that France had not yet responded to Ciano's invitation of 17 December 1938 to define its terms for a new accord. French truculence, he said, would not encumber Italian policy; " 'while awaiting satisfaction to its justifiable claims, Italy will refuse to underwrite any international engagement on arms limitation.' "[62] The king's remarks can be viewed as a heavy-handed goad for France to take a positive initiative toward negotiation.

Much more subtle pressure, however, began to arrive from France's cross-channel partner, whose actions in the past had so frequently frustrated Franco-Italian reconciliation. Perth, in particular, had become convinced that Britain must intervene somehow in an effort to ameliorate Franco-Italian relations—even though the French had in the past energetically rejected the idea of British mediation. The ambassador's alarm stemmed from information he had received to the effect that Mussolini would refrain from using his influence to restrain Hitler until the French demonstrated their willingness to talk. In short, Perth was convinced that "the French attitude toward Italy may well be the key to the situation." It is clear that Halifax shared the views of his ambassador in Rome. The latter reported on 19 April, based on information from a contact who knew Mussolini well, that the Duce would welcome a French initiative for negotiations. On that same day, the British Cabinet agreed that Halifax should encourage the French to respond with some positive action; the latter telegraphed such instructions to Phipps in Paris on 20 April. Perth also reported on that date that François-Poncet had requested British pressure on Daladier, who, according to the French ambassador, was " 'very obstinate' and 'frightened of the effect [of a diplomatic initiative] on left and extreme right opinion in France.'" François-Poncet corroborated the British judgment by reporting to Bonnet that the first secretary of the British Embassy in Rome had told his French counterpart that the Palazzo Chigi regarded the Franco-Italian imbroglio as essentially a moral problem, that a Franco-Italian conversation was "still desirable and possible, and that the Fascist Government had not definitively rejected an accord based on a moderated program of Italian claims." Moreover, an important letter from the English Embassy in Paris to the Quai d'Orsay, dated 21 April, spelled out the British position on the issue. The communication expressed the view that there was little sentiment in Italy for war with Great Britain and that Mussolini, if properly encouraged by the French, would be prepared to restrain Nazi Germany. In spite of the recent attack on Albania, the Duce had promised to withdraw all Italian troops from Spain following the 2 May victory celebration in Madrid. He also had pledged his loyalty to the Anglo-Italian accord of 1938 on maintaining the status quo in the Mediterranean. Given this situation, England formally requested the French to initiate some reasonable gesture toward Rome, while pledging "that the English government will give its full support to the French government to enable the latter to resist any unreasonable claims that Italy might advance. But the English government considers it essential to reestablish contact between the two governments as soon as possible and without awaiting the withdrawal of Italian troops from Spain."[63]

While the French government considered its response to this latest British intervention, François-Poncet met Ciano on 25 April to sign an addition to a commercial treaty. Ciano took the occasion to remark that there was nothing between France and Italy that could not be settled amicably. Pressed for details, the Duce's son-in-law said that Italy wanted a free port at Jibuti, shares in the Jibuti–Addis Ababa Railway, two directorships on the Suez Canal Board, and prolongation of the 1896 convention on Tunisia. He added spontaneously that Italy had no territorial claims to make against France. Although presented verbally and lacking in precision, Ciano's gesture was the closest an Italian official had yet come to broaching the subject of Franco-Italian détente through normal diplomatic channels. Bonnet, revealing the extent of his own isolation in the Cabinet, informed the British ambassador of François-Poncet's conversation with Ciano and then asked Phipps to reinforce to Daladier the extent to which the British government would value a Franco-Italian reconciliation. The British ambassador carried through, pointing out that the 26 April announcement of Britain's adoption of compulsory military training "would enable France to make . . . an approach [to Italy] from strength and not from weakness." All this was to no avail. Daladier's official response to London was a refusal to undertake any initiative in Rome. He believed that Mussolini would use any moderate compromise formula submitted by France as a jumping-off point for further demands—a result likely to have the worst possible effect on public opinion in France.[64]

The idea of a forthright French initiative had been definitively scotched. The French also rejected a papal proposal to mediate the Franco-Italian confrontation.[65] But Bonnet was successful in rallying Daladier to support a much more limited effort in Rome. François-Poncet had complained in the past about his lack of instructions on how to deal with Mediterranean questions, which left him in an awkward position when Ciano spontaneously put forth the Italian desiderata at their meeting of 25 April. Continued silence from him on the question of opening discussion risked being viewed in Rome as tantamount to rejection. Bonnet, therefore, finally persuaded Daladier on 3 May to authorize François-Poncet to invite Ciano to put Italian claims in writing as a basis for negotiation.[66] Taken a month or two sooner, when Italian chagrin at the Prague coup was at its zenith, this approach through normal diplomatic channels might have borne fruit. As it was, however, the French gesture proved both too limited and too late. François-Poncet met with Ciano briefly on 9 and 11 May, but the conversations proved indecisive. They coincided with Ribbentrop's arrival in Rome to negotiate what was to become the Pact of Steel. The French ambassador later revealed to his British counterpart in Rome that, following his last conversation with Ciano on the 11th, he received no further instructions from Paris.[67]

Why was France unable to come to terms with Mussolini in 1939? Bonnet has argued that the ideological differences between democracy and fascism proved insurmountable. In addition, the Anglo-Italian Mediterranean accords of April 1938, achieved without French consultation, undermined any serious Italian interest in an accord with France. The British pointed the finger of blame directly at Daladier, who remained unshakable in his opposition to negotiating with the Italians even in light of substantial evidence that the latter would be receptive to a French initiative. Daladier told Phipps that such a gesture would alienate Muslim support for France in North Africa and Syria, which had been encouraged by Italy's Albanian adventure. By mid-May 1939 the Franco-Italian imbroglio was probably beyond redemption. Quite aside from the psychological factor of neither side being willing to take the initiative and thereby risk the label of petitioner, many in France believed that Italy was already committed to Germany. That being the case, statesmen like Léger and Daladier saw little point in making even modest concessions to Italy as the price of normalization—even though their English allies energetically supported such a move.

PACT OF STEEL

Conversely, François-Poncet pointed out at the time that the true reason for Italian conduct derived from the fear that even if Italy advanced moderate claims against France, these would be summarily rejected because of the belief in Paris that Italy would align herself with Germany in any case. The stand-off engendered a dilemma neither side could resolve. In retrospect and with some irony—given his earlier anti-English bias—François-Poncet tended to endorse the English viewpoint. The French ambassador argued that the Quai d'Orsay had missed an excellent opportunity to split the Axis and reestablish contact with Rome. Hitler's occupation of Prague in March 1939 created consternation in Rome which the French failed to capitalize on, despite repeated appeals from the French ambassador and in the face of convincing evidence that Mussolini would have been receptive to a French proposal. France's reluctance was very likely due to the furor raised in the country over the untimely revelation of the Baudouin mission, the full intent of which was never revealed to the French ambassador.[68] Daladier would not risk another such initiative. Rather, in the wake of the Albanian adventure, Paris extended unilateral guarantees to Romania and Greece. Germany, on the other hand, congratulated Italy on the Albanian move. The lesson was clear enough; Italy had only one friend in Europe—Nazi Germany. The Pact of Steel was signed on 22 May 1939.

CHAPTER 13

To War

The signing of the Pact of Steel on 22 May 1939 guaranteed Hitler at least benevolent Italian neutrality should tensions between Germany and the western powers lead to war. But subsequent events revealed that, from Rome's point of view, the Pact was far from an ultimate commitment to the idea of fascist collaboration in building a "new order" in Europe. The notion of a Stresa-Front-type coalition against the ambitions of the Third Reich was dead. But western efforts to mitigate Italy's commitment to Berlin between 22 May 1939 and 10 June 1940 reveal weaknesses in both the Anglo-French relationship and ultimately in the credibility of the Third Republic itself.

In spite of the confident affirmations in the fascist press and statements by Italian officials that the Pact of 22 May increased Italy's freedom of action by "enhancing her role as arbiter in cases of European tension,"[1] some substantial doubts remained in official circles about how far Germany would be willing to go to support Italian claims against France in the Mediterranean. François-Poncet reported on 25 May that the underlying feeling in Rome was that the Pact of Steel rendered Italy subservient to Germany, and that a number of fascist officials "blame France and England for what has happened and accuse us of having thrown them into the arms of Germany." With regard to the question of whether the Duce had definitely decided on war, the French ambassador wrote: "I would not go so far as to say that. I would sooner believe that the chief of the Italian government still hopes that it will be possible, at the last moment, to avoid the general conflagration, without knowing himself how he will be able to achieve this."[2] In short, François-Poncet believed that Mussolini was counting on some unforeseen event that would allow him to escape an apparently inevitable conflict with his honor intact.

ITALIAN NONBELLIGERENCE

French sources also indicate that the road to Rome was not yet entirely closed. Cardinal Maglione assured the French chargé d'affaires on 27 May that his sources were convinced that Mussolini did not want war, and that Franco-Italian conversations were not only "possible" but were "opportune and necessary." He believed that the Italian government would be pleased to reach a nonterritorial regulation of the Jibuti, Tunisian, and Suez questions. The most substantial and direct indication of continued Italian interest in resolving matters with France came on 28 June in a note to the Quai d'Orsay from "Monsieur Nac." His visit the previous day to the Italian Embassy in Paris found officials there frustrated by the fact that France had not followed up on any of the initiatives launched by Italy during the previous few months. Nor had the French ambassador in Rome been charged with specific instructions to take to Ciano. M. Nac's contacts at the Italian Embassy insisted that Mussolini was anxious "to put an end to the Italo-French controversy and to achieve an accord which would normalize Italo-French relations." If, however, the French government did not move forward, Italy could only draw the conclusion that France did not wish to resolve differences peacefully. Without French initiative, "M. Mussolini will no longer make new proposals and will see himself forced to prepare a regulation of accounts with France by other means." Despite the thinly veiled threat, "M. Nac's" impression was that Italy wanted to negotiate.[3]

Daladier, however, remained unshaken in his refusal to initiate a specific proposal to Rome. That left the initiative once again in England's hands. British leaders, ever since the signing of the Italo-German alliance, had been considering yet another formal appeal from Chamberlain to encourage the French to break through the impasse. Vansittart doubted the wisdom of such an approach, given the number of times England had tried it already without success. But Halifax was more optimistic. "If it had been possible to induce better Franco-Italian relations," he wrote to Runciman on 3 July, "Italy might conceivably have been restrained from going the whole distance and signing a military alliance with Germany." In the event, Chamberlain sent a personal letter to Daladier on 13 July urging that the time had come to respond to Italian overtures and "to indicate that [France] would be prepared to hear more, and to listen to Italy's proposals." Chamberlain suggested that Daladier's domestic situation—especially with the Chamber of Deputies adjourned for the summer—was secure enough for such a move. Simply to ignore Italian "soundings" would encourage propaganda to the effect that the democracies were being cynical in their unwillingness to discuss differences. On the other hand, a move by France now might induce Mussolini to take a moderating role vis-à-vis Hitler with regard to Danzig and the deepening crisis over Poland.[4]

Although the British prime minister's proposal was modest, well-reasoned, and certainly worth pursuing, Daladier would not be moved. His response, delivered to London ten days later, was basically a lengthy refusal. Daladier wrote that in his radio speech of 29 March he had affirmed France's adherence to the accords of 1935, and he remained prepared to examine any new propositions that Italy cared to advance in the spirit of those accords. Furthermore, François-Poncet had invited Ciano shortly after the speech to define Italy's goals in specific detail; the only exception was that France would not entertain any proposal for the perpetual prolongation of the 1896 statutes on Tunisia. This, Daladier argued, had produced no specific response from the Italians, and he was, therefore, disinclined to make another appeal "for fear that any new initiative taken toward the government of Rome to lead it to formulate its views would only be interpreted by it as a solicitation, indicative of weakness."[5] Daladier's continued obduracy was no doubt conditioned by report after report arriving at the Quai d'Orsay, throughout the summer of 1939, attesting to Italian anxiety at the general European situation and describing Rome's efforts to moderate Hitler's posture over Danzig.[6] The Deuxième Bureau of the French General Staff summed up the entire summer of 1939 by saying that although the Italian press energetically affirmed the solidarity of the Axis, the actions of the Italian government were nevertheless *"deliberately pacific.* They demonstrated that this government was desirous of avoiding war and let it be understood that in spite of numerous previous declarations, it would work *to remain out of any eventual armed conflict."*[7]

Whereas indications like these encouraged British leaders to believe that a French appeasement of Italy might produce important dividends for the future, Daladier drew the opposite conclusion. These developments reinforced his determination to avoid any further moves toward Rome that the Duce might interpret as signs of weakness. Why bother, after all, if Mussolini was already working to restrain Hitler and if Italian neutrality in any subsequent conflict was likely without any concessions from France? It was a shortsighted policy which contravened advice from the British and also from Bonnet and François-Poncet.

As the international crisis heated up in August 1939, British policy became oriented increasingly toward the appeasement of Italy—perhaps to the point of neglecting crucial negotiations with the Soviet Union. Watt has maintained that British policy was encouraged principally by the Italians themselves and by François-Poncet and Bonnet. Percy Loraine, the new British ambassador in Rome, served as a vehicle for his French colleagues, and the effect was to keep open the possibility that Daladier could be pressured into negotiating directly with the Italians—a prospect mooted by Chamberlain after the Frenchman rejected his appeal of 13 July. British concern intensified considerably following the shocking announcement of the Nazi-Soviet Pact on 24 August 1939, and the imminence of war rekindled discussion in the Cabinet about pressuring the French to make concessions to assure Italian neutrality. At the very least British efforts may have dissuaded Daladier from making any sort of futile gesture likely to intensify Mussolinian propaganda, but Watt surely overstates the case when he suggests that British policy was in large measure responsible for the Italian decision of nonparticipation in the events of September 1939. The fact is that the Italians were unprepared for an immediate war. Italy's "nonbelligerency" has also been explained as the result of Mussolini's pique with Hitler at being kept in the dark about Germany's negotiations with the Soviet Union and about her plans for the assault on Poland.[8] Much more to the point, however, is de Felice's observation that in spite of the Pact of Steel and the failure to wring negotiated concessions from France, Mussolini "had not [yet] made a final decision of sides."[9]

De Felice's retrospective judgment magnifies the importance of the French diplomatic maneuvers of September 1939. Paul-Boncour, decrying the inertia of France's Italian policy during the summer, believed the time ripe, with Germany occupied in Poland, to take energetic measures to ensure a prolonged Italian neutrality. He observed that Italy, exhausted by her wars in Ethiopia and Spain, had no enthusiasm for becoming a German satellite. Therefore, a clearly defined Anglo-French policy would take advantage of Italy's difficult situation by presenting Mussolini with the alternative of choosing between the "consistent advantage" of continued neutrality and the perspective of an unwanted war. But events had cooled British ardor for the appeasement of Rome. When Mussolini floated his proposal to mediate the Polish crisis at a special conference among Great Britain, France, and Italy at San Remo on 5 September, Halifax was "glacial" in response. The British foreign secretary brushed aside the Duce's speculations that a negotiated settlement was possible and insisted that no negotiations could take place so long as German troops remained on Polish territory. Although Bonnet was decidedly more accommodating, offering words of encouragement to Ciano over the telephone and suggesting that Poland also be invited to San Remo, Daladier was flatly opposed. He told the British ambassador that he would rather resign than accept Mussolini's invitation to a second "Munich" in Italy. In the Cabinet meeting called to discuss the mediation offer, Bonnet and de Monzie spoke in favor of welcoming the Italian initiative; Gamelin's name was evoked in support as well. According to de Monzie's account, Daladier turned his back on Bonnet as soon as the latter started to speak, "an expression of mistrust or disgust on his face."[10] The French government nevertheless endorsed Mussolini's San Remo proposal on 31 August. But with no encouragement from London and obvious differences of opinion within the French cabinet on the issue, Mussolini was reluctant to push the matter of mediation in Berlin. Events were allowed to take their course.

The failure of Italy's mediation proposal induced some military figures in France to advocate preemptive military measures in northern Italy. It was even rumored that preparations were afoot to attack Libya some twenty-five days after mobilization. But the so-called "Gascons" (anti-Italians in the French government) could not overcome more moderate elements in the Daladier cabinet and the desire of Commander-in-Chief Gamelin to avoid unnecessary risks. With British encouragement, the French adopted a deliberately nonprovocative posture with regard to Italy, agreeing to avoid military measures and to restrain the French press from hostile or belittling editorials on the Italian stance of nonbelligerency—something sure to irritate the Duce's sensibilities. In early September, Paris offered to discuss with Italy all issues except Corsica, Nice, and Savoy. MacGregor Knox, citing British and Italian sources, recently maintained that Mussolini contemptuously ignored these overtures.[11] To be sure, the Italians were concerned about French military measures at Jibuti and in Syria and about rumored French military activity in the Balkans, an area regarded by Rome as within its sphere of influence.[12] French sources, however, indicate that the Italian response to French overtures was not nearly so negative as Knox implies.

French diplomacy, in effect, played on divisions within Italy and within the Fascist Party. It was known, for example, that General Badoglio clearly was opposed to the alliance with Germany. Moreover, key Italian diplomats like Ciano, Grandi, and Guariglia were by no means whole-hearted supporters of the Pact of Steel. This explains why, on 6 September, when François-Poncet delivered a note to the Italian foreign minister expressing France's appreciation for Italy's nonbelligerence and suggesting economic conversations between the two countries, Ciano accepted and even noted in his diary that the French gesture marked "a new step forward." On 8 September Bonnet received the Italian ambassador in Paris and expressed the hope that these commercial talks could tilt Italy toward a more active friendship with France. According to the French foreign minister, Guariglia expressed the view that "Italian neutrality can be prolonged and *perhaps even transformed*, provided that we follow a very careful diplomacy."[13]

At Ciano's insistence, the Franco-Italian economic conversations took place at San Remo rather than in Rome, lest details become known to the Germans. The resulting secret accord, hammered out on 14–15 September in negotiations between Amadeo Giannini, director of commercial affairs at the Italian Ministry of Foreign Affairs, and Hervé Alphand, director of commercial agreements at the French Ministry of Commerce and Industry, buoyed French optimism about eventually reversing Italian alliance commitments. Informing Bonnet of the details of the accord, François-Poncet gushed: "Italy's nonbelligerence was a remarkable success for us; it has been accompanied by a sudden and total turn toward us, since Italy has gone so far as to furnish us with powder, explosives, anti-tank mines and even airplanes."[14] Ciano, however, quickly balanced the picture. With frightening cynicism, he advised François-Poncet: "Don't wear yourself out propagandizing. Victories are the only propaganda! If you win victories, we will be with you. If you don't we will be against you."[15] Ciano's admonition dampened François-Poncet's initial enthusiasm. Nevertheless, the course of events during the opening months of the war encouraged pro-Italians at the Quai d'Orsay that a careful and "rigorously secret" diplomacy toward Italy[16] would bring rewards in the long run.

The San Remo economic agreement signalled the beginning of a remarkable record of Franco-Italian commercial exchanges extending from September 1939 until May 1940. The story has been uncovered only recently by a French scholar, Pierre Guillen, based on research in the unpublished files of the Ministry of Finance. France acquired from Italy important contraband war materiel, but Guillen argues that the system actually favored the Italians, who benefited from an overvalued currency and booming stock prices on the Paris Bourse. Italy also received vital deliveries of primary resources from France and the French colonies. Nevertheless, by April 1940 France had contracted for 1 billion francs' worth of airplanes (some 500 planes), 664 million francs of munitions, and 300 million francs in petroleum products. In order to save appearances with Germany, Italy insisted on not concluding contracts directly with the French government, but rather with a Portuguese purchasing company, Aereo Portugesa, which then delegated to Air France all power to represent it. Mussolini even went so far as to write personally to Hitler, averring disingenuously that "all deliveries [to France] of a typically military nature" had been prohibited and that a continued commercial relationship "permits us to acquire those raw materials without which we cannot complete our military preparations and which therefore ultimately benefit Germany as well." It was only on 24 May 1940 that Mussolini ordered a halt to armament exportation to France. In other words, a mutually beneficial Franco-Italian commercial relationship extended throughout the entire period of the "Phony War" in Europe and undergirded the continued optimism of those who believed it still possible to strip Mussolini from the Axis. De Monzie described in his diary on 4 December 1939 a warm meeting between Daladier, himself, and two representatives of an Italian importing consortium in France. He left that interview "with the feeling that business negotiations can serve as a prelude to political conversations."[17]

LA DRÔLE DE GUERRE

The ten-month period of Italian nonbelligerence can be divided into three rather distinct phases. The first, from September 1939 to January 1940, was marked by Mussolini's absence from center stage and corresponded to the period of Ciano's greatest influence. The second phase, marked by the Duce's reemergence on the public platform and an increasingly strident anti-French orientation in the Italian press, lasted from January to March. The last phase, from March until the 10 June declaration of war, corresponded with Mussolini's final determination to enter the war on Germany's side at a propitious moment. The stance of nonbelligerency was something virtually unprecedented—a condition of alliance but nonengagement—but certainly not "neutral" according to international law. The Allies were hard put to know exactly how to deal with it.

Three possible strategies presented themselves. Hardliners, such as Léger and Massigli, advocated the presentation of an ultimatum to Italy demanding that she clarify her posture (i.e., adopt formal neutrality). If Italy refused, France would attack. Out-and-out appeasers, such as de

Monzie, believed that Italian neutrality could be bought but that it would take more than friendly words and a profitable commerce; they advocated territorial cessions in Africa. The third path was necessarily more ambiguous. It was a long-range strategy whereby France would accept the stance of nonbelligerency and begin implementing policies toward Italy that might, over the course of time, lead that country on its own to move to a position of declared neutrality. It would play on the attitudes of Mussolini and Ciano and seek to provoke a negotiation—perhaps to be carried out by a plenipotentiary chosen from among the enthusiastic Italophiles in French political circles.[18]

On 9 September 1939, François-Poncet, recalled from Rome for consultations, met at the Quai d'Orsay with Bonnet, Daladier, President Albert Lebrun, and General Gamelin to discuss the various options and formulate strategy. Everyone agreed that the third path represented the only appropriate course of action. Gamelin in particular was delighted to be able to withdraw several divisions from the Italian frontier for redeployment against Germany. François-Poncet underscored his conviction that this policy necessitated "demonstrating to Italy that its abstention [from the war] would be fruitful and would bring substantial advantages." The ambassador further advised that such an approach must be carried out discreetly and with scrupulous rectitude, counsel that "was observed at the beginning. But the discipline and rigor that I had desired abated rapidly."[19] The rapid abatement deplored by François-Poncet began to be apparent at the Cabinet meeting of 13 September where the decision was made to remove the pacifist Bonnet from the Quai d'Orsay. Daladier himself assumed the duties of minister of foreign affairs along with those of the minister of national defense—a formidable set of responsibilities. This ministerial change gave virtually full power to Léger to run the Quai d'Orsay. The secretary general favored an openly hostile Italy to her continued unfriendly nonbelligerency. Why? Because Italy's active entry into the war would almost automatically bring in Turkey and other eastern countries on the allied side.[20] But for the moment, the more patient strategy advocated by François-Poncet prevailed. At the first meeting of the Supreme Interallied Council on 12 September, Daladier and Chamberlain rivaled each other with expressions of optimism and moderation. "All our information," said Daladier, "encourages us to push Italy to remain neutral." Chamberlain suggested that Italy must be given "all she needs, but no more." He added, "It is not inconceivable that she could one day find herself on the allied side." The French premier agreed.[21]

To a great extent François-Poncet's strategy depended upon his accurate assessment of Ciano. The latter had reached the apogee of his influence in

Italy, and François-Poncet regarded him as among the most moderate men in the Fascist Party, having little but contempt for "ultras" such as Achille Starace and Farinacci. The French ambassador saw Ciano frequently and actively cultivated his good will. Although completely loyal to his father-in-law, the Italian foreign minister had ideas of his own, and he frequently made them known to members of the Roman diplomatic corps through gestures or discreet silences. Although Ciano never said so openly, François-Poncet was convinced that his "secret wish is that, now that the struggle is engaged, Germany not emerge victorious"—a view confirmed by numerous citations in Ciano's own diary.[22]

Nevertheless, prewar formalisms and reticences proved difficult to break. Following up on his country's policy, François-Poncet saw Ciano on 16 September. He said that France would do everything possible to avoid incidents which might prejudice relations between the two countries and would avoid putting Rome in an embarrassing position with formal requests for Italy to define its attitude and intentions. He added that he had received instructions to go ahead with discussions aimed at a solution to all the problems still in suspense between France and Italy. But his instructions still contained the all-too-familiar caveat that, although prepared to talk and even to make important concessions, "because of present events, France will not take the initiative of proposing negotiations: it leaves Italy to choose the propitious moment." This led the British once again to consider pressuring the French to take the first step by offering specific concessions in Jibuti and Tunisia, since in any case "it was likely that they would agree to go a long way towards meeting the Italian point of view."[23]

These desultory communications, neither of which was followed up, typified the apparent lack of urgency with which the western powers dealt with anything concerning Italy—a confirmation of Mussolini's earlier complaints that Italian interests counted for little in Anglo-French diplomacy. It seems now almost incredible to note that, once the Allies had abandoned the so-called Salonika expedition early in the fall of 1939—largely for fear of pushing Italy into the war—the Supreme Interallied Council did not even discuss Italian affairs for a period of five months. At the session on 27 November Italy was not mentioned once in nineteen pages of minutes. At the 19 December session, Chamberlain evoked Italy only to reaffirm his opposition to any Balkan operation. On 5 February and 28 March 1940, Italy was not mentioned. On 19 April Italian issues constituted half a page out of eighteen pages of official minutes. Small wonder that, although François-Poncet continued to bombard the Quai d'Orsay with a voluminous correspondence and although he remained in frequent contact with Ciano, the ambassador could do little but conduct routine embassy business. He took care to keep the Italians informed of matters that might destabilize the condition of nonbelligerency. On 24 December, for example, he assured Ciano that although General Weygand's army was prepared to resist any attack in Syria from either Germany or Russia, Paris had no plans for further military operations in the eastern Mediterranean theater without a prior accord with Italy "in which France would recognize particular interests in this zone." Ciano regarded it as "significant that France has taken this initiative." Furthermore François-Poncet intervened on a couple of occasions to persuade the allied governments to allow shipments of German coal to pass through the allied blockade to Italy.[24] These were regarded as essential to the maintenance of Franco-Italian commercial relationships.

Certainly the most encouraging event of the opening months of the war was Ciano's well-publicized speech before the Chamber of Fasces and Corporations on 16 December 1939. Characterized by Lowe and Marzari as "a thoroughly self-conscious attempt to sabotage the alliance [with Germany]," the speech accused Germany of failing to fulfill obligations to Italy on several points—particularly her pledge of 22 May 1939 not to go to war for at least three years and her lack of consultation with Italy on Polish and Russian questions. All of these, Ciano asserted, fully justified Italy's decision to remain outside the conflict. The foreign minister's words rekindled the hopes of those who had still not ruled out the possibility that Italy would eventually make common cause with the western powers. They would certainly have been astonished at an extraordinary letter Mussolini addressed to Hitler on 5 January 1940, describing Ciano's speech as representing the Duce's thoughts " 'from the first to the last word.' " Furthermore, the Italian dictator expressed his uncertainty about forcing the British and French to their knees, suggesting that " 'the United States would never permit the total defeat of the democracies.' "[25]

Here was a fundamental divergence of views between the two Axis partners that might have been exploited more effectively by the Allies than was the case. Not only was Mussolini proposing a compromise peace in the west, he was simultaneously stressing the anti-Bolshevik aspects of his program by providing military aid to the Finns in their winter war against the USSR at the same time Hitler had publicly approved Russian aims in Finland. Apparently the western powers were diverted by the radical change of atmosphere Mussolini effected in his public posture during the first two months of 1940. The Duce reappeared in the limelight in his familiar role as truculent spokesman for a militant ideology, accompanied by a reappearance of violently anti-French and warmly pro-German campaigns in the fascist press. François-Poncet analyzed this phenomenon in his correspondence with the Quai d'Orsay. Both he and the French naval attaché in Rome pointed out that official anti-French diatribes contrasted starkly with opinions known to be held by the king, important military figures such as Marshal Badoglio, and above all the great mass of Italian people "who remain hostile to war, hostile to Germany, hostile to Russia."[26]

Three developments during the month of March 1940 set the final stage for the thrust of events leading to Italy's open declaration of war on France. First, on 1 March the British announced that in the future all shipments of German coal to Italy would be considered contraband merchandise and sequestered. Ciano immediately protested to the English envoy in Rome, lamenting that such action would only push Italy all the more quickly into Germany's arms. Sir Ronald Campbell reported from Paris that French officials expressed anxiety that Britain's decision to interdict coal deliveries to Italy "may impose a still greater strain on relations between the Allies and Italy." Second, on 18 March Hitler travelled to the Brenner frontier for a meeting with Mussolini. According to the official minutes of the conversation, the Führer did most of the talking, outlining in general his plans for spring offensives in Scandinavia and the Low Countries. It was here that Mussolini, flattered no doubt by the Nazi leader's attentions, formally announced his intention to enter the struggle—not because Germany would need his assistance, but because "the honor and the interests of Italy require his intervention in the war." The Duce, however, reserved the right to decide when his involvement would be most appropriate. The final event laying the foundation for Italy's move toward open military intervention was the vote of confidence lost by the Daladier government in the Chamber of Deputies on 21 March. He was replaced the following day as premier, minister of national defense, and foreign minister by Paul Reynaud, leader of the faction which had advocated a hard-line policy toward Italy since the beginning of the war. Because of his reputation, Reynaud apparently felt the need at first to reassure the Italians; he used that as an argument to keep the pro-Italian minister of public works, de Monzie, in his new government.[27]

PIERRE LAVAL . . . AGAIN

In late March 1940, the Deuxième Bureau of the Army prepared a long analysis of Italian propaganda, concluding that its current bellicosity was fully inconsistent with Ciano's statements that Italy would not be prepared for war for another three years. Furthermore, Italy's fundamental interests in the Mediterranean and the Balkans were antithetical to any permanent relationship with Germany. Therefore, one logical interpretation of Italy's current anti-French campaign was that it was inspired by Mussolini's so-called "realist" policy of "impressing the Allies and preparing them to accept 'a high price.' " The report concluded that "in the near future, it is probable that we shall see Italy offer, with threatening theatricality, the price for her alliance." Not many still believed, as apparently the author of this note did, that a reversal of Italian alliance commitments was possible. Nevertheless, the increasing tensions led to agitation in the French legislature and in the press for sending another special emissary to Rome to persuade Mussolini to maintain his nonbelligerence. Laval's name was mentioned frequently. Apparently Laval saw the Italian question as his route back from the political wilderness; the previous December he had approached Guariglia with a scheme for ending the war and reconstructing Europe on a federated, anticommunist basis. The Italian ambassador dismissed it as "useless and dangerous."[28]

Laval spoke a number of times on behalf of resurrecting Franco-Italian relations before the Foreign Affairs Committee of the Senate and in public. In March he met Daladier in the Senate and offered, "at his own risk and peril," to undertake a "private mission" to Rome. On 27 March the newspapers, *La Justice* and *L'Oeuvre*, bruited the possibility of a Laval mission and offered editorial support. The British ambassador in Paris, while personally regarding such an undertaking as dangerous, believed it "just conceivable that M. Reynaud might be tempted by it on the ground that it was something that had not hitherto been tried and that at the worst it could do no harm." Although Léger denied categorically to the British on 29 March that there was any truth in the story, which he dismissed as " 'une pure bêtise,' " nevertheless François-Poncet broached the idea to Ciano on 10 April. It was at this point that Ciano put an end to the speculation by showing the French ambassador a copy of instructions he had already sent to Guariglia in Paris. These asked him to dissuade the French government from pursuing such an unofficial mission; Mussolini would refuse to receive a French emissary " 'above all, if it were a question of M. Pierre Laval.' "[29]

This incident rendered all the more perplexing a mysteriously secret proposal tendered by Signor Donini-Feretti, an official at the Italian Embassy in Paris, to Captain Simon, Reynaud's military attaché, on 19 April 1940. The former suggested that, given the general European situation, Mussolini was reluctant to throw in his lot with Germany without first exploring all other options. Therefore, he judged the moment ripe for a French demarche to Italy specifying the concessions Paris was willing to make to assure Italian neutrality. These need not involve territorial cessions but should include: (1) guaranteed Italian access to key natural resources; (2) aid to Italy for the efficient exploitation of Ethiopia; (3) concessions on the Suez Canal; (4) a new statute for Italians in Tunisia; and (5) guaranteed access to Ethiopia via Jibuti. Donini-Feretti speculated that there were about twelve days ahead in which such a demarche would stand an even chance of success. Even more fascinating was his suggestion that the French concessions must be presented unofficially—but with the full concurrence of the French government—and that the ideal person to carry the program to Rome was none other than Pierre Laval.[30]

Given the categorical tone of Mussolini's earlier refusal to receive Laval, Reynaud was reluctant to launch another such initiative. There is no indication in the archives that any contact was made with the former premier, and therefore it is impossible to know whether or not this was a genuine Italian offer of settlement. But within the twelve-day grace period stipulated by Donini-Feretti, Reynaud wrote secretly a personal letter to Mussolini proposing conversations between the two leaders aimed at preparing a larger negotiation designed to keep the peace between their countries. "It must never be said [Reynaud wrote] that France and Italy came to clash on the field of battle without a total explanation [of the issues dividing them] and without a meeting between their leaders." Mussolini responded laconically on 24 April, explaining that Italy's alliance with Germany prevented him from accepting Reynaud's proposal for a meeting. The French premier described the Duce's letter quite simply as a "douche froide."[31]

THE FINAL ACT

The *drôle de guerre* came abruptly to an end on 10 May 1940. The Nazi *Blitzkrieg* against Belgium and the Netherlands marked the beginning of the final act in the drama of Franco-Italian relations—an episode characterized by ever more desperate measures to sustain Italy's nonparticipation in the war. The situation can perhaps be symbolized by a letter addressed to the Ministry of the Interior from Henri Labroue, a former deputy, on 17 May. The correspondent proposed changing the name of all public roads bearing the name of Matteotti, suggesting naively that "a measure of this nature would be likely to have fortunate repercussions on the Italian Government's disposition toward us." That the interior minister saw fit to forward such a ludicrous proposal to Daladier, who was reappointed to the Quai d'Orsay by Reynaud on 18 May, is a further indication of the sense of vulnerability prevailing in France. Daladier's reappointment coincided with the end of Léger's career as secretary general; he was replaced in mid-May by Charles-Roux. Before departing to take up his new duties in Paris,

Charles-Roux paid a farewell visit to François-Poncet at the Palazzo Farnese. The French ambassador's words offered a premonition of the difficult and distasteful tasks lying ahead: "Italy's nonbelligerence [he told Charles-Roux] is hanging only by a thread. Its chances of lasting diminish in proportion to the dangers we face. . . . If it is possible to prolong it, it will not in any case be by the same means we have employed up to now."[32]

For the moment, French efforts to secure continued Italian nonbelligerence focused on provoking an intervention by American President Franklin D. Roosevelt. The first such effort—to try to get Roosevelt to invite the Latin American chiefs of state, especially those of Brazil and Argentina where Italian economic and cultural interests were substantial, to present a collective appeal to the Duce for continued noninvolvement—came to naught. Roosevelt rejected the idea for fear that Mussolini would react badly to that sort of diplomatic pressure. He did agree, however, to contact Argentine and Brazilian heads of state and suggest that they address their own separate notes to Mussolini.[33] The second French initiative to secure a Washington mediation was decidedly more substantial. Between 21 and 26 May, as German forces under the command of General Heinz Guderian advanced toward Calais and Dunkirk, French and British statesmen thrashed out a proposal to President Roosevelt.

Although some British diplomats harbored considerable doubts about being able to buy Mussolini off, the gist of the Anglo-French proposal to Roosevelt was as follows. The American president would write directly to Mussolini telling him that he had reason to believe that the Allies, conscious of Italy's goals in the Mediterranean, "are disposed to take into consideration all her reasonable claims and to put themselves into accord with her on the terms of a regulation which would be effectuated at the end of the war." Italy was invited to outline her grievances to Roosevelt, who would then negotiate their fulfillment by France and Great Britain. Furthermore, Roosevelt was to offer his personal guarantee that such an agreement would be registered at the eventual peace conference, to which Italy would also be invited on an equal footing with the belligerent powers. The agreement thus arrived at was to be "dependent of course on Italy not entering the war against the allies."[34] The president accepted this formula and sent the note to Mussolini on 26 May. The latter did not even receive the American ambassador, leaving Ciano to make the refusal on his behalf. When, on 27 May, the English and French ambassadors inquired at the Palazzo Chigi about how Roosevelt's offer had been received, Ciano declared curtly, " 'The response was that there would be no response.' " If nothing else, this incident suggests that at least there was finally unanimity in Paris and London on the Italian question. But when Reynaud flew to London on 26 May to discuss with Halifax, Churchill, Chamberlain, Eden, and Labor Party leader Clement Attlee the kinds of concessions they would make to Italy should Roosevelt's appeal be welcomed, only Halifax was willing to endorse English participation in a plan involving territorial concessions. Churchill and Attlee were openly hostile to the idea, whereas Reynaud had been informed by de Monzie and Lieutenant Colonel Paul de Villelume, who was Gamelin's liaison officer at the Quai d'Orsay, that only vast territorial concessions in the Empire could now stop Italy from going to war.[35]

The 27th of May was a dark day indeed for the Third Republic. Mussolini rejected President Roosevelt's offer of mediation; Belgium capitulated to the Germans; and the evacuation of what remained of the British and French armies in the north began at Dunkirk. As the military situation worsened, continued Italian nonbelligerency seemed all the more essential. At a 10:00 P.M. Cabinet meeting, Daladier presented a proposal for a secret offer to Mussolini composed of the following: (1) cession of the French Somali coast as well as exploitation of the Jibuti–Addis Ababa Railway, reserving only rights for France in the port of Jibuti; (2) further substantial rectifications of the Libyan frontier; and (3) large territorial cessions between the hinterland of Libya and the Congolese coast. Furthermore, in case these concessions did not suffice, Daladier proposed that France be prepared to reform the statute on Tunisia "in such a way as to assure a confident collaboration of Italy and France in the French protectorate of the Regency"—in short, Franco-Italian condominium over Tunisia.[36]

Charles-Roux was awakened at 2:00 A.M. on the 28th and presented with the text. He absolutely opposed launching the proposal unilaterally and insisted that London must be consulted before such an offer were tendered to Italy. Reynaud, therefore, telegraphed the details to Churchill along with a thinly veiled invitation to Britain to add to the pot in order to make it a combined Franco-British offer.[37] Following a hasty Cabinet meeting, in which it was decided "to dissuade Reynaud from making his panicky appeal to Italy," Churchill telegraphed Paris with his negative reaction to France's list of concessions, maintaining that these would only encourage Mussolini's aggressive intentions by convincing him that Anglo-French backs were to the wall. The English prime minister indicated that France could send the offer to Rome on her own but that England refused association with it. Given the failure of British support, the telegram instructing François-Poncet to make the proposed concessions to Italy—which had already been drafted and coded for transmission to Rome—was withdrawn.[38]

In retrospect Bonnet noted the bitter irony of the situation with which France was now confronted. During his entire tenure at the Quai d'Orsay in

1938 and 1939, his efforts to achieve an administrative regulation of Mediterranean questions with the Italians without any territorial concessions had been strenuously and consistently opposed by Daladier. Yet, in May 1940, it was the latter who felt compelled by events to draw up the desperate list of territorial sacrifices deemed necessary to conserve Italian nonbelligerence: "Would it not have been better [Bonnet wrote] to have undertaken this negotiation at the time when our prestige was still intact instead of waiting and putting ourselves in a humiliating posture on the eve of defeat?"[39]

Reynaud later claimed that, when he became premier, he knew Italy was determined to enter the war and that further offers to preserve her nonbelligerence would be futile. Yet he devoted thirty-six pages of his book to describe the course of negotiations and the development of offers to Italy devised by others, which he did not feel he could oppose. The last of these was prompted by François-Poncet. On 27 May Ciano told the French ambassador that Mussolini was determined on war, and he did not think that even the richest gift could change the Duce's attitude. In his report to the Quai d'Orsay, however, François-Poncet added that Ciano was visibly anxious to know what such a gift might consist of—an impression characterized by the French ambassador as "a new and notable fact."[40] These observations were blue penciled for emphasis by officials at the Foreign Ministry.

On the strength of François-Poncet's observations, the French made one final effort to avert an Italian declaration of war. The British once again refused to be associated. On 30 May Daladier wrote a "solemn communication" to Guariglia which proposed a negotiation on Italian claims but made no precise offers. The text, authorized for formal presentation in Rome the following day, pledged to negotiate now but then to satisfy Italy's needs with regard to the Mediterranean and its outlets at the end of the war. Later in the day Guariglia told de Monzie, in a meeting in the latter's office, that this final French offer probably meant war. Without much conviction, de Monzie explained that one did not go to war without first declaring what he was fighting for. This last French note was an attempt to provoke a specific agenda from Italy. Subsequently, the Italian ambassador bitterly attacked "British intransigence" for blocking all substantive French offers to Rome. Looking at matters from the Italian perspective, he maintained that if precise offers had been extended by France, Mussolini would have been willing to take them into consideration. At the very least, Guariglia wrote in his memoirs in 1955, a concrete offer from the western democracies would squarely have confronted Mussolini with the dilemma of "whether to accept a revision of our Mediterranean and African colonial situation in accord with the two Mediterranean and African powers, France and England, or rather to try to impose it by force with the cooperation of an extra-Mediterranean and extra-African power like Germany." But the French made no concrete offers. Charles-Roux had few illusions that Daladier's letter would work; it was rather, he wrote after the war, a device to clear the consciences of those who could thereafter say that every conceivable effort had been expended to avoid war with Italy. In the event, Mussolini rebuffed this final, feeble gesture. No doubt impressed by the wave of *Wehrmacht* victories over France and envisioning the future annexation of territories that had been at issue for years, the Duce sent a message to Hitler on 30 May, the day of the French offer, that he intended to enter the war on 5 June. As it turned out, the timetable was set back several days at Hitler's insistence; on 10 June 1940, the day the French government abandoned Paris for Cangé near Tours, Italy declared war on France. The declaration of war hardly could have come as a surprise to François-Poncet, who remarked appropriately to Ciano: "You have waited until we were lying prostrate on the ground before stabbing us in the back."[41]

THE ARMISTICE

Implicit in French strategy vis-à-vis Italy from 1934 on was the assumption that Mussolini eventually would reject the position of German satellite; once he realized the scope of Nazi ambitions, the French thought he would turn toward France in order to preserve Italy's stature in the Mediterranean and eastern Europe. The oscillations of Italian diplomacy in the late 1930s demonstrate concern about the prospect of German continental hegemony, but the dramatic end to the "Phony War" and particularly the Nazi victories in May and June 1940 served to convince Mussolini that his own conquests, rather than any ties to a decadent and defeated France, would assure Italy's independence in the new world order. His main concern at the time of the declaration of war was that France would not fall too quickly to Germany, in order to allow time for the Italian army to take the field and position itself favorably for the armistice. As a sop to General Badoglio's pro-French sensibilities, the Duce ruled out air attacks on France, presumably because of alleged French air superiority, and delayed military operations until 20 June.[42] By then the war was all but over. The Germans had entered Paris on 14 June; Reynaud resigned on the sixteenth after moving the government to Bordeaux; Marshal Pétain was named head of government, and France sought armistice terms almost immediately.

Actually, Mussolini had formulated his armistice terms even before taking the field against the French, and he presented them to Hitler when the two dictators got together in Munich on 18 June. One can sense the full scope of Mussolinian ambition by glancing at this program. Among a myriad of minor provisions concerning merchant shipping, exchange of prisoners-of-war, and so forth, the Duce demanded the following:

1. Occupation of French territory from the Italian frontier to the Rhône River, including Toulon and Marseille and bridgeheads at Lyon, Valence, and Avignon
2. Occupation of Corsica, Tunisia, and Jibuti
3. Occupation of French naval bases at Algiers, Mers-el-Kebir, and Casablanca
4. Immediate transfer to Italy of all French ships, aircraft, and rolling stock in the occupied areas
5. Open access to French communication facilities
6. Neutralization of Beirut.

Hitler and Ribbentrop approved the Italian occupation zone to the Rhône but politely ignored the Duce's demands for Algerian and Moroccan territory. At this point the Germans were concerned to design armistice terms in such a way as to secure a French government functioning on French territory, thereby limiting the costs of occupation in terms of manpower, money, and materiel. As it turned out the Italians were forced to modify their program even more substantially than the discussions at Munich indicated. On 22 June 1940, Mussolini wrote to Hitler, "Führer: In order to facilitate the acceptance of the armistice by the French, I have not included among the clauses the occupation of the left side of the Rhône, or of Corsica, Tunis and Jibuti as we had intended at Munich. I have limited myself to a minimum, that is, to the demand for a demilitarized zone, 50 kilometers in width. I consider this to be an indispensable minimum, also in order to avoid incidents." The Franco-Italian armistice signed on 24 June, in addition to Mussolini's stipulated demilitarized zone, called only for Italian occupation of a small strip of French territory along the Menton front, which they had managed with some difficulty to overrun before the ceasefire. The armistice also provided for demilitarized zones of varying depth in Tunisia, Algeria, and French Somaliland and for the Italians to acquire full rights over the port of Jibuti and the French section of the Jibuti–Addis Ababa Railway. Additional clauses—such as those relating to the neutralization of the French fleet; demilitarization of naval bases at Toulon, Bizerta, Ajaccio, and Oran; surrender of arms, artillery, tanks, and armored cars; and the prohibition of the shipment of French war materiel to British territory—pretty much followed the pattern established by the Franco-

German armistice of 22 June.[43] Both instruments came into effect on 25 June.

What caused Mussolini's drastic reduction in armistice terms from the maximum program announced on 18 June to the bare minimum achieved just six days later? Various explanations have been offered, ranging from the ludicrous suggestion that the Duce was demonstrating his sportsmanship by refusing to claim more than he had occupied to the more plausible notion that Mussolini was so confident of eventual victory that he expected to realize all his war aims regardless of the armistice terms. Knox has examined these explanations and found them unsatisfactory. To be sure, Mussolini was embarrassed by the sluggish performance of his troops in the Alps, and some evidence suggests that the Duce anticipated a quick peace and was therefore willing to postpone full gratification temporarily. But Knox argues that Mussolini's principal concern was control of the Mediterranean. England must not be allowed to surrender before Italy had achieved mastery in the inland sea. Therefore, a quick peace with France was deemed essential. His views are buttressed by the contemporary British analysis of the Franco-Italian armistice. A Foreign Office minute, dated 26 June, observed that "the French have, by the acceptance of these specious terms—specious in the sense that they appear more lenient on the surface than in fact they are—delivered themselves hand and foot to the Italians, whose object it is in due course to annex all the French metropolitan and colonial territory they covet. For the moment their occupation is limited to the lines they occupy . . . but this is merely a presage and guarantee of occupations and annexations to come." Such draconian predictions were, of course, not to be realized. The Battle of Britain in the fall of 1940 failed to administer the anticipated coup de grâce to England, and the war continued. Mussolini eventually became hopelessly bogged down in the Balkans, the result of an ill-advised, ill-timed, and ill-prepared attack launched from Albania upon Greece on 28 October 1940. The evidence suggests that the Italian adventure against Greece—which marked the beginning of the end for "Mussolini's Roman Empire"—was motivated not only by concern about German penetration into Italy's Balkan sphere-of-influence but also by fear that Germany would, in the end, insist upon taking most of Italy's ultimate objectives from the victory over France.[44]

Much of this chapter has been devoted to documenting French efforts to maintain Italian nonbelligerence in the opening months of World War II. The military history of that struggle suggests that prolonged Italian nonbelligerence would not in all likelihood have altered the course of events a great deal. Therefore, the last couple of months of French diplomacy toward Italy are a classic example of appeasement at its worst; that is, concessions offered from a position of weakness, which are as often self-defeating as not. But what about the possibility of declared Italian neutrality, with all that that status implied about a potential repetition of the events of 1914–15? One wonders about the numerous opportunities tendered either directly or indirectly by Italy between 1936 and 1939, which might have weakened the Axis and thereby considerably altered the course of world events, but which were ignored in Paris either for ideological reasons, or misplaced amour-propre, or just plain contempt. One also recalls in this connection the testimony offered by François-Poncet to the commission investigating the origins of the war. He said that the formation of the Stresa Front in April 1935 was the only time in his entire tenure as French ambassador in Berlin that he ever saw Nazi leaders nervous or disconcerted about the potential constellation of powers arrayed against them.[45]

Assigning responsibility for the failure to keep Italy neutral involves a number of larger factors which were at play throughout the entire interwar period. These will be addressed in the conclusion. Here it is appropriate to cite the judgments of Léon Noël, France's ambassador to Warsaw in the 1930s, whose memoirs are more reliable and less obviously self-serving than most. He assesses responsibility in three categories of ascending importance. First, Noël blames Laval, not because of his foreign policy which he rates as good, but rather because Laval tended to value the Rome Accords of 1935 primarily as a step toward an eventual pact with Germany. Thus, the Italians were not taken fully seriously—an error shared by many other French statesmen in subsequent years. Second, Noël is very critical of American policy and particularly of Bullitt. Seeing matters in strictly ideological terms, he tended to view war between the two fascist dictators and the western democracies as inevitable from as early as 1937. Bullitt was quite influential in Paris, especially with the third and most important figure on Noël's list of villains, Léger. The latter, anti-Italian to the core, neglected nothing to encourage this state of mind in others. He told the Romanian ambassador in April 1939 that only when Mussolini had recognized the dangers of the German connection and made the effort to withdraw from Germany and seek a relationship with France—" 'only then will we be able to extend our hand.' "Noël's judgment that "it would be difficult to imagine a greater blindness" is one that can be extended to others as well.[46]

Another view of the mild Franco-Italian armistice, not to be wholly discounted given the long history of distrust between the two fascist dictators, posited that Mussolini was concerned about the role of France in any postwar configuration of power. He was anxious to balance German power on the continent and forestall the possibility of a Franco-German rapprochement. Therefore, the Duce responded favorably to an appeal from Baudouin, Pétain's foreign minister, for a peace that could serve as the foundation for future cooperation between the two nations. Guariglia indirectly corroborated this view, remarking in his memoirs that Mussolini had "an almost physical fear [of] a Franco-German entente . . . which would have left Germany a free hand in the east."[47] In one terribly ironic sense, therefore, those, such as Léger, who insisted that Italy recognize the dangers of the German connection before France would treat with her, were vindicated. All the more tragic that it required the collapse of the Third Republic to bring on this Italian epiphany.

CHAPTER 14

Conclusion

Toward the end of his reminiscence on his brief career at the Palazzo Farnese, François-Poncet wrote:

> The Franco-Italian war, in the little time that it lasted, was a fratricidal war. It is true that our disputes with Italy are not rare. They can even be burning and passionate. But they are quarrels between relatives, between Latin cousins. That they turned into a real war has always been, in my eyes, a kind of sacrilege. Don't we remember the last war when we vowed that such an episode would never again be allowed to recur, and let's not forget . . . that our attitude toward Italy has not . . . always been above reproach.

The ambassador's observation combines both sadness at the failure of his enterprise and barely concealed bitterness against those who had rendered his task so formidable. This formidability, however, was due not only to certain deficiencies in French statecraft. The record of the entire interwar period seems to show that the Versailles structure of 1919 was the only means conceivable at the time of containing German continental hegemony.

This same record also demonstrates that Versailles could be maintained only with the active cooperation of the three European allies who had won the war. Most French policymakers after 1923 realized this. Yet they had to contend with British counterparts who felt themselves buffered from any immediate German threat and who, therefore, proved slow to accept the fact that Germany's treaty violations constituted a threat to their own security. Even more stupefying was the blindness of some of the smaller nations on Germany's eastern border. Poland maintained virtually constant quibbles with all of her neighbors, while Czechoslovakia consistently refused to take seriously her relations with Italy—the only viable road through which western military support could come in the event of German aggression.[1] French efforts to maintain the wartime coalition, therefore, cannot be assessed in a vacuum.

The foregoing essay on France's relations with Fascist Italy can be divided into three reasonably coherent chronological periods. The first embodies the era from the end of the Great War to the collapse of the Weimar Republic in Germany. During the early 1920s the French, nervous and defensive about the burdens thrust upon them by what they regarded as an insufficient peace settlement and facing substantial resistance in London to their German policies, were inclined to take a conciliatory view of the nascent fascist movement led by Mussolini. The latter, although fiercely nationalist and a vocal exponent of many other Italians' embitterment at the "mutilated victory" for which they held France largely responsible, shared a common concern with Paris about the inherent potential for German continental resurgence. The two initiated an extraordinary, although fitful, period of mutual diplomatic cooperation evident in the Ruhr, Corfu, and Fiume crises and culminating in the Locarno Treaties of 1925. With the German danger momentarily quiescent under the leadership of Stresemann, other tensions between Rome and Paris resurfaced. During the late 1920s, the recrudescence of mutual acrimony over such hardy perennials as Tunisia and competition for influence in the Balkans clouded the atmosphere between France and Italy. That era of illusion in Europe demonstrated that, even when Anglo-French cooperation was reasonably close, the absence of an immediately apparent German threat blunted Mussolini's willingness to be conciliatory toward France even when presented with substantial overtures.

The second phase in the story of France's relations with Fascist Italy unfolded from roughly 1932 to the end of 1935. The rise of Hitler and the Nazis brought the common German danger back into focus and initiated the most fruitful period of Franco-Italian reconciliation. The first substantial achievements were those of Jouvenel during his mission to Rome in

CONCLUSION   291

1933. Barthou followed up these initial contacts during his tragically abbreviated tenure at the Quai d'Orsay. Assassinated on the eve of his projected visit to Rome in late 1934, Barthou was succeeded by Laval. The latter, although rejecting some aspects of his predecessor's "grand design," believed fervently in Franco-Italian cooperation. This period culminated in the famous Laval-Mussolini accords of 1935 and the subsequent Badoglio-Gamelin military understandings. The Stresa Front declarations of Laval, MacDonald, and Mussolini in April 1935, undertaken in the wake of unilateral German rearmament, revived the hopes of those who believed correctly that only a renewal of the First World War coalition could contain further Germany treaty violations. But the years from 1936 to 1940, the third and final phase of the Franco-Italian interwar relationship, belied all of these expectations. Everything that had been achieved in the way of Franco-Italian reconciliation by French statesmen and diplomats from Barrère and Poincaré through Barthou, Laval, and Flandin collapsed entirely. The period witnessed the gradual conjunction of the two fascist powers. It ended with the brief, fratricidal war that François-Poncet lamented so poignantly in his memoirs.

What went wrong? The conventional response, not entirely unsatisfactory, has been to focus on events. The Ethiopian War destroyed the League of Nations as a viable instrument for collective security. The Spanish Civil War, dragging on for an interminable three years from 1936 to 1939, hardened underlying ideological hostilities between the western powers and the central European dictatorships and provided the initial occasion for Mussolini's proclamation of the Axis between Rome and Berlin. But these specific events, and the way in which they were handled in Paris and London, undergird another principal thesis of this book—that good Franco-Italian relations were predicated upon mutual cooperation between Paris and London. Paul Cambon had made this observation as early as 1889; Barrère echoed it on numerous occasions until his retirement in 1924; Locarno and Stresa were cases in point.

But the record cited above for the 1930s reveals scant cooperation between the two Foreign Ministries, and English leaders must bear a heavy responsibility for this. Their attitude toward the French was frequently one of nonconsultation, if not outright contempt, unwittingly fostering the impression in Rome of western decadence. The Anglo-German Naval Accord of 1935, following so soon after Stresa, fostered a predictable discord between France and England which made it all the easier for Mussolini to consider a military solution to the Ethiopian question. The sudden resignation of Hoare following the premature revelation of the Hoare-Laval Plan, which the evidence suggests that Mussolini would have accepted, left the

French premier alone to weather the protest. In spite of the criticism it brought on Laval, he still received a vote of confidence in the French Chamber in December 1935—indicating that many believed his policies to be in the national interest.[2] The Anglo-Italian Easter Accord of 1938, from which France was systematically excluded, undoubtedly reinforced the conviction in Rome that the democracies lacked common resolve and could be split. The premature British effectuation of the Easter Accord in November, despite repeated pledges to France that such action would not occur until Italian soldiers had been withdrawn from Spain, undercut the dramatic effect of France's recognition of the Italian Empire in Ethiopia. These instances of Britain's apparent determination to play a lone hand in Italy undoubtedly complicated François-Poncet's ambassadorship from 1938 to 1940.

On the other side of the coin, French leadership cannot be entirely exonerated for the "mésentente cordiale" of the late 1930s. Laval, much more than Barthou, was inclined to take ultimate English support for granted and thus to direct his energies elsewhere.[3] From 1936 to 1938, with the notable exception of the Nyon Arrangement of September 1937, French Popular Front leaders were rarely content to see eye to eye with their British counterparts on how best to deal with fascist intervention in the Spanish Civil War. Daladier and Léger's intransigent refusal to initiate a conciliatory gesture toward Rome in 1939 sacrificed Britain's tardy decision to be cooperative.

Of all of these factors, the role of the Popular Front may have been the most damaging and decisive. From the inception of Blum's first ministry on 4 June 1936 to the collapse of his last prior to World War II on 10 April 1938, the Popular Front epoch in France occupied a pivotal position in the history of Franco-Italian relations between the wars. The period witnessed the outbreak of the Spanish Civil War, which found the two governments supporting opposing sides, the announcement of the Rome-Berlin Axis, Italy's withdrawal from the League of Nations, and the absorption of Austria into the Third Reich. The latter event, bringing Hitler's Germany to the Brenner frontier, wrote finis to the efforts of previous French statesmen to enroll Fascist Italy in a coalition with the western powers à la Stresa. Thereafter the only hope for undermining the Axis, and a slim one at that, lay in persuading the Italians to adopt a hesitant and unfriendly neutrality should general warfare erupt in Europe. Although the Popular Front regime was beset with numerous domestic challenges from all points of the political compass, one scarcely can avoid the conclusion that its fumbling and dilatory diplomacy cemented the Italo-German relationship that its predecessors had labored so energetically to forestall.

CONCLUSION

In the conclusion of her book on the military strategy of France in the 1920s, Judith M. Hughes argues that the French decision of 1929-30 to build the Maginot Line forced the country into even greater dependence upon England. Thus deprived of independent offensive capability, the Third Republic could do little to oppose German treaty violations in the 1930s so long as Great Britain was prepared to make substantial concessions. French diplomacy "could only drift, with no fixed point as a guide."[4] The foregoing pages of this volume—detailing the efforts of such varied statesmen as Paul-Boncour, Jouvenel, Barthou, Laval, Flandin, François-Poncet, and Bonnet to chart diplomatic courses designed to buttress the Anglo-French connection principally by strengthening France's ties to Mussolini's Italy—can be read in part as a corrective to Hughes's rather deterministic view.[5] Her judgments, however, seem apt when applied to the Popular Front government. Its unrelieved ideological hostility to fascism and its tendency to regard the Italian government with contempt, although intellectually honest, blinded its leaders to strategic and political reality. Delbos's decision to withdraw de Chambrun from Rome, contravening the advice of his own diplomats and even that of Italian Foreign Minister Ciano, deprived France of ambassadorial representation there for two crucial years. The prolonged stalemate made it impossible for the Quai d'Orsay to respond creatively to numerous Italian gestures of conciliation, especially those tendered during and after the *Anschluss* crisis of 1938.

From the French and British point of view, the likelihood of resurrecting the World War I alliance with Italy, or the Stresa Front, vanished for all intents and purposes after the failure of the Hoare-Laval Plan to resolve the Ethiopian crisis in December 1935. Similarly, even the maintenance of a threatening Italian neutrality in the event of war with Germany became less likely after the *Anschluss*. Nevertheless, the events described in this book compel a reassessment of Laval's foreign policy. Much of the blackness of his historical reputation lies, of course, in the role of collaboration with the Nazis that he played at Vichy from 1940 to 1944. His behavior during that era is not in question here.[6] But it should also be recalled that part of the indictment prepared against Laval in 1945 included charges of treason for his role in French foreign policy planning before the war. In this connection, his own defense of his policies, although clearly dissembling in what it left out, nevertheless strikes me as especially compelling. I hope, therefore, that the reader will forebear a rather lengthy quotation from the notes scribbled down by the condemned man in his prison cell at Fresnes.

> What I sought to do [Laval wrote] was to preserve a working agreement with Italy which would keep her on France's side in the event of a grave crisis in

> Europe. . . . The purpose [of the Rome Accords and military agreements of 1935] was precise: to defend Italy and France against a German invasion of Austria. This Treaty was of paramount importance; as long as Italy was France's ally we had a bridge leading to all those countries of Western and Eastern Europe which were then our allies. We could therefore not only benefit by whatever military strength Italy represented, but also by the added strength of Yugoslavia, Czechoslovakia, Poland and Rumania. . . .
>
> The real crime was not that of having been present when the humiliation of defeat was inflicted upon us. The real crime was to have launched France into a war, obviously lost in advance, since no preparation, either diplomatically or militarily, had been made to forestall defeat.
>
> My crime, if it were one, would have been the acceptance during the Occupation of those burdens which in justice should have been borne by those who were responsible for our disaster. My error was to have accepted the receivership in a bankruptcy which I myself had sought by every means to avoid. . . .
>
> [Laval goes on to say that the whole objective of his foreign policy had been] to encircle Germany politically.
>
> The real crime was to have broken the Italian agreements. There can be no explanation nor excuse for this blunder. The consequences were immediate and disastrous: the remilitarization of the Rhineland was the first signal of Hitler's devastating enterprise. This was the immediate consequence of breaking the political and military agreements that I had signed with Italy. . . .[7]

The first and last paragraphs of the quotation might well have been written by Barthou. But what Laval conveniently ignored here—a fact seized upon by critics and political opponents—was the undeniable fact that the original inspiration for his foreign policy was quite the opposite from that of his illustrious predecessor at the Quai d'Orsay. What he wanted was not to surround Germany with a ring of hostile alliances but rather to construct a diplomatic system strong enough to force Hitler to accept a rapprochement with France.[8] For this reason Laval's critics accused him of being pro-Nazi. What they failed to realize—or refused to admit—was that his policies were such that, if the Franco-German rapprochement he sought did not materialize, the system of accords he built had the further virtue of hemming in Nazi treaty violations. This is how Laval visualized his diplomacy after Germany's unilateral rearmament of 1935 and how he defended his actions in retrospect. There can be no denying the fact that the country was in a stronger position when he left office in January 1936 than when France ultimately went to war three and one-half years later.

Laval, a political protégé of Aristide Briand who lacked his mentor's congenial style and fluid oratorical gifts, acquired a well-earned reputation

CONCLUSION

as a manipulator, a devious and foxy politician totally lacking in ideals or moral values. A long-standing political joke had it that Laval had arranged to be born with a palindromic name that looked the same whether moving from left to right or right to left.[9] But most fundamentally he was a pacifist to the depths of his soul. Even his most ardent political opponents conceded that. Perhaps Laval answered his critics and revealed his motivations most clearly in the following statement: " 'I have been accused of lacking ideals, doubtless because I always believed and still believe that foreign policy, though it must take into account some imponderables, should always be based on solid realities. Regimes follow one another in solemn procession, governments undergo revolutions, but geography remains invariable. We will be neighbors of Germany forever.' "[10] The implication here, that Nazism was likely a passing phenomenon and that ultimate French security lay in coming to terms with her neighbor across the Rhine, seems unassailable in light of events since 1945. One is reminded of the poignant photograph that appeared in newspapers all over the world in the autumn of 1984, on the occasion of ceremonies commemorating French and German soldiers killed at Verdun in 1916. It depicted French President François Mitterrand and German Chancellor Helmut Kohl standing side by side at attention with hands clasped as their respective national anthems were played. Laval's error was not in seeking Franco-German reconciliation but rather in erroneously assessing the real nature of Nazism and the Third Reich. If such an error of judgment were legitimately treasonous, then many other of the world's statesmen of the 1930s would have stood in the dock beside him in 1945.

After bestowing a ritual paean of praise upon the policies of Barthou (the author of a true "*redressement* on the road of decadence"), Duroselle grudgingly admits that Laval's diplomacy was well founded. But then he flays it as hesitant—a series of "little steps" toward the USSR, Italy, Germany, and England without consistent follow-through on any of them.[11] But how, one might ask, could he commit France to any one or a combination of these courses without the British support deemed essential by every government since 1923? The uncertainties of British policy in the mid-1930s, wavering between appeasement and resistance to fascist aggression, made Laval more and more susceptible to the arguments of men such as de Brinon and de Monzie that French security lay in coming to terms with Germany and Italy.[12] But he was constrained by the conventional wisdom of French foreign policy and by his own predilections from moving completely in that direction. It is difficult to see how even Barthou, confronted with the same set of circumstances, could have done much differently.

Where Laval erred seriously was in his continued belief, beyond all reason and evidence, that a French alliance with Italy was still possible in 1939 and 1940. He vehemently argued the point with Bonnet in the Foreign Affairs Committee of the Senate on 16 March 1939, pointing out that the only way to prevent Hitler from taking over Europe was "to make the 'chain' stretch from London to Paris and on to Rome, Belgrade, Budapest, Warsaw, Bucharest, and Moscow."[13] Italy was the key link in such a "chain," and France, he urged, must make every effort and concession to secure Italy's position in it. Could Italy have been appeased at that late date? The record cited above indicates not, and the events of May–June 1940 show that even if Italy's nonbelligerency could have been prolonged, it would not have altered the outcome of the war. Denis Mack Smith has written recently that a better diplomat than Mussolini could have capitalized on England's and France's willingness to make concessions in August 1939 and in May 1940 to make substantial gains for Italy in exchange for neutrality. But that simply did not fit the model of Fascimo or ducismo. "Fatally flattered by Hitler and fascinated by Hitler's offer of a share in world dominion, he could hardly have been satisfied with just the fruits of appeasement."[14] After 1938 it was too late.

In his 16 March 1939 speech, cited above, Laval implied that it might be necessary for government leaders, such as Bonnet and Daladier, to circumvent legislative opposition to the appeasement of Italy by taking authoritarian action. For this, and for his wartime collaboration, Laval paid the ultimate price. But the real culprit in dismantling the entire interwar effort of men such as Poincaré, Barrère, Paul-Boncour, Jouvenel, Barthou, Laval, Flandin, Bonnet, and François-Poncet to build a workable Franco-Italian relationship was the stalemate engendered by the untimely recall of the French ambassador to Rome in 1936. Henry Kissinger observed recently in quite another context that " . . . prolonged stalemate will inevitably sap the will of a democracy."[15] Whether democracies are inherently more vulnerable to diplomatic stalemate than other systems of government is a question best left to political philosophers. But this particular impasse contributed to the ruin of the Third Republic and also, it might be added, most probably hastened the ultimate demise of Italian fascism.

Notes

ABBREVIATIONS USED IN NOTES

BFSP	Great Britain, Foreign Office, *British and Foreign State Papers*.
CAB	Great Britain, Unpublished Cabinet Papers, Public Record Office, Kew Gardens Branch.
DBFP	Great Britain, *Documents on British Foreign Policy, 1919-1939*, ed. Rohan Butler, J. P. T. Bury, et al. (London, 1947-1982).
DDF	France, Ministère des Affaires Étrangères, Commission de Publication des Documents Relatifs aux Origines de la Guerre 1939-45, *Documents diplomatiques français, 1932-1939*.
DGFP	U.S. Department of State, *Documents on German Foreign Policy, 1918-1945*.
DIA	*Documents on International Affairs*, ed. J.W. Wheeler-Bennett and J. Heald.
EMA/2	France, État-Major de l'Armée, Deuxième Bureau, Service Historique de l'Armée de Terre, "Rapports des Attachés Militaires," Vincennes Archives.
Évén.	France, Assemblée nationale, *Commission d'Enquête parlementaire*
Sur.	*sur les évènements survenus en France de 1933 à 1945*.
FO 371	Great Britain, Unpublished Foreign Office Papers, Public Record Office, Kew Gardens Branch.
FO 800	Great Britain, Foreign Office, Private Papers of Agents, Public Record Office, Kew Gardens Branch.
FRUS	U.S. Department of State, *Foreign Relations of the United States*.
HCAP	Great Britain, *House of Commons Accounts and Papers*.
JO, Ch.	France, *Journal Officiel de la République Française*, Chambre des Députés, *Débats*.
JO, Sén.	France, *Journal Officiel de la République Française*, Sénat, *Débats*.
MAE	France, Archives du Ministère des Affaires Étrangères, Unpublished documents from various subseries identified by name of country.
MAE, FN	France, Archives du Ministère des Affaires Étrangères, Fonds Nominatifs. Unpublished private papers.

CHAPTER 1

1. John C. Cairns, "March 7, 1936, Again: The View from Paris."

2. Cited in Gabriel Hanotaux, *Histoire des colonies françaises et de l'expansion de la France dans le monde* 4:633; Thomas F. Power, *Jules Ferry and the Renaissance of French Imperialism*, 50. For a discussion of the European diplomatic background to the Tunisian

expedition, see William I. Shorrock, "Prelude to Empire: French Balkan Policy, 1878-1881," 345-62.

3. Wilfred Knapp, *Tunisia*, 114-15; George W. Baer, *The Coming of the Italo-Ethiopian War*, 62-64.

4. C. J. Lowe and F. Marzari, *Italian Foreign Policy, 1870-1940*, 27-40.

5. Ibid., 49-50; Cambon cited in Léon Noël, *Les Illusions de Stresa: L'Italie abandonée à Hitler*, 23.

6. Cited in Lowe and Marzari, *Italian Foreign Policy*, 71.

7. René Albrecht-Carrié, *France, Europe and the Two World Wars*, 39.

8. The text of the 1896 accords can be found in Charles Monchicourt, *Les Italiens de Tunisie et l'accord Laval-Mussolini*, 8-9; see also Maurice Pernot, "Franco-Italian Relations."

9. Lowe and Marzari, *Italian Foreign Policy*, 80-88.

10. John F. Keiger, *France and the Origins of the First World War*, 32.

11. Harold Temperley, *A History of the Peace Conference of Paris* 4:289-91.

12. Cited in Christopher Andrew and A.S. Kanya-Forstner, *The Climax of French Imperial Expansion, 1914-1924*, 79.

13. The French position vis-à-vis Italy touched off an acrimonious dispute between Barrère, who championed a more assertive French response in Italy's behalf in the interests of future good relations between the two powers, and President Raymond Poincaré and Premier Clemenceau. Joel Blatt, "France and Italy at the Paris Peace Conference."

14. Temperley, *History of the Peace Conference* 4: 296.

15. Lowe and Marzari, *Italian Foreign Policy*, 160-61; René Albrecht-Carrié, *Italy at the Paris Peace Conference*, 141-49; Temperley, *History of the Peace Conference* 4:298-300.

16. Pierre-Etienne Flandin, *Politique française, 1919-1940*, 89. Flandin, a strongly pro-Italian French politician, became premier twice and foreign minister once during the turbulent period from 1934 to 1936. See also Comte Carlo Sforza, *Les Frères ennemis (l'Europe d'après guerre)*, 225-27; Lowe and Marzari, *Italian Foreign Policy*, 169-72.

17. See, for example, the excellent studies produced over the last decade by Stephen A. Schuker, *The End of French Predominance in Europe: The Financial Crisis of 1924 and the Adoption of the Dawes Plan*; Jacques Bariéty, *Les relations franco-allemandes après la première guerre mondiale: 10 novembre 1918-10 janvier 1925, de l'exécution à la négociation*; Marc Trachtenberg, *Reparation in World Politics: France and European Economic Diplomacy, 1916-1923*; Walter A. McDougall, *France's Rhineland Diplomacy, 1914-1924: The Last Bid for a Balance of Power in Europe*.

18. Albrecht-Carrié, *France, Europe and the Two World Wars*, 41; Bertrand de Jouvenel, *Après la défaite*, 70-72; Gerhard Weinberg, "The Defeat of Germany in 1918 and the European Balance of Power"; Schuker, *End of French Predominance*, 5. See also the review essay by Kathleen Burk, "Economic Diplomacy Between the Wars." Burk remarks that the opening of French diplomatic archives "has led historians to rearrange the pecking order of heroes and villains, with the major beneficiary being France" (1003).

19. MAE, "Italie," Z 374-4, vol. 96, pp. 34-48 ("Les Rapports Franco-Italiens de 1918 à 1924," 1 January 1925).

20. Opposition to the *Anschluss* was the single most important common denominator in French and Italian foreign policy at least until 1936. Sforza, *Les Frères ennemis*, 212-13; MAE, FN, "Papiers André Tardieu," vol. 66 (Paul Cambon to Foreign Minister Stephen Pichon, 26 February 1919).

21. Flandin, *Politique française*, 14; Monchicourt, *Les Italiens de Tunisie*, 8-16; Sforza, *Les Frères ennemis*, 228.

22. MAE, FN, "Papiers Camille Barrère," vol. 7, pp. 127-33.

CHAPTER 2

1. MAE, FN, "Papiers Barrère," vol. 7, pp. 66-72, 114-17; see also Georges Suarez, *Briand: sa vie, son oeuvre* 5:209.
2. For example, see MAE, "Italie," Z 375-1, vol. 212, pp. 12, 53-54, 59. This entire volume is devoted to German propaganda activities in Italy from 1918 to 1929.
3. MAE, FN, "Papiers Barrère," vol. 1, pp. 151-52; "Papiers François Charles-Roux," dossier 12, pp. 10-15 (Charles-Roux to Millerand). Barrère also had sounded an optimistic note in a letter to Millerand on 22 June 1920. MAE, FN, "Papiers Barrère," vol. 4, p. 108.
4. MAE, "Italie," Z 372-2, 3, 4, 5, vol. 74, pp. 17-19 (Barrère to Briand, 22 February 1921); p. 61 (communiqué to Quai d'Orsay from Sûreté Générale, 3 May 1921); Z 374-1, vol. 79, pp. 140-45 (Barrère to Briand, 15 March 1921); Z 372-1, vol. 60, pp. 20-25.
5. MAE, "Italie," vol. 59, pp. 56-58 (20 April 1920), pp. 67-69 (10 May 1920); vol. 60, pp. 9-12.
6. MAE, "Italie," Z 372-1, vol. 60, pp. 31-35.
7. Ibid., pp. 87-89, 121-23.
8. Ibid., Z 372-2, 3, 4, 5, vol. 74, p. 21 (1 March 1921); pp. 72-75 (4 July 1921); Z 372-1, vol. 60, pp. 141-42 (22 March 1921).
9. William A. Renzi, "Mussolini's Sources of Financial Support, 1914-1915." French subsidies were designed to encourage Mussolini's interventionist campaign in *Il Popolo d'Italia* after his dismissal as editor of the socialist newspaper, *Avanti!*
10. MAE, "Italie," Z 372-1, vol. 60, pp. 185-86.
11. Ibid., vol. 61, pp. 41-43, 131-32.
12. Ibid., vol. 61, pp. 166-67, 169; vol. 62, pp. 5-6.
13. Ibid., Z 374-9, vol. 125, pp. 51-52; Z 372-1, vol. 62, pp. 43-44 (Barrère to Poincaré, 11 October 1922).
14. *Le Temps*, 25 October 1922; *Le Petit Parisien*, 28 October; *Le Matin*, 24 October; *Le Gaulois*, 24 October; Pierre Milza, *L'Italie fascist devant l' opinion française, 1920-1940*, 22-25, 76.
15. Flandin, *Politique française*, 90; MAE, "Italie," Z 374-1, vol. 81, p. 31; Z 372-1, vol. 62, pp. 120, 122, 142-45; MAE, FN, "Papiers Charles-Roux," dossier 12, pp. 56, 62-65, 82-83 (Charles-Roux to Paris, 29 and 31 October, 2 November 1922).
16. John P. Diggins, *Mussolini and Fascism: The View from America*, 22-29. Diggins shows that a number of leading American newspapers, as well as mass circulation magazines like the *Saturday Evening Post*, took an initially favorable view of the nascent fascist experiment.
17. For example, see leading editorials in the following: *La Petite République*, 29 October 1922; *Le Temps*, 1 and 2 November; *Le Matin*, 31 October; *L'Intransigeant*, 31 October and 2 and 5 November; *Le Gaulois*, 31 October and 1 November; *Le Petit Parisien*, 3 November.
18. Comte Carlo Sforza, *Illusions et réalités de l' Europe*, 22-24 (see chapter three for details); Paul Cambon, *Correspondance* 3:421; Alan Cassels, *Mussolini's Early Diplomacy*, 9; MAE, FN, "Papiers Charles-Roux," dossier 12, p. 87 (Charles-Roux to Paris, 2 November 1922); MAE, "Italie," Z 374-1, vol. 81, pp. 33, 34-35 (two telegrams from Charles-Roux to Poincaré on 1 November 1922); ; Raffaele Guariglia, *La Diplomatie difficile, Mémoires, 1922-1946*, 4.
19. MAE, "Italie," Z 372-1, vol. 62, pp. 252-55 (Charles-Roux to Poincaré, 17 November 1922); Jules Laroche, *Au Quai d'Orsay avec Briand et Poincaré, 1913-1926*, 167; Cassels, *Mussolini's Early Diplomacy*, 15-16.
20. MAE, "Italie," Z 372-1, vol. 62, pp. 188-89 (3 November 1922); see also pp. 196-204 (6

November 1922), 232-42 (15 November 1922). The theme of governmental stability in Italy as a desirable prerequisite for the reestablishment of closer Italo-French relations can also be found in *Le Temps,* 7 December 1922. This leading article was written by Ludovic Naudeau, whose advocacy of an Italo-French entente is pursued in his book, *L'Italie fasciste ou l'autre danger,* esp. chapter 5.

21. MAE, "Italie," Z 372-2, 3, 4, 5, vols. 70-74.
22. Ibid., Z 372-1, vol. 62, p. 224 (Barrère to Poincaré, 11 November 1922); *Le Temps,* 11, 12, 18 November 1922.
23. MAE, "Italie," Z 372-1, vol. 63, pp. 64-73; Z 374-1, vol. 93, pp. 14-15, 22-23.
24. François Charles-Roux, "La France et l'Italie dès armistices à Locarno," 194-96; Cassels. *Mussolini's Early Diplomacy,* 16, 47; Jacques Chastenet, *Histoire de la Troisième République* 5:101; Comte de Saint-Aulaire, *Confession d'un vieux diplomate,* 643-44.
25. MAE, FN, "Papiers Barrère," vol. 3, pp. 218, 219 (letters dated 7 and 12 December 1922); MAE, "Italie," Z 374-1, vol. 81, pp. 90-95. (Charles-Roux expressed this possibility in a dispatch to Poincaré on 13 December 1922); Joel R. Blatt, "French Reaction to Italy, Italian Fascism, and Mussolini, 1919-1925: The Views from Paris and the Palazzo Farnese," 822.
26. Cassels, *Mussolini's Early Diplomacy,* 54-56; Sally Marks, "Mussolini and the Ruhr Crisis," 56-69.
27. MAE, "Italie," Z 374-1, vol. 81, pp. 101-5 (telegram to Poincaré); Arnold J. Toynbee, *Survey of International Affairs, 1920-1923,* 192-93.
28. McDougall, *France's Rhineland Diplomacy,* 265; MAE, "Italie," Z 374-4, vol. 93, pp. 48-52 (Foreign Ministry Note, 20 February 1923). Jouvenel's proposals had originally appeared in an article in *Le Matin.* They were reproduced in this Note for the Director of Political Affairs with instructions that they be communicated to the French Embassy in Rome.
29. Naudeau, *L'Italie fasciste,* 78-79; see also Chastenet, *Histoire de la Troisième République* 5:262.
30. MAE, "Italie," Z 374-1, vol. 83, pp. 34-42.

CHAPTER 3

1. Arnold J. Wolfers, *Britain and France Between Two Wars: Conflicting Strategies of Peace from Versailles to World War II;* Schuker, *End of French Predominance.*
2. The Franco-Czech alliance was signed on 25 January 1924 but military clauses were added only on 16 October 1925. The Franco-Romanian and Franco-Yugoslav treaties materialized in 1926 and 1927 respectively. The latter is discussed in detail toward the end of this chapter.
3. MAE, FN, "Papiers Tardieu," vol. 66, 14 February 1919; 24 February 1919; René Albrecht-Carrié, *Italy from Napoleon to Mussolini,* 112-21.
4. MAE, FN, "Papiers Tardieu," vol. 66, 17 March 1919.
5. MAE, "Italie," Z 374-1, vol. 79, pp. 21-26; Z 374-4, vol. 90, p. 156; Suarez, *Briand* 5:122-23.
6. Sforza, *Les Frères ennemis,* 250-51; Sforza, *Illusions et réalités,* 20.
7. France was one of the first countries to recognize the Treaty of Rapallo and one of the few to send immediate consular representation to Fiume. Thus the French consul's view of these events, a markedly anti-Italian one, is recorded in excruciating detail in MAE, "Fiume,"

NOTES TO CHAPTER 3

Z 933, vols. 1-3. See also Arnold J. Toynbee, *Survey of International Affairs, 1924,* 412-13; A. E. Moodie, *The Italo-Yugoslav Boundary: A Study in Political Geography,* 166-208.

8. MAE, "Fiume," Z 933, vol. 2, p. 92, 99-103.
9. Ibid., vol. 3, pp.1, 31-32, 87-88.
10. Cassels, *Mussolini's Early Diplomacy,* 81ff.
11. MAE, "Fiume," Z 933, vol. 3, pp. 109-10 (entire correspondence on this episode covers pp. 96-110).
12. MAE, "Italie," Z 374-6, vol. 107, pp. 166-67, 180.
13. Ibid., pp. 195-96, 203-7; Cassels, *Mussolini's Early Diplomacy,* 130-31; MAE, "Italie," Z 374-6, vol. 107, pp. 197-98.
14. Laroche, *Au Quai d'Orsay,* 173-74; Guariglia, *La diplomatie difficile,* 12; Pierre Renouvin, *War and Aftermath, 1914-1929,* 268; Cassels, *Mussolini's Early Diplomacy,* 95-103; Toynbee, *Survey, 1924,* 348-49.
15. MAE, "Italie," Z 374-10, vol. 128, pp. 29-30, 47-48.
16. See, for example, the editorial support extended to Mussolini's actions in the following: *Le Matin,* 31 August and 2 September 1923; *Le Temps,* 1 September; *L'Echo de Paris,* 1 September; *Le Petit Parisien,* 1 September; *L' Intransigeant,* 2 September.
17. MAE, "Italie," Z 374-10, vol. 128, pp. 43-44, 89-90.
18. Laroche, *Au Quai d'Orsay,* 174-77; MAE, "Italie," Z 374-10, vol. 128, p. 102.
19. Cassels, *Mussolini's Early Diplomacy,* 95-101; MAE, "Italie," Z 374-10, vol. 128, pp. 66-67; MAE, FN, "Papiers Hanotaux," carton 6, nos. 44-52; MAE, "Italie," Z 374-10, vol. 128, pp. 214-17.
20. MAE, "Italie," Z 374-10, vol. 128, pp. 231-34; MAE, FN, "Papiers Hanotaux," carton 6, nos. 68-72.
21. MAE, "Italie," Z 374-10, vol. 129, pp. 169-71; vol. 130, pp. 33-38, 94-95.
22. Ibid., vol. 129, pp. 78-82; MAE, FN, "Papiers Hanotaux," vol. 12, pp.154-56.
23. MAE, "Italie," Z 374-10, vol. 130, pp. 94-95, 219-21.
24. Toynbee, *Survey, 1924,* 354; Georges Christopolous, *La politique extérieure de l'Italie fasciste,* 21; MAE, "Italie," Z 374-10, vol. 129, pp. 124, 223-28; vol. 130, pp. 171, 215; vol. 131, pp. 13, 28-30; Z-374-4, vol. 94, pp. 12-18.
25. Ibid., Z 374-10, vol. 128, pp. 270-71; MAE, FN, "Papiers Hanotaux," vol. 12, pp. 144-45, carton 6; MAE, "Italie," Z 374-10, vol. 128, p. 274 (Foreign Office Note, 5 September 1923); MAE, FN, "Papiers Hanotaux," vol.12, pp.144-45.
26. MAE, "Italie," Z 374-10, vol. 129, pp. 250-51.
27. Maxwell H. H. Macartney and Paul Cremona, *Italy's Foreign and Colonial Policy, 1914-1937,* 93-94; Toynbee, *Survey, 1924,* 416-17; MAE, "Italie," Z 374-6, vol. 108, p. 109.
28. MAE, "Italie," Z 374-6, vol. 108, pp. 32, 62, 251-53; MAE, FN, "Papiers Barrère," vol. 3, p. 224.
29. Renouvin, *War and Aftermath,* 269; Moodie, *Italo-Yugoslav Boundary,* 172; MAE, "Fiume," Z 933, vol. 3, pp. 200-201.
30. MAE, "Italie," Z 374-6, vol. 108, pp. 209-11; vol. 118, pp. 53, 55-56, 63-64, 65, 66-68, 80-81.
31. Ibid., pp. 115-19, 181-82; also Z 374-6, vol. 109, pp. 48-49.
32. Ibid., Z 374-6, vol. 118, pp. 198-211; vol. 119, pp. 23-25.
33. Ibid., vol. 119, pp. 86-89; Z 374-1, vol. 83, pp. 44-47.
34. Ibid., Z 374-6, vol. 119, pp. 86-89; Z 374-9, vol. 125, pp. 172-82.
35. MAE, FN, "Papiers Alexandre Millerand," vol. 2, pp. 86-117 (Foreign Ministry note on Yugoslav questions, 23 May 1924).

36. Rome might well regard it as directed against Italy and thus poison the favorable atmosphere created by the Italo-Yugoslav agreement on Fiume. MAE, "Yougoslavie," Z 751-6, vol. 69, pp. 132-33 (Charles-Roux to Poincaré, 5 May 1924); pp. 146-47 (Foreign Ministry note, 5 June 1924).

37. Ibid., pp. 150-53; MAE, FN, "Papiers Millerand," vol. 2, pp. 214-20 (Foreign Ministry note, 31 May 1924).

38. MAE, "Yougoslavie," Z 751-6, vol. 69, pp. 169-71 (French minister in Belgrade to Briand, 3 October 1925); "Italie," Z 374-6, vol. 110, p. 72 (French minister in Belgrade to Briand, 26 November 1925); "Yougoslavie," Z 751-6, vol. 69, p. 197; vol. 70, pp. 4-5 (French minister in Belgrade to Briand, 12 January 1926); "Italie," Z 374-6, vol. 110, p. 107 (French minister in Belgrade to Briand, 19 February 1926); "Yougoslavie," Z 751-6, vol. 70, pp. 6, 16-18.

39. MAE, "Yougoslavie," Z 751-6, vol. 7 (Briand to Belgrade, 26 March 1927); see also MAE, "Italie," Z 374-6, vols. 110-12.

40. MAE, "Yougoslavie," Z 751-6, vol. 70, pp. 217-21 (Besnard to Briand, 9 November 1927); "Italie," Z 374-6, vol. 114, pp. 110-11 (Besnard to Briand, 10 November 1927).

41. MAE, "Italie," Z 374-9, vol. 127B, pp. 49-52 (Margerie to Briand, 14 November 1927); "Yougoslavie," Z 751-6, vol. 71, p. 93 (Berthelot to Belgrade, 15 November 1927); p. 113 (Roger in Rome to Briand, 17 November 1927); "Italie," Z 374-6, vol. 114, pp. 189-90 (Berthelot to Belgrade, 25 November 1927); MAE, "Yougoslavie," Z 751-6, vol. 72, pp. 18-20 (Fleuriau in London to Briand, 22 November 1927); pp. 45-51 (Briand to Fleuriau, 24 November 1927).

42. Roger de Dampierre, "Dix années de politique française à Rome (1925-1935)," 23.

43. Christopoulos, *La Politique extérieure,* 60; Monchicourt, *Les Italiens de Tunisie,* 15-16; Lowe and Marzari, *Italian Foreign Policy,* 169-72.

44. MAE, "Tunisie," P 362 sd, vol. 176, pp. 7-8 (Barrère to Briand, 24 June 1921); pp. 33-34 (text of the decree); pp. 62-63, 72-76 (Barrère to Briand, 8 and 14 December 1921).

45. MAE, FN, "Papiers Charles-Roux," côte 37, dossier 11, pp. 74-79 (letter from Jean Roger in Rome to Charles-Roux, 9 July 1922); MAE, "Tunisie," P 362 sd, vol. 176, pp. 160-62 (Barrère to Quai d'Orsay, 20 June 1922); vol. 174, pp. 213-16 (Barrère to Poincaré, 15 August 1922); see also pp. 152-53 (Charles-Roux to Poincaré, 10 June 1922); pp. 181-82 (Barrère to Quai d'Orsay, 15 July 1922); MAE, "Italie," Z 374-4, vol. 92, pp. 127-28 (Poincaré to Barrère, 20 July 1922).

46. MAE, "Tunisie," P 762 sd, vol. 328, p. 192 (20 November 1922); vol. 329, pp. 38-39 (15 February 1923); pp. 48-49 (3 March 1923); pp. 59-60 (5 March 1923); p. 64 (7 March 1923); P 362 sd, vol. 177, pp. 20-21.

47. Text of the proposed law, adopted by the Chamber on 12 July 1923 and by the Senate on 13 December (thus becoming law on that date), can be found in MAE, "Tunisie," P 362, vol. 167, pp. 81-90.

48. Ibid., vol. 177, pp. 43-44; "Italie," Z 374-4, vol. 93, pp. 160-65 (Charles-Roux to Poincaré, 28 August 1923); MAE, FN, "Papiers Barrère," vol. 2, pp. 187-88 (Barrère to Hermitte at Quai d'Orsay, 1 August 1923).

49. MAE, "Tunisie," P 362 sd, vol. 177, p. 128 (Poincaré to Rome and Tunis, 21 November 1923); P 362, vol. 168, pp. 3-9 (confidential background note from Quai d'Orsay to Senator Oran, 6 December 1923); vol. 177, pp. 156-59 (Barrère to Paris, 22 December 1923); see, for example, MAE, "Tunisie," P 762 sd, vol. 330 (January 1924–June 1925); Monchicourt, *Les Italiens de Tunisie,* 20-21.

50. MAE, "Italie," Z 374-4, vol. 94 (Poincaré to Barrère, 20 October 1923). For a fuller

discussion of Franco-Italian economic relations in the 1920s, see the excellent article by Pierre Guillen, "L'échec des tentatives d'entente économique avec l'Italie (1922-1929)."

51. MAE, "Tunisie," P 362, vol. 168, pp. 91-94 (Saint to Poincaré, 26 January 1924); pp. 131-37 (Saint to Herriot, 24 July 1924); vol. 169, pp. 103-6 (Foreign Ministry note, 19 December 1927); P 762 sd, vol. 331, p. 81 (Saint to Directeur général de l'Instruction publique, 10 November 1925); p. 84 (Saint to Directeur général des Travaux publics, 10 November 1925).

52. Ibid., P 362, vol. 168, p. 103 (Poincaré to Saint, 4 February 1924); P 762 sd, vol. 332, p. 55 (Besnard to Briand, 28 March 1926); vol. 334, pp. 34-35 (Besnard to Briand, 22 July 1926); vol. 331, pp. 77-78 (Minister plenipotentiary at Tunis to Monsieur le Contrôleur civil, 10 November 1925); vol. 336, pp. 72-89 (Saint to Briand, 30 April 1928); pp. 107-8 (Saint to Briand, 5 June 1928).

53. Ibid., P 362, vol. 168, pp. 177-214.

54. MAE, "Italie," Z 374-4, vol. 96, pp. 202-3 (Besnard to Paris, 28 January 1926); "Tunisie," P 762 sd, vol. 332, pp. 137-40 (Besnard to Briand, 23 April 1926); pp. 162-63 (Besnard to Briand, 29 April 1926).

55. MAE, "Italie," Z 374-4, vol. 98, pp. 2-3 (Besnard to Briand, 4 January 1927); ibid., p. 14; "Tunisie," P 362 sd, vol. 179, pp. 23-26.

56. MAE, "Tunisie," P 362 sd, vol. 179, pp. 43-45 (Berthelot to Rome, 20 March 1927); "Italie," Z 374-4, vol. 99, pp. 75-81 (Briand to London, 24 November 1927); pp. 96-98 (London to Briand, 29 November 1927); pp. 151-52 (Rome to Briand, 8 December 1927); Z 374-12, vol. 102 (Beaumarchais to Berthelot, 10 February 1928).

57. MAE, "Italie," Z 374-12, vol. 102, pp. 67-70; pp. 71-74 (Briand to Belgrade, 10 April 1928); pp. 75-78 (Beaumarchais's note on conversation with Poincaré, 21 April 1928); Z 374-1, vol. 85, pp. 245-48 (Beaumarchais to Briand, 5 June 1928); pp. 252-56 (Beaumarchais to Briand, 7 June 1928).

58. Ibid., Z 374-12, vol. 102, pp. 100-117 (Beaumarchais to Briand, 7 August 1928); text of the proposed Franco-Italian convention on Tunisia can be found in MAE, "Tunisie," P 362 sd, vol. 179, pp. 273-76 (13 October 1928); MAE, "Italie," Z 374-12, vol. 102, pp. 149-66; MAE, FN, "Papiers Henry de Jouvenel," dossier 5 (21 December 1928), pp. 36-43.

59. MAE, "Italie," Z 374-12, vol. 103, pp. 1-4 (Beaumarchais to Briand, 5 January 1929); ibid. (Beaumarchais to Briand, 20 June 1929); MAE, FN, "Papiers Jouvenel," dossier 5, pp. 44-50. The only fruitful achievement of six long years of negotiation on North African issues occurred on 25 July 1928, when Italy was accorded a position in the international organization of Tangiers. Since 1923, Mussolini had insisted that as a Mediterranean power, Italy was entitled to participation in the regulation of the international status of the Moroccan port city on the same footing as England, France and Spain. The French just as insistently maintained that a modification of the Statute of Tangiers to include Italy was not in conformity with the Franco-Italian accords of 1900, 1902, and 1912, whereby the two powers declared their mutual disinterest in Morocco and Tripolitania. Nevertheless, largely due to British and Spanish support for Italian involvement and the sympathy of French ambassadors in Rome, the Statute was revised in 1928 in such a way as to accord Italy an equal place in the international administration of Tangiers. It was clearly a victory for Italian diplomacy and a rather bitter pill for those in France who hoped that such a concession might soften Italian demands for the resolution of the status of Italians in Tunisia. Such was not the case. Lord Edgar D'Abernon, *An Ambassador of Peace: Pages from the Diary of Viscount D'Abernon* 3:249; Cassels, *Mussolini's Early Diplomacy,* 207-9, 237-39, 357-65.

60. This manner of thinking was reflected clearly in a dispatch from the French ambassador in Prague to Poincaré on 13 September 1923, in the midst of the Corfu crisis. The former

reported the virtually unanimous denunciation of French policy in the Czech press and concluded that "we cannot deny that our attitude in this affair has provoked in Czechoslovakia and, I believe, among her Little Entente allies, a certain uneasiness which it would be useful for us to dissipate." (MAE, "Italie," Z 374-10 vol. 129, pp. 250-51.) The sources for the period 1924-27 confirm the Prague ambassador's concern to refurbish French influence among the small nations of eastern Europe.

61. Henry de Jouvenel, later to become French ambassador to Rome in 1933, advocated continued close Franco-Italian relations in a series of articles for *Le Matin,* summarized in a Foreign Ministry note (MAE, "Italie," Z 374-4, vol. 93, pp. 48-52); see also Chastenet, *Histoire de la Troisième République* 5:262.

CHAPTER 4

1. MAE, "Italie," Z 374-1, vol. 84, pp. 61-63 (Besnard to Briand, 16 March 1926); pp. 72-73 (Besnard to Briand, 28 March 1926); Z 374-4, vol. 96, p. 228 (19 March 1926); Z 374-1, vol. 84, pp. 74-75 (29 March 1926).

2. Ibid., Z 374-4, vol. 99, pp. 60-65 (Jean Roger, chargé d'affaires in Rome, to Paris, 22 November 1927).

3. EMA/2, 7 N 2917, dossier 2 (13 September 1928); MAE, "Italie," Z 374-1, vol. 86, pp. 204-5 (30 November 1929).

4. MAE, "Tunisie," P 362, vol. 169, pp. 214-19 (Note sur la question des naturalisations en Tunisie, 10 December 1929); *DDF,* ser. 1, vol. 2, no. 41 (Roger de Dampierre to Herriot, 28 November 1932); Cassels, *Mussolini's Early Diplomacy,* 374. He discusses the *fuorusciti* on pp. 365-76.

5. MAE, "Yougoslavie," Z 751-6, vol. 72, pp. 171-74 (Roger to Paris, 15 December 1927).

6. EMA/2, 7 N 2915 (chargé in Brazil to Briand, 7 April 1925; Briand to Paul Painlevé, premier and minister of war, 8 May 1925); Général Maurice Gamelin, *Servir,* vol. 2, *Le Prologue du drâme, 1930-août 1939,* 162-63; MAE, "Italie," Z 374-4, vol. 96, p. 92 (Roger to Briand, 5 May 1925).

7. MAE, "Italie," Z 374-4, vol. 96, p. 100 (Besnard to Paris, 16 May 1925); p. 109 (Roger to Paris, 8 June 1925); p. 155 (Besnard to Briand, 14 November 1925); p. 126 (Foch to Briand, 25 June 1925).

8. EMA/2, 7 N 2915 (Besnard to Briand, 27 May, 1 June, 9 December 1926); MAE, "Italie," Z 374-9, vol. 127B, pp. 34-35 (Roger to Briand, 29 July 1927); Z 374-4, vol. 100, pp. 126-27 (Roger to Briand, 6 November 1928); pp. 151-53 (Beaumarchais to Briand, 28 December 1928); vol. 306, pp. 268-72 (French military attaché in Rome to EMA/2, 25 October 1930); vol. 96, pp. 186-87 (Besnard to Paris, 10 January 1926); p. 190 (Berthelot to Besnard, 14 January 1926); vol. 100 (Foreign Ministry note of 1 January 1928 in reference to a telegram from Briand to Besnard, 11 April 1927).

9. The material summarized in the following two paragraphs of the text consists of notes written by Robert de Caix detailing his conversations with the Marquis Theodoli from 1928 to 1932. These notes were collected and included as part of Henry de Jouvenel's "briefing book" prior to his departure for Rome as France's ambassador in January 1933. (MAE, FN, "Papiers Jouvenel," dossier 5, pp. 67-105) A less extensive compilation of these records can be found in *DDF,* I/2, no. 182 and accompanying annexes. It is also clear from reading the diary of Baron Aloisi that although Theodoli was speaking to de Caix and Joseph Avenol in an

unofficial capacity, he was working nevertheless with the knowledge and direction of the Palazzo Chigi. Baron Pompeo Aloisi, *Journal (25 juillet 1932-14 juin 1934)*, 27.

10. Milza, *L'Italie fasciste*, 139. The author cites editorials in *La Croix*, 16 February 1929; *Le Figaro*, 14 February 1929; *La Victoire*, 12 February 1929; *Le Temps*, 24 February 1929; MAE, "Italie," Z 374-4, vol. 305, pp. 8-9 (Beaumarchais to Paris, 27 February 1930); pp. 27-28 (Beaumarchais to Paris, 29 April 1930); vol. 306, pp. 134-41 (translation of article by Gayda, 17 August 1930).

11. FO 800/276, Orme Sargent's Papers, pp. 205-9 (letter from Sir Ronald Graham to Sargent, 29 January 1931); MAE, "Italie," Z 374-4, vol. 307, pp. 127-28 (Dard, minister in Belgrade, to Briand, 4 May 1931).

12. Noël, *Les Illusions de Stresa*, 30-34. Noël points out quite correctly that the archives at the Quai d'Orsay contain no mention of this Italian demarche. He found a few references to it in the Palazzo Farnese in Rome.

13. FO 800/274, Sargent Papers, pp. 257-61; Noël, *Les Illusions de Stresa*, 35-39.

14. Hubert de Lagardelle, *Mission à Rome: Mussolini*, 8. Lagardelle was posted to Italy from 1933 to 1937. See also Elizabeth R. Cameron, *Prologue to Appeasement: A Study in French Foreign Policy*, 28-29.

15. Gamelin, *Servir* 2:161.

16. Editor's introduction, Aloisi, *Journal*, x-xii; *DDF*, I/1, no. 119.

17. MAE, "Italie," Z 374-4, vol. 315, pp. 135-36 (Beaumarchais to Herriot, 7 November 1932), pp. 186-87 (Dampierre to Herriot, 21 November 1932; pp. 210-11 (Dampierre to Herriot, 29 November 1932. René Massigli, France's delegate to the Disarmament Conference in Geneva, also indicated to Berthelot on 10 November 1932 that the time was ripe for an official initiative toward Italy. (*DDF*, I/1, no. 317).

18. Joseph Paul-Boncour, *Entre deux guerres: Souvenirs sur la Troisième République* 2:337-40.

19. An interesting discussion of Jouvenel's career and his relationship to the Third Republic can be found in Rudolph Binion, *Defeated Leaders: the Political Fate of Caillaux, Jouvenel and Tardieu*, 117-94.

20. For a discussion of the significance of these various appointments, see Paul-Boncour, *Entre deux guerres* 2:337-40; George W. Baer, *The Coming of the Italo-Ethiopian War*, 62-64; Binion, *Defeated Leaders*, 178-80.

21. Lagardelle, *Mission à Rome*, 3-4; Charles-Roux, *Huit ans au Vatican*, 156.

22. MAE, FN, "Papiers Jouvenel," dossier 5, pp. 36-99. For background on Franco-Italian discussions of major issues between 1928 and 1932, see also *DDF*, I/2, no. 182 and annexes.

23. MAE, FN, "Papiers Jouvenel," dossier 5, pp. 1-6; *DDF*, I/2, no. 288.

24. Aloisi, *Journal*, 46, 60; MAE, FN, "Papiers Jouvenel," dossier 6, pp. 2-6, 21-27; *DDF*, I/2, no. 339.

25. MAE, FN, "Papiers Jouvenel," dossier 6, pp. 41-47; *DDF*, I/2, no. 368; Aloisi, *Journal*, 77-80.

26. Esmonde M. Robertson, *Mussolini as Empire-Builder: Europe and Africa, 1932-36*, 34-43.

27. Dampierre, "Dix années de politique française," 262; *DDF*, I/2, no. 382 (8 March 1933); no. 391.

28. *DDF*, I/3, no. 2; no. 7. See also Cameron, *Prologue to Appeasement*, 33-34; Paul-Boncour, *Entre deux guerres* 2:340-45.

29. *DDF*, I/3, no. 38; MAE, FN, "Papiers Jouvenel," dossier 6, pp. 89-94 (telegram to Paul-Boncour, 20 March 1933; personal letter to Émile Roche, in Émile Roche, *Caillaux que j'ai connu*, 66, cited in Binion, *Defeated Leaders*, 180.

30. MAE, FN, "Papiers Jouvenel," dossier 6, pp. 106-12; *DDF*, I/3, no. 44; Aloisi, *Journal*, 102.

31. *DDF*, I/3, no. 108, annex II; no. 112. Jouvenel's way of thinking was adopted by the Quai d'Orsay. On 19 May 1933, Paul-Boncour suggested to Jouvenel that an impending visit of Marshal Goering to Rome might endanger parliamentary willingness to endorse a Four-Power Pact. "We must not forget [he told his ambassador] that the point of departure and . . . the essential object of these negotiations has always been a rapprochement between France and Italy and conciliation between Italy and the Little Entente. It is to hasten the latter that we have agreed . . . to follow the path of the four-power pact" (*DDF*, I/3, no. 295).

32. Lagardelle, *Mission à Rome*, 45-46; MAE, FN, "Papiers Jouvenel," dossier 6, p. 268 (telegram from French ambassador in Prague to Quai d'Orsay, 6 May 1933); 223-26 (Jouvenel to Paul-Boncour, 24 April 1933); pp. 234-39 (Jouvenel to Paul-Boncour, 25 April 1933).

33. MAE, FN, "Papiers Jouvenel," dossier 6, pp. 307-18 (Jouvenel to Paul-Boncour, 20-21 May); pp. 325-30 (Jouvenel to Paul-Boncour, 23 May); *DDF*, I/3, no. 312 (Jouvenel to Paul-Boncour, 23 May). Another factor which played into Jouvenel's desire to move quickly on the Four-Power Pact was this: the Italians were especially concerned about the apparent precariousness of the Daladier ministry in France. The Italians believed, and Jouvenel apparently shared their concern, that Daladier could not stay in office more than a few months longer. His major political opponent was Edouard Herriot, who was outspokenly opposed to the Four-Power scheme. It was important, therefore, to speed the matter along before Daladier was defeated. Aloisi, *Journal*, 112.

34. *DDF*, I/3, no. 316 (24 May 1933); MAE, FN, "Papiers Jouvenel," dossier 6, pp. 369-71 (27 May); pp. 401-2 (30 May).

35. The complete text can be found in *DDF*, I/3, no. 330. See also Néré, *Foreign Policy of France*, 140-42, 311-13.

36. *DDF*, I/3, no. 335, no. 362; see also the discussion of the tension between Jouvenel and the Quai d'Orsay in Lagardelle, *Mission à Rome*, 46-47, and Dampierre, "Dix années de politique française," 2: 267.

37. *DDF*, I/3, no. 363; Lagardelle *Mission à Rome*, 48-49; Aloisi, *Journal*, 131 and note.

38. Gamelin, *Servir* 2: 93-95; Léon Blum, *L'Histoire jugera*, 59. Blum would have done well to follow his own advice when he became premier of the Popular Front from 1936-38.

39. Paul Raynaud, *Au Coeur de la mêlée, 1930-1945* (Paris, 1951), 62-65.

40. Paul-Boncour, *Entre deux guerres* 2: 353-57. According to Georges Bonnet, Paul-Boncour's subsequent claim that the Four-Power Pact, had it survived, "would have saved Europe," was typical of prewar politicians who sought to justify their actions in the tempestuous political climate of the post-liberation era. Georges Bonnet, *Le Quai d'Orsay sous trois républiques, 1870-1961*, 125-26.

41. *DDF*, I/3, no. 400 (Paul-Boncour to Jouvenel, 17 June 1933); no. 428 (Jouvenel to Paul-Boncour, 28 June); see also the discussion in Néré, *Foreign Policy of France*, 142-45, 316-19.

42. *DDF*, I/3, no. 478.

43. Rudolph Binion has concluded that Jouvenel's mission was important as an example: ". . . it was perhaps the most prodigious stunt of conciliation in diplomatic history. And if the stunt was not a starting point for peace, the fault was not his" (*Defeated Leaders*, 185). Mercifully, Jouvenel did not live to see the Italo-Ethiopian War bring his project to an end. He died of a heart attack on 5 October 1935, two days after Italy unleashed its attack on the east African kingdom.

44. Aloisi, *Journal*, 139-40; Paul-Boncour, *Entre deux guerres* 2:350-51; Charles de Chambrun, *Traditions et souvenirs*, 162.

CHAPTER 5

1. Paul-Boncour, *Entre deux guerres* 2:18-19; Dampierre, "Dix années de politique française," 2:269; Jean-Baptiste Duroselle, *La décadence, 1932-1939,* 70-75; MAE, FN, "Papiers Alexis Léger" (letter from Jouvenel to Léger, 12 June 1933); "Papiers Jules Cambon" (letter from de Chambrun to Cambon, 28 September 1933).
2. Aloisi, *Journal* (25 December 1932); MAE, FN, "Papiers Joseph Paul-Boncour," carton 1 (note titled "La Collusion Germano-Italienne," 22 November 1932).
3. EMA/2, 7 N 2903, dossier 1. This long, undated document from 1931 was probably prepared by the French military attaché in Rome. The quoted passage was underlined in red pencil in the original along with the marginal notation, "*Thèse italienne.*"
4. *DDF,* I/1, no. 266 (memorandum of the Ministry of the Navy, 21 October 1932).
5. Robertson, *Mussolini as Empire-Builder,* 56-58; *DDF,* I/4, no. 190 (de Chambrun to Paul-Boncour, 8 September 1933); I/5, no. 190 (de Chambrun to Paul-Boncour, 15 November 1933); Paul-Boncour, *Entre deux guerres* 2:360; Nére, *Foreign Policy of France,* 145-49; *DDF,* I/4, no. 180 (de Chambrun to Paul-Boncour, 5 September 1933); no. 293 (de Chambrun to Paul-Boncour, 11 October 1933).
6. Charles A. Micaud, *The French Right and Nazi Germany, 1933-1939: A Study of Public Opinion,* 28.
7. Paul-Boncour, *Entre deux guerres* 2:391; Robertson, *Mussolini as Empire-Builder,* 58.
8. Micaud, *French Right,* 29-32; *DDF,* I/4, no. 321 (de Chambrun to Paul-Boncour).
9. *DDF,* I/4, no. 376 (Paul Boncour to de Chambrun, 30 October 1933); Paul-Boncour, *Entre deux guerres* 2:352; *DDF,* I/5, nos. 48, 104 (Paul-Boncour to de Chambrun, 23 November and 11 December 1933); nos. 42, 53, 117, 133 (de Chambrun to Paul-Boncour, 22 and 24 November, 13 and 15 December 1933); no. 147 (Saurraut, Minister of the Navy, to Paul-Boncour, 16 December 1933); no. 184 (letter from Aloisi to de Chambrun, 2 January 1934); no. 199 (de Chambrun to Paul-Boncour, 6 January 1934); no. 206 (Paul-Boncour to de Chambrun, 8 January 1934); no. 317 (de Chambrun to Daladier, 3 February 1934); Aloisi, *Journal,* 154, 169-70 (entries for 20 October, 26, 27, 28 December 1933).
10. See Duroselle, *La décadence,* 88-92; Georges Dethan, review of *La décadence* in *Revue d'histoire diplomatique.*
11. André François-Poncet, *Souvenirs d'une ambassade à Berlin,* 168-81.
12. Dampierre, "Dix années de politique française," 2:271; *DDF,* I/6, no. 116 (Barthou to de Chambrun, 20 April 1934).
13. *DDF,* I/6, no. 155 (de Chambrun to Barthou, 29 April 1934) nos. 159, 164 (de Chambrun to Barthou, 1, 3, May 1934); no. 209 (Barthou, to Naggiar, 15 May 1934).
14. Ibid., no. 336 (de Chambrun to Barthou, 14 June 1934); Dampierre, "Dix années de politique française," 2:274-75.
15. *DDF,* I/6, no. 340 (Barthou to de Chambrun, 15 June 1934); nos. 372, 421 (de Chambrun to Barthou, 22 June, 16 July 1934).
16. Bennett Kovrig, "Mediation by Obfuscation: the Resolution of the Marseille Crisis, October 1934 to May 1935," 191-93; Maurice Pernot, "Franco-Italian Relations," 520-22.
17. MAE, "Italie," Z 372-1, vol. 62, pp. 1-3 (Charles-Roux to Poincaré, 1 September 1922); Z 374-1, vol. 83, pp. 210-12 (Besnard to Paris, 21 May 1925); Renouvin, *War and Aftermath,* 266; D'Abernon, *Ambassador of Peace* 3:223-24; Cassels, *Mussolini's Early Diplomacy,* 277; de Chambrun, *Traditions et souvenirs,* 102-3; Wolfers, *Britain and France Between Two Wars,* 145.
18. *DBFP,* ser. 2, vol. 2, pp. 7-10 (French note to London, 23 March 1931); *JO,* Ch., *Débats* (27 March 1931), 1525-26; *JO,* Sén., *Débats* (28 March 1931), 693; Paul-Boncour,

Entre deux guerres 2:178-80; Neville Waites, "The Depression Years," in *Troubled Neighbors: Franco-British Relations in the Twentieth Century*, 133-34.

19. William Evans Scott, *Alliance Against Hitler: The Origins of the Franco-Soviet Pact*, 124; *DDF*, I/2, no. 421 (Paul-Boncour to Jouvenel, 17 March 1933); Lagardelle, *Mission à Rome*, 18.

20. *DDF*. I/2, no. 382 (see also Lagardelle, *Mission à Rome*, 24-25); *DDF*, I/3, no. 107 (Note de la Direction Politique, 8 April 1933); no. 134 (Jouvenel to Paul-Boncour, 15 April 1933).

21. *DDF*, I/3, no. 158 (Puaux to Paul-Boncour, 21 April 1933); no. 163 (Paul-Boncour to Puaux, 22 April 1933); nos. 204, 223, 255 (28 April, and 1 May, 8 May 1933).

22. Ibid., no. 312 (Jouvenel to Paul-Boncour, 23 May 1933).

23. Ibid., no. 386 (Jouvenel to Paul-Boncour, 13/14 June 1933); no. 428 (Jouvenel to Paul-Boncour, 28 June 1933).

24. *DDF*, I/4, no. 82 annex (Paul-Boncour to French representatives in Berlin, Rome, Prague and Vienna, 4 August 1933); nos. 94, 98 (Rome to Paris, 7 and 9 August 1933); no. 101 (Angues Barthon de Montbas, chargé in Vienna, to Paul-Boncour, 10 August 1933); no. 129 (Paul-Boncour to Rome, Prague, Belgrade, Bucharest, 22 August 1933).

25. *DBFP*, II/5, no. 371 (28 August 1933); no. 322 (11 August 1933); see also no. 362 (25 August 1933); Aaron L. Goldman, "Sir Robert Vansittart's Search for Italian Cooperation Against Hitler, 1933-36."

26. *DDF*, I/4, no. 118.

27. Ibid., no. 180 (de Chambrun to Paul-Boncour, 5 September 1933); no. 193 annex (Paul-Boncour to de Chambrun, 10 September 1933).

28. Ibid., no. 288 (Pierre Arnal, chargé in Berlin, to Paul-Boncour, 6 October 1933); no. 404 (de Chambrun to Paul-Boncour, 7 November 1933); EMA/2, 7 N 2904, dossier 3 (Parisot, military attaché in Rome to EMA/2, 8 February 1934); *DDF*, I/5, no. 341 (de Chambrun to Daladier, 7 February 1934); see also de Chambrun, *Traditions et souvenirs*, 191, and Lagardelle, *Mission à Rome*, 75.

29. This interpretation acquires additional credence in the following anecdote. When Mussolini asked him for his frank assessment of the Austrian question, the Italian military attaché in Vienna replied that, given Austria's weakness, it might be best simply to recognize the fact that *Anschluss* was inevitable. Mussolini responded "'I understand your feeling, but to have fought the war and to have been victorious only to have Germany on my head . . . never!'" *DDF*, I/4, no. 374 (Beauverger, chargé in Budapest, to Paul-Boncour, 30 October 1933).

30. *DDF*, I/5, no. 399 (de Chambrun to Barthou, 17 February 1934); see also Lowe and Marzari, *Italian Foreign Policy*, 227.

31. Noël, *Illusions de Stresa*, 169-70; Robertson, *Mussolini as Empire-Builder*, 66-67.

32. *DDF*, I/5, no. 445 (de Chambrun to Barthou, 28 February 1934); no. 451 (Barthou to de Chambrun, 1 March 1934).

33. Ibid., no. 405 (Naggiar to Barthou, 19 February 1934).

34. François-Poncet, *Souvenirs*, 207; EMA/2, 7 N 2915 (de Chambrun to Quai d'Orsay, 16 June 1934); Lagardelle, *Mission à Rome*, 86; *DDF*, I/6, no. 511 [sic—misnumbered; it should be no. 512]; see also Scott, *Alliance Against Hitler*, 184.

35. *DDF*, I/7, nos. 1, 89 (Dampierre to Barthou, 27 July 1934; Piétri, interim minister of foreign affairs, to Dampierre, 10 August 1934); no. 108 (Piétri to Dampierre, 16 August 1934); Goldman, "Sir Robert Vansittart," 106; Noël, *Illusions de Stresa*, 171.

36. *DDF*, I/7, no. 24 (Dampierre to Barthou, 30 July 1934); Dampierre, "Dix années de politique française," 2:277-78.

37. Anthony J. Komjathy, *The Crises of France's East Central European Diplomacy, 1933-1938,* 80; François-Poncet, *Souvenirs,* 202-3; Charles-Roux, *Huit ans au Vatican,* 114.

CHAPTER 6

1. Duroselle, *La décadence,* 88.
2. Ibid., 88-112; Cameron, *Prologue to Appeasement,* 76-80.
3. Cameron, *Prologue to Appeasement,* 97; Scott, *Alliance Against Hitler,* 201; *DDF,* I/7, no. 205 (de Chambrun to Barthou, 1 September 1934); MAE, "Italie," Z 374-14, vol. 320, pp. 16-19 (Léger to de Chambrun, 14 September 1934); *DDF,* I/7, no. 347 (Barthou to de Chambrun, 5 September 1934).
4. *DDF,* I/7, nos. 265, 290 (de Chambrun to Barthou, 7 and 11 September 1934); MAE, "Italie," Z 378-14, vol. 320, pp. 26-30 (de Chambrun to Barthou, 19 September 1934); pp. 31-32 (de Chambrun to Paris, 23 September 1934).
5. MAE, "Yougoslavie," Z 751-1 sd 2, vol. 181, pp. 138-52 (Foreign Ministry note on "Affaires Yougoslaves," 29 September 1934); *DDF,* I/7, no. 409 (Barthou to de Chambrun, 3 October 1934); Aloisi, *Journal,* 221-22 (entry for 24 September 1934); MAE, "Yougoslavie," Z 751-1 sd 2, vol. 181, pp. 138-52; Flandin, *Politique française,* 103; Kovrig, "Mediation by Obfuscation," 193-94.
6. Chastenet, *Histoire de la Troisième République* 5:102-3; Robertson, *Mussolini as Empire-Builder,* 101.
7. Duroselle, *La décadence,* 125-30.
8. Ibid., 123-25; Flandin, *Politique française,* 169; Robertson, *Mussolini as Empire-Builder,* 86.
9. Kovrig, "Mediation by Obfuscation," 196-200; Aloisi, *Journal,* 227.
10. *DDF,* I/7, no. 492 (Naggiar to Laval, 19 October 1934); no. 488 (Laval to de Chambrun, 18 October 1934); no. 499 (Roger Cambon in London to Laval, 22 October 1934).
11. EMA/2, 7 N 2904, dossier 4 (Parisot to EMA/2, 18 November 1934); *DDF,* I/7, no. 566; MAE, "Italie," Z 374-12, 14, 15, vol. 318, pp. 54-85 (Laval to de Chambrun, 31 October 1934).
12. A week later, Suvich made a specific proposal on Tunisia the effect of which would delay for a generation the return of Italians to French law in the Regency. De Chambrun was very reserved in his reaction to the Italian formula but regarded it as of some importance in showing that Italy at least accepted the principle of the renunciation of the 1896 accords. MAE, "Italie," Z 374-14, vol. 320, pp. 43-44 (de Chambrun to Laval, 29 November 1934).
13. *DDF,* I/8, no. 97 (de Chambrun to Laval, 20 November 1934); Dampierre, "Dix années de politique française," 2:279.
14. *DDF,* I/8, no. 235 (de Chambrun to Laval, 12 December 1934); no. 246 (de Chambrun to Laval, 13 December 1934); Robertson, *Mussolini as Empire-Builder,* 91; Aloisi, *Journal,* 238 (entry for 14 December 1934).
15. *DDF,* I/8, no. 247 (Laval to de Chambrun, 13 December 1934); MAE, "Italie," Z 347-14, vol. 320, pp. 48-50 (Léger to Belgrade, 18 December 1934).
16. Aloisi, *Journal,* entries for 25, 29, 30 December 1934; Robertson, *Mussolini as Empire-Builder,* 109-10; *DDF,* I/8, nos. 323, 346 (Laval to Naggiar, 27 December 1934; Naggiar to Laval, 29 December 1934).
17. A substantial segment of *DDF,* I/8 deals with these negotiations.
18. Dampierre, "Dix années de politique française," 2:281; *DDF,* I/8, no. 267 (de Cham-

brun to Laval, 17 December 1934) (my emphasis); no. 332 (de Chambrun to Laval, 27 December 1934) (emphasis in original).

19. *DDF*, I/8, no. 327 (Laval to de Chambrun, 27 December 1934); no. 388 (Laval to Albert Bodard, French minister to Addis Ababa, 3 January 1935).

20. Milza, *L'Italie fasciste*, 155-73.

21. Geneviève Tabouis, *Ils l'ont appelée Cassandre*, 215; Elizabeth R. Cameron, "Alexis Saint-Léger Léger," in Gordon Craig and Felix Gilbert, eds., *The Diplomats, 1919-1939*, 384; Laval cited in Geneviève Tabouis, *Vingt Ans de suspense diplomatique*, 221; Alfred Mallet, *Pierre Laval* 1:70-72; Aloisi, *Journal*, 246 (entry for 6 January 1935); Tabouis, *Cassandre*, 222.

22. *DDF*, I/8, no. 420. The text of the public portion of the Laval-Mussolini Accords was published in *DIA 1935* (London, 1936), 1:18-24.

23. Cited in Geoffrey Warner, *Pierre Laval and the Eclipse of France*, 69.

24. *DDF*, I/8, no. 420. This particular volume was published only in 1979. See also D.C. Watt, "The Secret Laval-Mussolini Agreement of 1935."

25. Edouard Herriot, minister without portfolio in the Laval government, commented to his diary that he and others observed in the cabinet meeting of 10 January 1935—"and Laval does not deny it—that this accord on Ethiopia is very disturbing for the future" (*Jadis* 3:493-94). For more recent published assessments of the Ethiopian question, see the following: George W. Baer, *Test Case: Italy, Ethiopia and the League of Nations;* Lowe and Marzari, *Italian Foreign Policy;* Denis Mack Smith, *Mussolini's Roman Empire;* Charles O. Richardson, "The Rome Accords of January 1935 and the Coming of the Italian-Ethiopian War"; Robertson, *Mussolini as Empire-Builder*. An able review of much of this literature can be found in Denis Smyth, "Duce Diplomatico."

26. *DDF*, I/8, no. 434 (Laval to de Chambrun, 10 January 1935); no. 441 (François-Poncet to Laval, 10 January 1935); MAE, "Italie," Z 374-12, 14, 15, vol. 318 (François-Poncet to Laval, 8 January 1935); François-Poncet, *Souvenirs*, 221; Baer, *Coming of the Italo-Ethiopian War*, 87; *JO*, Ch., *Débats*, 23 March 1935, 1208; *JO*, Sén., *Débats*, 27 March 1935, 395; Blum, *L'Histoire jugera*, 100-102.

27. Reynaud, *Au coeur de la mêlée*, 102-6; Maurice Thorez, *Notre lutte pour la paix*, 39-40; Alexander Werth, *The Twilight of France, 1933-1940*, 39-40; Fred Kupferman, *Pierre Laval*, 40. It is interesting to note that in his recently published (1987) and expanded biography, Kupferman has considerably moderated his assessment of Laval's diplomacy (*Laval, 1883-1945*, 128-33).

28. *Le Procès du Maréchal Pétain*, 183; Pierre Laval, *Laval Parle*, 225; cited in Macartney and Cremona, *Italian Foreign and Colonial Policy*, 131-32.

29. These letters are fully reproduced in Lagardelle, *Mission à Rome*, 112-17, 275-87.

30. This view is not shared by all historians. Renzo de Felice published in 1974 evidence that he claimed exposed Laval's behavior as a ruse. *Mussolini il Duce*, vol. 1, *Gli anni del consenso, 1929-1936*, 525-33; see also Nicholas Rostow, *Anglo-French Relations, 1934-36*, 77. The French documents support Laval's claim, and Duroselle does not question them on this point. It is also interesting to note that Denis Mack Smith does not seem to regard De Felice's evidence too seriously (*Mussolini's Roman Empire*, 65).

31. *Le Procès Pétain*, 437-39; Guariglia, *La diplomatie difficile*, 60; Eden in *DBFP*, II/14, no. 327; Denis Mack Smith, *Mussolini*, 274-75; Bonnet, *Quai d'Orsay*, 136; Duroselle, *La décadence*, 132-33; Milza, *L'Italie fasciste*, 155-67.

32. FO 371/19496, pp. 96-99, 166-79 (Drummond to F.O., 8 January 1935); pp. 199-205 (minutes on cover of dispatch from Drummond to Sir John Simon, 8 January 1935); FO

371/19497, pp. 302-3 (Sir Eric Phipps in Berlin to Department, 21 January 1935); FO 800/274, Sargent Papers, pp. 291-97 (letter from British Embassy in Paris, 16 December 1934).

CHAPTER 7

1. EMA/2, 7 N 2904, dossier 4 (Parisot to EMA/2, 19 October 1934); *DDF,* I/8, no. 88 (Parisot to General Maurin, minister of war, 18 November 1934).
2. Lagardelle, *Mission à Rome,* 117; *DDF,* I/8, no. 454 (de Chambrun to Laval, 12 January 1935); I/9, no. 37 (Parisot to Maurin, 20 January 1935); EMA/2, 7 N 2905, dossier 1 (Parisot to Maurin, 20 January 1935); 7 N 2917, dossier 1; *DDF,* I/9, no. 99 (Maurin to Laval, 28 January 1935).
3. *DDF,* I/9, no. 86 (Laval to de Chambrun, 26 January 1935); EMA/2, 7 N 2905, dossier 1 (Parisot to Maurin, 29 January 1935).
4. EMA/2, 7 N 2905, dossier 1 (Note en vue d'une Réunion Éventuelle du Haut Comité Militaire, 8 February 1935); *DDF,* I/9, no. 112 (de Chambrun to Laval, 29 January 1935).
5. EMA/2, 7 N 2917, dossier 1 (Maurin to Laval, 8 February 1935).
6. Gamelin, *Servir* 2:163-64; *DDF,* I/9, no. 99 (Maurin to Flandin, 28 January 1935); EMA/2, 7 N 2917, dossier 1 (Instructions for Parisot, 8 February 1935); *DDF,* I/9, no. 288 (de Chambrun to Laval, 27 February 1935).
7. Warner, *Pierre Laval and the Eclipse of France,* 71; Laval cited in Duroselle, *La décadence,* 134-35, 136.
8. *DDF,* I/10, no. 69 (de Chambrun to Laval, 30 March 1935); no. 101 (de Chambrun to Laval, 3 April 1935).
9. Ibid., no. 103 (Laval to de Chambrun, 3 April 1935); *DBFP,* II/12, no. 697 (Clerk to Simon, 5 April 1935).
10. *DDF,* I/10, no. 112 (de Chambrun to Laval, 4 April 1935); no. 162 (Corbin to Laval, 10 April 1935). The text of the 3 February 1935 communiqué is in *DDF,* I/9, no. 144.
11. *DDF,* I/10, nos. 139, 162 (Corbin to Laval, 6 and 10 April 1935).
12. *DBFP,* II/12, no. 682 (Simon to Clerk and Drummond, 2 April 1935); no. 685 (Drummond to Simon, 3 April); no. 686 (Clerk to Simon, 3 April).
13. Text of the Stresa Agreements can be found in *DIA 1935* 1:80-82.
14. Flandin, *Politique française,* 177-78. Substantially the same view of this conversation appears in de Chambrun, *Traditions et Souvenirs,* 209; Lagardelle, *Mission à Rome,* 128-32; and Mallet, *Pierre Laval* 1:79.
15. Noël, *Illusions de Stresa,* 81-86; Robertson, *Mussolini as Empire-Builder,* 130-31.
16. Lagardelle, *Mission à Rome,* 132; *DBFP,* II/12, no. 722; see also Rostow, *Anglo-French Relations,* 145, 150.
17. *Le Temps* cited in Micaud, *French Right and Nazi Germany,* 40-45 (see also Wolfers, *Britain and France,* 147-48); François-Poncet, *Souvenirs,* 235; *DDF,* I/10, nos. 194, 200 (Prague and Belgrade to Laval, 15 and 16 April 1935).
18. Bonnet, *Quai d'Orsay,* 137-38; Chastenet, *Histoire de la Troisième République* 4:111-12; Aloisi, *Journal,* 265. See also *DDF,* I/10, no. 196 (de Chambrun to Laval, 15 April 1935) which reports enthusiastically favorable Italian press reaction.
19. Blum, *L'Histoire jugera,* 103-5.
20. Noël, *Illusions de Stresa,* 70-80. Given the thin documentation on Stresa at the Quai d'Orsay, Duroselle regards Noël as the most reliable witness (*La décadence,* 137).

21. Charles Bloch, "Great Britain, German Rearmament, and the Naval Agreement of 1935," in *European Diplomacy Between the Wars*, ed. by Hans Gatzke, 136; Michael Newman, "The Origins of Munich: British Policy in Danubian Europe, 1933-1939," 379.

22. Flandin, *Politique française*, 172-73. Flandin first disclosed that pledges of military aid had been exchanged at Stresa in a debate on the floor of the Chamber of Deputies on 26 February 1936 (*JO*, Ch., *Débats*, 26 February 1936, p. 640).

23. EMA/2, 7 N 2917, dossier 1 (2 April 1935); (Parisot to Maurin, 28 March 1935; Maurin to Parisot, 3 April 1935).

24. Robertson, *Mussolini as Empire-Builder*, 132; Noël, *Illusions de Stresa*, 183-87; *DDF*, I/10, no. 404 (Parisot to Maurin, 17 May 1935); no. 459 (de Chambrun to Laval, 26 May 1935).

25. General Staff negotiations can be followed on a day-by-day basis in the following file in the Army Archives at Vincennes: EMA/2, 7 N 2917, dossier 1.

26. Gamelin, *Servir* 2:165-66; EMA/2, 7 N 2917, dossier 1 (Maurin to Laval, 17 June 1935).

27. *DDF*, I/11, no. 179 and annex (Gamelin to Minister of War Fabry, 29 June 1935).

28. Ibid. (Note on "Cooperation Franco-Italienne," 14 June 1935); see also Robert J. Young, "French Military Intelligence and the Franco-Italian Alliance, 1933-1939," 159-62.

29. *JO*, Sén., comité secret (March 1940), 6-7; see also Jean Fabry, *De la Place de la Concorde au course de l'Intendance*, 133-38.

30. Gamelin, *Servir* 2:166; Warner, *Pierre Laval and the Eclipse of France*, 95-96.

31. Hines Hall, "The Foreign Policy-Making Process in Britain, 1934-1935, and the Origins of the Anglo-German Naval Agreement," 495-96.

32. A. J. Marder, "The Royal Navy and the Ethiopian Crisis of 1935-36," 1327-30; Paul Getizon, *Défense de l'Italie*, 129-31, 136; Mallet, *Pierre Laval* 1:80-81.

33. MAE, FN, "Papiers Edouard Herriot," vol. 35 (Léger to French ambassador in London, 17 June 1935); ibid (Note in Herriot's handwriting, 18 June 1935); Herriot, *Jadis* 2:562; Pierre Laval, *Diary of Pierre Laval*, 15. See also Flandin, *Politique française*, 175-76. A full discussion of the London Conference and the acrimonious negotiations that led to the 3 February 1935 declaration occurs in Rostow, *Anglo-French Relations*, 83-119.

34. *DGFP*, ser. C, IV, no. 275 (28 August 1935).

35. D.C. Watt, "The Anglo-German Naval Agreement of 1935: An Interim Judgment," 170; *DBFP*, II/13, no. 369; Bloch, "Naval Agreement," 125-51.

36. MAE, FN, "Papiers Gaston Doumergue," vol. 4, pp. 17-18 (letter dated 19 June 1935); Laval cited in Pierre Renouvin, "Les Relations franco-anglaises, 1935-1939: Esquisse provisoire," in *Les Relations Franco-Britanniques de 1935-1939*, 19.

37. Noël, *Illusions de Stresa*, 100; see also Flandin, *Politique française*, 177-79; Cameron, *Prologue to Appeasement*, 129; Werth *Twilight of France*, 51.

38. Bloch, "Naval Agreement of 1935," 145-46; Watt, "Anglo-German Naval Accord," 173-74.

39. CAB 23/82, Cabinet 33(35)4 (Cabinet Conclusions, 19 June 1935); *DBFP*, II/13, no. 362 (Clerk to Hoare, 21 June 1935); Robertson, *Mussolini as Empire-Builder*, 148-49.

40. Cited in Mario Toscano, "Eden's Mission to Rome on the Eve of the Italo-Ethiopian Conflict," in *Studies in Diplomatic History and Historiography*, ed. by A. O. Sarkissian, 132-34.

41. Ibid., 133-34.

42. FO 371/19499, R 4616-1937, pp. 176-79 (Neville Henderson in Belgrade to Hoare, 17 July 1935). An official in the Yugoslav Foreign Ministry had confidentially shown Henderson a document summarizing the results of Gamelin's visit to Rome and allowed him to copy it.

43. *DDF*, II/1, nos. 82, 83; Noël, *Illusions de Stresa*, 201-3; Duroselle, *La décadence*, 138;

Robert J. Young, *In Command of France: French Foreign Policy and Military Planning 1933-1940*, 90-91, 103.

44. EMA/2, 7 N 2917, dossier 1 (compte-rendu of a conversation between General Loizeau and François-Poncet, undated but it must have been written shortly after the outbreak of the Italo-Ethiopian War).

45. Fabry, *De la Place de la Concorde*, 66-67; *Évén. Sur.*, ser. 2, 7, p. 2057.

CHAPTER 8

1. In addition to the literature cited in Chapter 6, note 25, the reader's attention is also called to the following: Aaron L. Goldman, "Sir Robert Vansittart's Search for Italian Cooperation Against Hitler, 1933-36"; R. A. C. Parker, "Great Britain, France and the Ethiopian Crisis, 1935-1936"; James C. Robertson, "The Hoare-Laval Plan"; Rostow, *Anglo-French Relations*.

2. Rostow, *Anglo-French Relations*, 195. On 3 August the League Council added a fifth arbitrator to the Italo-Ethiopian arbitration commission in an effort to break the deadlock and agreed to reconvene in September to review the results. At that time, the Council would also consider wider issues such as Ethiopia and Italy's competing claims to sovereignty over the Ogaden.

3. Fabry, *De la Place de la Concorde*, 61; Maurice Beaumont, *Gloires et tragédies de la III République*, 365; see also Cameron, *Prologue to Appeasement*, 139-40.

4. *DDF*, 1/11, no. 54 (Guérin to Quai d'Orsay, 11 June 1935).

5. Ibid., no. 311 (Laval to de Chambrun and London, 19 July 1935; Aloisi, *Journal*, 280 (entry dated 23 June 1935); *DBFP*, II/14, no. 384 (Clerk to Hoare, 23 July 1935); see also FO 800/295, Samuel Hoare's Papers, pp. 8-10 (letter from Eric Drummond, 18 June 1935).

6. Lowe and Marzari, *Italian Foreign Policy*, 177-78; FO 371/19499, R 4928/1/67, pp. 227-31 (16 August 1935).

7. *DGFP*, ser. C, vol. 4, no. 194 (German ambassador in Rome to Wilhelmstrasse, 5 July 1935); Aloisi, *Journal*, entry for 31 July 1935; Lord Avon, *Facing the Dictators: The Memoirs of Anthony Eden*, 251-52.

8. Aloisi, *Journal* 297 (entry dated 17 August 1935); see also Robertson, *Mussolini as Empire-Builder*, 162.

9. Aloisi, *Journal*, 299 (entry dated 21 August 1935); FO 800/295, Hoare Papers, pp. 101-6 (Vansittart to Hoare, 19 August 1935); pp. 140-45 (Drummond to Hoare, 27 August 1935).

10. Fabry, *De la Place de la Concord*, 69-71; Lagardelle, *Mission à Rome*, 149.

11. MAE, FN, "Papiers Herriot," vol. 34 (Herriot's handwritten notes on the meeting of 28 August 1935); see also Herriot, *Jadis* 2: 574-75; Fabry, *De la Place de la Concorde*, 69-71.

12. Piétri cited in Renouvin, "Les Relations franco-anglaises," 22-23; Marder, "Royal Navy," 1332; Robertson, *Mussolini as Empire-Builder*, 166, 172-73. Robertson maintains that both Hoare and Laval admired Mussolini and feared that his downfall would lead to chaos in Italy with the consequent strengthening of communism in the Peninsula.

13. Avon, *Facing the Dictators*, 257-58.

14. *DDF*, I/12, no. 132 (Laval to Corbin in London, 8 September 1935); no. 145 (Corbin to Laval, 10 September 1935).

15. The matter was communicated by Hoare to the English Cabinet on 19 September. CAB 24/256, C.P. 177 (35), pp. 357-58.

16. See, for example, Robertson, *Mussolini as Empire-Builder*, 166-67.

17. MAE, FN, "Papiers Dommergue," vol. 4, p. 72 (letter dated 14 September 1935); Ro-

bertson, *Mussolini as Empire-Builder,* 174; MAE, FN, "Papiers Herriot," vol. 35 (Laval to de Chambrun, 19 September 1935); *DDF,* I/12, no. 192 (Laval in Geneva to Quai d'Orsay, 19 September 1935); Aloisi, *Journal,* 303 (entry dated 11 September 1935).

18. FO 800/295, Hoare Papers, pp. 219-27 (Hoare to the King, 14 September 1935); Marder, "Royal Navy," 1332; CAB 24/256, C.P. 179 (35), pp. 366-69; FO 800/295, Hoare Papers, pp. 241-46 (Hoare to Eden, 24 September 1935); CAB 23/82, Cabinet 43(35)1, pp. 198-203. Hoare believed that it would be difficult for France not to come to England's aid in such a situation because "the strongest elements in the [Laval] Government were led by M. Herriot."

19. *DDF,* I/12, no. 241 and annex (Hoare to Corbin, 26 September 1935). In his recent book, Nicholas Rostow gives a rather favorable assessment of British policy in this matter. He cites Hoare's response to Laval but does not point out his caveat about "unprovoked aggression" (*Anglo-French Relations,* 217).

20. MAE, sér. Y, "Intérnationale," vol. 443, pp. 48-50 (François-Poncet to Laval, 30 September 1935); Cameron, *Prologue to Appeasement,* 154, 159; Micaud, *French Right,* 56-58.

21. Gamelin, *Servir* 2:173.

22. Baer, *Test Case,* 2-10.

23. Milza, *L'Italie fasciste,* 188-209; Arthur H. Furnia, *The Diplomacy of Appeasement: Anglo-French Relations and the Prelude to World War II, 1931-1938.* 165-66n; Néré, *Foreign Policy of France,* 177-78; Chastenet, *Histoire de la Troisième République* 4:122; Gentizon, *Défense de Italie,* 139; FO 371/18811, C 7110/6562/62, pp. 7-14 (confidential memorandum from H. Lloyd Thomas, 7 October 1935); FO 800/295, Hoare Papers, pp. 269-70 (Eden to Hoare, 7 October 1935); Laval cited in Baer, *Test Case,* 63.

24. *DDF,* I/12, no. 326 (Corbin to Laval, 3 October 1935).

25. MAE, sér. Y, "Intérnationale," vol. 443, pp. 132-33 (Massigli in Geneva to Quai d'Orsay, 14 October 1935).

26. Werth, *Twilight of France,* 53-54.

27. *DBFP,* II/15, no. 79 (Hoare to Clerk, 14 October 1935); no. 81 (Clerk to Hoare, 15 October 1935); FO 800/295, Hoare Papers, pp. 304-6 (Hoare to Eden, 16 October 1935).

28. CAB 46 (35) minutes (cited in Marder, "Royal Navy," 1347). A similar discussion of the implications of Laval's response occurred among permanent officials at the Foreign Office. FO 371/18811, C 7211/6562/62, pp. 15-26 (Foreign Office minutes, 18 October 1935).

29. Goldman, "Sir Robert Vansittart," 120; Gamelin, *Servir* 2:166-76; John C. Cairns, "A Nation of Shopkeepers in Search of a Suitable France," 731.

30. MAE, sér. Y, "Intérnationale," vol. 443, pp. 139-45 (Corbin to Quai d'Orsay, 18 October 1935).

31. FO 432/1, pt. 4, no. 47; ibid., nos. 64, 66, 73 (27 November 1935); FO 371/19166, pp. 479-81 (5 December 1935); Marder, "Royal Navy," 1346.

32. MAE, sér. Y, "Intérnationale," vol. 444, pp. 13-15 (aide-mémoire from Italian Embassy to Quai d'Orsay, 8 November 1935); Lagardelle, *Mission à Rome,* 184.

33. MAE, sér. Y, "Intérnationale," vol. 444, pp. 10-12, 20-24 (aide-mémoire from Quai d'Orsay to Italian Embassy, 14 November 1935; my emphasis); MAE, FN, "Papiers Herriot," vol. 35 (Laval to de Chambrun, 9 November 1935).

34. Laval cited in Cameron, *Prologue to Appeasement,* 166; Largardelle, *Mission à Rome,* 183.

35. EMA/2, 7 N 2905, dossier 2 (Parisot to Minister of War, 18 November 1935); Gamelin, *Servir* 2:177-82; EMA/2, 7 N 2905, dossier 2 (Parisot to Minister of War, 19 November 1935).

36. Count Jan Szembek, *Journal, 1933-1939,* 138.

37. This was the characterization of the French Minister of War, Jean Fabry, (*De la Place de la Concorde,* 72).

38. Mallet, *Pierre Laval* 1:110; Viscount Templewood, *Nine Troubled Years,* 179-81; CAB 24/257, C.P. 233(35), pp. 319-20 (7 December 1935); C.P. 235(35), pp. 322-24 (8 December 1935).

39. Marder, "Royal Navy," 1341-42. Monsell made these observations in a personal letter to Marder. The latter noted that Ramsey MacDonald was the only other member of the cabinet to support the Admiralty chief.

40. Cabinet Conclusions 53(35), 10 December 1935. Laval may also have been impressed by the fact that Mussolini had withdrawn Italian divisions from the Brenner frontier as a countermeasure against the threatened oil sanctions. The Hoare-Laval Plan would perhaps result in their reinstatement. *DGFP,* ser. C, vol. 4, no. 457 (memorandum recording conversation between a German official and Count Magistrati, first secretary of the Italian Embassy in Berlin, 12 December 1935).

41. Herriot, *Jadis* 2:261.

42. MAE, FN, "Papiers Herriot," vol. 35 (Laval to de Chambrun, 10 December 1935).

43. Aloisi, *Journal,* 328-29; FO 371/19169, p. 6; FO 401/35, pt. 25, no. 263 (cited in Baer, *Test Case,* 138); *DGFP,* ser. C. vol. 4, no. 457 (Foreign Ministry memorandum, 12 December 1935).

44. Mallet, *Pierre Laval* 1:111 and note; Tabouis, *Cassandre,* 158-60; Aloisi, *Journal,* 331 (entry dated 17 December 1935); EMA/2, 7 N 2905, dossier 3 (Air attaché in Rome to Minister of Air, 20 December 1935). Fred Kupferman ably summarizes the demise of the Hoare-Laval Plan and suggests, although concrete evidence is lacking, that important officials at the Quai d'Orsay such as Pierre Comert, chief of press services, or even Léger himself, might have been responsible for the sabotage (*Laval, 1883-1945,* 162-63).

45. The evidence indicates that the British Cabinet vastly underestimated the depth of public revulsion against Hoare-Laval. Thus, even though a large majority of the Cabinet approved in advance the concessions Hoare made, he alone was allowed to accept the blame. The chief beneficiary was Anthony Eden, named foreign minister by Baldwin on 22 December. Parker, "Great Britain, France and the Ethiopian Crisis," 302-24.

46. Aloisi, *Journal,* 331 (entry dated 18 December 1935).

47. The texts of these two letters are reproduced in Lagardelle, *Mission à Rome,* 275-78.

48. François-Poncet, *Souvenirs,* 299.

49. Cecil cited in Gaetano Salvemini, *Prelude to World War II,* 495; Jules-François Blondel, *Ce que mes yeux ont vu de 1900 à 1950* 2:76-77.

50. Delbos cited in John Dreifort, *Yvon Delbos at the Quai d'Orsay: French Foreign Policy During the Popular Front, 1936-1938,* 28; Reynaud, *Au coeur de la mêlée,* 115-19 (see also Reynaud, *La France a sauvé l'Europe* 1:162; Blum, *L'Histoire jugera,* 138.

51. Laval cited in Gentizon, *Défense de l'Italie,* 146-47. The entire course of the debate on the confidence motions can be reviewed in *JO,* Ch., *Débats,* 27 and 28 December 1935, passim.

52. MAE, sér. Y, "Intérnationale," vol. 444, pp. 61-62 (Dampierre to Laval, 3 January 1936); EMA/2, 7 N 2906, dossier 1 (Military attaché in Rome to EMA/2, 10 January 1936).

53. Blum, *L'Histoire jugera,* 147; Herriot, *Jadis* 2:635-37; Warner, *Pierre Laval,* 129.

54. *Le Temps,* 24 January 1936.

55. For example, see Warner, *Pierre Laval,* 130-31; Alexander Werth, *France, 1940-1955,* 101-2; Robert Frankenstein, "The Decline of France and French Appeasement Policies, 1936-39," in *The Fascist Challenge and the Policy of Appeasement,* ed. Wolfgang Mommsen and Lothar Kettenacker, 237.

56. Reynaud, *La France a sauvé l'Europe 1:175;* Pierre Renouvin, *Histoire des Relations Intérnationales: Les crises du XXe siècle* 8, pt. 2:85; Duroselle, *La décadence,* 131, 136, 149; René Remond, review of *La décadence,* in *Revue historique,* 415-24. Duroselle describes

Laval's policies as "half measures" and "little steps" and ascribes his failures not so much to wrongheadedness as to an inability or unwillingness to commit himself to a single line of policy and then pursue it energetically.

57. Such linkage was common in books and memoirs published during and shortly after the war. It was implicit in Laval's trial in 1945. The most recent example in a book published in 1984 in which the author concluded that Laval's acrimonious disputes with the British over Ethiopia "were steps to Vichy and collaboration after 1940; to his imprisonment and death after the war; and to the crystallisation of his reputation as an amoral manipulator and traitor" (Rostow *Anglo-French Relations*, 78).

58. *DGFP*, ser. C, vol. 4, no. 480 (Hassell to Wilhelmstrasse, 2 January 1936); Chastenet, *Histoire de la Troisième République* 6:125.

59. *DDF,* II/1, no. 99 (Laval to Mussolini, 23 January 1936).

CHAPTER 9

1. Parker, "Great Britain, France and the Ethiopian Crisis," 325.
2. Esmond M. Robertson, "Hitler and Sanctions: Mussolini and the Rhineland," 421.
3. Ibid., 420; MAE, sér. Y. "Intérnationale," vol. 444, pp. 108-11 (de Chambrun to Flandin, 25 January 1936); p. 117 (Léger to de Chambrun, 29 January 1936); EMA/2, 7 N 2906, dossier 1 (Parisot to EMA/2, 29 January 1936), emphasis in original.
4. *DGFP,* ser. C, vol. 4, nos. 553, 579; EMA/2, 7 N 2906, dossier 2 (Financial attaché in Rome to Minister of Finance, 6 February 1936); MAE, FN, "Papiers Doumergue, vol. 4, p. 190 (letter dated 15-16 February 1936); *DDF,* II/1, no. 209 (de Chambrun to Flandin, 20 February 1936).
5. Aloisi, *Journal,* 352 (entry dated 24 February 1936); *DDF,* II/1, no. 224 (de Chambrun to Flandin, 25 February 1936).
6. *DDF*, II/1, no. 239 (de Chambrun to Flandin, 27 February 1936); Largardelle, *Mission à Rome,* 235-37; EMA/2, 7 N 2906, dossier 2 (Parisot to Minister of War, 28 February 1936).
7. *DDF,* II/1, no. 283 annex (Flandin to Eden, 3 March 1936); Reynaud, *La France a sauvé l'Europe,* 174-75; *DDF,* II/1, no. 295 (Corbin to Flandin, 6 March 1936).
8. Aloisi, *Journal* (entry dated 10–11 March 1936).
9. *DDF,* II/1, no. 442 (de Chambrun to Flandin, 16 March 1936); nos. 368, 371 (François-Poncet to Flandin, 10 March 1936); see also no. 353 (Charles-Roux at the Vatican to Flandin, 9 March 1936), and no. 378 (de Chambrun to Flandin, 10 March 1936); no. 248 (Léon Noël in Warsaw to Flandin, 28 February 1936).
10. Robert J. Young, "Preparations for Defeat: French War Doctrine in the Inter-war Period," 167-68; Rostow, *Anglo-French Relations,* 243-44; *DDF,* II/1, no. 518 (de Chambrun to Flandin, 27 March 1936); EMA/2, 7 N 2906, dossier 3 (Parisot to Minister of War, 29 March 1936).
11. *DGFP,* ser. C, vol. 5, no. 180 (German chargé in Paris to Wilhelmstrasse, 22 March 1936); EMA/2, 7 N 2907, dossier 4 (Air attaché in Rome to Minister of Air and EMA/2, 20 and 30 March 1936).
12. *DDF,* II/1, no. 526; II/2, no. 17 (de Chambrun to Flandin, 29 March and 3 April 1936).
13. Flandin, *Politique française,* 189-90.
14. *DDF,* II/1, no. 533 (Corbin to Flandin, 20 April 1936); CAB 24/262, p. 68, C.P. 122(36), 27 April 1936.

15. *DDF*, II/2, no. 98 (de Chambrun to Flandin, 20 April 1936); see also MAE, "Italie," Z 374-4, vol. 308, pp. 112-14 (de Chambrun to Flandin, 17 April 1936).
16. *DDF*, II/2, no. 173 (de Chambrun to Flandin, 7 May 1936); Aloisi, *Journal*, 385 (entry dated 13 May 1936); *DDF*, II/2, no. 189 (Flandin to de Chambrun, 9 May 1936); MAE, "Italie," Z 374-1 sd 1, 2, 3, vol. 303, p. 26 (de Chambrun to Paris, 9 May 1936); *DDF*, II/2, no. 199 (Massigli to Flandin, 12 May 1936).
17. *DDF*, II/2, no. 220 (Note for the Council of Ministers, 16 May 1936).
18. Ibid., no. 248 (de Chambrun to Flandin, 26 May 1936); no. 210 (de Chambrun to Paris, 14 May 1936); no. 234 (Puaux in Vienna to Flandin, 23 May 1936).
19. EMA/2, 7 N 2907, dossier 1 (Parisot to Minister of War, 30 May 1936). Badoglio repeated this message in a subsequent conversation with Parisot on 9 June 1936. See dossier 2.
20. MAE, "Italie," Z-374-1 sd 1, 2, 3, vol. 303, pp. 125-26 (de Chambrun to Flandin, 30 May 1936).
21. Paul-Boncour, *Entre deux guerres* 3:49-52.
22. Flandin, *Politique française*, 191; Blum cited in Werth, *Twilight of France*, 89; Dreifort, *Yvon Delbos*, 24; *DDF*, II/2, no. 233 (Flandin to Corbin, 23 May 1936).
23. Paul-Boncour, *Entre deux guerres* 3:52-54; Baer, *Test Case*, 263-64; Goldman "Sir Robert Vansittart's Search," 126-28.
24. *DDF*, II/2, no. 275 (Note by Massigli, 5 June 1936).
25. EMA/2, 7 N 2917, dossier 1 (Note by the Political Director titled "Tendence de la politique italienne," 4 June 1936). This important document was not published in *DDF*, and I was unable to locate a copy of it in the Archives of the Ministry of Foreign Affairs. A handwritten note accompanying the document at the Army Archives at Vincennes, dated 18 October 1963, says that the original at the Quai d'Orsay was marked "Remis aux 3 chefs d'état-major." Thus, it may be the document referred to by General Gamelin in *Servir* 2: 223-24. Massigli, when asked about it on 18 October 1963, said he did not remember.
26. *DDF*, II/2, nos. 339, 359 (Blondel to Delbos, 23 and 26 June 1936); Bonnet, *Le Quai d' Orsay*, 176-78; Frankenstein, "The Decline of France," in Mommsen and Kettenacker, eds., *The Fascist Challenge*, 239-40; Lagardelle, *Mission à Rome*, 240.
27. *DDF*, II/2, nos. 346 and 368 (de Chambrun to Delbos, 24 and 29 June 1936).
28. Yvon Delbos, *L'expérience rouge*, 228; Bonnet, *Le Quai d'Orsay*, 178; Dreifort, *Yvon Delbos*, 153; *DDF*, II/1, no. 432 (de Chambrun to Flandin, 14 March 1936).
29. EMA/2, 7 N 2915 (de Chambrun to Quai d'Orsay, 10 June 1936); *DDF*, II/2, no. 278 (François-Poncet to Delbos, 6 June 1936); no. 374 (Parisot to Daladier, Minister of National Defense and War, 30 June 1936); *DGFP*, ser. C, vol. 5, no. 457 (Von Hassell to Wilhelmstrasse, 17 July 1936); text of Austro-German agreement reproduced in ser. D, vol. 1, no. 152.
30. MAE, "Italie," Z 374-1 sd 1, 2, 3, vol. 303, pp. 150-51 (Blondel to Delbos, 20 June 1963); sér. Y, "Intérnationale," vol. 444, p. 141 (de Chambrun to Delbos, 5 July 1936).
31. *DDF*, II/2, no. 408 (Delbos to London and Rome, 8 July 1936); MAE, sér. Y, "Intérnationale," vol. 444, pp. 148-51 (François-Poncet to Delbos, 10 July 1936); pp. 175-80 (Corbin to Delbos, 28 July 1936.
32. *DDF*, II/2, no. 415 (Corbin to Delbos, 9 July 1936); no. 479 (Delbos to Rome, Berlin, London, Brussels, 18 July 1936).
33. Dante A. Puzzo, *Spain and the Great Powers*, 42-43; *DDF*, II/3, no. 46 (French resident general in Rabat to Delbos, 30 July 1963); John F. Coverdale, *Italian Intervention in the Spanish Civil War*, 3-5.
34. Coverdale argues that Mussolini's primary goal in Spain was the negative one of interdicting the transshipment of French colonial forces rather than a positive desire to obtain new bases for Italy (Coverdale, *Italian Intervention*, 89-90, 388-89).

35. *DDF,* II/3, nos. 33, 34, 36 (Delbos to Minister of Finance, 26 July; to French ambassador in Madrid, 27 July; circular to major embassies, 27 July). See also Malcolm Muggeridge, ed., *Ciano's Diplomatic Papers,* 22-23.

36. *DDF,* II/3, no. 56 (Delbos to Rome, London, 1 August 1936). While this message was being delivered to Rome and London, the French Cabinet revealed its ambivalence by secretly authorizing Pierre Cot, the minister of air and the most outspoken pro-Spanish member of the Popular Front coalition, to ship aircraft directly to Spain. This action was a response to Italian and German aid to the rebels. Some 38 French aircraft reached the Republic (Coverdale, *Italian Intervention,* 89-92 and notes).

37. *DDF,* II/3, nos. 111, 112 (Delbos to major embassies and the Minister of Finance, 9 August 1936).

38. On 3 November 1935, Alfred Mallet, the editor-in-chief of *Petit Journal,* published the results of a public opinion survey in France similar to the "Peace Ballot" in England. The Patenôtre Press offered its readers three choices with regard to the Ethiopian crisis. The results were as follows: (1) absolute neutrality (530,000), (2) graduated economic sanctions (310,000), (3) military sanctions (10,000). Source: Kupferman, *Pierre Laval,* 49.

39. Cameron, "Léger," in Craig and Gilbert, eds., *The Diplomats* 2:391. This view is accepted by Puzzo, *Spain and the Great Powers,* 86-88, and can also be found in Wolfers, *Britain and France Between Two Wars,* 151-52. See also *Évén. Sur.* 1:217.

40. David Carlton, "Eden, Blum and the Origins of Nonintervention," 40-55; M. D Gallagher, "Léon Blum and the Spanish Civil War," 56-64; Coverdale, *Italian Intervention,* 92; Werth, *Twilight of France,* 117; Micaud, *French Right,* 108-32.

41. Sir Basil Liddell Hart, *The Liddell Hart Memoirs* 2:127-28; see also Jean Lacouture, *Léon Blum,* 326.

42. Dreifort, *Yvon Delbos,* 48-50. A good summary of the nonintervention debate in France can be found in Helmut Gruber, *Léon Blum, French Socialism, and the Popular Front: A Case of Internal Contradictions,* 19-26.

43. *DDF,* II/3, no. 49 (de Chambrun to Delbos, 30 July 1936); no. 81 (François-Poncet to Delbos, 5 August 1936); nos. 90, 104, 143, 144, 173 (de Chambrun to Delbos, 14 August 1936).

44. Ibid., no. 185 (de Chambrun to Delbos, 21 August 1936); Puzzo, *Spain and the Great Powers,* 131-33.

45. Coverdale, *Italian Intervention;* see also Smyth, "Duce Diplomatico," 999; *FRUS, 1936* 2:510-11; *DDF,* II/3, no. 186 (de Chambrun to Delbos, 21 August 1936).

46. *DDF,* II/3, no. 229 (de Chambrun to Delbos, 8 September 1936); Paul Reynaud, *Mémoires,* vol. 2, *Envers et contre tous,* 122.

47. Blondel, *Ce que mes yeux* 2:83-85; *DDF,* II/3, no. 318 (de Chambrun to Delbos, 7 October 1936); MAE, "Italie," Z 374-1 sd 1, 2, 3, vol. 303, pp. 208-11 (Delbos to de Chambrun, 13 October 1936); de Chambrun, *Traditions et souvenirs,* 227; Lagardelle, *Mission à Rome,* 247.

48. Noël, *Illusions de Stresa,* 109; de Chambrun, *Traditions et souvenirs,* 228.

49. Raymond J. Sontag, *A Broken World, 1919-1940,* 298.

50. Young, "Preparations for Defeat," 168. Scepticism about the Franco-Soviet accord was not shared by the entire French right wing; politicians such as Paul Reynaud, Georges Mandel, and Ernest Pezet in the Chamber of Deputies and journalists such as Pertinax, Georges Bidault, and De Kerillis believed the Russian connection necessary to contain the German danger (Micaud, *French Right,* 70).

51. Cited in Neville Thompson, *The Anti-Appeasers: Conservative Opposition to Appeasement in the 1930s,* 35-36.

52. Marder, "Royal Navy," 1351-56.

53. MAE, FN, "Papiers Doumergue," vol. 4, p. 270 (letter dated 23 July 1936); *DDF,* II/3, no. 381 (de Chambrun to Delbos, 20 October 1936).

CHAPTER 10

1. MAE, "Italie," Z 374-4, vol. 308, pp. 124-27 (de Chambrun to Delbos, 30 October 1936).
2. *DDF,* II/4, no. 175 and note (Delbos to Blondel, 19 December 1936); no. 182 (Blondel to Delbos, 21 December 1936); no. 222 (Blondel to Delbos, 29 December 1936); MAE, "Italie," Z 374-1 sd 1, 2, 3, vol. 304, p. 18 (Blondel to Paris, 24 February 1937).
3. EMA/2, 7 N 2909, dossier 4 (Note by Parisot on "Mussolini et la France," 20 April 1937); MAE, "Italie," Z 374-4, vol. 308, pp. 139-42 (Dampierre to Delbos, 20 April 1937).
4. EMA/2, 7 N 2908, dossier 1 (17 August 1936); dossier 2 (30 September 1936); dossier 5 (17 December 1936).
5. *DDF,* II/3, no. 464 (Dampierre to Delbos, 10 November 1936); II/5, no. 89 (Blondel to Delbos, 10 March 1937).
6. Ibid., II/5, no. 153 (Dampierre to Delbos, 23 March 1937).
7. Ibid., no. 154 (Delbos to Dampierre, 23 March 1937).
8. Ibid., no. 40 (French minister in Prague to Delbos, 27 February 1937); EMA/2, 7 N 2909, dossier 4 (Parisot to Ministry of War, 1 April 1937); MAE, "Italie," Z 374-6, vol. 325, pp. 105-9 (Dampierre to Delbos, 27 March 1937).
9. Avon, *Facing the Dictators,* 472-75; Coverdale, *Italian Intervention,* 127, 198; *DGFP,* ser. D, vol. 3, pp. 132-33; *DIA, 1936,* 346-47; *1937,* 86.
10. *JO,* Ch., *Débats,* 5 December 1936, 3346-62; Milza, *Italie fasciste,* 210-11; Micaud, *French Right,* 123-24; see also Flandin, *Politique française,* 217-18.
11. *DDF,* II/4, no. 11 (Blondel to Delbos, 20 November 1936).
12. *DIA, 1937,* 86; *HCAP, 1936-37,* vol. 29, pp. 441ff; London *Times,* 22 December 1936; *DDF,* II/4, no. 30 (Corbin to Delbos, 24 November 1936); no. 139 (Note du Ministre, 12 December 1936).
13. *DDF,* II/4, no. 41 (Corbin to Delbos, 26 November 1936); no. 170 (Delbos to Corbin, 18 December 1936).
14. *BFSP 1937,* vol. 141, pp. 387-89.
15. *DGFP,* ser. D, vol. 3, p. 204.
16. Patricia A. M. van der Esch, *Prelude to War: the International Repercussions of the Spanish Civil War,* 90; *DGFP,* ser. C, vol. 3, pp. 230, 580; Grandi cited in John C. DeWilde, "The Struggle Over Spain," 17; *HCAP 1936-37,* vol. 28, pp. 687-707.
17. EMA/2, 7 N 2915 (Blondel to Quai d'Orsay, 20 March 1937); 7 N 2917, dossier 5 (22 May, 26 May, 29 May, 8 June 1937); *DDF,* II/5, no. 415 (François Charles-Roux to Delbos, 9 May 1937); no. 417 (Blondel to Delbos, 10 May 1937); II/6, no. 47 (François-Poncet, 10 June 1937); EMA/2, 7 N 2915 (20 March 1937); 7 N 2917, dossier 5 (April 1937); *DDF,* II/5, nos. 415, 417, 451, annex I (Delbos to Blondel, 22 May 1937); EMA/2, 7 N 2917, dossier 5 (Information for Deuxième Bureau, 22 July 1937).
18. EMA/2, 7 N 2917, dossier 5 (Note for Deuxième Bureau on the "possible attitude of Italy in the event of conflict," April 1937).
19. Roy Douglas, "Chamberlain and Eden, 1937-38." Corbin described a further split between Conservatives and the Liberal/Labor opposition over the question of recognizing the Italian conquest of Ethiopia. MAE, "Italie," Z 374-1 sd 1, 2, 3, vol. 304, pp. 43-48 (Corbin to Delbos, 27 May 1937).
20. Dreifort, *Yvon Delbos,* 60.

21. *House of Commons Debates*, ser. 5, vol. 326, col. 1804; *Ciano's Diplomatic Papers*, 132; *FRUS 1937* 1:357 (Bullitt to Secretary of State, 26 August 1937); *DDF*, II/6, no. 315 (François-Poncet to Delbos, 4 August 1937); no. 331 (Charles-Roux to Delbos, 13 August 1937); EMA/2, 7 N 2917, dossier 5 ("Propos du Cardinal Pacelli sur les rapports entre l'Allemagne et l'Italie," 26 August 1937).
22. *DDF*, II/6, no. 333 (Chautemps to London and Rome, 14 August 1937).
23. Ibid., no. 345 (Roger Cambon, chargé in London, to Delbos, 20 August 1937); no. 289 (Delbos to Corbin, 29 July 1937).
24. Ciano bragged about the torpedoings in his diary. See Count Galeazzo Ciano, *Hidden Diary*, ed. Malcolm Muggeridge, 9-11.
25. *Ciano's Diplomatic Papers*, 137n.
26. FO 371/21358, W 16229/23/41 (Eden to Lloyd Thomas in Paris, 26 August 1937); W16299/23/41 (Cambon to Eden, 30 August 1937).
27. Avon, *Facing the Dictators*, 519.
28. Cited in Arnold J. Toynbee, *Survey of International Affairs 1937* 2:345. See also Puzzo, *Spain and the Great Powers*, 196-200; Dreifort, *Yvon Delbos*, 60-76; Coverdale, *Italian Intervention*, 320-26.
29. *HCAP 1936-37* (28:385-406).
30. *House of Commons Debates*, ser. 5, vol. 327, col. 58.
31. Avon, *Facing the Dictators*, 468-71; Anthony Eden, *Foreign Affairs*, 228; *Le Temps*, 13 September; *La Dépêche de Toulouse*, 13 September; *La Lumière*, 17 September; *Le Populaire*, 12 September; *L'Action Française*, 12 September; Winston Churchill, *The Gathering Storm*, 246-48; A. J. P. Taylor, *The Origins of the Second World War*, 125; Louis Fischer, *Men and Politics: An Autobiography*, 445-47; Van der Esch, *Prelude to War*, 97; Dreifort, *Yvon Delbos*, 76-78.
32. Hugh Thomas, *The Spanish Civil War*, 447; Ciano, *Hidden Diary*, 15; *DGFP*, ser. D, vol. 3, p. 445.
33. London *Sunday Times*, 12 June 1938 (cited in Dreifort, *Yvon Delbos*, 76).
34. EMA/2, 7 N 2911, dossier 2 (Parisot note on "Les Possibilités de l'Armée italienne," 8 November 1937); *DDF*, II/7, no. 17 (Daladier to Delbos, 4 October 1937); no. 279 (Delbos to Blondel, 27 November 1937).
35. *DDF*, II/7, no. 288 (Charles-Roux to Delbos, 29 November 1937); no. 292 (Blondel to Delbos, 30 November 1937).
36. Pierre Renouvin, "Les relations de la Grande Bretagne et de la France avec l'Italie en 1938-1939," *Les Relations Franco-Britanniques*, 297; CAB 23/90, Cabinet 45 (37)5, pp. 215-23; MAE, "Italie," Z 374-1 sd/4, vol. 278, p. 1 (Quai d'Orsay to Rome, 5 December 1937).
37. *DDF*, II/7, no. 326 (Blondel to Delbos, 9 December 1937); no. 418 (Holy See to Paris, 9 January 1938).
38. EMA/2, 7 N 2915 (MAE to Minister of National Defense and War, 3 February 1938); MAE, "Italie, " Z 374-1 sd 1, 2, 3, vol. 304, pp. 113-14 (Blondel to Paris, 22 January 1938). Much of this entire volume of documents is devoted to reports from representatives in countries which made the decision to recognize the Italian conquest.
39. See, for example: EMA/2, 7 N 2909, dossier 4 (Note by General Parisot, 10 April 1937); *DDF*, II/5, no. 243 (Parisot to Daladier, 10 April 1937); II/7, no. 8 (François-Poncet to Delbos, 1 October 1937); no. 30 (Montbas, chargé in Vienna, to Delbos, 7 October 1937); no. 50 (Blondel to Delbos, 10 October 1937).
40. *DDF*, II/3, no. 473 (Puaux, minister in Vienna, to Delbos, 12 November 1936); II/4, no. 212 (Blondel to Delbos, 26 December 1936); II/5, no. 184 (Puaux to Delbos, 27 March 1937); EMA/2, 7 N 2915 (Delbos to Daladier, 25 March 1937); 7 N 2919, dossier 1 (Note for

the Deuxième Bureau on the Austrian crisis, 10 March 1938); *DDF,* II/5, no. 458 (Montbas to Delbos, 26 May 1937).
   41. *DDF,* II/7, no. 387 (Puaux to Delbos, 26 December 1937).
   42. Ibid., II/8, nos. 154, 186 (Puaux to Delbos, 13 and 17 February 1938); Perth to Eden, 16 February 1938 (cited in Douglas, "Chamberlain and Eden," 110).
   43. *DDF,* II/8, no. 190 (Delbos to Corbin, 17 February 1938); Young, *In Command of France,* 195.
   44. Avon, *Facing the Dictators,* 662-70; *Ciano's Diplomatic Papers,* 182-83; Renouvin, "Les Relations franco-anglaises," *Relations Franco-Britanniques,* 37-38; *DDF,* II/8, no. 304 and annex (Delbos to Corbin, 2 March 1938).
   45. *JO,* Ch., *Débats,* 25-26 February 1938, 595-646; Flandin, *Politique française,* 236; Micaud, *French Right,* 137-42; Werth, *Twilight of France,* 143-45.
   46. *DDF,* II/8, no. 213 (Blondel to Delbos, 19 February); no. 237 (Blondel to Delbos, 22 February); no. 239 (Puaux to Delbos, 22 February); nos. 263, 264 (Blondel to Delbos, 24 February); no. 321 (Charles-Roux to Delbos, 5 March 1938); no. 330 (Puaux to Delbos, 7 March 1938); Gabriel Puaux, *Mort et transfiguration de l'Autriche 1932-1945;* Renouvin, "Les relations de la Grande Bretagne et de la France," *Les Relations Franco-Britanniques,* 299; *DDF,* II/8, 369 and note (Blondel to Delbos, 11 March 1938); EMA/2, 7 N 2919, dossier 1 (minutes of conversation between Léger and Phipps).
   47. *DDF,* II/8, no. 414 (Blondel to Delbos, 13 March 1938); D. C. Watt, "Britain, France and the Italian Problem, 1937-1939," *Les Relations Franco-Britanniques,* 280.
   48. *DDF,* II/8, nos. 388, 414 (Blondel to Delbos, 12 and 13 March 1938); no. 486 (Blondel to Paul-Boncour, 17 March 1939); II/9, no. 87 (Blondel to Paul-Boncour, 30 March 1938); EMA/2, 7 N 2915 (French consul in Turin to Paul-Boncour, 17 March 1938; *DDF,* II/9, no. 87 (Blondel to Paul-Boncour, 30 March 1938); Blondel, *Ce que mes yeux ont vu,* 119.

CHAPTER 11

   1. FO 371/22402, R 852/23/22, p. 174 (Cranborne to Foreign Office, 28 January 1938); FO 371/22402, R 1055/23/22, R 1083/23/22, R 1054/23/22 (Perth to Foreign Office, 4 and 7 February 1938); *DBFP,* II/19, no. 557 (minutes dated 19 February 1938 on French proposal of the previous day).
   2. MAE, "Italie," Z 374-1 sd/4, vol. 278, pp. 49-50 (Corbin to Delbos, 23 February 1938); pp. 57-59 (Delbos to Corbin, 24 February 1938); FO 371/22404, R 1784/23/22 (Phipps to Foreign Office, 24 February 1938).
   3. *DBFP,* II/19, no. 589 (Halifax to Phipps, 25 February 1938); FO 371/22404, R 1788/23/24 (F. O. memorandum by Mr. Nichols, 25 February 1938); R 2110/23/22 (F. O. minutes and memoranda, 28 February 1938).
   4. MAE, "Italie," Z 374-1 sd/4, vol. 278, pp. 76-83 (Corbin to Delbos, 4 March 1938); *DBFP,* II/19, no. 621 (Phipps to Halifax, 5 March 1938); FO 371/22405, R 2188/23/22 (Perth to Foreign Office, 7 March 1938); MAE, "Italie," Z 374-1 sd/4, vol. 278, pp. 115-17 (Corbin to Delbos, 10 March 1938); *DBFP,* II/19, no. 626 (Halifax to Phipps, 10 March 1938); *DDF,* II/8, no. 420 (Note du Départment, 13 March 1938).
   5. *DDF,* II/8, no. 354 (Blondel to Delbos, 9 March 1938).
   6. FO 800/274, Sargent Papers, p. 335 (minute by Sargent, 17 March 1938); FO 371/22407, R 2840/23/22; R 2982/23/22; FO 371/22408, R 3283/23/22 (Perth to Foreign Office, 18, 19, 25 March 1938—minutes by Ingram and Sargent); FO 371/22409, R

3591/23/22 (Perth to Halifax, 3 April 1938); MAE, "Italie," Z 374-1 sd/4, vol. 278, pp. 144-58 (Note on Anglo-Italian negotiations, 22 March 1938).

7. *DDF,* II/9, no. 53 (Noël to Paul-Boncour, 26 March 1938); no. 86 (Charles-Roux to Paul-Boncour, 30 March 1938); EMA/2, 7 N 2918, dossier 1 (intelligence reports from Rome, 28 and 30 March 1938); 5 N 579, dossier 3 (Buisson's memo titled "L'Alliance France-Italie," cited in Young, "French Military Intelligence," 164).

8. MAE, "Italie," Z 374-12, 14, 15, vol. 318, pp. 236-38 (Blondel to Paul-Boncour, 5 April 1938); see also equally urgent dispatches in ibid., pp. 241-55 (8 April 1938), and *DDF,* II/9, nos. 75, 110 (29 March, 4 April 1938).

9. Paul-Boncour, *Entre deux guerres* 3:102.

10. The British initially had proposed a resolution calling for "recognition" of the Italian conquest. The French, however, felt this wording would hurt her bargaining position with Italy and suggested instead a resolution freeing member nations to decide for themselves what "consequences to draw from the situation of fact existing in Ethiopia." London accepted the French wording. *DBFP,* II/19, no. 641 (Halifax to Phipps, 29 March 1938); *DDF,* II/9, nos. 111, 150 (exchange of French and British notes, 5 and 9 April 1938).

11. *DDF,* II/9, no. 99 (Paul-Boncour to Blondel, 1 April 1938); no. 119 (Blondel to Paul-Boncour, 6 April 1938); no. 129 (Massigli to Blondel, 7 April 1938); see also no. 160 (Note du Direction Politique, 11 April 1938).

12. *HCAP 1937-38* vol. 31, cmd. 5726.

13. MAE, "Italie," Z 374-12, 14, 15, vol. 318, pp. 268-69 (Blondel to Bonnet, 14 April 1938); *DDF,* II/9, no. 180 (Blondel to Bonnet, 14 April 1938). Ciano apparently told the German ambassador in Rome that Italy had no intention "of letting herself be led into negotiations with France through any side roads. The French should first send an ambassador, then the rest could follow." *DGFP,* ser. D, vol. 1, no. 737 (Mackensen to Wilhelmstrasse, 15 April 1938).

14. *DDF,* II/9, no. 183 (Bonnet to Rome and London, 15 April 1938). Ciano remarked to Perth that he was glad that the French had abandoned the idea of a nonofficial envoy; he liked Blondel and was happy that eventual conversations would be with him. FO 371/22426, R 3947/23/22 (Perth to F.O., 16 April 1938).

15. *DDF,* II/9, no. 194 (Blondel to Bonnet, 16 April 1938).

16. Ibid., no. 213 (Blondel to Bonnet, 20 April 1938); see also EMA/2, 7 N 2917, dossier 4 ("État d' esprit après l'Anschluss," 27 April 1938). It is also worth noting that whereas the Germans displayed little alarm at the conclusion of the Anglo-Italian accord, they were much more suspicious of French approaches to Italy, which seemed to them to be an effort to revive the Stresa Front. The German press reaction also betokened lack of confidence in Italy. FO 371/22426, R 4148/240/22 (Henderson to F.O., 21 April 1938).

17. Ciano, *Hidden Diary,* 104-5 (entries for 20-22 April 1938); Georges Bonnet, *De Washington au Quai d'Orsay,* 145; Jules Blondel, *Au fil de la carriè*re, 380.

18. *DDF,* II/9, no. 214 (Bonnet to Blondel, 21 April 1938). For background on the preparation of this agenda see ibid., no. 195 (Note du Directeur Politique, 16 April 1938).

19. Noël, *Illusions de Stresa,* 123-24; FO 371/22426, R 4132/240/22 (Phipps to F. O., 21 April 1938); see also Sargent's minute in R 4241/240/22 (23 April 1938).

20. *DDF,* II/9, no. 217 (Blondel to Bonnet, 22 April 1938); MAE, "Italie," Z 374-12, 14, 15, vol. 319, pp. 44-47 (Blondel to Bonnet, 30 April 1938); *DDF,* II/9, no. 260 (Blondel to Bonnet, 1 May 1938).

21. Blondel expressed these convictions to the British ambassador in Rome. FO 371/22426, R 4409/240/22 (Perth to F.O., 30 April 1938).

22. *DDF,* II/9, no. 241 (Bonnet to Corbin, 26 April 1938); CAB 24/276, C.P. 109 (38), (Record of Chamberlain-Halifax/Daladier-Bonnet conversations, 28-29 April 1938); CAB 23/93, Cabinet 22(38)2 (Cabinet Conclusions, 4 May 1938). Shortly after the formation of Blum's second cabinet, the premier issued a secret order opening the frontier. Daladier maintained the open frontier for some time after the fall of the Popular Front. During April and May, 1938, some 300 Soviet aircraft and 25,000 tons of war materiel crossed the Pyrenees into Spain (Coverdale, *Italian Intervention,* 354-55).

23. FO 371/22426, R 4781/240/22 (minutes by Nichols, Cadogan, Roberts, and others on Perth's dispatch of 12 May 1938).

24. *DDF,* II/9, nos. 313, 315, 332 (Blondel to Bonnet, 11 and 13 May 1938); EMA/2, 7 N 2919, dossier 1 (military attaché in Geneva to General Colson, chief of Army General Staff, 13 May 1938).

25. Lowe and Marzari, *Italian Foreign Policy,* 310-11; *DDF,* II/9, no. 339 and note (Blondel to Bonnet, 14 May 1938); no. 357 (Blondel to Bonnet, 17 May 1938); MAE, "Italie," Z 374-12, 14, 15, vol. 319, pp. 133-36 (Blondel to Bonnet, 20 May 1938; FO 371/22419, R 4865/43/22 (Perth to Halifax, 14 May 1938); CAB 23/93, Cabinet 24(38)5 (Cabinet Conclusions, 18 May 1938); *DGFP,* ser. D, vol. 1, no. 763 (Welczeck to Ribbentrop, 16 May 1938); FO 371/22426, R 4824/240/22 (Phipps to Halifax, 15 May 1938).

26. *DDF,* II/9, no. 351 (Bonnet to Blondel, 16 May 1938); FO 371/22426, R 4929/240/22 (Record of Cadogan/Corbin interview, 17 May 1938); *DDF,* II/9, no. 369 (Blondel to Bonnet, 18 May 1938); MAE, "Italie," Z 374-12, 14, 15, vol. 319, pp. 114-18 (Bonnet to Corbin, 19 May 1938).

27. *DDF,* II/9, no. 373 (Bonnet to Corbin and Blondel, 19 May 1938); no. 433 (Note on Bonnet/Prunas audience, 23 May 1938); MAE, "Italie," Z 374-12, 14, 15, vol. 319, pp. 149-50 (Bonnet to Corbin, 24 May 1938).

28. MAE, "Italie," Z 374-12, 14, 15, vol. 319, pp. 156-57 (Blondel to Bonnet, 2 June 1938); EMA/2, 7 N 2912, dossier 3 (Résumé by Parisot of "La Politique Étrangère de l'Italie," 9 June 1938); FO 371/22426, R 5293/240/22, R 5301/240/22 (Phipps to F.O. on notes handed to him by Bonnet, 3 June 1938).

29. MAE, "Italie," Z 374-12, 14, 15, vol. 319, pp. 179-82 (Bonnet to Corbin, 20 June 1938); Z 374-1 sd/4, vol. 279, pp. 28-31 (Corbin to Bonnet, 20 June 1938); FO 371/22427, R 5606/240/22 (Phipps to F.O., 15 June 1938); R 5954/240/22 (Phipps to F.O., 30 June 1938); R 5738/240/22 (Phipps to F.O., 21 June 1938); R 5392/240/22 (Halifax to Phipps, 14 June 1938); *DDF,* II/10, no. 62 (Corbin to Bonnet, 20 June 1938); no. 67 (Blondel to Bonnet, 21 June 1938); CAB 23/94, Cabinet 29(38)4 (Cabinet Conclusions, 22 June 1938); MAE, "Italie," Z 374-12, 14, 15, vol. 319, pp. 185-86 (Corbin to Bonnet, 24 June 1938); EMA/2, 7 N 2918, dossier 1 (25 June 1938); see also Renouvin, "Les Relations de la Grande Bretagne," *Relations Franco-Britanniques,* 303.

30. *DDF,* II/10, no. 108 (Blondel to Bonnet, 28 June 1938); FO 371/22413, R 5978/23/22 (Perth to F. O., 2 July 1938); MAE, "Italie," Z 374-12, 14, 15, vol. 319, pp. 194-97 (Blondel to Bonnet, 5 July 1938); CAB 23/94, Cabinet 31(38)5 (Cabinet Conclusions, 6 July 1938); EMA/2, 7 N 2913, dossier 2 (note by Parisot on "La Politique Extérieure de l'Italie, 9 July 1938); FO 371/22413, R 6020/23/22 (Perth to Halifax and minutes, 6 July 1938); *DGFP,* ser. D, vol. 1, no. 799 (Welczeck to Ribbentrop, 16 August 1938).

31. See, for example, EMA/2, 7 N 2915 (French consul in Naples to Foreign Ministry, 1 June 1938); 7 N 2918, dossier 4 (French military attaché in Rome to EMA /2, 30 August 1938); *DDF,* II/10, no. 418 (Blondel to Bonnet, 19 August 1938); no. 421 (Charles-Roux to Blondel, 20 August 1938); no. 466 (Blondel to Bonnet, 26 August 1938).

32. Young, *In Command of France*, 206-7.
33. EMA/2, 7 N 2917, dossier 4; 7 N 2919, dossiers 1 and 2 (documents dated 12, 13, 14, 28 September 1938); *DDF*, II/10, no. 425 (Blondel to Bonnet, 20 August 1938).
34. André François-Poncet, *Au Palais Farnèse: Souvenirs d'une ambassade à Rome, 1938-1940*, 9.
35. Robert J. Young, "The Aftermath of Munich: The Course of French Diplomacy, October 1938 to March 1939," 312. Young's source for this information was a personal letter to him from General Olivier Poydenot recalling this incident.
36. *DDF*, II/11, no. 521 (Blondel to Bonnet, 2 October 1938); II/12, no. 31 (Note of EMA/2 on daily meeting at Quai d'Orsay, 5 October 1938); Georges Bonnet, *Fin d'une Europe*, 2:63-64.
37. *DBFP*, III/3, no. 329 (Perth to Halifax, 3 October 1938); MAE, "Italie,"Z 374-1 sd/4, vol. 279, pp. 97-98 (Blondel to Bonnet, 4 October 1938); FO 371/22415, R 8578/23/22 (extract from Cabinet Conclusions, 26 October 1938); *DBFP*, III/3, no. 355 (Halifax to English representatives, 26 October 1938).
38. *DBFP*, III/3, no. 357 (Halifax to Phipps, 26 October 1938); nos. 363, 369 (Phipps to Halifax, 29 and 31 October 1938).
39. MAE, "Italie," Z 374-1 sd/4, vol. 279, pp. 130-33 (Corbin to Bonnet, 3 November 1938); pp. 161-67 (text to Anglo-Italian declarations, 16 November 1938); *DDF*, II/12, no. 236 (Blondel to Bonnet, 28 October 1938).

CHAPTER 12

1. Anthony Adamthwaite, "France and the Coming of War," *Fascist Challenge*, ed. Mommsen and Kettenacker, 246-56.
2. René Massigli, *La Turquie devant la guerre: Mission à Ankara*, 17-21. Anatole de Monzie maintained that Bonnet never worked toward Léger's dismissal for fear of creating a lasting and bitter personnel situation at the Quai d'Orsay (De Monzie, *Ci-devant*, 54 [entry for 13 November 1938]).
3. A useful corrective to Adamthwaite is Robert Young, *In Command of France*, 216-17.
4. Ciano, *Hidden Diary*, 190 (entry for 5 November 1938); *DGFP*, ser. D, vol. 4, no. 335 (Mackensen to Ribbentrop, 6 October 1938); François-Poncet, *Au Palais Farnèse*, 13, 44-49.
5. Guariglia, *La Diplomatie difficile*, 83. As one reads through the entire chapter devoted to his ambassadorship in Paris (pp. 79-169), it seems that he was studiously ignored by Ciano and Mussolini and left virtually without instructions.
6. EMA/2, 7 N 2918, dossier 5 (19 November 1938). The French military attaché clarified this statement by explaining that what Ciano really meant was that Italy had not *increased* the size of her effectives in Spain; those withdrawn had been replaced but not increased (EMA/2, 7 N 2913, dossier 6, 16 November 1938).
7. *DDF*, II/12, no. 288 (François-Poncet to Bonnet, 10 November 1938).
8. Ibid., no. 330 (François-Poncet to Bonnet, 19 November 1938); EMA/2, 7 N 2918, dossier 5 (6 December 1938); *DDF*, II/12, nos. 433, 434 (François-Poncet to Bonnet, 29 November 1938); FO 371/22427, R 9268/240/22 (F.O. memo, 18 November 1938); R 9294/240/22 (Orme Sargent memo, 25 November 1938); *DDF*, II/12, no. 318 (François-Poncet to Bonnet, 16 November 1938); also no. 379 (23 November 1938).
9. MAE, "Italie," Z 374-4, vol. 308, pp. 224-25 (François-Poncet to Bonnet, 30 November 1938); *DDF*, II/13, no. 1 (François-Poncet to Bonnet, 1 December 1938); François-Poncet,

Au Palais Farnèse, 21-22; Young, "Aftermath of Munich," 315-16; Charles-Roux, *Huit ans au Vatican,* 311.

10. Bonnet, *Fin d'une Europe* 2:68; *DDF,* II/13, nos. 2, 3 (Bonnet to François-Poncet, 1 December 1938); MAE, "Italie," Z 374-4, vol. 309, pp. 79-84; *DDF,* II/13, no. 15 (François-Poncet to Bonnet, 3 December 1938); Bonnet, *Fin d'une Europe* 2:65.

11. *DDF,* II/13, nos. 5, 9; MAE, "Italie," Z 374-4, vol. 309, pp. 27-33 (François-Poncet to Bonnet, 1 December 1938); MAE, "Italie," Z 374-4, vol. 309, pp. 85-91 (François-Poncet to Bonnet, 3 December 1938); EMA/2, 7 N 2917, dossier 4 (note dated 1 December 1938); *DGFP,* ser. D, vol. 4, no. 421 (Ciano to Ribbentrop, 2 January 1939).

12. MAE, "Italie," Z 374-4, vol. 309, pp. 1-4 (François-Poncet to Bonnet, 1 December 1938).

13. *DGFP,* ser. D, vol. 4, no. 369 (text of Franco-German declaration of 6 December 1938); MAE, "Italie," Z 374-4, vol. 310, pp. 30-31 (Bonnet to François-Poncet, 12 December 1938); EMA/2, 7 N 2913, dossier 6 (note by General Toussaint, French military attaché in Rome, 14 December 1938).

14. *DDF,* II/13, no. 50 (Hughes Barthan de Montbas, chargé in Berlin, to Bonnet, 7 December 1938); no. 63 (Toussaint to Daladier, 7 December 1938); *DBFP,* III/3, nos. 473, 474, 476 (Perth to Halifax, 4, 5, 14 December 1938); no. 469 (Halifax to Perth, 3 December 1938); FO 371/22428, R 9870/240/22 (minute by Noble on telegram from Perth to Halifax, 10 December 1938); MAE, "Italie," Z 374-4, vol. 309, pp. 251-53 (François-Poncet to Bonnet, 9 December 1938).

15. *DDF,* II/13, nos. 110, 130.

16. MAE, "Italie," Z 374-4, vol. 309, pp. 92-100 (François-Poncet to Bonnet, 3 December 1938).

17. MAE, "Italie," Z 374-4, vol. 309, pp. 117-19 (François-Poncet to Bonnet, 4 December 1938). It is worth mentioning that the Chamberlain/Halifax visit to Rome was planned without consultation with the French government. The latter was not even informed until an embarrassing press leak made it necessary for London to do so (FO 371/22417, R 9749/23/22 [26 November 1938]; FO 371/22416, R 9511/23/22 [28 November 1938]).

18. MAE, "Italie," Z 374-4, vol. 309, pp. 111-15, 117-19 (François-Poncet to Bonnet, 4 December 1938).

19. Ibid., pp. 120-22 (Bonnet to François-Poncet, 4 December 1938); *DDF,* II/13, no. 281 (François-Poncet to Bonnet, 4 December 1938); MAE, "Italie," Z 374-4, vol. 309, pp. 160-63; EMA/2, 7 N 2918, dossier 5.

20. *DDF,* II/13, no. 102 (Note by Léger, 12 December 1938); no. 115 (Note by Bonnet, 13 December 1938); no. 102 (Foreign Ministry note initialed by Léger, 12 December 1938); no. 115 (note by Bonnet, 13 December 1938).

21. This was the position articulated by Sir Alexander Cadogan, permanent undersecretary at the Foreign Office, to the French ambassador in London on 10 December 1938 (MAE, "Italie," Z 374-4, vol. 309, pp. 272-73).

22. *DDF,* II/13, no. 123; MAE, "Italie," Z 374-4, vol. 310, pp. 50-51 (François-Poncet to Bonnet, 14 December 1938); *JO,* Ch., *Débats,* 13 December 1938; Duroselle, *La décadence,* 391.

23. MAE, "Italie," Z 374-14, vol. 320, pp. 52-54; Bonnet, *Le Quai d'Orsay,* 249; Néré, *Foreign Policy of France,* 233-34.

24. MAE, "Italie," Z 374-14, vol. 320, pp. 55-56 (François-Poncet to Bonnet, 18 December 1938); *DDF,* II/13, no. 223 (Bonnet to Ciano, 25 December 1938).

25. *DDF,* II/13, no. 184 (Robert Coulondre, French ambassador in Berlin, to Bonnet, 20

December 1938); MAE, "Italie," Z 374-4, vol. 311, pp. 214-16 (François-Poncet to Bonnet, 9 January 1939).

26. *DDF*, II/13, no. 215 (François-Poncet to Bonnet, 23 December 1938). The French ambassador's particular concern about Tunisia and Jibuti was based upon military intelligence information indicating Italian troop concentrations in Eritrea and a concerted propaganda campaign among Italian communities in the Regency (EMA/2, 7 N 2918, dossier 4 [Toussaint to War Minister, 23 and 27 December 1938]).

27. *DDF*, II/13, no. 227 (François-Poncet to Bonnet, 26 December 1938); MAE, "Italie," Z 374-4, vol. 311, pp. 16-18 (Bonnet to Roger Cambon in London, 27 December 1938); *DDF*, II/13, nos. 229, 230, 231 (Bonnet to Cambon, 27 December 1938); see also Renouvin, "Les Relations . . . 1938-1939," *Les Relations Franco-Britanniques*, 306-8; Bonnet, *Fin d'une Europe* 2:68; *DBFP*, III/3, no. 484 (Phipps to Halifax, 26 December 1938).

28. Lengthy background reports on Franco-Italian rivalry over the past three years were prepared both by Phipps and by officials at the Foreign Office. *DBFP*, III/3, no. 479 (Phipps to Halifax, 19 December 1938); FO 371/22429, R 10108/240/22 (F.O. report on Tunisia, 17 December 1938).

29. FO 371/22429, R 10125/240/22 (minute by Ingram on telegram from Perth to Halifax, 20 December 1938); see also FO 371/22417, R 10223/23/22 (draft statement to Cabinet, 20 December 1938).

30. Bonnefous, *Histoire politique* 7:3; MAE, "Italie," Z 374-4, vol. 311, pp. 117-20 (Corbin to Bonnet, 4 January 1939); pp. 200-201 (François-Poncet to Bonnet, 7 January 1939).

31. *DDF*, II/13, no. 248 (François-Poncet to Bonnet, 29 December 1938); no. 256 (31 December 1938); no. 315 (note of the sous-directeur d'Europe, Henri Hoppenot, 8 January 1939); EMA/2, 7 N 2913, dossier 6 (note by Toussaint, 29 December 1938); MAE, "Italie," Z 374-4, vol. 311, pp. 134-36 (François-Poncet to Bonnet, 4 January 1939).

32. David Dilks, ed., *The Diaries of Sir Alexander Cadogan, 1938-1945*, 135; CAB 24/282, C.P. 8(39), 10 January 1939; *DDF*, II/13, no. 359 (François Poncet to Bonnet, 13 January 1939); MAE, "Italie," Z 374-1 sd/4, vol. 280, pp. 173-75 (Bonnet to Corbin, 15 January 1939); FO 800/319, Halifax Papers, pp. 3-6 (personal account of visit to Rome, 11-14 January 1939); De Monzie, *Ci-devant*, 75 (entry for 11 January 1939).

33. *DDF*, II/13, no. 360 (François-Poncet to Bonnet, 13 January 1939); no. 373 (16 January 1939); MAE, "Italie," Z 374-1 sd/4, vol. 280, pp. 195-96 (16 January 1939); *DDF*, II/13, no. 465 (Corbin to Bonnet, 30 January 1939). On the evolution of British policy, see FO 371/22429, R 10221/240/22 (Phipps to Halifax, 21 December 1938, with minutes by Ingram, Sargent and Cadogan on 31 December and 3 January).

34. FO 371/23792, R 961/7/22 (Perth to Halifax, 9 February 1939); *DBFP*, III/4, no. 330 (Perth to Halifax, 10 February 1939); Young, *In Command of France*, 224.

35. *DDF*, II/13, nos. 398, 434 (François-Poncet to Bonnet, 19 and 26 January 1939).

36. MAE, "Italie," Z 374-4, vol. 312, pp. 115-24 (François-Poncet to Bonnet, 2 February 1939).

37. *Évén. Sur.*, ser. 2, vol. 7, 2057-58; Bonnet, *Fin d'une Europe* 2:69; Paul Baudouin, "Un voyage à Rome (fevrier 1939)," 69-74. In the latter retrospective, Baudouin points out that while Bonnet exuded confidence in the project, Daladier was decidedly more reserved and skeptical.

38. *Évén. Sur.*, ser. 2, vol. 9, 2729-30 (Bonnet testimony); Noël, *Illusions de Stresa*, 139-40. Noël's judgement is shared by Duroselle, *La décadence*, 393-94.

39. *DDF*, II/14, no. 46 (review of Boudouin/Ciano conversations, 2-3 February 1939); Bonnet, *Quai d'Orsay*, 249-50.

40. MAE, "Italie," Z 374-4, vol. 312, pp. 198-99 (London to Paris, 16 February 1939);

Robert Coulondre, *De Staline à Hitler: Souvenirs de deux ambassades, 1936-1939; DDF,* II/14, no. 159 (Bonnet to François-Poncet, 21 February 1939); Bonnet, *Fin d'une Europe* 2:69n.

41. *DDF,* II/14, nos. 130, 131 (François-Poncet to Bonnet, 16 February 1939); Baudouin, "Un voyage à Rome," 80.

42. *DDF,* II/14, no. 238 (François-Poncet to Bonnet, 1 March 1939); MAE, "Italie," Z 374-4, vol. 312, pp. 275-76 (Bonnet to Corbin, 2 March 1939); vol. 313, pp. 83-85 (Corbin to Bonnet, 12 March 1939); pp. 88-89 (François-Poncet to Bonnet, 13 March 1939). The British were, however, surprised by the press revelations concerning the Baudouin mission and complained about not being kept informed (FO 371/23793, R 1243/7/22 [Perth to Halifax, 21 February 1939]; R 1379/7/22 [F.O. minutes, 23-24 February 1939]; R 1457/7/22 [Phipps to Halifax, 2 March 1939]).

43. *DDF,* II/14, no. 281 (Corbin to Bonnet, 8 March 1939); MAE, "Italie," Z 374-4, vol. 313, p. 104 (Corbin to Bonnet, 15 March 1939). This contrasts starkly with Baudouin's own assessment. He shows, quite correctly, that the Germans were fully informed immediately of the Baudouin project and hints that the Germans deliberately torpedoed it by orchestrating the premature press leak (Baudouin, "Un voyage à Rome," 81-82; see also *DGFP,* ser. C, vol. 4, no. 447 [Mackensen to Ribbentrop, 4 February 1939]).

44. Duroselle, *La décadence,* 412-13; Lowe and Marzari, *Italian Foreign Policy,* 325; MAE, "Italie," Z 374-4, vol. 313, pp. 105-6 (François-Poncet to Bonnet, 15 March 1939); see also pp. 107-9, 110-11.

45. *Ciano Diaries,* 46; MAE, "Italie," Z 374-4, vol. 313, p. 126 (François-Poncet to Bonnet, 17 March 1939).

46. Cited in René de Chambrun, *Pierre Laval devant l'histoire,* 95-98; MAE, "Italie," Z 374-4, vol. 313, p. 127 (François-Poncet to Bonnet, 18 March 1939).

47. FO 371/23794, R 2164/7/22 (Campbell to Sargent, minute by Noble, 25 March 1939); see also R 1932/7/22 (Campbell to Sargent, 20 March 1939) and R 1939/7/22 (F.O. minutes, 21 March 1939).

48. *DDF,* II/15, no. 91 (Daladier to Baudouin, 20 March 1939); Baudouin, "Un voyage à Rome," 82.

49. *DDF,* II/15, no. 110 (Gentizon to François-Poncet, 21 March 1939); MAE, "Italie," Z 374-4, vol. 313, p. 137 (François-Poncet to Bonnet, 21 March 1939); pp. 140-41 (Charles-Roux to Bonnet, 21 March 1939).

50. MAE, "Italie," Z 374-4, vol. 313, p. 144 (François-Poncet to Bonnet, 23 March 1939); Baudouin, "Un voyage à Rome," 84-85.

51. *DDF,* II/15, no. 162 (François-Poncet to Bonnet, 26 March 1939).

52. Ibid., nos. 166, 175 (François-Poncet to Bonnet, 27 and 28 March 1939); see also Duroselle, *La décadence,* 412-13.

53. MAE, "Italie," Z 374-4, vol. 313, p. 202 (Charles-Roux to Bonnet, 28 March 1939); Bonnet, *Fin d'une Europe* 2:72n; *DDF,* II/15, no. 190 (Noël to Bonnet, 29 March 1939).

54. Bonnet, *Fin d'une Europe* 2:72-73; Noël, *Illusions de Stresa,* 144-45; *DDF,* II/15, no. 193 (Note from "M. Nac" to Quai d'Orsay, 29 March 1939); EMA/2, 7 N 2917, dossier 6 (4 April 1939).

55. *DDF,* II/9, no. 75 (Blondel to Paul-Boncour, 29 March 1938); MAE, "Italie," Z 374-4, vol. 313, pp. 224-34 (François-Poncet to Bonnet, 29 March 1939).

56. See MAE, "Italie," Z 374-4, vols. 318-19.

57. Edouard Daladier, *Défense du pays,* 171-75; *DDF,* II/15, no. 165 (Note du président du Conseil, 26 March 1939); p. 293, note 2.

58. *DDF,* II/15, no. 201 (Corbin to Bonnet, 30 March 1939); MAE, "Italie," Z 374-4, vol.

314, pp. 5-6 (Bonnet to François-Poncet, 1 April 1939); vol. 313, pp. 257-62 (François-Poncet to Bonnet, 31 March 1939).
  59. *DDF,* II/15, no. 250 (M. de Vaux Saint-Cyr to Bonnet, 4 April 1939); *DBFP,* III/5, no. 73; nos. 76, 79 (see also D.C. Watt, "Britain, France and the Italian Problem, 1937-1939," *Les Relations Franco-Britanniques,* 289); *DDF,* II/15, no. 261 (François-Poncet to Bonnet, 5 April 1939).
  60. *DDF,* II/15, no. 409 (François-Poncet to Bonnet, 15 April 1939).
  61. Ciano cited in Mario Toscano, *The Origins of the Pact of Steel,* 232; see also Guariglia, *La diplomatie difficile,* 106.
  62. MAE, "Italie," Z 374-4, vol. 314, p. 77 (François-Poncet to Bonnet, 18 April 1939).
  63. FO 800/319, Halifax Papers, pp. 16-17 (Perth to Halifax, 19 April 1939); see also *DBFP,* III/5, no. 132 (Perth to Halifax, 11 April 1939); also nos. 194, 214, 228, 238, 328; CAB Conclusions 21(39)8; FO 371/23794, cited in Watt, "Britain, France and the Italian Problem," *Les Relations Franco-Brittaniques,* 289; *DDF,* II/15, no. 454 (François-Poncet to Bonnet, 20 April 1939); no. 465 (letter extracted from Bonnet papers, 21 April 1939).
  64. FO 371/23795, R 3350/7/22 (Phipps to Halifax, 27 April 1939); CAB 23/99, Cabinet 24(39)4, (Cabinet Conclusions, 26 April 1939); FO 371/23795, R 3323/7/22 (Note by Ingram, 26 April 1939).
  65. MAE, "Italie," Z 374-4, vol. 314 (Bonnet to Charles-Roux, 13 May 1939). The offer was rejected on the grounds of consistency, since France had previously rejected British mediation. Besides, the Vatican had proposed to link the resolution of the Franco-Italian problem with that of the German-Polish problem. The French quite rightly insisted that these were wholly separate issues.
  66. *DDF,* II/16, no. 21 (Bonnet to François-Poncet, 3 May 1939); no. 43 (François-Poncet to Bonnet, 4 May 1939); see also no. 76 and annex (Note du ministre, 5 May 1939); Bonnet, *Au Quai d'Orsay,* 250; Cameron, "Léger," in Craig and Gilbert, *The Diplomats* 2:398.
  67. *DBFP,* III/5, no. 603 (Loraine to Halifax, 23 May 1939).
  68. Bonnet, *Au Quai d'Orsay,* 251-52; *DBFP,* III/5, no. 255 (Phipps to Halifax, 22 April 1939); FO 371/23795, R 3675/7/22 (minute by Sargent, 10 May 1939, on telegram from Phipps to Halifax, 5 May 1939); *DDF,* II/16, no. 223 (François-Poncet to Bonnet, 18 May 1939); François-Poncet, *Au Palais Farnèse,* 92-102.

CHAPTER 13

  1. *DDF,* II/16, no. 328 (Coulondre to Bonnet, 1 June 1939). The Italians also blustered about the salutary effect of the Pact of Steel on Italo-Yugoslav relations. Fascist leaders felt that Yugoslavia had been effectively neutralized, its frontiers sufficiently weak to conform to Axis directives yet strong enough to resist—in accord with Italy—any eventual pressure from Germany toward the Adriatic (*DDF,* II/16, nos. 371, 400 [François-Poncet to Bonnet, 8 and 12 June 1939]).
  2. *DDF,* II/16, no. 282 (François-Poncet to Bonnet, 25 May 1938).
  3. MAE, "Italie," Z 374-4, vol. 314, pp. 172-73; *DDF,* II/17, no. 35 (Note de "M. Nac," 28 June 1939).
  4. FO 371/23795, R 4436/7/22 (Loraine to Halifax, 23 May 1939); R 4410/7/22 (Halifax to Phipps, 27 May 1939); R 4872/7/22 (minutes and drafts of proposed letter from Chamberlain to Daladier, 8-15 June 1939); R 5631/7/22 (Phipps to Halifax, 11 July 1939); CAB 23/99, Cabinet 31(39)4 (Cabinet Conclusions, 7 June 1939); FO 800/319, Halifax Papers, pp. 30-33

(Halifax to Runciman, 3 July 1939); *DBFP*, III/6, no. 317; *DDF*, II/17, no. 199 (Chamberlain to Daladier, 13 July 1939).

5. *DBFP*, III/6, no. 428; *DDF*, II/17, no. 293 (Daladier to Chamberlain, 24 July 1939).

6. See, for example, the following reports from Rome, Berlin, the Vatican and Warsaw for the period from 7 July to 12 August 1939: *DDF*, II/17, nos. 134, 332, 408, 423, 466, 478, 485, 498, 521, 523, 536.

7. EMA/2, 7 N 2919, dossier 3 (30 September 1939). Emphasis in original.

8. Watt, "Britain, France and the Italian Problem," *Les Relations Franco-Britanniques*, 288; *DBFP*, III/6, no. 536; *DDF*, II/17, no. 416 (Chamberlain to Daladier, 3 August 1939); CAB 53/11 (Chiefs of Staff 312th meeting, 24 August 1939); CAB 21/565 (Halifax to Campbell, 22 August 1939); *DGFP*, ser. D, vol. 7, no. 529 (memo by Weizsacker, German State Secretary, 1 September 1939). Pierre Renouvin has explained that Italy opted for "nonbelligerency" rather than "neutrality" in order to affirm solidarity with Germany while at the same time not enforcing the Pact of Steel (*Histoire des Relations Internationales* 8:242-43).

9. Renzo de Felice, *Fascism: An Informal Introducton to Its Theory and Practice*, 88.

10. Paul-Boncour, *Entre deux guerres* 3:166-67; Bonnet, *Quai d'Orsay*, 299-303; François-Poncet, *Au Palais Farnèse*, 130-35; *DBFP*, III/7, no. 604 (Phipps to Halifax, 31 August 1939); De Monzie, *Ci-devant*, 145-49 (entry for 31 August 1939); see also Bonnet's preface to Guariglia, *La Diplomatie difficile*, iii-iv.

11. *DBFP*, III/7, nos. 610, 653 (Loraine to Halifax, 31 August and 1 September 1939); MacGregor Knox, *Mussolini Unleashed, 1939-1941: Politics and Strategy in Fascist Italy's Last War*, 45-46. See also Charles-Roux, *Huit Ans au Vatican*, 335-36; Lowe and Marzari, *Italian Foreign Policy*, 359.

12. EMA/2, 7 N 2919, dossier 3 (confidential print, 15 November 1939); Lowe and Marzari, *Italian Foreign Policy*, 358-59.

13. Galeazzo Ciano, *Journal politique, 1939-1943* 1:147-48; Bonnet, *Fin d'une Europe* 2:382-83.

14. Bonnet, *Fin d'une Europe* 2:382-83. See also François-Poncet, *Au Palais Farnèse*, 146.

15. Bonnet, *Quai d'Orsay*, 311. See also *Fin d'une Europe* 2:75-80, 382-83.

16. MAE, "Italie," Z 374-4, vol. 314, pp. 221-22 (François-Poncet to Paris, 18 September 1939).

17. Pierre Guillen, "Le coopération économique entre la France et l'Italie de septembre 1939 à juin 1940," unpublished manuscript, 1980, cited in Jean-Baptiste Duroselle, *L'Abîme, 1939-1945*, 125-26; *DGFP*, ser. D, vol. 8, no. 504 (Mussolini to Hitler, 3 January 1940); De Monzie, *Ci-devant*, 183.

18. Duroselle, *L'Abîme*, 35.

19. François-Poncet, *Au Palais Farnèse*, 139-41.

20. Paul de Villelume, *Journal d'une défaite, avril 1939-juin 1940*, 16. Lieutenant Colonel Villelume was Gamelin's liaison officer at the Quai d'Orsay and, as such, in close touch with day-to-day policy formulation.

21. Quotations from the English official proceedings cited in François Bédarida, *La stratégie secrète de la drôle de guerre: le conseil suprême interallié, septembre 1939-avril 1940*, 97-98.

22. François-Poncet, *Au Palais Farnèse*, 111-17, 141-42; Ciano, *Journal politique* 1:192, 201-2 (citations for 31 December 1939 and 18 January 1940). Sir Percy Loraine also indicated that Ciano believed Italy's best interests lay in understanding and cooperation with England and France (FO 800/319, Halifax Papers, p. 157 [Loraine to Halifax, 29 December 1939]).

23. Count Galeazzo Ciano, *Les Archives secrètes du Comte Ciano, 1936-1942*, 309-10; CAB 65/1, War Cabinet 61(39)7 (War Cabinet Conclusions, 26 October 1939).

24. Bédarida, *La stratégie secrète*, 475ff; Ciano, *Journal politique* 1:177-78, 182, 188, 199; *DGFP*, ser. D, vol. 8, no. 504 (Mussolini to Hitler, 3 January 1940).

25. Lowe and Marzari, *Italian Foreign Policy*, 350-52, 362.

26. EMA/2, 7 N 2914, dossier 3 (Naval attaché in Rome to Admiral of the Fleet, 19 February 1940); François-Poncet, *Au Palais Farnèse*, 155-61.

27. Ciano, *Journal politique* 1:216 (1 and 2 March 1940); FO 371/24958, R 2813/438/22 (Campbell to F.O., 2 March 1940); Ciano, *Archives secrètes*, 362-67 (see also *Journal politique* 1:224 [18 March 1940]); De Monzie, *Ci-devant*, (22 March 1940).

28. EMA/2, 7 N 2919, dossier "propagande italienne" (no date, but context of documents suggests late March 1940); Duroselle, *L'Abîme*, 122.

29. Mallet, *Pierre Laval* 1:133; FO 371/24958, R 3871/438/22 (Campbell to F.O., 27 March 1940); R 3822/438/22 (Campbell to F.O., 27 March 1940 and Cadogan to Perth, 29 March 1940); François-Poncet, *Au Palais Farnèse*, 169-70; *DGFP*, ser. D, vol. 9, no. 84 (Mackensen to Ribbentrop, 10 April 1940).

30. EMA/2, 7 N 2915 (Note from Count Larnaudis to General Gamelin, 19 April 1940). Donini-Feretti further specified that Laval's presence in Rome must be made to appear entirely fortuitous and suggested the ruse of engine trouble forcing a landing in Rome en route to a mission elsewhere.

31. Reynaud, *La France a sauvé l'Europe* 2:183-85; *Au Coeur de la mêlée*, 596; *DGFP*, ser. D, vol. 9, no. 172 (Mackensen to Ribbentrop, 27 April 1940).

32. MAE, "Italie," Z 374-4, vol. 317, pp. 164-65 (Interior to Foreign Ministry, 23 May 1940); Charles-Roux, *Huit ans au Vatican*, 389-90. There is some indication that Charles-Roux's appointment was made in order to secure the use of his contacts in Rome and at the Vatican to work toward a last-minute papal intervention with Mussolini (MAE, "Italie," Z 374-1, 1A, 4, 5, 6, vol. 281, pp. 108-10 [Charles-Roux to Paris, 18 May 1940]); Reynaud, *La France a sauvé l'Europe* 2:200.

33. MAE, "Italie," Z 374-1, 1A, 4, 5, 6, vol. 281, p. 113 (Daladier to Saint Quentin, 20 May 1940); pp. 123-24 (Saint Quentin to Daladier, 21 May 1940).

34. FO 371/24958, R 6198/438/22 (Campbell to F.O., 21 and 23 May 1940); Knox, *Mussolini Unleashed*, 113; MAE, "Italie," Z 374-1, 1A, 4, 5, 6, vol. 281, pp. 172-73 (Daladier to François-Poncet, 27 May 1940); FO 371/24958, R 6198/438/22 (text of Franco-British note, 26 May 1940). Prior communications in this same file describe how the exact wording of the proposal to Roosevelt was arrived at between 23 and 25 May.

35. François Charles-Roux, *Cinq mois tragiques aux Affaires Étrangères: 21 mai–1 novembre 1940*, 8-9; Villelume, *Journal d'une défaite*, 353. He accompanied Reynaud to London. See also Reynaud, *La France a sauvé l'Europe* 2:200-204; CAB 66/7, WP(40)170 (War Cabinet Memorandum, 26 May 1940).

36. Reynaud, *La France a sauvé l'Europe* 2:209-11; Duroselle, *L'Abîme*, 150-51.

37. FO 371/24959, R 6308/438/22 (Reynaud to Churchill, 28 May 1940). Previous documents in this file had discussed the possibility of England's promising to demilitarize and internationalize the Gibraltar Straits and the Suez Canal, but these had been rejected as tantamount to surrendering Britain's predominance as a sea power in the Mediterranean.

38. Dilks, *Cadogan Diaries*, 290-91 (entries for 27 and 29 May 1940); Charles-Roux, *Cinq mois tragiques*, 10-13. The frantic search through several departments of the Quai d'Orsay to recover all copies of François-Poncet's cancelled instructions before one was erroneously transmitted is told in Duroselle, *L'Abîme*, 151-52.

39. Bonnet, *Quai d'Orsay*, 324. A similar analysis of opportunities missed was made at the time by Sir Percy Loraine, Britain's ambassador in Rome (FO 800/320, Halifax Papers [Loraine to Halifax, 28 May 1940]).

40. Reynaud, *La France a sauvé l'Europe* 2:190-226; MAE, "Italie," Z 374-1, 1A, 4, 5, 6, vol. 281, pp. 169-70 (François-Poncet to Paris, 28 May 1940). See also Ciano, *Journal politique* 1:255-56; *DGFP*, ser. D, vol. 9, no. 340 (Mackensen to Ribbentrop, 28 May 1940).

41. De Monzie, *Ci-devant*, 241 (entry for 30 May 1940); Guariglia, *La Diplomatie difficile*, 156-57, 160; Charles-Roux, *Cinq mois tragiques*, 15-18; François-Poncet, *Au Palais Farnèse*, 178.

42. Knox, *Mussolini Unleashed*, 122.

43. *DGFP*, ser. D, vol. 9, no. 479 (record of Hitler-Mussolini conversation at Munich, 18 June 1940); Knox, *Mussolini Unleashed*, 126-27; *DGFP*, ser. D, vol. 9, no. 525 (memorandum by Weizsäcker, 22 June 1940); EMA/2, 7 N 2915 (text of Franco-Italian armistice, 24 June 1940).

44. Knox, *Mussolini Unleashed*, 131-33; FO 371/24348, C 7411/7362/17, pp. 59-60 (unsigned F.O. minute, 26 June 1940); FO 371/24959, R 8142/438/22 (many documents in this file demonstrate increasing disagreement between Mussolini and Hitler about the treatment of France).

45. *Évén. sur.* 3:765.

46. Noël, *Illusions de Stresa*, 143-44, 157-65.

47. J. Benoist Mechin, *Procès Benoist Mechin* 2:293, cited in Lowe and Marzari, *Italian Foreign Policy*, 370; Guariglia, *La Diplomatie difficile*, 92 (see also p. 95).

CHAPTER 14

1. François-Poncet, *Au Palais Farnèse*, 186; Néré, *Foreign Policy of France*, 260-61.
2. Richardson, "Rome Accords," 57.
3. Rostow, *Anglo-French Relations*, 61.
4. Judith M. Hughes, *To the Maginot Line: The Politics of French Military Strategy in the 1920s*, 240.
5. In this context one might also place Robert J. Young's volume, *In Command of France* (1978). Its very title constitutes a striking counterpoint to J-B. Duroselle's *La décadence*, published just one year later.
6. Robert O. Paxton, *Vichy France: Old Guard and New Order, 1940-1944*, and Paxton and Michael R. Marrus, *Vichy France and the Jews*, present compelling indictments of the moral shortcomings of Vichy leaders, particularly Laval. These views have been challenged most recently by René de Chambrun, *Pierre Laval devant l'histoire*, translated into English as *Pierre Laval, Traitor or Patriot?* A new biography by the French scholar Fred Kupferman, *Laval, 1883-1945*, presents a balanced and nuanced portrait of this extraordinarily complex personality.
7. Pierre Laval, *The Unpublished Diary of Pierre Laval*, 34-35, 178-179.
8. Flandin, *Politique française*, 104; Warner, *Pierre Laval*, 63; David Thomson, *Two Frenchmen: Pierre Laval and Charles DeGaulle*, 52-53.
9. Nicholas Rostow cites a great number of these unflattering character references in *Anglo-French Relations*, 58-59. See also Geneviève Tabouis, *Vingt Ans de suspense diplomatique*, 216, and Massigli, *La Turquie devant la guerre*, 33.
10. Blum, *L'Histoire jugera*, 122; Laval cited in Thomson, *Two Frenchmen*, 11.
11. Duroselle, *La décadence*, 152. See also Dethan's review of *La décadence* in *Revue d'histoire diplomatique*, vol. 93 (1979), 368-70.
12. Thomson, *Two Frenchmen*, 52-53.

13. Cited in de Chambrun, *Pierre Laval*, 95-98. On Laval's continued conviction that Italy could be detached from Germany, see Alexander Werth, *France, 1940-1955*, 101-2.

14. Denis Mack Smith, "Appeasement as a Factor in Mussolini's Foreign Policy," in Mommsen and Kettenacker, eds., *The Fascist Challenge*, 266.

15. Henry A. Kissinger, "Vietnam: A Noble Goal by a Flawed Strategy," *International Herald Tribune* (8 April 1985), 5.

Bibliography

DOCUMENTARY SOURCES

Unpublished Material

France. Archives du Ministère des Affaires étrangères. Paris. Série P: Tunisie, 1917–29. Includes P 91–93 (Étrangèrs en Tunisie); P 362 sd (Nationalité—Naturalisation: Italiens en Tunisie); and P 762 sd (Presse et publication: Presse et propagande italiennes).

———. Archives du Ministère des Affaires étrangères, Paris. Série Y: Intérnationale, 1918–40 (Y s/d 2 — Pacte de la S.D.N.).

———. Archives du Ministère des Affaires étrangères, Paris. Série Z: Europe, 1918–40.

Sous-série "Fiume," Z 933.
Sous-série "Italie 1918–29, 1930–40"
    Z 366-1 (Presses française et italienne et relations entre les deux pays)
    Z 366-2 (Analyse de la presse italienne)
    Z 372-1 (Politique intérieure: Dossier général)
    Z 372-2, 3, 4, 5 (Partis politiques, socialistes, action pacifistes et revolutionnaire)
    Z 373-3 (Relations avec la St. Siège)
    Z 374-1 (Politique étrangère: Dossier général)
    Z 374-1 sd (Accords anglo-italiens; différend italo-éthiopien)
    Z 374-1, 1A, 4, 5, 6 (Politique étrangère: Dossier général, discours, accords anglo-italiens, etc.)
    Z 374-4 (Politique étrangère: Relations avec la France)
    Z 374-5 (Limitation des armaments)
    Z 374-6 (Politique étrangère: Relations avec la Yougoslavie—Adriatique)
    Z 374-9 (Politique étrangère: Relations avec l' Allemagne)
    Z 374-10 (Politique étrangère: Relations avec la Grèce)
    Z 374-11 (Corse)
    Z 374-12, 14, 15 (Négotiations franco-italiennes)
    Z 374-13 (Tyrol méridional)
    Z 374-14 (Négotiations franco-italiennes—supplémentaire)
    Z 375-1-5 (Propagandes)
    Z 398-1 (Colonies)

Sous-série "Yougoslavie, 1918–29, 1930–40"
   Z 751-1; Z 751-1, 5, 7; Z 752-1, 2; Z 753-1 (Politique étrangère: Dossier général)
   Z 751-1 sd 2 (Politique étrangère: Voyage en France du roi de Yougoslavie . . .)
   Z 751-1 sd 3 (Politique étrangère: Conséquences politiques de l'attentat de Marseille)
   Z 751-6 (Politique étrangère: Accord politique franco-yougoslave)
———. Archives du Ministère des Affaires étrangères, Paris. Série: Fonds Nominatifs.
   Papiers Camille Barrère
   Papiers Jules Cambon
   Papiers François Charles-Roux
   Papiers Gaston Doumergue
   Papiers Aimé de Fleuriau
   Papiers Gabriel Hanotaux
   Papiers President Herriot
   Papiers Henry de Jouvenel
   Papiers Pierre Jacquin de Margerie
   Papiers Alexandre Millerand
   Papiers Joseph et Jean Paul-Boncour
   Papiers André Tardieu
———. Service Historique de l'Armée, Vincennes. EMA/2 [État-Major de l'Armée, Deuxième Bureau]. Rapports des Attachés militaires.
   7 N 2900–2914 (Dossier général, 1919–40)
   7 N 2915 (Correspondance diplomatique, 1924–40)
   7 N 2917–2919 (Politique intérieure et extérieure, 1928–40)
   7 N 2953–2955 (Colonies et politique coloniale italienne, 1919–39)
Great Britain. Cabinet Papers. Public Record Office, Kew Gardens Branch. Includes CAB 23/77-100 (Cabinet Conclusions) and CAB 24/256-282 (Confidential Print)
———. Foreign Office. Public Record Office, Kew Gardens Branch.
   FO 371/18811–24959 (General Correspondence)
   FO 800 (Private Papers of Agents)
      FO 800/274–276 (Sir Orme Sargent's Papers)
      FO 800/292 (Lectures on Foreign Policy by Mr. R. F. Wigram)
      FO 800/295 (Sir Samuel Hoare's Papers)
      FO 800/318–320 (Lord Halifax's Papers)

Published Documents

France. Annexes (Dépositions). *Témoinages et documents recueillis par la commission d'enquête parlementaire.* 9 vols. Paris, 1951–52.
———. Assemblée Nationale, 1946–58. Session de 1947. Commission chargée

d'enquêter sur les événements survenus en France de 1933 à 1945. No. 2344. *Rapport fait au nom de la commission . . . par M. Charles Serre, rapporteur general.* 2 vols. Paris, 1952.

───. *Journal officiel de la république française, 1870–1940. Chambre des députés. Débats parlementaires.* Paris, 1881–1940.

───. *Journal officiel de la république française, 1876–1940. Chambre des députés. Documents parlementaires. Annexes aux procès- verbaux des séances.* Paris, 1881–1939.

───. *Journal officiel de la république française. Sénat, 1876–1940. Débats parlementaires.* Paris, 1881–1940.

───. *Journal officiel de la république française. Sénat, 1876–1940. Documents parlementaires. Annexes aux procès verbaux des séances.* Paris, 1881–1939.

───. Ministère des Affaires Étrangères. Commission de publication des documents relatifs aux origines de la guerre 1939–45. *Documents diplomatiques français.* First Series (1932–35) and Second Series (1936–39). Paris, 1963–86.

Germany. Auswärtiges Amt. *Documents on German Foreign Policy, 1918–1945.* Series C and D. Washington, 1957–66.

Great Britain. Foreign Office. *British and Foreign State Papers, 1937.* Vol. 141. London, 1950.

───. *Documents on British Foreign Policy, 1919–1939,* eds. Rohan Butler, J. P. T. Bury, et al., London, 1947–82.

───. *House of Commons Accounts and Papers, 1936–37.* Vol. 18. London, 1938.

United States. Department of State. *Foreign Relations of the United States.* Washington, 1861–.

Documents on International Affairs, 1935, 1936, 1937. J. W. Wheeler-Bennett and S. Heald, eds. London, 1936, 1937, 1938.

NEWSPAPERS

L'Echo de Paris (Conservative and Nationalist)
Le Gaulois (Conservative and Catholic)
L'Intransigeant (Radical)
Le Matin (Moderate)
La Petite République (Socialist)
Le Petit Parisien (Sensational but politically moderate)
Le Temps (Moderate)

MEMOIRS, DIARIES, SPEECHES, RECOLLECTIONS

Aloisi, Baron Pompeo. *Journal (25 juillet 1932–14 juin 1936).* Edited by Mario Toscano. Paris: Plon, 1957.

Avon, Lord. *The Memoirs of Anthony Eden.* Vol. 2, *Facing the Dictators.* Boston: Houghton Mifflin Co., 1962.

Baudouin, Paul. "Un voyage à Rome (fevrier 1939)." *Revue des deux mondes* (1 May 1962): 69-85.

Blondel, Jules-François. *Au fil de la carrière: Récit d'un diplomate, 1911-1938.* Paris: Hachette, 1960.

———. *Ce que mes yeux ont vu de 1900 à 1950.* 2 vols. Arras: Impr. centrale de l'Artois, 1965.

Blum, Léon. *L'Histoire jugera.* Montreal: Editions de l'Arbre, 1943.

———. *L'Oeuvre de Léon Blum.* Paris: Editions Albin Michel, 1964-65.

Bonnet, Georges. *Défense de la paix: De Washington au Quai d'Orsay.* Geneva: Editions du Cheval ailé, 1946.

———. *Fin d'une Europe.* 3 vols. Geneva: Editions du Cheval ailé, 1948.

———. *Vingt ans de vie politique, 1918-1939: De Clemenceau à Daladier.* Paris: Fayard, 1969.

Briand, Aristide. *Discours et écrits de politique étrangère.* Paris: Plon, 1965.

Charles-Roux, François. *Cinq mois tragiques aux Affaires étrangères (21 mai-1 novembre 1940).* Paris: Plon, 1949.

———. *Huit ans au Vatican, 1932-1940.* Paris: Flammarion, 1947.

———. *Souvenirs diplomatiques: Une grande ambassade à Rome, 1919-1925.* Paris: Fayard, 1961.

Ciano, Count Galeazzo. *Les archives secrètes du Comte Ciano, 1936-1942.* Paris: Plon, 1948. English translation, *Ciano's Diplomatic Papers.* Edited by Malcolm Muggeridge. London: Oldham's Press, 1948.

———. *Hidden Diary, 1937-1938.* Edited by Malcolm Muggeridge. New York: Dutton, 1953.

———. *Journal politique, 1939-1943.* 2 vols. Neuchâtel: Editions de la Baconnière, 1948. English translation, *The Ciano Diaries, 1939-1943.* Edited by Hugh Gibson. Garden City, N.Y.: Doubleday, 1946.

Coulondre, Robert. *De Staline à Hitler: Souvenirs de deux ambassades, 1936-1939.* Paris: Hachette, 1950.

D'Abernon, Edgar. *An Ambassador of Peace: Pages from the Diary of Viscount D'Abernon.* 3 vols. London: Holter and Stoughton, 1929-30.

Daladier, Edouard. *Défense du Pays.* Paris: Flammarion, 1939.

Dampierre, Robert de. "Dix années de politique française à Rome (1925-1935)." *Revue des deux mondes,* pt. 1 (1 November 1953): 14-38, pt. 2 (15 November 1953): 258-83.

De Chambrun, Charles. *Traditions et souvenirs.* Paris: Flammarion, 1952.

Delbos, Yvon. *L'Expérience rouge.* Paris: Au Sans Pareil, 1933.

Dilks, David, ed. *The Diaries of Sir Alexander Cadogan, 1938-1945.* London: Cassell, 1971.

Fabry, Jean. *De la Place de la Concorde au course de l'Intendance.* Paris: Editions de France, 1942.

Flandin, Pierre-Etienne. *Politique française (1919-1940).* Paris: Les Editions nouvelles, 1947.

François-Poncet, André. *Au Palais Farnèse: Souvenirs d'une ambassade à Rome, 1938-1940.* Paris: Fayard, 1961.

———. *Souvenirs d'une ambassade à Berlin, septembre 1931–october 1938.* Paris: Flammarion, 1946.
Gafencu, Grégoire. *Derniers jours de l'Europe: Un voyage diplomatique en 1939.* Paris: L.U.F., 1946.
Gamelin, General Maurice Gustave. *Servir.* 2 vols. Paris: Plon, 1946.
Guariglia, Raffaele. *La diplomatie difficile: Mémoires, 1922–1946.* Paris: Plon, 1955.
Herriot, Edouard. *Jadis.* Vol. 2, *D'une guerre à l'autre.* Paris: Flammarion, 1952.
Jouvenel, Bertrand de. *Après la défaite.* Paris: Plon, 1941.
Lagardelle, Hubert de. *Mission à Rome: Mussolini.* Paris: Plon, 1955.
Laroche, Jules. *Au Quai d'Orsay avec Briand et Poincaré, 1913–1926.* Paris: Hachette, 1957.
Laval, Pierre. *Laval parle: Notes et mémoires rédigés à Fresnes d'août à octobre 1945.* Paris: Librairie Ch. Béranger, 1948. English translation, *The Diary of Pierre Laval.* New York: Scribner's 1948.
Liddell Hart, Sir Basil. *The Liddell Hart Memoirs.* Vol. 2. New York: Putnam, 1966.
Massigli, René. *La Turquie devant la guerre: Mission à Ankara, 1939–1940.* Paris: Plon, 1964.
Monzie, Anatole de. *Ci-devant.* Paris: Flammarion, 1941.
Noël, Léon. *Les Illusions de Stresa: L'Italie abandonnée à Hitler.* Paris: Editions France-Empire, 1975.
Paul-Boncour, Joseph. *Entre deux guerres: Souvenirs sur la troisième république.* 3 vols. Paris: Plon, 1945–46.
Puaux, Gabriel. *Mort et transfiguration de l'Autriche, 1932–1945.* Paris: Plon, 1956.
Reynaud, Paul. *Au coeur de la mêlée, 1930–1945.* Paris: Flammarion, 1951.
———. *La France a sauvé l'Europe.* 2 vols. Paris: Flammarion, 1947.
———. *Mémoires.* 2 vols. Paris: Flammarion, 1960–63.
Saint-Aulaire, Comte de. *Confession d'un vieux diplomate.* Paris: Flammarion, 1953.
Sforza, Comte Carlo. *Illusions et réalités de l'Europe.* Neuchâtel: Ides de Calendes, 1944.
Szembeck, Jan. *Journal, 1933–1939.* Paris: Plon, 1952.
Tabouis, Geneviève. *Ils l'ont appelée Cassandre.* New York: Editions de la Maison Française, 1942.
Tardieu, André. *Notes de semaine, 1938: L'année de Munich.* Paris: Flammarion, 1939.
Templewood, Viscount (Samuel Hoare). *Nine Troubled Years.* London: Collins, 1954.
Thorez, Maurice. *Notre lutte pour la paix.* Paris: Editions sociales internationales, 1938.
Villelume, Paul de. *Journal d'une défaite avril 1939–juin 1940.* Paris: Fayard, 1976.

CONTEMPORARY STUDIES

Bonnet, Georges. *Le Quai d'Orsay sous trois républiques, 1870–1961.* Paris: Fayard, 1961.
Breal, August. *Philippe Berthelot.* Paris: Gallimard, 1937.
Cameron, Elizabeth R. *Prologue to Appeasement: A Study in French Foreign Policy.* Washington: American Council on Public Affairs, 1942.
Charles-Roux, François. "La France et l'Italie dès armistices à Locarno." *Revue des deux mondes* (1 March 1926): 188–207.
Chastenet, Jacques. *Vingt ans d'histoire diplomatique, 1919–1939.* Geneva: Editions du milieu monde, 1945.
Christopolos, Georges. *La politique extérieure de l'Italie fasciste.* Paris: L. Rodstein, 1936.
Cot, Pierre. "La politique extérieure de la troisième république." In *L'Oeuvre de la troisième république,* edited by Jean Benoit-Levy and Gustave Cohen, 39–66. Montreal: Editions de l'Arbre, 1943.
_____. *Triumph of Treason.* Chicago and New York: Ziff-Davis Publishing Co., 1944.
Currey, Muriel. *Italian Foreign Policy, 1918–1932.* London: Nicholsen and Watson, 1932.
DeWilde, John C. "The Struggle Over Spain." *Foreign Policy Reports* 14, no. 2 (April 1938).
Géraud, André (pseud. Pertinax). "The Anglo-French Alliance." *Foreign Affairs* 18 (1939–40): 601–13.
_____. "France and the Anglo-German Naval Treaty." *Foreign Affairs* 14 (1935–36):51–61.
_____. *The Gravediggers of France.* New York: Doubleday, 1944.
_____. "Les risques du gentleman's agreement." *L'Europe nouvelle* 20 (9 January 1937):33.
_____. "What England Means to France." *Foreign Affairs* 17 (Janury 1939): 362–73.
Hanotaux, Gabriel. *Histoire des colonies françaises et de l'expansion de la France dans le monde* Vol. 4. Paris: Société de l'histoire nationale, 1932.
Lasturel, Pierre. *L'Affaire greco-italienne de 1923: étude critique avec des documents inédits.* Paris: L'Ile de France, 1925.
Marabini, Camillo. *Le problème France-Italie.* Paris: Editions européenes, 1931.
Monchicourt, Charles. *Les Italiens de Tunisie et l'accord Laval-Mussolini.* Paris: Librairie du Recueil Sirey, 1938.
Naudeau, Ludovic. *L'Italie fasciste ou l'autre danger.* Paris, 1927.
Pernot, Maurice. "Franco-Italian Relations." *International Affairs* 13 (July–August 1934): 508–22.
Recouly, Raymond. *De Bismarck à Poincaré: Soixante ans de diplomatie républicaine.* Paris: Les Editions de France, 1932.

Sforza, Count Carlo. *Dictateurs et dictatures de l'après guerre.* Paris: Gallimard, 1931.

———. *Les frères ennemis (l'Europe d'après-guerre).* Paris: Gallimard, 1933.

Soltau, Roger. *French Parties and Politics, 1871-1930.* New York: Oxford Univ. Press, 1930.

Suarez, Georges. *Briand, sa vie, son oeuvre,* 6 vols. Paris, L'Artisan de la Paix, 1938-41.

Temperley, H. W. V. *A History of the Peace Conference of Paris.* 6 vols. London: Frowde, Hodder and Stoughton, 1920-24.

Thomson, David, "French Foreign Policy." Oxford Pamphlets on World Affairs No. 67. London, 1944.

Torrès, Henry. *Pierre Laval: la France trahie.* New York: Oxford Univ. Press, 1941.

Toynbee, Arnold J. *Survey of International Affairs, 1920-1923, 1924.* London: Oxford Univ. Press, 1927, 1928.

———. *The World After the Peace Conference.* London: Milford, 1926.

Ward, Barbara. "Italian Foreign Policy." Oxford Pamphlets on World Affairs No. 48. London, 1942.

Werth, Alexander. *France and Munich: Before and After the Surrender.* New York, London: Harper and Brothers, 1939.

———. *The Twilight of France, 1939-1940.* New York: Harper and Brothers, 1942.

HISTORICAL STUDIES

Adamthwaite, Anthony. *France and the Coming of the Second World War, 1936-1939.* London: Frank Cass, 1977.

Albrecht-Carrié, René. *France, Europe and the Two World Wars.* Geneva: E. Droz, 1960.

———. *Italy at the Paris Peace Conference.* Reprint, Hamden, Conn.: Archon Book, 1966.

———. *Italy from Napoleon to Mussolini.* New York: Columbia Univ. Press, 1950.

Andrew, Christopher M., and A. S. Kanya-Forstner. *The Climax of French Imperial Expansion, 1914-1924.* Stanford: Standford Univ. Press, 1981.

Auffray, Bernard. *Pierre de Margerie (1861-1942) et la vie diplomatique de son temps.* Paris: Klincksieck, 1976.

Baer, George W. *The Coming of the Italian-Ethiopian War.* Cambridge, Mass.: Harvard Univ. Press, 1967.

———. *Test Case: Italy, Ethiopia and the League of Nations.* Stanford: Hoover Institution Press, 1976.

Barclay, Glen St. J. *The Rise and Fall of the New Roman Empire: Italy's Bid for World Power, 1890-1943.* London: Sedgwick and Jackson, 1973.

Barros, James. *The Corfu Incident of 1923: Mussolini and the League of Nations.* Princeton: Princeton Univ. Press, 1965.

Baumont, Maurice. *Gloires et tragédies de la IIIe République.* Paris: Hachette, 1956.

Bédarida, François. *La stratégie secrète de la drôle de guerre: le conseil suprême intérallié, septembre 1939-avril 1940.* Paris: Centre National pour la Recherche Scientifique, 1979.

Bell, J. Bowyer. "French Reaction to the Spanish Civil War, July-September 1936." In *Power, Public Opinion and Diplomacy*, edited by L. P. Wallace and W. C. Askew, 267-96. Durham, N.C.: Duke Univ. Press, 1959.

Binion, Rudolph. *Defeated Leaders: the Political Fate of Caillaux, Jouvenel and Tardieu.* New York: Columbia Univ. Press, 1960.

Blatt, Joel. "France and Italy at the Paris Peace Conference." *The International History Review* 8, no. 1 (February 1986): 27-40.

———. "French Reaction to Italy, Italian Fascism, and Mussolini, 1919-1925: The Views from Paris and the Palazzo Farnese." Ph.D. diss., University of Rochester, 1977.

Bloch, Charles. "Great Britain, German Rearmament, and the Naval Agreement of 1935." In *European Diplomacy Between Two Wars, 1919-1939*, edited by Hans Gatzke, 125-51. Chicago: Quadrangle Books, 1972.

Bonnefous, Edouard. *Histoire politique de la Troisième République.* Vol. 6 and 7. Paris: Presses Universitaires de France, 1965, 1967.

Braddick, Henderson B. "The Hoare-Laval Plan: A Study in International Politics." *The Review of Politics* 4, no. 3 (July 1962): 342-64.

Burk, Kathleen. "Economic Diplomacy Between the Wars." *The Historical Journal* 24, no. 4 (December 1981): 1003-15.

Cairns, John C. "March 7, 1936, Again: The View from Paris." *International Journal* 20 (Spring 1965): 230-46.

———. "A Nation of Shopkeepers in Search of a Suitable France: 1919-40." *American Historical Review* 79, no. 3 (June 1974): 710-43.

Carlton, David. "Eden, Blum and the Origins of Non-Intervention." *Journal of Contemporary History* 6, no. 3 (1971): 40-55.

Cassels, Alan. *Mussolini's Early Diplomacy.* Princeton: Princeton Univ. Press, 1970.

Chastenet, Jacques. *Histoire de la Troisième République.* Vols. 5 and 6. Paris: Hachette, 1952.

———. *Raymond Poincaré.* Paris: Julliard, 1948.

Cobban, Alfred. "Laval and the Third Republic." *The Cambridge Journal* 2 (February 1949): 279-87.

Cole, Hubert. *Laval: A Biography.* New York: G. P. Putnam's Sons, 1963.

Coverdale, John F. *Italian Intervention in the Spanish Civil War.* Princeton: Princeton Univ. Press, 1975.

Craig, Gordon, and Felix Gilbert, eds. *The Diplomats, 1919-1939.* Princeton: Princeton Univ. Press, 1953.

De Chambrun, René. *Pierre Laval devant l'histoire.* Paris: Editions France-Empire, 1983. English translation by Elly Stein. *Pierre Laval: Traitor or Patriot?* New York: Charles Scribner's Sons, 1984.

Dethan, Georges. Review of Jean-Baptiste Duroselle's *La Décadence, 1932-1939.* *Revue d'histoire diplomatique* 93 (1979): 368-70.

Diggins, John P. *Mussolini and Fascism: The View from America.* Princeton: Princeton Univ. Press, 1972.
Douglas, Roy. "Chamberlain and Eden 1937-38." *Journal of Contemporary History* 13, no. 1 (January 1978): 97-116.
Dreifort, John E. *Yvon Delbos at the Quai d'Orsay: French Foreign Policy During the Popular Front, 1936-1938.* Lawrence, Kans.: Univ. Press of Kansas, 1973.
Duroselle, Jean-Baptiste. *L'Abîme 1939-1945.* Paris: Imprimerie Nationale, 1982.
———. *La Décadence (1932-1939).* Paris: Imprimerie Nationale, 1979.
———. *La politique extérieure de la France de 1914 à 1945.* Paris: Centre de documentation universitaire, 1965.
Felice, Renzo de. *Fascism: An Informal Introduction to Its Theory and Practice.* New Brunswick, N.J.: Transaction Books, 1977.
———. *Mussolini il Duce.* Vol. 1, *Gli anni del consenso, 1929-1936.* Turin: Einaudi, 1974.
Furnia, Arthur H. *The Diplomacy of Appeasement: Anglo-French Relations and the Prelude to World War II, 1931-1938.* Washington, D.C.: University Press, 1960.
Gallagher, M. D. "Léon Blum and the Spanish Civil War." *Journal of Contemporary History* 6, no. 3 (1971): 56-64.
Gentizon, Paul. *Défense de l'Italie.* Lausanne: Editions de l'Aiglon, 1949.
Gilbert, Martin. *The Roots of Appeasement.* London: World Publishing Co., 1966.
Gilbert, Martin, and Richard Gott. *The Appeasers.* London: Weidenfeld and Nicholson, 1963.
Goguel, François, *La politique des parties sous la IIIe République.* Paris: Editions de Seuil, 1946.
Goldman, Aaron L. "Sir Robert Vansittart's Search for Italian Cooperation Against Hitler, 1933-36." *Journal of Contemporary History* 9, no. 3 (July 1974): 93-130.
Gruber, Helmut. *Léon Blum, French Socialism, and the Popular Front: A Case of Internal Contradictions.* Cornell Studies in International Affairs No. 17. Ithaca: Cornell Univ. Press, 1986.
Guillen, Pierre. "L'échec des tentatives d'entente économique avec l'Italie (1922-1929)." *Relations Internationales* 13 (Spring 1978): 51-69.
Hall, Hines H., III. "The Foreign Policy-Making Process in Britain, 1934-1935, and the Origins of the Anglo-German Naval Agreement." *The Historical Journal* 19, no. 2 (June 1976): 477-99.
Howard, J. E. *Parliament and Foreign Policy in France, 1919-1939.* New York: Cresset Press, 1948.
Hughes, Judith M. *To the Maginot Line: The Politics of French Military Preparation in the 1920s.* Cambridge, Mass.: Harvard Univ. Press, 1971.
Jacobson, Jon. *Locarno Diplomacy: Germany and the West, 1925-1929.* Princeton: Princeton Univ. Press, 1972.
———. "Strategies of French Foreign Policy After World War I." *Journal of Modern History* 55, no. 1 (March 1983): 78-95.

Jarausch, Konrad H. *The Four Power Pact, 1933*. Madison, Wis.: State Historical Society of Wisconsin, 1965.
Kaiser, David E. *Economic Diplomacy and the Origins of the Second World War: Germany, Britain, France and Eastern Europe, 1930-1939*. Princeton: Princeton Univ. Press, 1981.
Keiger, John F. *France and the Origins of the First World War*. New York: St. Martin's Press, 1983.
Knox, MacGregor. *Mussolini Unleashed, 1939-1941: Politics and Strategy in Fascist Italy's Last War*. New York: Cambridge Univ. Press, 1982.
Komjathy, Anthony Tihamer. *The Crises of France's East Central European Diplomacy, 1933-1938*. New York: Columbia Univ. Press, 1976.
Kovrig, Bennett. "Mediation by Obfuscation: The Resolution of the Marseille Crisis, October 1934 to May 1935." *The Historical Journal* 19, no. 1 (March 1976): 191-221.
Kupferman, Fred. *Pierre Laval*. Paris: Messon, 1976.
———. *Laval, 1883-1945*. Paris: Editions Balland, 1987.
Lacouture, Jean. *Léon Blum*. Trans. George Holloch. New York and London: Holmes and Maier, 1982.
Lammers, Donald N. "Britain, Russia, and the Revival of 'Entente Diplomacy': 1934." *Journal of British Studies* 6, no. 2 (May 1967): 99-123.
Laurens, Franklin D. *France and the Italo-Ethiopian Crisis 1935-1936*. The Hague: Mouton, 1967.
Leffler, Melvyn P. *The Elusive Quest: America's Pursuit of European Stability and French Security, 1919-1933*. Chapel Hill: Univ. of North Carolina Press, 1979.
Lowe, C. J., and F. Marzari. *Italian Foreign Policy 1870-1940*. London: Routledge and Kegan Paul, 1975.
Macartney, Maxwell H. H., and Paul Cremona. *Italy's Foreign and Colonial Policy, 1914-1937*. Reprint, New York: Howard Fertig, Inc., 1972.
McDougall, Walter A. *France's Rhineland Diplomacy, 1914-1924: The Last Bid for a Balance of Power in Europe*. Princeton: Princeton Univ. Press, 1978.
Mack Smith, Denis. *Mussolini*. New York: Alfred A. Knopf, 1982.
———. *Mussolini's Roman Empire*. New York: Penguin Books, 1977.
Mallet, Alfred. *Pierre Laval*. 2 vols. Paris: Amiot-Dumont, 1955.
Marder, A. J. "The Royal Navy and the Ethiopian Crisis of 1935-36." *American Historical Review* 75, no. 5 (1970): 1327-56.
Marks, Sally. "Mussolini and Locarno: Fascist Foreign Policy in Microcosm." *Journal of Contemporary History* 14 (1979): 423-39.
———. "Mussolini and the Ruhr Crisis." *International History Review* 8, no. 1 (February 1986): 56-69.
Micaud, Charles A. *The French Right and Nazi Germany, 1933-1939: A Study of Public Opinion*. Reprint, New York: Octagon Books, 1964.
Michael, Robert. "The Foreign Policies of the French Radicals, 1933-1939." *Third Republic/Troisième République* 10 (Fall 1980): 45-91.
Milza, Pierre. *L'Italie fasciste devant l'opinion française, 1920-1940*. Paris: A. Colin, 1967.

Mommsen, Wolfgang, and Lothar Kettenacker, eds. *The Fascist Challenge and the Policy of Appeasement.* London: George Allen and Unwin, 1983.
Moodie, A. E. *The Italo-Yugoslav Boundary: A Study in Political Geography.* London: George Philip and Son, 1945.
Murray, Williamson. *The Change in the European Balance of Power, 1938-1939: The Path to Ruin.* Princeton: Princeton Univ. Press, 1984.
Néré, Jacques. *The Foreign Policy of France from 1914 to 1945.* London: Routledge and Kegan Paul, 1975.
Newman, Michael. "The Origins of Munich: British Policy in Danubian Europe, 1933-1937." *The Historical Journal* 21, no. 2 (June 1978): 371-86.
Northedge, F. S. *The Troubled Giant: Britain Among the Great Powers, 1916-1939.* London: London School of Economics, 1966.
Parker, R. A. C. "Great Britain, France and Ethiopian Crisis, 1935-1936." *English Historical Review* 89 (1974): 293-332.
Power, Thomas F. *Jules Ferry and the Renaissance of French Imperialism.* New York: Octagon Books, 1966.
Puzzo, Dante A. *Spain and the Great Powers, 1936-1941.* New York: Columbia Univ. Press, 1962.
Queuille, Pierre. "Le décisif armistice franco-italien (23-24 juin 1940)." *Revue d'histoire diplomatique* 92 (January-June 1976): 100-11.
Les Relations franco-britanniques, 1935-1939: Colloques Anglo-Français, 1971, 1972. Paris: Centre National de la Recherche Scientifique, 1975.
Rémond, René. Review of Jean-Baptiste Duroselle's *La Décadence (1932-1939). Revue historique* 534 (April-June 1980): 415-24.
Renouvin, Pierre. *Histoire des relations internationales.* Vol. 8, *Les crises du XXe siècle.* Paris: Hachette, 1958.
──────. "La politique extérieure de la France de 1933 à 1939: Progrès et lacunes de l'information historique." *Bulletin de la classe des lettres et des sciences morales et politiques* 49 (1963): 199-221.
──────. *War and Aftermath, 1914-1929.* New York: Harper and Row, 1968.
Renzi, William A. "Mussolini's Sources of Financial Support, 1914-1915." *History* 56 (June 1971): 189-206.
Richardson, Charles O. "The Rome Accords of January 1935 and the Coming of the Italian-Ethiopian War." *The Historian* 41, no. 1 (November 1978): 41-58.
Robertson, Esmonde M. "Hitler and Sanctions: Mussolini and the Rhineland." *European Studies Review* 7, no. 4 (October 1977): 409-35.
──────. "Mussolini and Ethiopia: The Prehistory of the Rome Agreement." In *Studies in Diplomatic History in Memory of D. B. Horn,* edited by M. S. Anderson and R. Hattan, 339-56. London: Longmans, 1970.
──────. *Mussolini as Empire-Builder: Europe and Africa, 1932-36.* New York: St. Martin's Press, 1977.
Robertson, James C. "The Hoare-Laval Plan." *Journal of Contemporary History* 10, no. 3 (July 1975): 433-64.
Rostow, Nicholas. *Anglo-French Relations, 1934-36.* New York: St. Martin's Press, 1984.

Rusinow, Dennison I. *Italy's Austrian Heritage, 1919-1946*. Oxford: Oxford Univ. Press, 1969.
Schmidt, Royal J. *Versailles and the Ruhr: Seedbed of World War II*. The Hague: Martinus Nijhoff, 1968.
Schuker, Stephen A. *The End of French Predominance in Europe: The Financial Crisis of 1924 and the Adoption of the Dawes Plan*. Chapel Hill: Univ. of North Carolina Press, 1976.
──────. "France and the Remilitarization of the Rhineland, 1936." *French Historical Studies* 14, no. 3 (Spring 1986): 299-338.
Scott, William Evans. *Alliance Against Hitler: The Origins of the Franco-Soviet Pact*. Durham: Duke Univ. Press, 1962.
Shorrock, William I. "France and the Rise of Fascism in Italy, 1919-1923." *Journal of Contemporary History* 10, no. 4 (October 1975): 591-610.
──────. "France, Italy and the Eastern Mediterranean in the 1920s." *International History Review* 8, no. 1 (February 1986): 70-82.
──────. "La France, l'Italie fasciste et la question de l'Adriatique (1922-1924)." *Revue d'histoire diplomatique* 94 (January-September 1980): 86-110.
──────. "The Jouvenel Mission to Rome and the Origins of the Laval-Mussolini Accords, 1933-1935." *The Historian* 45, no. 1 (November 1982): 20-30.
──────. "Prelude to Empire: French Balkan Policy, 1878-1881." *East European Quarterly* 16, no. 3 (September 1982): 345-62.
──────. "The Tunisian Question in French Policy Toward Italy, 1881-1940." *International Journal of African Historical Studies* 16, no. 4 (1983): 631-51.
Smyth, Denis. "Duce Diplomatico." *The Historical Journal* 21, no. 4 (December 1978): 981-1000.
Sontag, Raymond J. *A Broken World, 1919-1934*. New York: Harper and Row, 1971.
Stafford, P. R. "The French Government and the Danzig Crisis: The Italian Dimension." *International History Review* 6, no. 1 (February 1984): 48-87.
Tabouis, Geneviève. *Vingt ans de suspense diplomatique*. Paris: A. Michel, 1958.
Thompson, Neville. *The Anti-Appeasers: Conservative Opposition to Appeasement in the 1930s*. Oxford: Clarendon Press, 1971.
Thomson, David. *Two Frenchmen: Pierre Laval and Charles De Gaulle*. London: Cresset Press, 1951.
Toscano, Mario. "Eden's Mission to Rome on the Eve of the Italo-Ethiopian Conflict." In *Studies in Diplomatic History and Historiography*, edited by A. O. Sarkissian, 126-52. London: Longmans, 1961.
──────. *The Origins of the Pact of Steel*. Baltimore: Johns Hopkins Univ. Press, 1968.
Van der Esch, Patricia A. M. *Prelude to War: The International Repercussions of the Spanish Civil War*. The Hague: Martinus Hijhoff, 1951.
Villari, Luigi. *Italian Foreign Policy Under Mussolini*. New York: Devin-Adair Co., 1956.

Waites, Neville, ed. *Troubled Neighbors: Franco-British Relations in the Twentieth Century.* London: Weidenfeld and Nicholson, 1971.
Wandycz, Piotr S. *France and Her Eastern Allies, 1919-1925: French-Czechoslovak-Polish Relations from the Paris Peace Conference to Locarno.* Minneapolis: Univ. of Minnesota Press, 1962.
Warner, Geoffrey. *Pierre Laval and the Eclipse of France.* New York: Macmillan, 1968.
Watt, D. C. "The Anglo-German Naval Agreement of 1935: An Interim Judgement." *Journal of Modern History* 28 (June 1956): 155-75.
———. "The Secret Laval-Mussolini Agreement of 1935." *The Middle East Journal* 15 (Winter 1961): 69-78.
Weinberg, Gerhard. "The Defeat of Germany in 1918 and the European Balance of Power." *Central European History* 2 (1969): 248-60.
Werth, Alexander. *France, 1940-1955.* Reprint, Boston: Beacon Press, 1966.
Wolfers, Arnold. *Britain and France Between Two Wars: Conflicting Strategies of Peace from Versailles to World War II.* Reprint, New York: Norton, 1966.
Young, Robert J. "The Aftermath of Munich: The Course of French Diplomacy, October 1938 to March 1939." *French Historical Studies* 8, no. 2 (Fall 1973): 305-22.
———. "French Military Intelligence and the Franco-Italian Alliance, 1933-1939." *Historical Journal* 28, no. 1 (March 1985): 143-68.
———. *In Command of France: French Foreign Policy and Military Planning, 1933-1940.* Cambridge, Mass.: Harvard Univ. Press, 1978.
———. "Preparations for Defeat: French War Doctrine in the Inter-war Period." *Journal of European Studies* 2, no. 2 (June 1972): 155-72.
———. "Soldiers and Diplomats: The French Embassy and Franco-Italian Relations, 1935-6." *Journal of Strategic Studies* 7 (1984): 74-91.

Index

Abyssinia. *See* Ethiopia
Adowa: battle of, 5, 159
Albania, 9, 44, 91–92, 101; alliance with Italy (1927), 62, 49; Ciano's visit to, 227–28; and Corfu crisis, 37; Italian interests in, 60, 70, 71; Italian invasion of, 263–65, 267; and Italian invasion of Greece, 286; territorial integrity of, 47–48, 199–200
Alexander, King (Yugoslavia), 102, 118
Alfieri, Dino, 211
Aloisi, Baron Pompeo, 71, 100, 106; appointed secretary general of Palazzo Chigi, 67; and Ethiopian crisis, 109, 144–45, 146, 149, 162–63, 172; impressions of Laval, 103; Jouvenel mission, assessment of, 78; and Stresa Front, 127
Alphand, Hervé, 273
Anglo-German Naval Agreement, 133–37, 148, 291; and Ethiopian crisis, 142, 147
Anglo-Italian Easter Accord (1938): implementation of, 225–33, 235–36, 238, 240, 242; and Italian demands on France, 243, 245; mentioned, 265, 266, 292, 322n. 16; negotiation of, 220–25; possible French adherence to, 227–30; signing of, 251
Ansaldo, Giovanni, 249, 257
Anschluss, 48, 147, 184, 214–19, 223, 229, 293; Franco-Italian opposition to, 66, 71, 78, 87–98; and role of Laval, 167; and Stresa Front, 201
Attlee, Clement, 282
Attolico, Bernardo, 263
Austria, 11, 26, 60, 82; agreement with Germany, 184; and Danubian confederation, 95; and Ethiopian crisis, 155, 179; and Franco-Italian rapprochement of 1934, 100, 105, 106; independence of, 71, 74–75, 87–98, 150; Italian influence in, 77; and Rhineland crisis, 177; and Stresa Front, 123, 124–25, 128. See also *Anschluss*
Austria-Hungary, 2, 4–5, 7, 9
Austro-Prussian War, 2
L'Avenir, 54
Avenol, Joseph, 137, 147
Avezzana, Baron Romano, 37, 51

Badoglio, General Pietro, 64, 65, 173, 184; as Italian military attaché in Rio de Janeiro, 62–63; named chief of Italian General Staff, 63; and Franco-Italian military rapprochement, 118–21, 129–33; and Italo-Ethiopian War, 158, 159, 179–80; and Italian nonbelligerency, 273, 278; and Franco-Italian armistice, 284. See also Gamelin-Badoglio Agreements
Balbo, Marshal Italo, 186
Baldwin, Stanley, 156, 187
Bardo, Treaty of, 3
Barrère, Camille, 17, 30, 58, 78, 238, 291, 296; as ambassador to Italy, 5; before World War I, 6, 7, 14, 15–16; and Fiume question, 33–37, 43; at Paris Peace Conference, 298 n. 13; and relations with Yugoslavia, 44–46; and rise of Italian fascism, 18, 19, 20–30; and Tunisian question, 50–52
Barthou, Louis, 58, 103, 186, 291, 292, 294, 295, 296; appointed French foreign minister, 84; assassination of, 100–102, 170; and Austrian Nazi coup of 1934, 97; and Danubian confederation, 95, 99–100; as delegate to Reparations Commission, 23, 39; opposition to Four-Power Pact, 76

INDEX

Bastianini, Giuseppe, 160
Baudouin, Paul, 258, 259; and Franco-Italian armistice, 288; and Italian invasion of Ethiopia, 139–40; secret mission to Rome of, 252–55, 267, 326n. 37
Beaumarchais, Maurice, 55–57
Belgium, 28, 40
Beneš, Eduard, 42
Béranger, Henri, 86; and *Anschluss* crisis, 218; and Four-Power Pact, 76; and Franco-Italian rapprochement of 1934, 67–68, 100
Berlin, Congress of, 3
Berthelot, Philippe, 18, 32, 47, 59, 63, 67; resignation of, 69
Besnard, René, 47, 48, 49, 54–55, 58, 59–60, 63
Bey of Tunis, 3
Bidault, Georges, 318n. 50
Bismarck, Otto von, 3, 4, 5
Blondel, Jules, 202, 205, 261; and Anglo-Italian rapprochement, 211–13, 222–26, 230; and *Anschluss* crisis, 215, 217–19; and Hoare-Laval Plan, 164; and Munich crisis, 234; urges recognition of Italian conquest of Ethiopia, 197, 214, 222–24, 235
Blum, Léon, 153; and Anglo-Italian Easter Accord, 223–24; and Four-Power Pact, 76; and Hoare-Laval Plan, 165; and Laval-Mussolini Agreement, 112; and lifting of sanctions on Italy, 182–83; resignation of, 225; and resignation of Laval, 166; and retirement of De Chambrun, 192; and rise of Popular Front, 180, 181; and Spanish Civil War, 187–91, 323n. 22; and Stresa Front, 127–28. *See also* Popular Front
Bonaparte, Louis Napoleon, 2
Bonnet, Georges, 58, 206, 242, 257, 293, 296; and Anglo-Italian Easter Accord, 225, 228–31, 236; and appeasement of Italy, 238, 241, 260–61, 263–66, 271; and Baudouin mission to Rome, 253–55, 326n. 37; and British mediation between France and Italy, 246, 248; and Four-Power Pact, 306n. 40; and Italian nonbelligerency, 273, 275, 282–83; and Laval-Mussolini Agreements, 115, 247; named foreign minister, 225; and Polish crisis, 272; and recognition of Italian conquest of Ethiopia, 226–28, 235–36; removed from Quai d'Orsay, 275
Bordonaro, Antonino, 60
Boucher, Marcel, 217
Briand, Aristide, 57, 58, 61, 63, 65, 294; in first Laval ministry, 66; and Franco-Italian relations, 63; and Franco-Yugoslav Treaty, 49; opposition to *Anschluss*, 88; and rise of Italian fascism, 20–21; and Tunisian question, 50, 54–55
Brinon, Fernand de. *See* De Brinon, Fernand
Buisson, Colonel, 223
Bulgaria, 60, 127
Bullitt, William, 207, 287

Cadogan, Alexander, 221, 230, 245, 250, 325n. 21
Caillaux, Joseph, 76
Caix, Robert de. *See* De Caix, Robert
Cambon, Jules, 5, 7, 40
Cambon, Paul, 4, 5, 7, 15, 293
Cambon, Roger, 208, 248
Campbell, Sir Ronald, 278
Caporetto: battle of, 9
Carr, Edward Hallett, 128–29, 133
Cavour, Count Camillo di, ix, 2
Cecil, Lord Robert, 40, 151, 164
Cerruti, Vittorio, 157, 160, 207
Chamberlain, Sir Austen, 48–49, 135
Chamberlain, Neville, 231, 238, 256; and Anglo-German Naval Agreement, 133; and Anglo-Italian rapprochement, 207, 210–11, 228, 244–51, 325n. 17; and appeasement of Italy, 269–71; and Italian nonbelligerency, 275–76, 282; and resignation of Eden, 206, 216–17
Chamber of Fasces and Corporations, 277
Chambrun, Charles de. *See* De Chambrun, Charles
Charles-Roux, François, 51, 58, 61, 211; and *Anschluss* crisis, 217; and Austrian Nazi coup of 1934, 97–98; and Corfu crisis, 38–40; and Fiume crisis, 35–36; and Franco-Yugoslav Treaty, 46–49; and Germany's Prague coup, 259, 260; and Italian nonbelligerency, 281–84; named ambassador to Holy See, 59; named secretary general

of Quai d'Orsay, 280–81, 330n. 32; and resignation of Sforza, 24; and rise of Italian fascism, 18, 19, 21–28
Chautemps, Camille, 206, 207, 216, 223
Churchill, Winston: and Anglo-German Naval Agreement, 135–36; and Italian nonbelligerency, 282; opposes implementation of Anglo-Italian Easter Accord, 236; and Spanish Civil War, 210
Ciano, Count Galeazzo, 184–85, 191; and Anglo-Italian Easter Accord, 225–26, 227, 230–32, 235, 236; and *Anschluss* crisis, 214; appointed Italian foreign minister, 183; and appointment of François-Poncet to Rome, 238; and Baudouin mission to Rome, 253–54; denunciation of Laval-Mussolini Agreements, 246–47, 248–50, 252; and French Popular Front, 194; and French recognition of Italian conquest of Ethiopia, 197, 201, 226; and Germany's coup in Prague, 256–57, 259, 261, 263, 265–66; and Italian demands on France, 240–42, 245, 269–70; and Italian nonbelligerency, 273–80, 281, 283–84; and Italo-Yugoslav relations, 199–200; and Polish crisis, 272; pro-German sentiments of, 211; and retirement of de Chambrun, 191–92, 293; and Spanish Civil War, 203–4, 211, 239
Clemenceau, Georges, 10, 32, 47, 298n. 13
Clerk, Sir George: and Anglo-German Naval Agreement, 134; and Ethiopian crisis, 144, 153, 155; and Stresa Front, 123
Colrat, Maurice, 51
Comert, Pierre, 238, 315n. 44
Contarini, Salvatore, 24, 26, 36, 63, 44–45; resignation of, 59–60
Corbin, Charles, 262; and Anglo-Italian rapprochement, 207, 221, 230, 245, 250–51; and *Anschluss* crisis, 216; and Ethiopian crisis, 149–50, 154, 156, 174, 180, 319n. 19; and Spanish Civil War, 202–3; and Stresa Front, 123
Corfu, 32, 290, 303; crisis of 1923, 37–44
Corriere d'Italia, 48, 53
Cot, Pierre, 187–88, 318n. 36
Coulondre, Robert, 154
Crispi, Francesco, 4, 5, 6

Curzon, George Nathaniel, Lord, 25
Czechoslovakia, 290; and Corfu crisis, 42, 304n. 60; and Franco-Italian military rapprochement, 130–32; and Laval-Mussolini Agreements, 113; in Laval's diplomacy, 294; and Little Entente, 32; Locarno Treaties and, 47; and Munich crisis, 233–35; and Stresa Front, 127

Daily Mail (London), 38
Daily Telegraph (London), 163
Daladier, Edouard, 166, 278, 280, 296; and Anglo-Italian Easter Accord, 228–29, 236; and Baudouin mission to Rome, 253–55, 326n. 37; and Four-Power Pact, 72–73, 306n. 33; and Italian claims on France, 246, 250; and Italian nonbelligerency, 274–75, 282–84; and Munich crisis, 233–34; named prime minister, 225; opposes appeasement of Italy, 237–38, 258, 262–67, 269–72, 292; and Spanish Civil War, 187–88, 323n. 22
Dampierre, Roger de, 61, 67–68, 106, 107, 166, 198–200
D'Annunzio, Gabriele, 23, 33–34, 43–44
Dawes Plan, 58
De Bono, General Emilio, 159
De Brinon, Fernand, 254, 295
De Caix, Robert, 64–65, 101, 103, 115, 304n. 9
De Chambrun, Charles Pineton, 78, 79–80, 185; and Austrian Nazi coup of 1934, 88–94; and Danubian confederation, 82; and Ethiopian crisis, 138, 144, 147, 157, 158, 162–63, 171–72, 173, 178, 179, 182, 197; and Franco-Italian rapprochement, 83–84, 85–87, 100–107, 119; and German withdrawal from League of Nations, 83; impressions of Mussolini, 80; and Laval-Mussolini Agreements, 109, 111; retirement of, 191–92, 194–95, 196, 293; and Rhineland crisis, 175–76; and Spanish Civil War, 189–91; and Stresa Front, 122; and Tunisian question, 309n. 12
Delbos, Yvon, 205, 211, 293; and Anglo-Italian rapprochement, 206–7, 212, 220–21; and *Anschluss* crisis, 215–18; appointed

foreign minister, 181; and Hoare-Laval Plan, 164-65; and inception of Popular Front, 182-87; and Italo-Yugoslav relations, 199-200; opposition to recognition of Italian conquest of Ethiopia, 197-98; and Spanish Civil War, 187-91, 208-11. *See also* Popular Front

Delcassé, Theophile, 5, 6, 9

De Monzie, Anatole, 250, 295; and *Anschluss* crisis, 218; and Italian nonbelligerency, 274-75, 282, 283; and Polish crisis, 272; in Reynaud cabinet, 278

Denain, General, 129, 146

Deutsche Allgemeine Zeitung, 151

Dodecanese Islands, 7

Dollfuss, Engelbert, 89-90, 92-96

Donini-Feretti, Signor, 279-80, 330n. 30

Doumergue, Gaston, 84, 136, 220, 222

Drummond, Sir Eric: and Anglo-Italian Easter Accord, 230, 232, 236; and *Anschluss* crisis, 215-16; and British mediation between France and Italy, 245, 248, 251; and Italian demands on France, 243, 244-45; and Laval-Mussolini Agreements, 115-16; and Spanish Civil War, 203; urges appeasement of Italy, 263-64

Dupuy, Pierre, 94

L'Echo de Paris, 136, 151, 163

Eden, Anthony, 173, 211, 220, 246; and Anglo-German Naval Agreement, 135, 137, 206-7; and Anglo-Italian rapprochement, 212-13, 221, 236; and Ethiopian crisis, 114-15, 138, 144-45, 147, 154-55, 174, 176-77, 181, 184, 315n. 45; and Italian nonbelligerency, 282; resignation of, 206, 216-17, 221; and Spanish Civil War, 187, 202-3, 208-10

Egypt, 213

England. *See* Great Britain

Ethiopia, 5, 12, 64, 205, 251, 291; and Anglo-German Naval Agreement, 134-36, 137-40; and Franco-Italian rapprochement, 69-70, 101, 105, 107-8, 109-16, 132-33; incorporated into Italian Empire, 178; and Italo-Ethiopian crisis of 1935, 141-69; and League of Nations sanctions on Italy, 172, 184; recognition of Italian conquest of, 196, 213, 234, 239, 292, 319n. 19, 322n. 10; and Rhineland crisis, 175; and Stresa Front, 125-26. *See also* Hoare-Laval Plan; Italo-Ethiopian War; Laval-Mussolini Agreements

Fabry, Colonel Jean, 83, 142, 146

Fagiuoli, Vincenzo, 253, 258, 259

Farinacci, Roberto, 243, 276

Ferry, Jules, 3

Fiume, 7, 9, 10, 32, 39, 45, 57, 290; claimed by Italy, 15; claimed by Yugoslavia, 10; at Paris Peace Conference, 11; postwar crisis in, 33-37; resolution of postwar crisis, 42-44; and Treaty of Rapallo, 300n. 7. *See also* D'Annunzio, Gabriele; Rapallo, Treaty of

Flandin, Pierre Etienne, 134, 192, 206, 293, 298; and *Anschluss* crisis, 217; appointed to Quai d'Orsay, 170; and Ethiopian crisis, 153, 154, 174, 177, 178, 180; and Franco-Italian military rapprochement, 129; and Laval's foreign policy, 103; and Rhineland crisis, 175, 176-77; and Stresa Front, 124-25

Foch, General Ferdinand, 63

Four-Power Pact, 71-77, 79, 90, 172, 194, 225, 306n. 31, 33, 40; and Austrian Nazi coup of 1934, 91, 92; and German rearmament, 81; and German withdrawal from League of Nations, 82. *See also* Jouvenel, Henry de

Fourteen Points, 10

Franco, General Francisco, 203-4, 208, 226, 229, 250, 252; and outbreak of Spanish Civil War, 186-91. *See also* Spanish Civil War

Franco-Czechoslovakian Treaty (1924), 44, 46-47, 300n. 2

François-Poncet, André, 58, 184, 196, 289, 291, 293, 296; and Austrian Nazi coup of 1934, 97; and Baudouin mission to Rome, 253-55; and British mediation between France and Italy, 245-46, 249-50; and Ethiopian crisis, 112, 139, 150-51, 239; and German rearmament, 84; and Ger-

many's coup in Prague, 256–57; and Italian denunciation of Laval-Mussolini Agreements, 247–48; and Italian nonbelligerency, 273, 275–79, 281–84; and Munich crisis, 235; named ambassador to Italy, 235–36, 238–39; and Pact of Steel, 268–69; and Spanish Civil War, 239, 252; and Stresa Front, 127, 287; urges appeasement of Italy, 240–43, 244, 253, 258–67, 270–71
Franco-Prussian War, 2
Franco-Romanian Treaty (1926), 300 n. 2
Franco-Soviet Treaty (1935), 135, 159, 192–93, 201, 222, 318 n. 50
Franco-Yugoslavian Treaty (1927), 44, 46–49, 55, 60, 62, 75, 200, 300 n. 2
Franklin-Bouillon, Henri, 83

Gafenco, Grégoire, 260
Gamelin, General Maurice, 67, 317 n. 25; and Ethiopian crisis, 145, 146, 151–52, 156, 158; and Four-Power Pact, 76; and Franco-Italian military rapprochement, 120, 129–33; as French military attaché in Rio de Janeiro, 62–63; and Hoare-Laval Plan, 159; and Italian nonbelligerency, 272, 275, 282; and Munich crisis, 235; and Polish crisis, 272. *See also* Gamelin-Badoglio Agreements
Gamelin-Badoglio Agreements, 131–32, 138, 291; and *Anschluss* crisis, 218; impact of Ethiopian crisis on, 145, 158, 178, 198
Garibaldi, Giuseppe, 2
Garnier, Jean-Paul, 234
Le Gaulois, 23
Gayda, Virginio, 65–66, 171, 243, 257, 262–63
Gazetta del Popolo, 149, 249
Gentizon, Paul, 258
Gentleman's Agreement, 193, 201–5, 206, 207, 210, 212, 225
George, General, 147
George V, King (England), 150
Géraud, André (pseud. Pertinax), 163, 254–55, 318 n. 50
Germany, 2–3, 4–5, 5–6, 7, 9, 13–14, 16, 17, 64, 80–81, 184; and Anglo-Italian Easter Accord, 322 n. 16; and Austrian Nazi coup of 1934, 92–97; and Baudouin mission to Rome, 327 n. 43; and Ethiopian crisis, 144, 150–51; and Four-Power Pact, 71–77; and Franco-Italian rapprochement, 70, 118–21; in Laval's diplomacy, 112, 295; and Little Entente, 32; and Pact of Steel, 268–69; and Paris Peace Conference, 10–12, 15; and Prague coup, 256–57; propaganda of, in Italy, 18, 21, 22; rearmament of, 74, 81, 121–22; rise of Hitler in, 65; and Ruhr occupation, 26–29, 38; and Spanish Civil War, 190, 204; and Tunisian question, 51; withdrawal from League of Nations of, 82–83. *See also* Anglo-German Naval Agreement; Hitler, Adolf; Rhineland
Giannini, Amadeo, 273
Giolitti, Giovanni, 18, 19, 20, 21, 23, 34
Giornale d'Italia, 48, 60, 65–66, 171, 243, 257, 262
Goering, Marshal Hermann, 204, 306 n. 31
Gömbös, Julius, 95
Grandi, Count Dino: and Anglo-Italian rapprochement, 206, 213; and Ethiopian crisis, 158, 160; and Italian nonbelligerency, 273; and resignation of Eden, 216–17; and Spanish Civil War, 202; and Stresa Front, 123, 24
Grat, Felix, 201
Great Britain, 4–5, 9, 14, 21, 29–30, 66, 87, 89, 193, 295; and Anglo-German Naval Agreement, 121, 124, 129; and Anglo-Italian rapprochement, 212–14, 220–32, 244–51; and Austrian Nazi coup of 1934, 92–97; and Baudouin mission to Rome, 327 n. 42; and Corfu crisis, 37–42; and Ethiopian crisis, 112–16, 123, 142–67, 184, 315 n. 45, 322 n. 10; and Four-Power Pact, 71–77; and Franco-Italian armistice, 286; and Italian nonbelligerency, 272; and Locarno Treaties, 30, 47; and Munich crisis, 233–35; at Paris Peace Conference, 10–12; and Rhineland crisis, 175–76; and Ruhr occupation, 25–29, 35, 39; and Spanish Civil War, 187–88, 202–4, 208–10; and Stresa Front, 122–29; urges French appeasement of Italy, 264–66, 271–72. *See also* Anglo-German Naval Agreement; Anglo-Italian Easter Accord; Chamberlain, Neville; Churchill, Winston; Gentleman's Agreement; Hoare-Laval Plan

INDEX

Greece: and Corfu crisis, 37–42; Italian invasion of, 286
Guariglia, Raffaele, 56, 260, 261; and Franco-Italian armistice, 288; and Italian nonbelligerency, 273, 279, 283–84; and Laval-Mussolini Agreements, 114; named Italian ambassador to France, 239, 324 n. 5
Guderian, Heinz, 281
Guérin, Hubert, 143

Halifax, Viscount: and Anglo-Italian Easter Accord, 221–22, 228, 229, 232, 235–36; and British mediation between France and Italy, 244–50, 325 n. 17; and Italian nonbelligerency, 282; and Polish crisis, 272; urges French appeasement of Italy, 264, 270
Hanotaux, Gabriel, 5, 39, 40, 42
Herriot, Edouard, 57, 67–68, 151, 181, and Anglo-German Naval Agreement, 134–35, 137; and Four-Power Pact, 306 n. 33; and Ethiopian crisis, 147, 153, 162, 310 n. 25; and rapprochement with Italy, 87; resignation of, from Laval cabinet, 166–67
Hitler, Adolf, 30, 58, 71, 118, 184, 210, 211, 241, 243, 274, 277, 294; and *Anschluss* crisis, 214–19; appeasement of, 262; and Ethiopian Crisis, 151, 164; and German rearmament, 121–22; and Italian nonbelligerency, 278; and Laval-Mussolini Agreements, 112; and Munich crisis, 233–34; Mussolini's distrust of, 171, 174; and Pact of Steel, 268–69; and Polish crisis, 270–72; and Prague coup, 256, 257; and Rhineland crisis, 175; rise to power of, 65, 67, 70, 77, 290; visits to Italy of, 85–86, 225, 227–29; withdrawal from League of Nations, 77; World War II armistice, 284–85. *See also* Germany
Hoare, Samuel, 291; and Ethiopian crisis, 147–50, 153–54, 155–56, 314 n. 18, 315 n. 45; resignation of, 163–64. *See also* Hoare-Laval Plan
Hoare-Laval Plan, 154, 158–67, 170, 177, 255, 291, 293; failure of, 171, 315 n. 45; and League of Nations sanctions against Italy, 315 n. 40; map, 160
Hungary, 60, 77; and Austrian independence, 91; Barthou's assassination, involvement in, 103; and Danubian confederation, 95; and Munich crisis, 234, and Stresa Front, 127

Ingram, E. M. B., 249
L'Intransigeant, 136
Italo-Ethiopian War, 152–69, 171, 176–79. *See also* Hoare-Laval Plan
Italo-Turkish War, 7
Italo-Yugoslavian Treaty (1924), 43, 45, 46, 48

Jibuti-Addis Ababa Railway, 64, 105, 107–8, 241; and Baudouin mission to Rome, 254; in Ethiopian crisis, 137, 139, 152, 159; in Franco-Italian armistice, 285; Italian ambitions in, 249, 261, 263, 265, 282; in Laval-Mussolini Agreements, 111, 240, 244, 247
Le Jour, 83
Jouvenel, Bertrand de, 182
Jouvenel, Henry de, 29, 58, 69, 80, 85, 115, 293, 296; as ambassador to Rome, 68–78, 290; death of, 306 n. 43; and Four-Power Pact, 73–77, 79, 306 nn. 31, 33; and opposition to *Anschluss*, 89–91. *See also* Four-Power Pact
La Justice, 279

Kellogg-Briand Pact, 72, 73, 246
Kingdom of Serbs, Croats and Slovenes. *See* Yugoslavia
Kohl, Helmut, 295
Krofta, Kemil, 200

Labroue, Henri, 280
Lagardelle, Hubert de, 182–83, 184–85, 198
Laroche, Jules, 25, 42
Lateran Treaties, 65
Lausanne Conference, 25, 27
Laval, Pierre, 58, 65, 79, 173, 186, 188, 192, 194, 235, 287, 291, 292; and Anglo-German Naval Agreement, 133–37; and assassination of Barthou, 103–4; assessment of for-

eign policy of, 167–69, 293–96, 315–16nn. 56, 57, 331n. 6; and Ethiopian crisis, 111–16, 138–40, 141–69, 315n. 40; first ministry of, 66–67; and Franco-Italian rapprochement, 102–8, 129–33; and Italian nonbelligerency, 278–80, 330n. 30; resignation of, 170; and Stresa Front, 122–29; urges appeasement of Italy, 257–58. *See also* Hoare-Laval Plan; Laval-Mussolini Agreements

Laval-Mussolini Agreements, 6, 61–62, 78, 108–16, 123, 169, 198, 225, 253, 287, 291, 294; and Anglo-German Naval Agreement, 134; and Anglo-Italian Easter Accord, 220; denunciation of, by Italy, 242, 244, 246–47, 248–50, 252, 255, 262; and Ethiopian crisis, 142–43, 144, 149, 154, 158, 165, 171, 178, 179; and Franco-Italian military rapprochement, 117–21; ratification of, by France, 126

League of Nations, 12, 15, 100, 107, 291; and Austrian Nazi coup of 1934, 94; Corfu crisis and, 37–42, 69; and Danubian confederation, 81–82; and Ethiopian crisis, 64, 108, 142–67, 172–81, 182, 184; and Fiume crisis, 43; and Four Power Pact, 72, 77, 79; and Franco-Italian military rapprochement, 129, 132–33; and Franco-Italian rapprochement, 68; in Laval's foreign policy, 105; and recognition of Italian conquest of Ethiopia, 196, 198, 224–25, 228–29, 231; and Spanish Civil War, 208; and Stresa Front, 123, 125, 128; withdrawal from, of Germany, 82, 94; withdrawal from, of Italy, 173, 178–79, 196, 292

Lebrun, Albert, 275

Lefebvre du Prey, Edmond, 167

Léger, Alexis Saint-Léger, 69, 106, 206, 211, 238; and Anglo-German Naval Agreement, 134; anti-Italian bias of, 287; and Ethiopian crisis, 137, 158, 171–72, 180, 227, 315n. 44; and Franco-Italian armistice, 288; and Italian nonbelligerency, 274–75, 279; and Laval-Mussolini Agreements, 109; opposes appeasement of Italy, 257–58, 266, 292; resignation of, 280; and Spanish Civil War, 187–88

Leygues, Georges, 18, 19

Libya, 9, 71, 84, 106, 226, 272; in Barthou's foreign policy, 85; boundary rectifications for, 56–57, 64, 68; and Franco-Italian rapprochement, 86, 100; and Italian nonbelligerency, 282; Italian troop concentrations in, 211, 213, 256; and Jouvenel mission to Rome, 69–70; in Laval-Mussolini Agreements, 110–11; in Laval's foreign policy, 105

Little Entente, 32, 42, 45–46, 48, 55, 58, 60, 70, 77; and Anglo-Italian Easter Accord, 223; and assassination of Barthou, 104; and Austrian Nazi coup of 1934, 93–94; and Corfu crisis, 304n. 60; and Danubian confederation, 95; and Franco-Italian military rapprochement, 118–20; and Italo-Yugoslav relations, 200; and opposition to *Anschluss,* 91; and Popular Front, 199

Lloyd George, David, 10, 17

Locarno, Treaties of, 30, 31, 33, 47, 49, 58, 63, 82, 90, 290, 291; and Ethiopian crisis, 156, 158, 171–72; and Franco-Italian rapprochement, 129, 133; and German rearmament, 122, 123; and Rhineland crisis, 174; and Stresa Front, 124

London Conference (1922), 27

London, Treaty of, 6, 34, 57, 101; article 13 of, 9, 12, 15; and Italian war aims, 9; map, 8; and postwar Italian colonial claims, 12; provisions of, 7–9; rejection of, at Paris Peace Conference, 10–11

Loraine, Sir Percy, 271, 329n. 22, 330n. 39

MacDonald, Ramsay, 124–27, 291, 315n. 39

Maginot, André, 51

Maginot Line, 81, 293

Maglione, Cardinal, 259, 260, 269

Malvy, Jean-Louis, 182–83

Mandel, Georges, 83, 256, 318n. 50

Margerie, Pierre de, 48

Marin, Louis, 83, 201, 217

Massigli, René, 90, 317n. 25; and Anglo-Italian Easter Accord, 220; and *Anschluss* crisis, 218; and Ethiopian crisis, 154–55, 179; and Italian nonbelligerency, 274; and Popular Front, 182; and recognition of Italian Empire in Ethiopia, 224; removal of, from Quai d'Orsay, 238; and Spanish Civil War, 202

INDEX

Le Matin, 23, 69, 83, 151
Matteotti, Giacomo, 112, 183, 280
Maurin, General Joseph, 118-20
Mazzini, Giuseppe, 2
Messagero, 60
Millerand, Alexandre, 15, 27, 50, 51
Mistler, Jean de, 218
Mitterrand, François, 295
Il Mondo, 21
Monsell, Eyres, 162, 315n. 39
Monsieur Nac, 260-61, 269
Montbas, Hugues Barthon de, 214-15
Monzie, Anatole de. *See* De Monzie, Anatole
Morocco, 4, 6, 114; international administration of port of Tangiers in, 52, 55, 303n. 59; in Italian armistice terms, 285; in Laval's foreign policy, 105; and Spanish Civil War, 186
Munich crisis, 167, 233-35

Naggiar, Emile, 95, 103-4
Napoleon III, Emperor (France), ix, 2
Nazi-Soviet Pact, 271
Neurath, Baron Constantin von, 121, 201
Ninchich, Momchilo, 47
Nitti, Francesco, 17, 18, 19, 20, 22, 24
Noble, Sir Andrew, 258
Noël, Léon: and Anglo-German Naval Agreement, 136; assessment of French diplomacy by, 287; and Baudouin mission to Rome, 253-54; as Laval's chief of staff, 66-67; and recognition of Italian Empire in Ethiopia, 192, 227; and Stresa Front, 125, 128; urges appeasement of Italy, 260
Nonintervention Committee, 189-90, 204, 208-9, 222, 228, 230. *See also* Spanish Civil War
Nyon Conference, 208-11, 292. *See also* Spanish Civil War

L'Oeuvre, 109, 163, 279
Orlando, Vittorio, 10, 11, 17, 33

Pact of Steel, 244, 266-67, 268-69, 271, 273, 328n. 1

Il Paese, 22
Paris Conference (on reparations), 28
Parisot, General H.: and Ethiopian crisis, 159, 173; and Franco-Italian military rapprochement, 117-21, 131; and military relations with Italy, 198-99
Paris Peace Conference. *See* Saint-Germain, Treaty of; Trianon, Treaty of; Versailles, Treaty of
Paris-Soir, 182, 191
La Patria, 22
Paul-Boncour, Joseph, 58, 115, 151, 293, 296; and Anglo-Italian Easter Accord, 223-24; and Ethiopian crisis, 178, 180; and Four-Power Pact, 73-77, 79, 306nn. 31, 40; and French military stature, 80; and French opposition to *Anschluss*, 89-93; and German withdrawal from League of Nations, 82; and Jouvenel mission to Rome, 68-78, 83; named premier and minister of foreign affairs, 68; and Polish crisis, 271
Paul, Prince (Yugoslavia), 102, 127
Pavelič, Ante, 103
Perth, Lord. *See* Drummond, Sir Eric
Pertinax. *See* Géraud, André
Pétain, Marshal Philippe-Henri, 113, 114, 253, 284, 288
Le Petit Parisien, 23
Pezet, Ernest, 201, 217, 318n. 50
Pflugl, Emerich von, 90
Phipps, Sir Eric, 221, 227, 231-32, 264-66
Piétri, François, 100, 137, 146, 147
Pingaud, Albert, 14
Pius IX, Pope, 2
Plombières, Conference of, 2
Plymouth, Lord, 230
Poincaré, Raymond, 30, 57, 58, 69, 78, 206, 291, 296; and Corfu crisis, 37-42, 303n. 60; and Fiume crisis, 35-37, 43; at Lausanne Conference, 25; at London Conference on reparations, 27; and occupation of Ruhr, 29, 39; and Paris Peace Conference, 298n. 13; and relations with Yugoslavia, 44-46, 46-49; and rise of Mussolini, 21, 23; and Tunisian question, 51-53
Poland, 70, 71, 290; French alliance with, 32; and Hoare-Laval Plan, 160; in Laval's diplomacy, 294; and Laval-Mussolini Agree-

ments, 113; Locarno Treaties and, 47; and Munich crisis, 234; and outbreak of World War II, 270–72
Poliakoff, 66–67
Popolo d'Italia, 171, 257
Popular Front, 167, 170, 197, 222; assessment of diplomacy of, 292–93; and deteriorating relations with Italy, 191–95; inception of, and relations with Italy, 180, 181–86; resignation of, 219, 225; and Spanish Civil War, 186–191, 239, 323 n. 22. *See also* Blum, Léon; Delbos, Yvon
Primo de Rivera, Miguel, 186
Prinetti, Giulio, 6
Prunas, Renato, 230–31
Puaux, Gabriel, 90, 215, 217–18
Puricelli, Senator, 224

Quilici, François, 163

Rapallo, Treaty of (1920), 34, 35–37, 42, 300 n. 7
Reparations Commission, 27–29, 35, 39, 57
Revue des Vivants, 69
Reynaud, Paul, 76, 191, 318 n. 50; and *Anschluss* crisis, 217; and Germany's coup in Prague, 256; and Hoare-Laval Plan, 165; and Italian nonbelligerency, 279–83; and Laval-Mussolini Agreements, 112–13; named premier, 278; resignation of, 284
Rhineland, 10, 32, 122, 123; French evacuation of, 58; German remilitarization of, 129, 174–77, 193, 199, 294
Ribbentrop, Joachim von, 241, 242, 266, 285
Roatta, General Mario, 159
Robilant, Carlo di, 4
Romania, 32, 113, 294
Rome Agreements. *See* Laval-Mussolini Agreements
Roosevelt, Franklin D., 281–82
Rossoni, Edmondo, 117–18
Rudinì, Antonio di, 5
Ruhr, occupation of, 26–29, 31, 32, 36, 37, 38–39, 41, 51, 290
Runciman, Lord Walter, 245, 270
Russia (pre-1922), 5, 7, 9, 29, 32. *See also* Union of Soviet Socialist Republics

Saar, 10, 102, 118, 122
Saint-Aulaire, Comte de, 27
Saint-Germain, Treaty of, 11, 32
St. Jean de Maurienne Agreement, 12
Saint, Lucien, 53
Salandra, Antonio, 7, 40
Santa Margherita Accords, 34, 35–36
Sargent, Orme, 145, 202, 221
Sarraut, Albert, 102, 170–71, 179, 180, 181
Schmidt, Guido, 215
Schuschnigg, Kurt von, 215, 216, 218
Seipel, Monsignor Ignaz, 88
Selassie, Haile, 65, 108; and Ethiopian crisis, 138, 142, 173, 177–78; and Hoare-Laval Plan, 159, 160; and Stresa Front, 125. *See also* Italo-Ethiopian War; League of Nations
Serbia, 9
Sforza, Count Carlo: and Fiume crisis, 34; as Italian foreign minister, 18, 34; resignation of, as Italian ambassador to France, 24, 36
Simon, Sir John, 112, 123–28, 133
Soleri, Marcello, 87–88
Sonnino, Sidney, 7, 10, 11
Sotelo, José Calvo, 186
Spanish Civil War, 200–206, 208–11, 239, 291, 292; and Anglo-Italian Easter Accord, 226, 229–31; end of, 252; outbreak of, 186–91; withdrawal of Italians from, 226–27. *See also* Franco, Francisco; Nonintervention Committee; Nyon Conference
Starace, Achille, 276
Stein, Boris, 205
Stojadinovich, Milan, 166, 200
Strang, William, 221
Stresa Front, 121–29, 173, 175, 198, 217, 223, 287, 291, 293; and Anglo-German Naval Agreement, 133–35; demise of, 194; and Ethiopian crisis, 142, 152, 158, 171–72; and Rhineland crisis, 176; and Spanish Civil War, 201–202
Stresemann, Gustav, 48, 290
Sunday Times (London), 211
Supreme Interallied Council, 276
Suvich, Fulvio, 70, 78, 86, 94, 108; and Ethiopian crisis, 138, 146, 171, 172; and Franco-Italian rapprochement, 101; and Laval-Mussolini Agreements, 109; and lifting of

INDEX

League of Nations sanctions on Italy, 179; and Stresa Front, 122, 124; and Tunisian question, 309 n. 12
Szembeck, Count Jan, 260

Tabouis, Geneviève, 109, 163
Taittinger, Pierre, 201
Tardieu, André, 67, 87
Tellini, General Enrico, 37-38, 39
Le Temps, 22-23, 26, 122, 126, 136, 258
Theodoli, Marquis A., 64-65, 101, 103, 106, 115, 304 n. 9
Thomas, H. Lloyd, 177
Thorez, Maurice, 113
Times (London), 66
Tittoni, Tommaso, 17
Trasformismo, 3, 4
Trianon, Treaty of, 32, 87-88
Tribuna, 48, 60
Triple Alliance, 4, 5, 6, 7
Tripolitania. *See* Libya
Tunisia, 3, 4, 35, 84, 106, 270, 290; in Barthou's foreign policy, 85; in Baudouin mission to Rome, 254; and conventions of 1896, 6, 15, 49-50; as focus of Franco-Italian difficulties in 1920s, 49-57; and Franco-Italian rapprochement, 68, 86, 100; Italian aims in World War I in, 9; Italian ambitions in, 241, 242-43, 253, 260, 261, 263, 265; in Italian armistice terms, 285; and Italian nonbelligerency, 276, 280, 282; and Jouvenel mission to Rome, 69-70; in Laval-Mussolini Agreements, 110-11, 239-40, 244; in Laval's foreign policy, 105; naturalization of Italians in, 64; and recognition of Italian Empire in Ethiopia, 226-27; rights of Italians in, 6, 15, 29, 45, 61, 104, 246. *See also* Laval-Mussolini Agreements
Turkey, 12, 29, 235, 275

Union of Soviet Socialist Republics (USSR), 100, 271, 277, 295. *See also* Franco-Soviet Treaty
United States, 10-12, 24, 53, 277. *See also* Roosevelt, Franklin D.; Wilson, T. Woodrow
Ustashi, 102, 103

Vansittart, Robert, 66, 181; and Anglo-German Naval Agreement, 135; and Anglo-Italian Easter Accord, 232; and Austrian Nazi coup of 1934, 93-97; and British military weakness, 146; and Ethiopian crisis, 148, 153, 157, 160; and Laval-Mussolini Agreements, 116; and Stresa Front, 123-24; urges appeasement of Italy, 270
Versailles, Treaty of, 18, 26, 28, 48, 92, 289-90; and Anglo-German Naval Agreement, 135, 136; and German rearmament, 122; perceived inadequacies of, in France, 14; and Rhineland crisis, 174; and Stresa Front, 125
Vichy, 112, 253, 293
Victor Emmanuel III, King (Italy), 178, 239, 258-59, 264
Villafranca, Treaty of, 2
Villelume, Lieutenant Colonel Paul de, 282, 329 n. 20
Visconti-Venosta, Emilio, 5, 6
Von Neurath, Baron Constantin. *See* Neurath, Baron Constantin von

Washington Naval Conference, 66, 103
Welczeck, Count Johannes von, 232
Weygand, General Maxim, 80, 277
Wilson, T. Woodrow, 10-11, 33

Ybarnégaray, Jean, 201, 217
Young Plan, 58
Yugoslavia, 15, 24, 32, 66, 70, 102, 199; and Danubian confederation, 60, 80; and Ethiopian crisis, 166; and Fiume question, 11, 33-37, 42-44; and Franco-Italian rapprochement, 86, 101, 106-7, 118-21, 130-32; and Franco-Yugoslavian Treaty, 44-46, 47-49; in Laval's diplomacy, 113, 294; and Munich crisis, 234, and Pact of Steel, 328 n. 1; and rise of Mussolini, 23; and Tunisian question, 55. *See also* Fiume; Franco-Yugoslavian Treaty; Little Entente

Zay, Jean, 256
Zogu, Ahmed Bey, 47-48. *See also* Albania
Zollverein, 88

William I. Shorrock is Professor of History at Cleveland State University, Cleveland, Ohio and author of *French Imperialism in the Middle East: The Failure of Policy in Syria and Lebanon, 1900-1914.*